God Knows All Your Names

STORIES IN AMERICAN HISTORY

Third Edition

PAUL N. HERBERT

authorHOUSE®

AuthorHouse™
1663 Liberty Drive
Bloomington, IN 47403
www.authorhouse.com
Phone: 1-800-839-8640

First published by AuthorHouse 12/15/2010

ISBN: 978-1-4389-4512-5 (sc)
ISBN: 978-1-4389-4513-2 (dj)
ISBN: 978-1-4520-1634-4 (e)

Printed in the United States of America

This book is printed on acid-free paper.

Dedication

To Dad, the gambling maverick, and to my mother, for whom the Indian word 'vomonte' fits perfectly. It means good to everybody.

And to Eileen, who has the wisdom to learn and the courage to stand out within a herd of wicked conformity.

Contents

Part II: The Civil War

Part III: Other Stories

Columbia ever will know you,
From her glittering towers;
And kisses of love will throw you,
And send you wreaths of flowers.

Ever in the realms of glory,
Shall shine your starry fame;
Angels have heard your story,
God knows all your names.

Monument inscription honoring soldiers
from Michigan's Upper Peninsula

Preface

The four horsemen of the Apocalypse gallop wildly through these pages. War carves its ugly name in tales of terror and tragedy. Famine wields its thunder too, especially in stories about the baker-general's heroic attempt to feed the army as well as the miserable conditions leading to a near-insurrection of Continental soldiers. Pestilence covers bone-weary soldiers with disease-laden blankets, malignantly befriending those too weak to reject its choking and destructive embrace. And death, violently swinging its hard scythe of finality, rides last.

But these stories also tell humorous, obscure and fascinating tales. That road you're driving on might have been built by slave labor and captured Revolutionary War Hessian troops. That non-descript building in Alexandria, Virginia that thousands of cars pass everyday once held auctions of human beings. Over two thousand vessels sank in the Civil War, including eleven in Chinese waters alone. You may not know it, but the Civil War started and ended at the residences of a couple named Wilmer and Virginia McLean. Imagine any historic event, let alone a civil war, starting and ending in your house.

Was there really an attempted slave insurrection in Fairfax three decades before John Brown went to Harper's Ferry? Everyone knows John Brown, but who ever heard of John Windover? Who knew a monument was erected in Virginia to honor the brave deeds of a slave, six years before the Civil War? With stories of Mary Todd Lincoln's oft-repeated spending habits, how did Mr. Lincoln save the tidy sum of $84,000 during his presidency?

An instructor who can't make history fascinating should find another vocation. Once you peel away the decades to get to the personalities, you find it's page turning stuff, almost like fiction. In fact, a fellow named Andre Gide, who is long forgotten, if in fact he was ever known in the first place, said: "Fiction is history that might have taken place, and history fiction that has taken place."

Time shortens when learning about the people who walked before us. The Civil War was fought almost a century and a half ago, which sounds like a very long time until you realize that anyone born in 1959 was alive when its last soldier was still living; until very recently, a couple Civil War widows were still alive. We are five years from the Centennial Anniversary of the start of World War One, a long time indeed, but alas, a few (precious few) doughboys have not yet gone over the top, or as they said at that time, "gone west." It's probable that someone living now had a grandfather who fought in the Mexican War. It wasn't that long ago.

Researching these stories has been an incredible joy. It's amazing how quickly the hours pass while poring over dusty, barely legible documents in old town hall basements. It's not work at all when you put the stories together a little at a time never knowing when, where or how you'll find the next precious details. It may be an account of a property bought or sold, or a last will and testament where your grandfather with eight greats in front of his name left instructions for how his nine-dollar estate should be divided. Once rescued from "that great dust-heap called history" these fragments go from forgotten to memorable.

Herodotus of Halicarnassus (now Bodrum, Turkey) earned the sobriquet "'the Father of History" for writing about the Greeks twenty-five-hundred years ago. His purpose in writing was so "the vestiges of humankind might withstand the erosion of time and that great and wonderful exploits might be saved from ignoble obscurity." Two and half centuries later, that still perfectly summarizes the purpose of history. The parents of history, if there were such a thing, according to one writer, were epic poetry and science. An Arab historian named

Ibn Khaldun who lived through the Black Plague of the Fourteenth Century wrote: "On the surface history is no more than information about political events, dynasties, and occurrences of the remote past, elegantly presented and spiced with proverbs...The inner meaning of history, on the other hand, involves speculation and an attempt to get at the truth, subtle explanations of the causes and origins of existing things, and deep knowledge of the how and why of events."

Sometimes we learn from history. But sometimes we don't. Hegel said the only thing man has learned from history is that man hasn't learned anything from history.

Historian William Thayer provided this motive for those trying to provide accurate portrayals of the past:

"We need to know the words actually spoken, the speech actually delivered,--not the expurgated or embellished revision, purveyed by Hansard or by the *Congressional Record*,--because those words were integral strands in the web of history. We need to know each actor's estimate of his fellows: for however unjust, mistaken, or over-favorable that estimate may be, it determined action ...Unless the historian comes to this knowledge, the past will be dead to him, an affair of mummies, a deciphering of mummy-cases, which no display of erudition concerning economics, commercial statistics or documents can bring to life."

Appreciate the quest for knowledge, possibly the most enjoyable journey that life offers. As DeWitt Clinton eloquently expressed in his 1823 Phi Beta Kappa Address:

"Pleasure is a shadow, wealth is vanity, and power a pageant; but knowledge is ecstatic in enjoyment, perennial in fame, unlimited in space, and infinite in duration. In the performance of its sacred offices it fears no danger, spares no expense, omits no exertion. It scales the mountain, looks into the volcano, dives into the ocean, perforates the earth, wings its flight into the skies, encircles the globe, explores sea and land, contemplates the distant, examines the minute, comprehends the great, and ascends to the sublime. No place too remote for its grasp; no heavens too exalted for its reach. Its seat is the bosom of God; its voice the harmony of the world. All things in heaven and earth do it homage, the very least as feeling its care, and the greatest as not exempt from its power. Both angels and men and creatures, of what condition soever, though each in different sort and manner, yet all, with uniform consent, admiring it as the parent of peace and happiness."

Once you understand that past really is prologue, it becomes clear President Truman was onto something when he said the only thing new in the world is the history you don't know. Or maybe the writer William Faulkner captured the essence of history best: "The past is never dead; it's not even past."

For many of us, the past keeps drawing us back. We go back frequently. Back to 1783 when our new nation almost self-destructed because there was no money to pay Revolutionary War soldiers, or to 1795 when Americans, livid with the Jay Treaty and the Whiskey Rebellion, almost went to civil war, or to 1804 when the Northern States threatened civil war because of the Louisiana Purchase.

The past is there. "So," as F. Scott Fitzgerald summarized in the final line of *The Great Gatsby,* "we beat on, boats against the current, borne back ceaselessly into the past."

We go back because the past enlightens. It even *entertains.* Everything can be found in history. Humor and tragedy and irony are there. Even, as the author Bernard DeVoto eloquently stated, romance is found there:

"If the mad, impossible voyage of Columbus or Cartier or LaSalle…is not romantic, if the stars did not dance in the sky when the Constitutional Convention met, if Atlantis has any landscape stranger than the other side of the moon or any lights or colors or shapes more unearthly than the customary homespun of Lincoln or the morning coat of Jackson, well, I don't know what romance is. Ours is a story mad with the impossible, it is chaos out of dream, it began as a dream and it has continued as a dream down to the last headlines you read in a newspaper. And of our dreams there are two things above all others to be said, that only madmen could have dreamed them or would have dared to - and that we have shown a considerable faculty for making them come true. The simplest truth you can ever write about history will be charged and surcharged with romanticism, and if you are afraid of the word you better start practicing seriously on your fiddle."

Everyone has a collection of incredibly interesting stories in their past. We all share history. If you had ancestors here in America during the Revolutionary War, be assured without question, they were out there, perhaps providing medicine or comfort to a Continental soldier; they were there burying their meager foods and silver in the back yard so the enemy would not steal them. They were not hiding all day in their homes. They were out buying wares and selling vegetables, greeting people, transacting commerce, doing what people have always done.

They saw and lived through experiences and incidents that would astonish you. They were cheering as a Loyalist got tarred and feathered; they were dazzled as John Hancock, Patrick Henry or one of the other Founding Fathers made a stirring speech. Their stories, and hopefully the stories in this book, bring them back.

Paul N. Herbert
pnh9202@verizon.net
P.O. Box 2111
Fairfax, VA 22031

Part I:
The American Revolution

Benjamin Church: Revolutionary War Doctor Spy

Five years before Benedict Arnold tried to sell the fort at West Point to the enemy, a year before America declared its independence, a Boston physician with impeccable professional and patriotic credentials committed treason by divulging sensitive information to the British Army.

Just as the Revolutionary War started, a secret group of ardent patriots plotting a revolution in taverns like the *Salutation* and the *Green Dragon* were alerted they had a spy in their midst. But who? Certainly it couldn't be Sam Adams, John Adams or John Hancock, the soul, mind and bank of the Rebellion; it couldn't be Paul Revere, the 'midnight rider;' not Dr. Benjamin Church, Jr., the surgeon-general of the American Army, the poet who wrote pro-rebellion verse, the hardened patriot who proudly showed off his blood-stained socks after the Battle of Lexington.

Dr. Church, "witty, high strung and bombastic," according to Esther Forbes in her 1942 Pulitzer Prize-winning biography about Paul Revere, was simply an odd duck. In retrospect he should have quickly been identified as the spy. He consorted with a British officer, and in 1775 just as the war began he had a sudden increase in wealth, spending lavishly on a house and a mistress. Whether he was ever confronted about the pecuniary or the peccadillo is lost to history, but as for his association with the British officer, he dismissed it as a clumsy ruse to try and obtain secret information. With that simple explanation the man Forbes described as the noisiest patriot in Boston avoided detection for several months.

A spy is always an instant away from being caught. Every activity, every letter, every communication is like a card precariously placed on top of an already tipsey double-decker house of them. It all came tumbling down in July or August 1775 when Church misplayed the 'use mistress to pass a letter to the enemy' card. Unable to get a ciphered note to the British, the desperate doctor directed his mistress to have one of her friends forward the note. Deeply perplexed by this unusual request, the friend, a Newport, Rhode Island baker named Godfrey Wenwood put the note aside, not sure what to do.

Weeks passed. Dr. Church somehow learned the letter had not been delivered. It might have been tossed on the pile of unrecorded history except for the fact that the worried doctor, acting like the rank clandestine amateur that he was, seemingly lost his senses over the undelivered letter and directed his mistress to inquire again with the baker. Add poor judgment to the list of crimes and indiscretions committed by the conspiratorial doctor and his pesky girlfriend.

Like leaven to flour this additional ingredient to the mix made Wenwood's suspicions rise. The good baker passed the original note to the American Army and the doctor quickly became toast.

General George Washington initiated an investigation. When asked about the letter, the mistress hemmed and hawed, claimed to know nothing. Perhaps the threat of the gibbet made her give up Dr. Church. When interviewed, the not-so-good doctor simply lied. Yes, he wrote the letter to the British and yes, he gave it to his mistress to pass on. But no, the cipher contained nothing sinister, it was simply an innocuous code which Church, for unexplained reasons, wouldn't share with Washington.

Clearly some evil-doing had been done. But before anyone went to the gallows, Washington had to get the letter deciphered. He assigned that task to Reverend Samuel West, who later served as a delegate to the Constitutional Convention in 1787; working independently as a second team were Elisha Porter of the Massachusetts militia and Elbridge Gerry, the future fifth vice president of the United States.

The cipher must have been astonishingly elementary. Both teams quickly broke it and came to the same results. The note divulged American troop strengths, plans and movements, and ended with the warning: "Make use of every precaution or I perish."

Confronted with this incontrovertible evidence, the physician lied again. The letter, which in fact overestimated troop strength and arms, was designed according to Church to intentionally mislead the British. Something smelled in the Hamlet of Boston and the traitorous skunk was brought to trial before a packed and cynical throng. Future First Lady Abigail Adams summed up the public consensus: "You may as well hope to bind up a hungry tiger with a cobweb as to hold such debauched patriots in the visionary chains of decency."

Although found guilty of holding criminal correspondence with the enemy, Church could not be executed. Incredibly, that penalty for treason was not in effect at the time. The doctor spent a few years in jail before eventually being exiled to the West Indies, never allowed back to America. Nothing was ever heard again of the ship or Church. In *The Codebreakers*, David Kahn succinctly summed up Church's likely fate: "The first American to have lost his liberty as a result of cryptanalysis evidently lost his life because of it as well." Church's wife later moved to England and filed a pension, citing the work her husband had done for the British Army. She was granted a British pension of 150 pounds per year.

The first printed book on cryptology, the science of analyzing and deciphering codes and ciphers, was *Polygraphiae,* written in 1518 by Abbott Johannes Trithemius. Two thousand years earlier, Spartans of early Greece first used cryptology in military operations.

Years earlier the great Chinese military leader Sun Tzu opined, "To remain in ignorance of the enemy's condition is the height of inhumanity…One who acts thus is no leader of men…[and] no master of victory." Chia Lin, another Chinese military strategist echoed the same theme when he compared an army without spies to a man without eyes or ears.

Washington had no love of New Englanders in general, having called them "an exceeding dirty and nasty" bunch.

Soon afterwards, on November 7, 1775, the Articles of War were amended "to suffer death" to "all persons convicted of holding a treacherous correspondence with, or giving intelligence to the enemy."

John Champe's
Audacious Adventure

In Loudoun County, Virginia, a street, historical marker and monument commemorate the bravery of the principal figure of a daring and obscure Revolutionary War scheme involving George Washington, Benedict Arnold and Henry Lee.

Here was the home of Sergeant John Champe
Continental Army
who risked the inglorious death of a spy
for the independence of his country.

The mission was set into motion by Benedict Arnold, one of the finest officers to wear an American uniform, his military excellence widely recognized. "Of all the Americans," the British secretary of state proclaimed, Arnold was "the most enterprising and dangerous." He had performed magnificently in every assignment. He was the mastermind, who along with Ethan Allen, captured Fort Ticonderoga; his brilliant leadership resulted in victory at the Battle of Saratoga; and he came very close to capturing Quebec and all of Canada, despite enduring unspeakable hardships just to get there. He held off the overwhelming forces of the British Navy on Lake Champlain, giving the colonists critical time to fight another day.

On September 23, 1780, five years into the war, the hyper-sensitive Arnold, motivated by greed and revenge for having his feelings hurt one time too many, fled command of American-held West Point and became a traitor. Many historians have opined the prickly, thin-skinned general, who just wanted to feel appreciated, defected because he got only grief and political backstabbing. His switch to the British in New York City caused immediate fury among the American soldiers and officers as well as the citizens. In Philadelphia, an angry mob paraded an effigy of the despicable traitor through town before hanging and burning it.

General George Washington probably could not have been more shocked and irate. The loss was devastating. If Washington's stoicism ever faltered and left him throwing a chair against the wall, this was the time. Arnold had almost sold West Point to the enemy, a move that would have pretty much guaranteed the colonists' defeat. More than anyone, Washington knew the man and the fort were critical to America's military success. The war at that time, like at most times, was not going well. It could only get worse with Arnold now wearing the British redcoat.

Henry "Light-Horse Harry" Lee is probably best known as Robert E. Lee's father and for delivering the profound words at Washington's eulogy: "First in war, first in peace and first in the hearts of his countrymen, he was second to none in the humble and endearing scenes of private life...vice shuddered in his presence and virtue always felt his fostering hand." But the advisor, respected officer and friend of Washington was much more. Washington was thrilled to have the talented Lee, who specialized in, "the carefully calculated coup, the surprise, the raid that damaged a stronger enemy who then had too little time to strike back." His soldiers loved him because he protected and cared for them. To Lee, they mattered.

At the time of Arnold's defection, Lee and his cavalry unit were stationed outside Passaic, New Jersey. To wrest Arnold back, Washington and Lee hatched a plot so secretive that only one other man could know about it. That man was the soldier assigned to carry it out.

Sergeant John Champe, about twenty-three years old, was described by Lee as "full of physical power, with a countenance grave and thoughtful." Given the hazardous task of faking his own desertion from the ranks, riding his horse through the forty-mile barrier to New York City and making it safely to the British camp, this "very promising youth of uncommon taciturnity and invincible perseverance" then had to convince British General Clinton to believe his fake defection was sincere. Once that was done, he had to work with another American spy (who used the surname of Baldwin) already in New York City to drag, carry or coerce the smart, rugged, physically-fit contemptible traitor across the Hudson back to New Jersey. Insisting Arnold be returned alive, Washington bristled, "my aim is to make a public example of him."

Champe was initially reluctant to accept the perilous challenge. If his fellow soldiers believed he was really defecting, they would try to stop him even if it meant killing him. He had probably seen many hangings in the American camp for desertion and he undoubtedly knew about Nathan Hale, a young American hanged in a British camp a few years earlier. (The British executed 275 American prisoners in New York City alone during the war.) Champe knew that if detected he would be hanged in either the American or the British camp. And Champe knew that despite his officers' involvement, they would have to disavow any knowledge of the plot, unable to save his life if things went badly.

More than the risk of danger, however, the "ignominy of desertion," according to Lee, deterred the intrepid Champe, but with some patriotic persuasion, Lee enticed him to accept, assuring him that his "reputation would be protected...should he be unfortunate." He would be "hailed as the avenger of the reputation of the army, stained by foul and wicked perfidy." Lee "excited [Champe's] thirst for fame by impressing on his mind the virtue and glory of the act."

As for the danger, Lee promised to do everything possible to give Champe a head start by delaying the inevitable chase. True to his word, at about 11:00 p.m. on October 20, 1780, Champe fled Lee's cavalry at Tappan, New Jersey for the Hudson River. Within minutes, guards reported the escape to Lee. The normally intelligent and decisive Lee, acting befuddled and confused, delayed as long as practicable. He did not order an immediate chase like he normally would have. Instead, he directed the remaining men be checked to determine who was missing. When advised of the deserter's identity, Lee instigated a lengthy soliloquy wondering why a man like Champe would desert.

Eventually Lee ordered the chase when it was apparent any longer delay might have caused enough suspicion to lead to the plot's unraveling.

As expected, Champe's compatriots, believing he was deserting, had killing on their mind. Consuming additional time because he had to "zig-zag" to avoid patrols along the route, Champe barely beat the chase team to water's edge where he jumped in and swam to the safety of a British ship. The Light Horse riders who had chased Champe returned to camp several hours later, Champe's horse in tow. Lucky Champe had survived the first danger: his fellow soldiers, pursuing him with a vengeance.

Having previously rehearsed with Lee, Champe told the British exactly what they wanted to hear: morale and conditions in the colonists' ranks were so bad that many Americans would soon be switching allegiances. Champe talked his way into the confidence of the British leadership and was assigned to assist recruiting other American soldiers and Loyalists. He soon met the newly-minted British officer in charge of this recruiting unit: Benedict Arnold.

To encourage Americans to defect to the British, Arnold penned the following piece of propaganda. It appeared in the *New York Royal Gazette* twice a week, every week from late October through December of 1780:

> "His Excellency, Sir Henry Clinton, has authorized me to raise a corps of cavalry and infantry, who are to be clothed, subsisted and paid as the other corps are in the British service, and those who bring in horses, arms, or accoutrements are to be paid their value, or have liberty to sell them. To every non-commissioned officer and private a bounty of three guineas will be given, and as the Commander-in–Chief is pleased to allow me to nominate the officers, I shall with infinite satisfaction embrace this opportunity for advancing men whose valor I have witnessed, and whose principles are favorable to a union

with Britain and true American liberty...Friends, fellow soldiers and citizens, arouse and judge for yourselves—reflect on what you have lost—consider to what you are reduced, and by your courage repel the ruin that still threatens you... what is America but a land of widows, beggars, and orphans? —and should the parent nation cease her exertions to deliver you, what security remains to you for the enjoyment of the consolations of that religion for which your fathers braved the ocean, the heathen, and the wilderness?...But what need of arguments to such as feel infinitely more misery than language can express? I therefore only add my promise of the most affectionate welcome and attention to all who are disposed to join me."

Champe charmed Arnold and convinced him of his sincerity. This new-found treasonous kinship must have thrilled the lonely and isolated Arnold, whose reception in the British Army had been frosty and unwelcome, due to the execution of John André, a very popular British officer. Andre had been working with Arnold and had the grievous misfortune of being captured by the Americans on September 23, 1780. He was executed a week later. Many British soldiers and officers believed Arnold should have offered himself to the Americans in exchange for the release of Andre to the British. Washington had proposed such an Andre for Arnold exchange, but it had been rejected.

Finally, a month and a half after Champe had arrived, everything was in place to make Arnold's next night in New York his last. Champe and Baldwin would capture Arnold at about midnight as he took his nightly trip to the outhouse, a brick privy located in an alley on a path from his residence at the south end of Broadway to the Hudson. They would knock their quarry out, gag and carry him to the river. If questioned, they would claim to be taking a drunken sailor to the guard-house. The traitor would be returned to New Jersey where a noose would be slipped around his neck. A boat was readied under the moonless sky of December 11, 1780.

Arnold, however, was an incredibly lucky man. Before nightfall on December 11th, British troops, Champe included, were ordered to board ships to prepare for a voyage and attack upon Virginia. The opportunity squandered, the chagrined Champe would not be returning to New Jersey, with or without Arnold. Instead, he was stuck in a British uniform, along with 1,600 British soldiers, Hessians and Loyalists in a flotilla of forty-two ships, headed to his home State of Virginia where he would have to take up arms against his fellow compatriots.

Four months later, in April 1781, Champe managed to escape from the British ranks and rejoined his own unit. He received an honorable discharge and most likely a monetary reward. Washington had a financial account for such activity.

Masks, invisible ink, drop dead locations, ciphers, deception, and hidden compartments were effectively and extensively utilized during the American Revolution.

Information had to get communicated between people and armies and the ground between the senders and recipients was a no-man's land dotted with thieves, spies and scoundrels adept at stealing messages. So it shouldn't be surprising that messages were transmitted in all types of unique ways, including in the soles of shoes, the lining of coats, the hollow space of double bottom canteens, inside cloth covers of buttons, and even, and according to the author, this is actually documented-- in a bullet. One spy hid a note in a secret compartment underneath various botanical plants, which is a clever idea except for the fact that moisture eventually seeped into the note. When all else failed, and the message absolutely had to get sent across hostile forces, notes were actually tied to arrows and shot into the city.

Not much is known about the spy referred to as Baldwin or how Washington, Lee or Champe communicated with him. It's probable, however, they employed the secret code developed in 1779 by the American spy-master Benjamin Tallmadge, which assigned a number from 1-763 for various words, people and places.

The word soldier was 613 and General Washington was number 711. There were several other codes used during the war and in those Washington was referred to as "James," 596, 572, 206, 4576, or the Roman numerals LXVIII. In various codes, the Colony/State of Virginia was referred to as 739, 583, 558, 205, and XXXII.

Although no such orders existed, had someone written a coded note: 591-642-736-641, the discerning reader would know it instructed: Send the traitor to New Jersey for trial.

Here is a sample of some of the codes for words starting with the letter S:

Sail	586
See	587
Sea	588
Scheme	589
Set	590
Send	591
Ship	592
Safe	593
Same	594
Shy	595
Secret	596
Seldom	597
Sentence	598
Servant	599
Signal	600
Silent	601
Suffer	602
Sudden	603
Surprise	604
Summer	605
Speaker	606
Steady	607
Submit	608
Surpass	609
Sanction	610
Sensible	611
Singular	612
Soldiers	613

A lot of effort was spent deciphering--sometimes without much success. John Adams complained: "I am on this occasion, as on all others hitherto, utterly unable to comprehend the sense of the passage in cipher." On another occasion he wrote that he had received a recent letter, "some dismal ditty," but that it was "unintelligible in ciphers." As for the letter's meaning, the frustrated Adams's lamented, "I know not what."

Abigail Adams remarked about this same deciphering problem when she that her husband was "no[t] adept in investigating ciphers and hates to be puzzled for a meaning." Ben Franklin, who published a book in 1748 written by George Fisher which contained a section on the use of ciphers and codes also had occasional trouble: "If you can find the key and decipher it, I shall be glad, having myself tried in vain."

Often the sender and recipient used an agreed upon book to send messages. The books varied, but both parties had to be extra careful not only that they had the same book, but that they had the same edition of that book. Both Americans and Britons used the Thirteenth Edition of *Entick's Spelling Dictionary*. Another book used was Nathan Bailey's *Universal Etymological English Dictionary--* twenty-first and twenty-fifth editions.

After his discharge from the military, Champe returned to Loudoun County and eventually moved to what is now West Virginia. He is buried at Prickett's Cemetery in Marion County. He never received a war pension but in 1837 his eighty-year-old widow was awarded an annual pension of $120. An unknown poet penned *A Ballad of the Revolution* to honor Champe's gallantry:

"Come sheathe your swords! My gallant boys,
And listen to the story,
How Sergeant Champe, one gloomy night,
Set off to catch the Tory.

Bold Champe, when mounted on Old Rip,
All buttoned up from weather,
Sang out "Goodbye", cracked off his whip,
And soon was in the heather.

He galloped on toward Paulus Hook,
Improving every instant-

Until a patrol, wide awake,
Descried him in the distance.

On coming up, the guard called out,
And asked him where he's going-
To which he answered with his spur
And left him in the mowing.

The bushes passed him like the wind,
And pebbles flew asunder.
The guard was left, far, far behind
All mixed with mud and wonder.

The Sergeant missed 'em, by good luck,
And took another tracing,
He turned his horse from Paulus Hook,
Elizabethtown facing.

It was the custom of Sir Hal
To send his galleys cruising,
And so it happened just then,
That two were at Van Deusen's.

"Twas just at eve the troopers reached
The camp they left that morning.
Champe's empty saddle, unto Lee,
Gave an unwelcome warning.

If Champe has suffered, 'tis my fault
So thought the generous Major.
"I would not have his garment touched
For millions on a wager."

And so it happened that brave Champe
Until Sir Hal deserted,
Deceiving him, and you, and me,
And into York was flirted.

He saw base Arnold in his camp,
Surrounded by the legion,
And told him of the recent prank,
That threw him in that region.

Then Arnold grinned and rubbed his hands
And e'enmost choked with pleasure,
Not thinking Champe was all the while
'A-taking of his measure.'

Full soon the British ship set sail,
Say, wasn't that a pity?
For thus it was brave-Sergeant Champe
Was taken from the city.

Most of what is known about this incident comes from Henry Lee's *Memoirs of the War in the Southern Department of the United States.*

The Newburgh Conspiracy

At the end of the Revolutionary War, General George Washington, calling on his keen leadership skills, innate wisdom and good judgment, diffused a powder keg known in history as the Newburgh Conspiracy, the closest America has ever come to a coup de etat. The not-prone-to-exaggerating future president warned: "The predicament was as critical and delicate as can well be conceived," one that could plunge the nation "into a gulph of civil horror."

The sun had shone on young America, flush with pride and optimism from its victorious battle for independence. Now, mired in debt estimated at $25 million, only darkness and "the forebodings of evil" loomed ahead. An impost (tax) to raise money had just been defeated. The States were not going to voluntarily make payments and Congress could not force them. Robert Morris, the superintendent of finances, cleverly stated the Articles of Confederation gave Congress "the privilege of asking for everything" but gave the States "the prerogative of granting nothing." Believing the very survival of America in jeopardy, many felt corrective action, no matter how extreme, was necessary. Money, not patriotism, paid the bills. But there was none.

Politicians' whining about money is one thing. But they weren't alone. Army officers also felt the crisis. Intrepid soldiers who had spent years fighting and suffering feared they would get neither their long overdue back-pay nor future pay, that is, the pensions they had been promised. "Pay must be found for the army," lamented future

President James Madison, who maddeningly wondered, "where it is to be found God knows."

Time was working against the army. Fighting had ceased months earlier and American diplomats in Europe were hammering out a peace treaty. Once signed, few would pay attention to the army or its complaints. When their guns were taken away, their leverage and voice would go too. Henry Knox warned that if not paid, the army might "be so deeply stung by the injustice and ingratitude of their country as to become...tygers and wolves."

Playing a very dangerous game, the conspirators threatened that money be raised quickly by the government, or else. The 'or else' was an implied coup, contained in an anonymous letter, actually written by John Armstrong Jr., an officer loyal to General Horatio Gates, an archenemy of Washington. Gates, Armstrong and a few others had conspired for years to embarrass, criticize and smear Washington. This threat of a coup meant that in addition to forcing Congress to raise money to pay the army, there now existed the added possible bonus of achieving their long-held dream: Gates replacing Washington as commander of the American Army.

It was a perilous time. Fifteen years afterwards, Secretary of War Benjamin Lincoln recalled that he "tremble[d] for his country." But the Sage of Mount Vernon, who called the incident "distressing beyond description" knew how to use words as weapons. His arsenal didn't include the sheer brilliance or eloquence of some other statesmen of his era, but he wielded the finely honed sword and scepter of persuasion and wisdom.

Sure, the soldiers were angry. They were also, as Private Joseph Martin wrote, "starved, ragged and meager...[without] a cent to help themselves." Another lamented "the insults and neglects of the cowardly countrymen" who would "damn the world rather than part with a dollar for their army." But these soldiers were still the same good men who had sacrificed tremendously. They had weathered the war's adversities and hardships. Just as importantly, Washington knew, with very few exceptions, his soldiers and officers revered him.

Washington's handling of the incident should be mandatory reading in management textbooks. The anonymous letter, circulated on Monday morning, March 10th, called for officers to meet the following day to redress their grievances, specifically, "the coldness and severity of government" towards the soldiers who had put the country "in the chair of independence." The mutinous letter criticized their own country which "tramples upon your rights, disdains your cries and insults your distresses."

Washington had been forewarned by Alexander Hamilton that some deviltry was brewing:

> "...I have often thought...that the public interest might be benefitted, if the Commander in Chief of the Army was let more into the political and pecuniary state of our affairs than he is...where there is a want of information there must be a chance medley; and a man may be upon the brink of a precipice before he is aware of the danger, when a little foreknowledge might enable him to avoid it. But this by the by."

Washington acted quickly. He authorized the officers to discuss the matter among themselves, but changed the meeting to Saturday the 15th. For the element of surprise, Washington gave the impression he would not attend the meeting, leaving General Gates, the second in command in charge.

The meeting site-the New Windsor Cantonment, called the Temple of Virtue, or simply the Temple, included approximately seven hundred huts, which could hold about seven thousand soldiers and a few family members.

The meeting started as planned on the 15th—the Ides of March. Washington walked into the mutinous den of hostility and deftly cured the mad beast with a powerful concoction of shame, pride and patriotism. He called on the soldiers to recall why they had fought so long and implored them to avoid dangerous mischief caused by a few anonymous malcontents. He appealed to their sense of honor, forcefully pointing out the folly being contemplated as wrong and dangerous. He asked for a little more patience, requesting they "give one more distinguished proof of unexampled patriotism and patient virtue." He played on their sympathies, reminding them that he also had suffered greatly for eight long years. Certainly it was well understood that if things had gone the other way, Washington's neck would have been the first one with a rope around it.

He brought out of his pocket and began reading a letter. From Congressman Joseph Jones of Virginia, the letter was dated February 27, 1783. The 'Father of our Country,' who had seen some tough times, pulled out a pair of spectacles, something no one had seen him with before. Military battles a thing of the past, his youth a fading memory, the old war-horse who had done so much with so little for so long simply was losing the battle of time. Those not swept over with shame upon hearing the sentence about soldiers "who harbour wicked designs…to lessen [Washington's] popularity in the Army," certainly were flooded with guilt when Washington (having a hard time reading the letter) quietly said, "I have grown gray in the service of my country and now find myself going blind." The tears on many soldiers' faces washed away the conspiracy.

Washington then left the room and that was that. The officers agreed to immediately terminate the matter. Without fanfare, an incident that could have destroyed America quietly slipped into history. One historian lamented the evil plans of some of the soldiers in the Newburgh Conspiracy "disrobed [the Temple] of its mantle of purity."

The Plot to Kidnap George Washington

A week before America declared its independence, an American soldier- a member of the elite Commander-in-Chief's Guard no less- was executed for conspiring to assist the British in destroying the American Army and capturing and/or killing General George Washington. Having met the elite guard's qualifications of "sobriety, honesty and good behavior...from 5' 8" to 5' 10"...handsomely and well made...clean and spruce," Thomas Hickey, born in Ireland, found himself living in New York City when the Revolutionary War broke out.

Teeming with staunch Loyalists, New Yorkers drank the defiant elixir of sabotage at taverns such as *Corbie's*, the *Highlander* and *Robin Hood*. British agents funded the owners of these 'grog shops' or what early American writer Washington Irving called "a network of corruption and treachery" to entice New Yorkers to join the Loyalist ranks and spring into action when the British landed in the city. The going offer: five guineas and the promise of two hundred acres of land for the recruit and one hundred acres for his wife. Intoxicated by too many toasts to the ruination of the rebel army, Hickey brashly spewed threats and promises he would someday come to regret. That day got closer when a patriotic patron named William Collier reported to authorities comments Hickey had made at the *Sergeant Arms Tavern*.

In June 1776, eighteen-year-old Private Hickey "got bewitched after hard money" (George Washington's expression) and tried to pass counterfeit currency. There was a lot of counterfeiting going on; even the British Navy was believed to have been printing mounds of it on its vessels blockading New York. The British were not counterfeiting American currency to make money—they were doing so to get so much currency in the system that it would lose its value and hence undermine the war effort. In complaining about British counterfeiting efforts, George Washington complained that: "No artifices are left untried by the enemy to injure us," and Thomas Paine called this counterfeiting: "A new vice to the military catalogue" which no earlier enemy had been "mean enough to even think of it." Paine was incorrect: printing counterfeit currency to undermine the enemy's war effort had been going on for centuries.

Back to Thomas Hickey, who landed in prison after his jail chatter was reported to authorities. Before the month was out, the young miscreant was hanged from a tree located near the present day intersection of Christie and Grand Streets.

Fellow convict Isaac Ketchum heard Hickey's comments and knew he had a get-out-of-jail-card. Ketchum claimed he was so "deeply imprest with shame and confusion for his [own] past misconduct" that he wanted to report "nothing concearning my afair but entirely on another subgyt." The subject: his cellmate named Hickey had boasted that he enlisted seven hundred people to help the British defeat what he called the "damnably corrupted" American Army.

By June 1776, hundreds of Loyalists had already been reported to American authorities and a 'Committee to Detect Conspiracies' had been formed in New York. Those found guilty of providing information or supplies to the British were jailed or banished to another colony.

The committee had been established "for the hearing and trying of disaffected persons and those of equivocal characters." Most of the characters knew enough to be discreet, or as John Adams said, "durst not show their heads."

Hickey, however, dursted. His loud, indiscreet and brash threats in bars and behind bars made him a prime target. He was tried on June

26 before thirteen officers for "exciting and joining in a mutiny and sedition, and treacherously corresponding with, enlisting among, and receiving pay from the enemies of the United American Colonies."

Four defendants, Ketchum included, were called to prove Hickey's guilt; it appears they were given leniency for their testimony. Gilbert Forbes, one of the plot's moneymen, testified he had paid Hickey. William Green and William Welch stated they had had conversations about the plot with Hickey and heard him say: "This country was sold...the enemy would soon arrive, and it was best for us old countrymen to make our peace ... or they would kill us all." Hickey did not offer any evidence in his defense. He claimed he was merely trying to cheat the Tories and "get some money from them."

Washington hoped Hickey's "unhappy fate" would "produce many salutary consequences and deter others from entering into like traitorous practices." Hickey, the guard's fallen star had somehow plunged into a netherworld galaxy of convicts and con men. And some unsavory women too. The real source of Hickey's downfall, however, might have been members of the opposite sex. Washington laconically lamented: "Lewd women...first led [Hickey] into practices which ended in an untimely and ignominious death."

It is not known if Washington still had Hickey in mind fourteen months later when he wrote in general orders: "Officers...will take every precaution...to prevent an inundation of bad women from Philadelphia."

Aaron Burr, another American officer, who later went on to become vice president of the United States complained about women spies during the Revolution: "There are a number of women here of bad character, who are continually running to New York and back again. If they were men, I would flog them without mercy."

Years later, David Mathews, the Loyalist mayor of New York at the time of the 'Hickey Plot' (described by writers at the time as: hellish, vile, horrid, and most barbarous and infernal), stated in a sworn deposition that George Washington was to have been stabbed.

Whatever it was called, this scheme to assist the British upon their arrival was foiled just in time. On the morning of June 29, 1776, a staggering armada of British ships was sighted. One witness wrote:

"The whole bay was full of shipping … I thought all London was afloat." But Thomas Hickey would not be there to assist the British. A day earlier, before a crowd of approximately 20,000, Hickey became the first of an estimated one hundred soldiers executed during the American Revolution.

Loyalists were also referred to as Tories. The word Tory was Irish and originally meant outlaw. Those against the British were called Patriots or Whigs. One Continental Army officer complained that Loyalists "are destroying the army by their conduct much faster than [the British] can possibly do by their fighting." Famed Green Mountain Boy Ethan Allen complained that "Tories…measured their loyalty to the English king by the barbarity, fraud and deceit which they exercise towards the Whigs." One anonymous wit defined a Loyalist as "a thing whose head is in England, whose body is in America and whose neck needs stretching."

Thomas Paine poetically illuminated the importance of the patriot's fight in his book *Common Sense*: "The sun never shined on a cause of greater worth," and in *The American Crisis*: "Let them call me rebel...but I should suffer the misery of devils, were I to make a whore of my soul by swearing allegiance to one whose character is that of a sottish, stupid, stubborn, worthless, brutish man...There are cases which cannot be overdone by language, and this is one." And since this was, after all, the 18th Century where everything was exclaimed in verse, Paine had this to add:

"In a chariot of light from the regions of day,
The Goddess of Liberty came;
Ten thousand celestials directed the way,
And hither conducted the dame.
A fair budding branch from the gardens above,
Where millions with millions agree,
She brought in her hand as a pledge of her love,
The plant she named Liberty Tree.
But hear, O ye' swains, 'tis a tale most profane,
How all the tyrannical powers;
Kings, Commons, and Lords are uniting again,
To cut down this guardian of ours:

From the east to the west blow the trumpet to arms,
Through the land let the sound of it flee,
Let the far and the near, all unite with a cheer,
In defense of our Liberty Tree."

Of course the Loyalists were not without their own passionate beliefs. They "fought independence bitterly with the pen, the Bible, their wealth and the sword. They denounced it as the direst calamity, supreme folly, diabolically wicked and suicidal...Engineered by debtors, smugglers, republicans and the illiterate rabble, [it] would end in making the colonists slaves of some foreign tyrant." And like the passionate patriots, they also wrote poetry to verse their views:

"Ye Tories all rejoice and sing
Success to George our gracious king:
These hardy and stupid fools,
Some apish and pragmatic mules:
Good Lord! Disperse this venal tribe,
Their doctrine let no fools imbibe:
There's Washington and all his men,
Where Howe had one, the goose had ten:
Prepare, prepare, my friends prepare,
For scenes of blood, the field of war,
To royal standard we'll repair
And curse the haughty Congress."

An Early America
Health Care Crisis

The Dogs of War were unleashed in the American Revolution and the meanest, nastiest one of all was named Disease. "The smallpox! The smallpox!" John Adams shrieked, "what shall we do with it?" Benedict Arnold believed this "King of Terror" would ruin the army and George Washington warned its "calamitous consequences" were more deadly than "the sword of the enemy."

Widely believed responsible for more than two-thirds of all American casualties, "it raged," one historian noted, "in the streets and cantonments." It led to rioting in the towns. It also led to the first government-wide immunization program.

After a ten to fourteen day incubation period, the highly contagious disease (which felt at first like a bad flu) ran its course in a month, with widely varied fatality rates. Victims were left dead within two weeks, survivors often left maimed or blind, usually scarred and always with a life-time immunity.

George Washington carried slight facial pockmarks the remainder of his life after contracting the disease in Barbados in 1751 on his first and only foreign trip. It had taken, to name a few, a child of Benjamin Franklin's, a delegate to the 2nd Continental Congress and Ethan Allen's son.

One scribe noted how the infected were quarantined: "The

smallpox raged…in a violent manner. There was a pest-house provided for every one that was taken with it, a little distance from the town." Inoculations were sporadically available, but were dangerous and controversial.

Although sometimes deadly, inoculations (or variolation), were much safer than getting the disease the "natural way." Inoculations were introduced in America in the 1720s after a slave named Onesimus explained how the process had been successfully used in Africa for many years. "Pus (also called the venom) from the ripe postules" of a patient was inserted into the inoculee's open cut, usually in the arm or finger.

In the Revolution, the British and the epidemic attacked Boston at about the same time. A group of thirty-six citizens (called "the Committee of Thirty Six Persons") personally inspected all houses to determine who had contracted the disease "the natural way, & by inoculation, & how many of each have died?" To keep this enemy outside the gate, those infected were sent to pesthouses. People who refused (like Paul Revere who wouldn't let his daughter be taken away) found their yards fenced in with red warning flags hung outside.

Bostonians smitten with "taking" the disease went "inoculation-mad." Abigail Adams gleefully reported: "Such a spirit of inoculation never before took place. The town and every house in it, are as full [of recovering patients] as they can hold."

A journal written by a Bostonian reflected the terror felt in the city: "…PS I fear the Small Pox will spread universally as Boston is shut up with it & people flocking in for innoculation…the times look dark and gloom[y] upon the account of the wars. I believe this year will decide the fate of America, which way it will turn God only knows…"

In the end, almost 5,000 people were inoculated in Boston, of which twenty-eight died.

But the inoculations were not without controversy. Numerous anti-inoculation riots blazed from the 1720s up to and through the Revolution. Some years earlier, one rioter launched a stone and warning through Cotton Mather's window (the man who owned

Onesimus): "You dog, damn you. I'll inoculate you with this, with a pox to you."

It seemed too strange, too unnatural. However, it was primarily money, or the lack of it, provoking this health care controversy. It pitted the haves against the have-nots. By getting inoculated, people brought the disease into their community, potentially exposing everyone to get it the natural (and more deadly) way. It may or may not have otherwise come into their community.

But not everyone could get inoculated. The poor, alas, were left out. Left out because the lengthy recovery period (about a month) precluded many who could ill-afford to leave their jobs for that long. Left out also because it was expensive. "The expence of having the operation performed by a surgeon," grumbled Benjamin Franklin, "has been pretty high in some parts of America."

The conditions-teems of exhausted, hungry soldiers packed in squalor -were tailor made for the pox. At one point, a third of all soldiers were believed ill from the disease. The threat lurked in every town and regiment. It sailed on ships and hovered in campsites. The crisis forced George Washington to make a critical decision, one that would seriously impact his soldiers:

To inoculate or not to inoculate? That was the paradox the pugnacious general wrestled with. At length. Getting the disease through inoculation was the safest way, so it seemed like a good idea. But was it too dangerous? What if the British learned there would be a staggering percentage of Continental soldiers recuperating in hospitals, too weak to fight? Even on a good day, American forces were stretched thin.

Spreading inoculations over a wider expanse of time would minimize troop shortages at any given time. But this would also significantly increase the risk to those waiting their turn. That is, the recently inoculated troops, who were contagious for a month, might pass it along to others. How do you covertly carry out a massive project like this, knowing spies and British Loyalists skulked everywhere?

The decision went back and forth. There were periods during the war when soldiers could be inoculated, and times when they should not. For awhile it was strictly forbidden, penalized by death. During these periods, soldiers discreetly inoculated themselves (or each other) in the thigh to avoid detection. One soldier who inoculated his comrades recounted the secrecy involved in the process: "As this was against orders, they were sent into [the] room blindfolded, were inoculated, and sent out in the same condition. Many lives were saved...as none thus inoculated died."

Finally, Washington ordered the troops to get inoculated. Private Joseph Martin recounted:

"I was soon...ordered off, in company with about four hundred others of the Connecticut forces, to a set of old barracks, a mile or two distant in the Highlands, to be inoculated with the smallpox...after two or three days [we] received the infection. I had the smallpox favorably as did the rest, generally. We lost none, but it was more by good luck or rather a kind Providence interfering, than by my good conduct that I escaped with life...I left the hospital on the sixteenth day after I was inoculated, and soon after joined the regiment."

Private Martin went on to say he immediately got very sick from several other illnesses (which he attributed to leaving the hospital too soon after the inoculation).

In the end, the army managed to stealthily pull it off, without letting the enemy know their battle readiness had significantly, albeit temporarily, decreased. This army-wide effort in 1777 and 1778 turned out to be America's first widespread government-mandated immunization program.

Almost two decades later, Thomas Jefferson expressed his appreciation to Dr. Edward Jenner, the man who discovered the smallpox vaccine:

"You have erased from the calendar of human afflictions one of its greatest. Yours is the comfortable reflection that mankind can never forget that you have lived. Future nations will know by history only that the loathsome small-pox has existed and by you has been extirpated."

Christopher Ludwick:
the Baker-General

In 1776, a fifty-six-year-old Philadelphia baker enlisted in the Revolutionary War and before it was over had baked thousands of pounds of bread for the American Army and persuaded untold Hessian soldiers to leave the British Army. Christopher Ludwick immigrated to America in 1754 and quickly became a very successful businessman. Before the war his fellow Pennsylvanians, about a third German, had elected the gregarious and patriotic 'baker-general' to several community positions.

Slightly fewer than 30,000 Hessian soldiers served in America as hired mercenaries for the British during the Revolutionary War. England's original endeavor to hire 20,000 Russian troops was denied by Catherine the Great. That England would hire mercenaries to quell an American rebellion stung the Continental Congress enough to include it as a complaint in the Declaration of Independence: "He [King George III] is at this time transporting large armies of foreign Mercenaries to compleat the works of death, desolution and tyranny..."

The sting of paying foreign soldiers, "slavish Hessian guards," according to Ethan Allen, "who were sent to America for no other design but cruelty and desolation" pulsated through patriotic rhetoric, including this from Thomas Paine's *American Crisis*:

"I know our situation well...by perseverance and fortitude

we have the prospect of a glorious issue; by cowardice and submission, the sad choice of a variety of evils—a ravaged country—a depopulated city, habitants without safety, and slavery without hope—our homes turned into barracks and bawdyhouses for Hessians, and a future race to provide for, whose fathers we shall doubt of."

There was no Germany at the time, but instead a very loose confederation of German-speaking provinces or territories, six of which negotiated treaties with the British. They are collectively referred to as Hessians because the Hessian government provided, by far, the most soldiers. Had Waldeck provided the most, the generic term would probably be Waldeckers. Each territory negotiated the best terms it could extract (the going rate was seven pounds, four shillings and four pence sterling for each soldier) and some even contained a 'blood clause' requiring an additional payment in the event of a soldier's death or maiming. The first treaty was signed on January 9, 1776 with the Duke of Brunswick. The number of men each sent to America:

Brunswick:	5,723
Hesse-Cassel:	16,992
Hesse-Hanau:	2,422
Anspach-Bayreuth:	2,353
Waldeck:	1,225
Anhalt-Zerbst:	1,160
Total	29,875

British Officer "Gentleman" Johnny Burgoyne emphasized in a letter the need for hiring foreign soldiers: "Such a pittance of troops as Great Britain and Ireland can supply will only serve to protract the war, to incur fruitless expense and insure disappointment."

England leasing Hessians soldiers was nothing new; by 1776 it had already been done five times in the 18th Century. But it was not without controversy. Frederick the Great pitied "the poor Hessians who end[ed] their lives unhappily and uselessly in America." "The conduct," he charged, "was caused by nothing but dirty selfishness." Another warned "the treasury...was filled with blood and tears."

But money talks and in 1776, the "damnable money" spoke German. One leader who acknowledged the distastefulness of the practice argued the treaty's benefits "far outweigh the hatefulness of the business." He believed once people "see foreign money flowing into our poor country…they will be enchanted, and will acknowledge that the troops…have conquered our worst enemy—our debts."

It was then up to the recruiters, described thusly in a book in 1876: "All countries, especially all German countries, are infested with a new species of predatory two-legged animals—Prussian recruiters. They glide about, under disguise if necessary; lynx-eyed, eager almost as the Jesuit hounds are; not hunting the souls of men… but the bodies, in a merciless, carnivorous manner."

The Hessians fought bravely and valiantly in America. One American soldier lamented their losses: "The skulls and other bones and hair were scattered about the place. Here were Hessian skulls as thick as a bombshell. Poor fellows! They were left unburied in a foreign land. They had, perhaps, as near and dear friends to lament their sad destiny as the Americans who lay buried near them."

Christopher Ludwick must have been very disturbed to see German-speaking soldiers from his ancestral homeland fighting German-speaking Americans. There were two ways to skin a panther, or in this case, lessen the leased Hessian forces: defeat them or entice them to desert from the army, move to the peaceful Pennsylvania countryside and start a new life. While General Washington struggled with the former, the baker-general deftly handled the latter.

The skilled propagandist named Ludwick convinced many Hessian prisoners of war to desert from the army and take up residence among a welcoming German community only a few miles away. 'Farm, don't fight' would have been the bumper sticker, if such a thing existed. How many he persuaded will never be known, but it worked. It worked for the reason Ludwick explained to the Continental Congress: "The many Hessians…are so well pleased with this country…that at all events they would rather prefer to settle here than to return to the dreary abodes of bondage from whence they came."

In addition to the POWs, the audacious Ludwick, posing as a deserter, snuck into the Hessian Camp at Staten Island and made the same quality of life spiel, including a plea that Pennsylvania offered "a complete farm except for the frau." Sometimes, as shown in one Hessian's diary, the product sold itself: "America is a wonderful land, where the industrious hand of the worker never goes unrewarded, and those who work never want." This particular soldier seemed surprised with early American recreation: "The Americans, from their youth on, participate in vigorous body exercise, and when nothing else is to be done, they hit a ball." Another Hessian remarked, "the Americans are bold, unyielding, and fearless. They have always lived in plenty, and we cannot block their resources [nor] their indomitable ideas of liberty."

In July 1776, Pennsylvania began hiring Hessian POWs to make ammunition. A month later, the federal government formed a committee to "encourage Hessians...to quit [their] iniquitous service." Rewards would be offered to those who "choose to accept lands, liberty, safety, and a communion of good laws and mild government in a country where many of their friends and relations are already happily settled, rather than continue exposed to the toils and dangers of a long and bloody war." By 1778, the Americanization of Hessians was at full boil: the government offered fifty acres for any Hessian to desert. The pot was sweetened for captains who brought forty Hessians with him: 800 acres, four oxen, one bull and two cows.

In England, James Luttrell, a Member of Parliament worried of this exact thing happening. He pointed out the British were simply providing "an excellent opportunity for our hired troops to desert, because they most likely will be offered lands and protection."

The following broadside was written in German and circulated to Hessians:

"Christian Gentlemen and Fellow Brethren!

Because our implacable enemies, the ministers of Great Britain, consider it impossible, to conquer us with their own and unwilling troops, they have turned to your Landlords, who have left you to them, in order by your assistance in a probable manner to execute the cruel plan to subjugate us and to make slaves of us. Because we are fighting for nothing else but what nature, reason, and the British constitution demand, we are completely justified, and can do the same with the greatest joy, to commend our cause into the hands of Him who executes justice, and helps the oppressed. We have turned to heaven, hence we do not fear that which men can do to us. Yes, because our enemies are exerting themselves to the utmost to annihilate us, we consider it our duty to address you and to adjure you by all that is holy, to consider, how you will on the frightful day of divine judgment answer for the innocent blood that you must shed, if you decide to support our enemies. You cannot have any reason for insults from our side; we have never done you the least injury, and you did not know a thing about the unhappy causes of our quarrels. Because, however, with our enemies you are taking part in this war, which can be defended neither on the basis of Christianity, nor according to the basis of wisdom and honor, we hope that you will contribute nothing to the suppression of an oppressed people. Your countrymen, when they pressed at home, in American found a secure place of refuge, and still have the enjoyment of it, under the shade of their own vineyards and fig trees, in the most complete freedom. We offer you the same. All those who lay down their arms and want to unite with us shall receive sufficient land, and all conveniences with complete freedom from taxes for ten years shall be granted them. You shall have all the privileges of native Americans and the most complete freedom of religion. If, however, none of the above-named causes will be effective among you and you will continue to assist our enemies, we shall not look upon you as people of honor and as soldiers, and give our men the sharpest orders not to give a single one of you quarter. John Hancocks (sic) President.

Dr. Benjamin Rush, one of our nation's Founding Fathers, praised Ludwick for showing Hessians "the difference between the privileges and manner of life of an American freeman and those of a Hessian slave," and for providing "the most captivating descriptions of the affluence and independence of their former countrymen in the German counties of Pennsylvania." George Washington believed that well-treated Hessian POWs "so fraught with a love of liberty," who were returned to the enemy would "create a disgust to the service among the remainder of the foreign troops and widen that breach which is already opened between them and the British."

In May 1777, Ludwick was appointed superintendent of bakers. American soldiers were generally allotted ¾ to 1 ¼ pounds of flour daily. Sometimes they baked their own bread, commonly known as fire cakes: "the [flour] mixed with cold water, then daubed upon a flat stone and scorched on one side." Often, however, they traded their flour for rum or bread, "hard enough to break the teeth of a rat," according to one soldier. Hard bread was preferable to soft because it lasted longer and was easier to carry. The soldiers were usually, as characterized by one poet:

"Riddled with hunger, grey of face
And weakly cursing the deadly place."

Sometimes it seemed that when they had food it was only bread. One soldier wrote that he had nothing but fire-cakes and water, meal after meal, eating so much of it until his "glutted gutts are turned to pasteboard."

Almost single-handedly, Ludwick rescued the critical operation of getting the staff of life to soldiers too familiar with getting a loaf of nothing. "His deportment," according to Washington, "has afforded unquestionable proofs of his integrity and worth." With utmost dedication and honesty, the baker-general could just as well have been called the baker-saint.

He died at the age of eighty on June 17, 1801, and is buried in the Lutheran Cemetery in Germantown. His epitaph says it all:

"Art thou poor, Venerate his character,
Art thou rich, Imitate his example."

According to *The Guide Book of Historic Germantown*, Christopher Ludwick's house in Germantown, Pennsylvania was on the south side of Haines Street, the first house east of Chew Street, about ¾ of a mile east of Main Street.

The English-language
Controversy

Fifteen years after Ludwick died, fifty-nine German-speaking Americans in Pennsylvania were charged with assault and conspiracy for harassing a group of fellow congregants who wanted to introduce English services into their shared church.

Prior to these criminal charges, a riot of two to three hundred people had broken out in Philadelphia over this language argument. The defendants were found guilty and ordered to pay fines of $5 to $50 each. Pennsylvania Governor (a German-American) Simon Snyder subsequently upheld the convictions, but dropped the fines and court costs.

Today's debates about immigrants speaking (or refusing to speak) English is nothing new in America. As early as 1755 Benjamin Franklin, a friend to everyone and every group, expressed disappointment over a group of German-Americans who refused to learn or speak English. "Why should the Palatine Boors," Franklin asked, "be suffered to swarm into our settlements, and by herding together establish their language and manners to the exclusion of ours? Why should Pennsylvania, founded by the English, become a Colony of Aliens, who will shortly be so numerous as to Germanize us instead of us anglifying them?"

The language debate centered in heavily German-concentrated areas of Pennsylvania but were not restricted there. In 1795, Germans in Virginia initiated a debate to have federal documents printed in German. The House of Representatives, presided over by Frederick Muhlenberg, a German-American from Pennsylvania rejected the proposal on the grounds it was too expensive. The Constitution was silent on the subject of language but during the Confederation period (1781-1789), various federal government documents were printed in German, French, Dutch and Swedish. Federalist #2 (written by John Jay) included a sentence that: "Providence has been pleased to give this one connected country, to one united people...speaking the same language."

An early historian wrote in 1789 that "the English language is the one which is universally spoken in the United States, in which business is transacted, and the records kept." People would, he predicted, "become so assimilated, as that all nominal distinctions shall be lost in the general and honorable name of AMERICANS."

John Adams weighed in with an argument for English to be spoken by everyone: "Language...influences not only the form of government, but the temper, the sentiments, and manners of the people." Years later President Teddy Roosevelt proclaimed that every immigrant to the United States "should be required within five years to learn English or leave the country."

Noah Webster opined, "English is the common root or stock from which our national language will be derived. All others will gradually waste away—and within a century and a half, North America will be peopled with hundred millions of men, all speaking the same language...a national language is a national tie, and what country wants it more than America?" Certainly Webster was right about the part of his prediction that the United States of America would someday have hundreds of millions of people.

Revolutionary War Finances

"**M**oney! Money! Money! … I want money so much that I would do almost anything for some." These comments were written by the paymaster-general of the American Army during the Revolutionary War, John Pierce. Having received no money for his department for six months, he warned that without funds, military operations "may entirely cease." If these were the times that tried mens' souls, as Thomas Paine wrote, it was also the wretched epoch that obliterated hope. Emptiness permeated the treasury, want shadowed the soldiers, and desperation snuffed out any flicker of success. There was no money. Letter after letter said so.

George Washington wrote in 1775: "If the evil is not immediately remedied…the army must absolutely break up." The next year: "I think the game is pretty near up." In 1778: Without more money the army would "starve, dissolve or disperse." In 1779: "A dissolution of the army…is unavoidable." In 1780: "If our condition should not undergo a very speedy…change…it will be difficult to point out all the consequences." In 1781: "The aggravated calamities and distresses… are beyond description," and without "a foreign loan our present force…cannot be kept together." In perhaps a moment of resignation he wondered: "But why need I run into the detail…we are at the end of our tether…now or never our deliverance must come."

Thomas Paine claimed that even if the army had the necessary provisions, they didn't have enough money to transport them. Ben Franklin knew, as people in Boston wondered, why soldiers in Boston had not fired their cannons: "We could not afford it." (Franklin was not joking when he suggested that soldiers be supplied with bows and arrows.) James Madison was shocked in 1780 to find "the public treasury empty, public credit exhausted," and one historian noted that at one point in 1782, "there was not a single dollar in the treasury."

A Board of Treasury originally handled government finances, but proved ineffective because of endless political squabbling. In June 1781, Robert Morris, named superintendent of finances, took over. Along with the money shortage, he faced the confusion of multiple coins and currencies, making for easy counterfeiting and fraud. The poem *'Death of the Paper Money'* included this verse:

"He made our wives and daughters fine
And pleas'd most everybody;
He bought the rich their costly wine
The poor their flip and toddy."

A British officer observed that New York money was no good in New Jersey, New Jersey money no good in Pennsylvania, "and so on." Each state "entertained little opinion as to the value of their neighbor's money." In addition, there were:

"Ninepences and fourpence-ha'-pennies, there were bits and half bits, pistareens, picayunes, and fips. Of gold pieces there were the johannes, or joe, the doubloon, the moidore, and pistole, with English and French guineas, carolins, ducats, and chequins. Of coppers there were English pence and half-pence and French sous."

The war cost approximately $135-170 million, excluding amounts expended by foreign governments. Finances became especially desperate and inflation skyrocketed in 1777 when the Continental dollar collapsed, hence the expression 'not worth a continental.'

Many blamed profiteers and speculators. Government price controls were attempted, but as Thomas Paine explained, when they tried regulating the price of goods, like salt, "the consequence was that no salt was brought to market." Simply put, price fixing, "reprobated by many and obeyed by few," proved ineffective. Washington berated army contractors and speculators ("as active and wicked as the Devil") and proclaimed he'd like to "hang them all on a gallows higher than Haman." Thomas Jefferson laid the blame on the money glut, calling other explanations "non-sensical quackery."

The soldiers got hit the hardest. With little or no food, supplies or clothes, they were according to General Nathaniel Greene, "naked as the day they were born." Baron De Kalb said those who had not "tasted the cruelties" felt by soldiers in the war, "know not what it is to suffer." A private complained, "we vent[ed] our spleen at our country...our government...and then ourselves for our imbecility in staying there and starving...for an ungrateful people."

Finding money was critical, but nothing seemed to work as one Congressional delegate lamented: "One hypothesis has been piled upon another...scheme has been tacked to scheme, and system succeeded system...and finally all [the] pretty...schemes crumbled away."

According to John Adams, taxes were the "radical cure." He urged his wife to pay every tax even if it meant selling "my books, or clothes or oxen, or your cows, to pay it." But Congress didn't have the power to enforce taxes, and most states, even if required, didn't have the money to pay. By 1781, the Massachusetts debt was eleven million pounds; in Virginia "there is not a shilling in the treasury...nor is it probable there will be..."

Privateering (essentially government-sanctioned piracy) brought in money and goods, but the national government ended up competing against the states. Men who would have otherwise served on military vessels were enticed to serve instead on more lucrative private ventures.

A national lottery was tried, without much success, again largely due to competition from the states, which had their own lotteries, including two for *Loyalist causes*. Not surprisingly, the fact that the prizes were paid in paper money or certificates stymied ticket sales.

To halt inflation Congress replaced and revalued at 40:1 the Continentals with new State dollars. Many states followed suit, including Pennsylvania which revalued its currency at 75:1. However, these efforts also proved ineffective.

It was as if a thirteen-member team, with a different state written on each jersey, blocked every play. Not knowing what else to do, Congress punted—they printed more money. And by printing reams and reams of paper, they shanked the punt. In the war's first three years $38 million had been printed. In 1778 and 1779, another $188 million was printed, making for such a worthless glut of paper that even soldiers sometimes tried to refuse to take continentals on those few occasions it was given.

Washington, who noted: "a waggon load of money could scarcely buy a waggon-load of provisions," was left to ponder: "When a rat in the shape of a horse could not be bought for less than 200 pounds, what funds can stand the present expenses of the army?"

By 1779, the continental's value had declined 97%, corn prices increased 1255% in one year and $4,000 Continentals bought $1 in gold. By 1781, a soldier paid $1,200 for a quart of rum, Sam Adams spent $2,000 for $20 worth of clothes, Thomas Paine bought a pair of socks for $300, and a cavalry horse cost $150,000.

Foreign loans were sought, but even that was fraught with competition from the states. John Adams complained that many states had representatives "running all over Europe, asking to borrow money." Efforts to raise foreign money proved difficult. Adams voiced his frustration that seeking loans made him feel like "a man in the midst of the ocean negotiating for his life among a school of sharks." In the end, trade and a raft of loans from France, Spain and Holland kept the struggling country afloat in a bloody sea of red ink.

The Revolutionary
War Lottery

When the long arm of the tax-man comes up a little short, governments have often lured the beguiling Goddess of Chance to use her charming wiles of lotteries to replenish the bare coffers of the treasury. In the American Revolution, Congress beckoned her to help fund the war.

> "That none can 'reap who never sow,'
> Requires no argument to show;
> Alike 'tis clear—none prizes gain
> Who never plough the lottery main."

England had used lotteries since 1569 (to strengthen "the Realme, and towardes such other publique good workes") and the nascent Colony of Virginia benefited from them in 1612 "for the more effectual advancing of the said Plantation." John Smith heralded lotteries as the "reall and substantiall food, by which Virginia hath been nourished." About 8,000 pounds of lottery revenue fed the entire 17,800-pound Virginia budget of 1620.

> "The Merchants of Virginia now,
> Hath nobly tooke in hand,
> The bravest golden lottery,
> That ere was in this land."

State-approved gambling evoked controversy then as well as now. Puritans, not surprisingly, enacted the first anti-gambling laws in America (in 1638). Quakers quickly followed suit, outlawing "such… enticing…evil sports and games." Eventually various state legislatures voiced concerns. Pennsylvania warned of "mischievous and unlawful games, called lotteries…which…ruin…many poor families." Georgia chided "idle, loose, disorderly persons [who] …support themselves in a dishonest, dissolute course of life," and Massachusetts urged "children, servants…and other unwary people" to avoid this "vain and foolish expense of money."

One person incurring a foolish gambling expense was British General Johnny Burgoyne, who "wagers Charles Fox one pony (fifty guineas) that he will be home victorious from America by Christmas Day, 1777." Had Gentleman Johnny been back in England rather than at the Saratoga battlefield, he might have won it back in the stock market. Some English investors profited by shorting stocks whenever there was a remote likelihood that bad war news might be received.

The British, who used lotteries to support wartime efforts against the colonies, also had its dissenters, one who wrote to an acquaintance in America: "These cursed…lotteries…are big with 10,000 evils. Let the Devil's children have them all to themselves."

It's likely the Devil's children (if that meant Americans) did have lotteries mostly to themselves. Although not 10,000, one historian calculated that before the Revolutionary War, one hundred fifty seven towns and colonies sanctioned lotteries to fund hospitals, roads, bridges and churches. Rhode Island, with the majority (by far), could have called itself the Lottery Colony. In fact, a lottery in 1750 for land prizes resulted in a town known today as Lotteryville.

"The silly man may buy a ticket
Perhaps 'twill open reason's wicket.
The lucky are accounted wise,
And so they are—in folly's eyes.
Who nought but fortune deifies."
"Those who will not, when fortune offers,
Hold to her hand their empty coffers;

May well lament when others gain,
What they've neglected to obtain."

George Washington gambled in several lotteries in his lifetime. As an officer in the French and Indian War, he had been ordered to control excessive gambling among his men. During the Revolution he frequently issued orders to try and stop gambling, but without much luck. It was said that starving soldiers at Valley Forge rolled dice to win acorns to eat. In one directive, Washington ordered, "all officers, non-commissioned officers and soldiers are positively forbid playing cards, or other games of chance. At this time of public distress, men may find enough to do, in the service of their God and their country, without abandoning themselves to vice and immorality."

Thomas Jefferson believed "gaming corrupts our dispositions," but made an exception for lotteries, which he considered "useful in certain occasions." Lotteries were an accepted, albeit controversial way to raise money.

So it shouldn't have surprised anyone to find general orders from George Washington posted like girl scout cookie sales on office bulletin boards. In April 1778 he reported: "A few Continental lottery tickets to be sold at the Orderly Office;" seven months later: "A few tickets in the second class of the United States lottery are received and ready for sale...adventurers are requested to apply." Indeed, the word adventurer described the type of person who would bet on a government madly issuing mounds of worthless money.

Congress hoped the lottery would provide, after prizes and operating expenses, $1.5 million in cash and a $7 million loan. Small prizes (less than $20) were paid in cash but large prize-winners got an IOU payable in five years with 4% interest (later increased to 6%). The lottery "for carrying on the present most just and necessary war in defence of...lives, liberties and property" commenced in Philadelphia in November 1776 with seven appointed managers. The top prize was $50,000. In addition there were two $30,000 prizes, two at $25,000, two at $20,000, two at $15,000 and ten at $10,000.

Lotteries were set up like raffles with buyers receiving consecutively numbered tickets rather than selecting their own numbers. Two wheels were used to select winners--one had all the tickets in it, the other had pieces of paper, some with prizes written on them. A ticket from one wheel was drawn and matched with a winning ('prize') or losing ('blank') ticket from the other. There were four classes of drawings with 100,000 tickets available for each class. The ticket prices were $10, $20, $30 and $40 for each class, respectively. Several months passed between each class of drawings.

"Thanks to the state for every favor past
And this indulgence, greater than the last;
The richest wheel e'er offered to your view
The prizes many, and the blanks but few."

Losing tickets could be 'reused' for subsequent drawings, i.e. with a losing 1st round ticket and another $10, a buyer could obtain a new ticket for the 2nd drawing. If that ticket lost in the 2nd round, he could (for his losing ticket and $10 more) obtain a ticket for the 3rd drawing. Same thing for 4th and last round.

The lottery was disbanded in December 1782 with mixed reviews. It did generate some money--at least $135,000 in lottery revenues were Congressionally appropriated for military expenses.

Competition and inconsistent management thwarted its success. During the eight-year war there were twenty-four state-operated lotteries, five of which were for military causes. There were even two lotteries for Loyalist causes. People willing to gamble could do so in their home town or colony--without the involvement of a Congress comprised of people primarily from other states. High turnover of managers didn't help, but is understandable--at one point the managers stopped working because they weren't getting paid!

The collapse of the currency hurt ticket sales the most. With the low value of money, even a winning ticket might be a loser. The Goddess of Chance might pump up hopes of riches but rampant inflation would burst the bubble.

Revolutionary War Privateers

Ill winds swept through Revolutionary War America, with conditions, to borrow a phrase, better imagined than described. As the formidable British armada cut through ocean waves sending currents of shock and misery through the colonies, beleaguered troops funded by worthless currency, led by a weak Congress, and sabotaged by way too many Loyalists, valiantly fought on land just to survive.

But things were different at sea. War and commerce came together to form a splendid storm called privateering. Private citizens, at their own risk and peril, appetites whetted by the thrill of the hunt for lucrative rewards, gorged on the plunder of British resupply vessels, fattening coastal seafaring towns with rich harvests of cargo. And all "at Johnny Bull's expense."

The men who went on to become our first three presidents each favored privateering and realized its benefits. George Washington opined after the war that victory pivoted on the success of privateers. Thomas Jefferson happily reported in July 1775, "the New Englanders are fitting out light vessels of war by which it is hoped we shall not only clear the seas and bays...but that they will visit the coasts of Europe and distress the British trade in every port of the world. The adventurous genius and intrepidity of these people is amazing."

"Thousands of schemes for privateering are afloat in American imaginations," John Adams wrote, and from these, "many fruitless and some profitable projects will grow." They grew to wildly phenomenal levels after March 1776 when Congress authorized privateering. There was money to be had. Lots of it. One unidentified scribe provided this description of the excitement:

"Oh, what prizes these cruisers brought into port! There are no items in the newspapers of that day... [except] lists of prizes. When these half-pirates came in, cannon were fired, the whole town turned out, and the taverns were filled with rejoicings. The names of the ships and their captains were household words. The captured cargoes were carried ashore; inventories were posted in the taprooms, and often the goods were sold within the welcoming tavern doors."

Advertisements screamed along the waterfronts, recruiters barked promises of riches, and slogans and poems cleverly persuaded:

"Come all you young fellows of courage so bold,
Enter on board and we will clothe you with gold."

"All you that have bad masters,
And cannot get your due,
Come, come, my brave boys,
And join our ship's crew."

"Brave boys, to the Rendezvous in Fore Street, where you will find your jolly Companions, and receive greater Advantages than in any private ship whatever."

A single cruise could result in anything or everything. There was money and gold and:

"lumber, spars, pitch and tar. There were hogsheads of sugar and molasses, and puncheons of Jamaica rum. There was cider and wine, London porter, Bristol ale, and casks of vinegar and oil. There was indigo and flaxseed, oats and wheat, flour, kegs of bread, bags of coffee, cocoa, and boxes of tea. From the holds, too, came barrels of pork, cheeses, oysters, almonds, lemons, figs, ceramics, glassware, linens and dry goods."

Robert Morris, Revolutionary War moneyman, spoke of privateers making huge fortunes "in a most rapid manner." Many young and inexperienced boys, some who "could not find a rope in the night" became very wealthy, including one fourteen-year old who received from a single voyage: one ton of sugar, 30 to 40 gallons of rum, 20 pounds of cotton, 20 pounds of ginger and about $700.

Residents of Tom's River, New Jersey were said to have spent almost all their time just dividing up the prizes. So profitable were these efforts that late in the war with the end of privateering in sight, "there were a great many persons...dejected on the return of peace."

A popular poem and drinking song honoring famed privateer John Manley included these verses, each ending with the refrain "and a privateering we will go:"

Brave Manley he is stout, and his men have proved true,
By taking of those English ships, he makes their Jacks to rue;
To our ports he sends their ships and men, let's give a hearty cheer,
To him and all those valiant souls who go in privateers.

O all ye gallant sailor lads, don't never be dismayed,
Nor let your foes in battle never think you are afraid,
Those dastard sons shall tremble when our cannon they do roar,
We'll take, or sink, or burn them all, or them we'll drive on shore.

Our heroes they're not daunted when cannon balls do fly
For we're resolved to conquer, or bravely we will die,
Then rouse all you New England Oaks, give Manley now a cheer,
Likewise those sons of thunder who go in privateers.

They talk of sixty ships, lads, to scourge our free-born land,
If they send out six hundred we'll bravely them withstand,
Resolve we thus to conquer, boys, or bravely we will die,
In fighting for our wives and babes, as well as liberty.

Then cheer up, all my hearty souls, to glory let us run,
Where cannon balls do rattle with sounding of the drum;
For who would cowards prove, or even stoop to fear,
When Manley he commands us in our bold privateer.

Privateering had been around for centuries and was an internationally accepted practice. The goal: capture an enemy vessel, and obtain a predetermined and contractually agreed upon share of the 'prize.' The pursued ship was 'the chase,' a single voyage (or cruise) usually lasted six weeks. Privateers had to have a commission, provided by the states or Congress, after posting a $5,000 bond. Many vessels were off limits, including as Thomas Jefferson noted, "fisherman, husbandmen, and citizens unarmed and following their occupations in unfortified places."

The pursuer could use deception during the chase, including flying false flags, no flags or even the flag of the chase. The first man sighting the chase received double prize money; the first to board got triple. The capturing vessel determined which port to take the prize. Cargo could only be opened if perishable or in case of emergency. Violation of rules could lead to the loss of the seized ship and cargo, monetary fines, loss of bond and the loss of the commission.

The privateer did not formally obtain the spoils until a court legally condemned the ship and cargo. George Washington originally handled condemnation cases until the states took over and established their own courts. Some states were deluged with cases; others had few. Thomas Jefferson remarked that in Virginia, "a British prize would be a more rare phenomenon than a comet."

If more than one vessel was involved in the capture, the prize would be split among all ships in sight at the time of capture. It was a common practice to send a man to the masthead with a scope to sweep the horizon at the moment the chase surrendered so he could later testify in prize court. Numerous lawsuits occurred to resolve whether a ship was actually in sight at the critical moment.

Privateering investors bought and sold shares and partial shares, betting on the success of an upcoming cruise. Like studying a business before investing in its stock, they gambled on the likelihood of success by considering factors such as the crew's competence, the ship's guns, and the captain's track record.

Privateering came with much controversy and had at least one tangible drawback. The American Navy lost many likely recruits. Men who would have enlisted and served on Navy vessels chose instead the much more lucrative privateers. One historian tabulated that between 1778 and 1782 the number of privateers increased from 115 to 323. Yet in the same period the number of commissioned ships in the Continental Navy dropped from twenty-one to seven. It was called "folly, chimerical and phantastick" to attack the world's largest navy at sea. Samuel Chase of Maryland called it "the maddest idea in the world."

And then there was the intangible issue of morality. The practice was believed to make people greedy, like hired mercenaries. "Think," urged one dissenter, "of the effect privateering would have on the morals of American seamen! They would grow mercenary, bloodthirsty altogether."

But John Adams suggested that instead of getting wrapped up in morality, people should consider the benefits: "It is not prudent to put virtue to too serious a test. I would use American virtue as sparingly as possible lest we wear it out." With Adams' support, Congress approved the practice.

Risks like getting captured or killed by the enemy or the sea lurked everywhere. But these bold seafarers dared, and in the process lined their own pockets and provided a desperately needed boost to the war effort. In all more than 2,000 privateers filled the oceans, "eat[ing] out," as Thomas Jefferson said, "the vitals of British commerce." It was "the dagger which strikes at the heart of their enemy."

The success of the privateers resulted in another unintended benefit. To deal with the real harm and danger caused by the privateers, Parliament passed a very controversial act, known as the "Pirate Act" in March 1777, which fueled strong anti-war sentiment in England. This new act took away the prisoner of war status for captured privateers.

While in Europe, Ben Franklin issued commissions for three vessels, French-owned and staffed mostly by Irish smugglers, which in one eighteen-month period captured 114 British vessels. A British citizen in the West Indies observed eighty-two captured English ships in port, the *General Mifflin* captured six prizes in the Irish Sea and the *Pilgrim* took eight prizes in one cruise off the Irish coast. All in all, as John Adams happily remarked, it was "a short, easy and infallible method of humbling the English…and bringing the war to a conclusion."

The privateers swarmed enemy ships, veritable floating treasure chests of sweets, like bees to honey. As an example of the impact on the war effort, consider that in the winter of 1775-1776 only eight of the forty transport ships sent by England to Boston made it to their destination.

In February 1778, less than three years into the war, the House of Lords in England heard a report that seven hundred and thirty-three ships had been captured or destroyed by American privateers.

"Had it not been for our privateers," one historian opined, "the Stars and Stripes would have been completely swept from the seas." It may have been the most important factor in ending the war.

These "piratical sea-dogs" proved to be like a Brinks money truck backing up to the gates of the British Treasury, convincing British merchants that the war cost more than it was worth and eventually forcing Parliament to end its war in America. That very plan had been spelled out in August 1776 by the Continental Congress: "We expect to make…their merchants sick of a contest in which so much is risked and nothing gained."

The Revolutionary War
Draft in Virginia

"It is an old maxim," George Washington wrote during the American Revolution, "that the surest way to make a good peace is to be well prepared for war." During the Rebellion in the colonies a dwindling supply of soldiers made a military draft the last hope for victory. Although controversial, he warned the draft would appear necessary, "when the capital of your state is in the enemy's hands."

America was defended by a professional army as well as a much larger militia, a rag-tag collection of sixteen to fifty-year-old free males, who were required to be five feet four inches tall, healthy, strong-made, and well-limbed, not deaf, or subject to fits.

The war dragged on, the militia thinned. Enticements grew with the expanding ranks of deserters, casualties and departing soldiers whose expired terms were "by no means punctually filled." Recruits should be persuaded of the "utility and necessity of strongly reinforcing the Continental Army," Washington suggested, "in the warmest terms."

Soldiers were originally promised one hundred acres and exemption from taxes during their continuance in the service; incentives eventually swelled to three hundred acres and a lifetime exemption from all taxes. Bounties skyrocketed from ten dollars to $12,000 (not a typo), but the deflated currency lost its luster. It was in this "unhappy depreciated light in which the Soldiery view the money." Among other benefits, recruits were offered a gill of spirits per day gratis.

"Experience has shewn that a preemptory draft will be the only effectual one," Washington wrote before laying out the options: "We have only to decide, whether the States shall be loaded with the enormous expense of Militia...capable only of making a feeble defence...or the Army compleated by coercive methods." Coercion, of course, meant the draft, which Thomas Jefferson called, "the most unpopular and impractical thing that could be attempted." Jefferson added, "our people...had learnt to consider it as the last of all oppressions."

The draft "may produce convulsions in the people," Washington warned, before adding they might be enticed: "Many incentives of immediate interest may be held up to the people to induce them to submit to it. They must begin to consider the repeated bounties they are obliged to pay as a burden, and be willing to get rid of it, by sacrificing a little more, once and for all." They might even welcome the draft: "The hopes of the people elevated by the prospects before them will induce a chearful (sic) compliance, with this and all other measures of vigor." If properly handled, "it would not be deemed a hardship," and "the people would not complain."

The country, "standing on too precarious and uncertain a footing," needed soldiers fast. The language justifying the draft in Virginia captured its urgency: "It is of the greatest moment to the cause of America that the continental army be speedily completed... be it therefore enacted...that a just and equal draught of men should speedily take place." Only the counties of Kentucky, Ohio, Monongalia and Yohogania were relieved from quota requirements.

In 1777, Fairfax, Prince William and Loudoun Counties were required to draft thirty-eight, thirty-two, and sixty-eight men, respectively; by 1780 their quotas were increased to forty-nine, forty-eight, and one hundred seventeen.

Potential draftees assembled to "draw a paper fairly out of (a) hat or vessel, the same remaining covered, and being frequently shaken." They were drafted if the word 'service' was written on their piece of paper; the word 'clear' meant they had dodged the musket ball.

Soldiers who deserted "with public arms" faced the death penalty; those who simply deserted faced punishment "not touching life or member." Harboring deserters brought severe penalties, except for a son protecting his father, a wife protecting her husband, or a mother protecting her son. Rewards were paid to those reporting deserters, "one moiety... to the informer... the other moiety to the commonwealth." Individuals who apprehended and returned deserters were given sixty pounds as well as one dollar per mile for their trouble and expense.

Property was transferred to the heirs of those using force to oppose the draft. Ironically, these protestors who believed they were preventing battle deaths, were declared "civilly dead."

The Raid on Monkton and Weybridge, Vermont

Along the western banks of Lake Champlain, in Monkton, Vermont, the Revolutionary War landed at the doorstep of John and Rachel Bishop's humble abode on Monday, November 9, 1778. With their sons, Timothy, John Jr., Elijah and Napthala, the Bishops lived along the edge of Monkton Pond, now known as Cedar Lake, in an area easily accessible to friend and foe alike due to its close proximity to the nearby Otter Creek. During the War, Vermont provided a geographic buffer between British-held Canada and the American colonists.

The British made periodic attacks into upstate and central Vermont to prevent colonists from gaining a foothold and taking the war north to Canada. This military sojourn consisted of about 355 British soldiers and officers as well as approximately one hundred Indians.

The Otter Creek raid in the fall of 1778 was led by British General Christopher Carlton (who was married to an Indian), under the command of General Frederick Haldimand. General Haldimand spelled out his rationale for conducting the raid:

"...I mean still to prosecute this design, as there are some settlements upon the borders of Lake Champlain, Otter Creek, and about Tyconderoga and Crown Point that may furnish many conveniences and necessaries which would facilitate the approach of the enemy. I propose to send a respectable party, which will be covered by some of the ships and gun-boats, and that it shall be as late as possible in going out as the damage it may then do to the enemy will be irreparable this season."

Vermonters, Haldimand warned:

"are in every respect better provided than the Continental troops, and in their principals (sic) more determined. These considerations, with the impossibility of acting from this province except in great force have always made me anxious to prevent the Union they seem so bent upon accomplishing... Such is the enthusiasm of the vulgar for their idol, independence, that nothing but unavoidable necessity will ever induce them to relinquish it...This extensive province [of Vermont]...is in its present condition quite open to the insults and ravages of the colonies in actual rebellion...The rebels have explored every part of the country and know it well... What will become of the fur trade and how long may we expect to keep possession of the lower and cultivated part? If this goes, America most probably will be lost to Great Britain for ever.

Should the rebels undertake a winter expedition against this province, they have many advantages over us. The Germans are heavy troops, unused to the snowshoe, to handling the axe and the hatchet, only fit for garrison duty. The English troops have only been two winters in the country and therefore cannot be so expert at these as the Americans; these are trained to the woods from their infancy, know well how to shelter themselves from the cold, and are excellent marksmen..."

John Bishop and his neighbors had earned the wrath of the British for having previously captured a group of Loyalists. Bishop served:

"Under the command of James Bentley in taking thirteen

Tories in Monkton (at the Tory Rocks) on their way to Canada, viz. Benjamin Cole, and his party, and for bringing them before the committee at Neshobe (Brandon) and guarding them to Ticonderoga."

"Approaching the place in Monkton where the Tories were encamped, Bentley's detachment waited until their enemies slept, then rushed upon them with a great noise and made them all prisoners. The next day a court was convened at Neshobe (Brandon), the trial lasting two and one-half days, the prisoners being sentenced to be delivered to the American garrison at Ticonderoga, where they were taken by Captain Bentley and his detachment."

James Bentley received ninety pounds and nine shillings to pay his twenty soldiers. Bishop received five pounds and eight shillings for twelve days' service.

Perhaps more troubling to the British might have been an "Association Bill" signed in 1777 by Bishop and sixty-five other Otter Creek residents. Modeled after the Declaration of Independence, this Association Bill proclaimed Otter Creek residents would:

"Voluntarily and cheerfully determine to render every assistance in our power to the Northern Army of the United States of America, either by taking up Arms, if thereto required; by giving information of all the motions of the enemy, with which our situation of being acquainted with; by carefully watching all suspicious persons amongst our selves, or, by any other method whatsoever on our power…"

A couple years earlier, before his defeat at the Battle of Saratoga, British General Johnny Burgoyne wrote his view of the rebels in the Vermont (New Hampshire grants) area. He called it "a country unpeopled, and almost unknown, in the last war [which] now abounds in the most active and the most rebellious race of men on the continent, and hangs like a gathering storm on my left."

The raid started from Canada at the northern tip of Lake

Champlain on October 24th and ended on December 12th. By November 8th, fifteen days into the expedition, the British had taken thirty-five prisoners and a large amount of cattle and supplies. The expedition had been hugely successful and the winter freeze was about to begin. But instead of ending the expedition and returning to Canada, Carlton felt compelled to spend additional time sending troops further into the area around Monkton.

Haldimand wrote in his journal the rationale for the Monkton detour:

> "My principal motive for destroying this township (Monkton), tho it delayed me twelve hours was because I knew it to be a remarkable rich one and a nest of the greatest Rebels in that part of the country, besides I could be fortunate enough to catch Wintress Howick, the Indian interpreter."

This side trip resulted in the capture of John Bishop, 47, John Bishop, Jr., 21, Timothy Bishop, 17, at the northeast edge of Monkton Pond, where Monkton Ridge Road meets Starksboro Road. Most importantly, the British were indeed fortunate enough to capture Winthrop Hoyt, the Indian interpreter (sometimes referred to as Winter Hoit, Winchip Hoit, Wintress Howett and Winter Howick). Years earlier in the French and Indian War, Hoit (originally from Epping, New Hampshire) had been taken captive and spent several years in Canada as an adopted son with the Caughnawaga Indian tribe. (Hoyt had been one of Ethan Allen's Green Mountain Boys and was a signer of the Association Bill).

Not all the Bishops, however, were taken captive. Elijah, about ten years old, was not captured because he "feigned lameness." Rachel (nee: Ruggles) Bishop, forty-six years old:

> "...repelled the Indians from burning their hay stacks and wheat stacks, knowing them to be her main dependence, by having a kettle of hot water handy and throwing it upon the Indians. They seemed to admire her courage and spared the stacks."

This unlikely defense worked. The Indians fled without the entire Bishop clan. Afterwards, Rachel took her sons Elijah and Napthala to the safety of Fort Ranger in nearby Rutland, where they lived for nineteen months. Constructed in the spring of 1778, the oval-shaped fort covered at least two acres and could accommodate almost three hundred people. At the fort, Rachel cooked for the troops. Elijah's younger brother Napthala, served as a drummer.

In 1903 the Daughters of the American Revolution erected a marker in Rutland commemorating Fort Ranger. The marker was later moved and is now where Route 4 (West Street) intersects East Proctor Road and goes under the railroad tracks.

The captives were taken to ships on Lake Champlain for transport to prison camps in Canada, where they would be held until July 1783. Benjamin Everest, one of the captives, tried to make an early escape, as described by Ralph Nading Hill in *Lake Champlain, Key to Liberty*:

"Having in the meantime collected thirty-nine men and boys as prisoners, Major Carleton concluded to take (Benjamin) Everest to Canada before he was tried, and ordered him on board the vessel just ready to sail to Canada. It was now the latter part of November; a severe storm from the northeast came on, sleet and snow, with the wind blowing furiously. The vessel had run up to Ticonderoga to take on board some freight. During the day Everest had bribed one of the sailors to bring on board a bottle of liquor, which was secreted by Everest. At sunset the vessel was taken into the middle of the lake and anchored there. The night was very wild and tempestuous. At the solicitation of the prisoners the captain had ordered a tent pitched on deck to shield them from the storm.

Everest now proposed to his fellow prisoners to try to escape. They were anchored about half a mile north of the bridge that crossed the lake at that place, and he proposed to invite the sentry to take a drink or two out of the bottle and shelter themselves from the storm, while they watched the opportunity to let themselves into the lake and to swim to the bridge. Only two dared to think of trying it. When everything was quiet Everest gave the sentry a drink out of the bottle, and in a little while asked him to come under the tent and have another glass. This was complied with and in a short time Everest, saying "What a storm it is!" went out as if to take a look. He took off his clothing and tied it about his head, let himself down into the water near the stern, and struck out for the bridge. It almost made him cry out loud when he first went into the water, it was so piercing cold. Spaulding followed next, but the water was so cold when he touched it that he shrank back and crawled on board again. No other one attempted it."

The Bishops may have had prior knowledge of the raid. The same group of enemy intruders had attacked the nearby Town of Weybridge the day before. Prisoners taken there included Claudius Brittel and his son, Claudius, Jr. History doesn't record whether the Bishops and Brittels knew each other at the time, but years later, Claudius Brittel's daughter Elizabeth, married Elijah Bishop's son, Basil Bishop.

An eight-foot marble monument now commemorates the Brittel capture site. Erected about a century after the Otter Creek raid, the monument is located on the site of a root cellar where some Weybridge residents hid to evade capture. Located along the Otter Creek on Route 23 (Weybridge Road) between Thompson Road and Prunier Road, the monument is inscribed:

"November 8, 1778, a marauding party of British, Indians and Tories, invaded the quiet homes of four families in this vicinity, being the only inhabitants of Weybridge, burned their houses and effects, killed their cattle and hogs, and took Thomas Sanford, and his son Robert, David Stow and his son Clark, Claudius Brittel and his son Claudius, and Justus Sturdevant and carried them prisoners to Quebec. The four wives and their young children, for eight to ten days, occupied an out-door cellar of Mr. Sanford, at this place, till our troops from Pittsford came to their rescue. David Stow died in prison, December 31st, 1778. Thomas Sanford, and two others from

Vermont, Gifford and Smith, escaped from prison, and after wandering through Maine and New Hampshire, reached their families."

Haldimand triumphed the mission's success to Lord George Germain:

"...there remain no more of these traitors on either side of Lake Champlain from near Tyconderoga to Canada, and considerable settlements of them along Otter Creek have been destroyed on this occasion. Among these, some hoards of arms and ammunition were found, besides great quantities of provisions and forage.

The Indians of this party brought off some cattle & killed a great many & between thirty and forty prisoners were made, one of whom proved to be an Indian interpreter, inhabitant of the neighbourhood of Otter Creek, long known in this country to have been employed by the Rebels...and never could be taken until now. I annex the copy of an Association taken from these people, with their names signed. Those marked are the prisoners upon this occasion. This paper clearly shows that there was necessity to rid ourselves of these neighbours."

On April 22, 1780, the Bishops, along with Winthrop Hoyt and Claudius Brittel Jr. were moved from Quebec to Malbaie Bay. The occupations for all three Bishops were listed as masons. Brittel and Hoyt were listed as farmers. John, John Jr., and Timothy Bishop were imprisoned in Canada until their release at Whitehall on July 18, 1783. The Bishops went back to Monkton. Hoyt moved to Swanton, Vermont, where he showed up in the 1810 federal census.

After the raid, diplomatic measures were attempted to get the prisoners back. George Washington wrote on August 30, 1780 to Colonel Ethan Allen:

Sir: I have been favored with yours of 16th instant. I cannot, without deviating from the rule of conduct which I have constantly observed, exchange the officers of Colonel Warner's regiment at this time, because there are a great many who have been much longer in captivity, and have therefore a just right to a preference. But, to endeavor to afford the best relief the nature of the case will admit, I have written to General Haldimand, and proposed to him to send them and the other prisoners in his possession to New York, where we can furnish them with supplies of different kinds, which we cannot, from the great distance, forward to Quebec, and where they will be exchanged in due course. I have also represented to General Haldimand what you report of the treatment of our prisoners in Canada; and I hope my remonstrance will have the desired effect, should the cause of complaint be well grounded.

The military expedition was an overwhelming British success. However, there was a problem with paying the Indians for their assistance. The Indians were clamoring for greater pay for the cattle they brought in. They had been promised eight dollars for each oxen, and, as their part of the bargain, they had not taken the human scalps which they wanted to take.

Disputes about this Indian compensation continued long after the raid. The particulars of this early American labor problem resulted from the fact that one fourth (twenty out of eighty) of the cattle taken during the raid died during transport. The Indians believed they should have been paid for the eighty head they took whereas the British believed payment should relate to only the number that survived transport.

As late as a year later, the Indians threatened, if not paid, to go back into Otter Creek to get the scalps they so graciously passed on in November 1778. Haldimand was advised on January 17, 1779, that "the Indians have demanded to be sent to Otter Creek to take some scalps." In a letter to Carlton three days later, Haldimand expressed his concerns about the Indians' request to go back to Monkton to gather scalps. He agreed Indians could go back to take more prisoners but they must "contain themselves within the bounds of humanity towards [their captives], otherwise they must not be suffered to go."

General Carlton kept a journal during the raid, which included these comments:

On Saturday the 24th of October...

> At half past six in the morning, I left the Isle aux Noix; the wind fresh down the lake with small rain, prevented our getting on very much; with great difficulty I reached the upper end of Isle a Motte where wee encamped. Most of the Indians arrived soon after.

Sunday the 25th...

> I was detain'd untill eight o'clock in the morning waiting for the last of the Indians, I feared if I went on without them they might turn back, as I was inform'd they were not pleas'd with coming so far the night before.

Monday the 9th of November...

> I sent back the two gun boats with orders to make the best of their way down to the Isle Aux Noix. I sett off at 7 and at ten arrived at the falls four miles from dead Creek I found that Captain Jones with his twenty men had been detached agreeable to my directions to destroy the Township of Moncktown which lay eight miles back paralel to the lake. My principal motive for destroying this township tho' it delay'd me twelve hours was because I knew it to be a remarkable rich one and a nest of the greatest Rebels in that part of the country besides if I could be fortunate enough to catch Wintress Howick the Indian interpreter the only person who negociates the Congress business with the villages in Canada from thence I should do an essential service. At 4 o'clock Captain Jones return'd with several prisoners of which Howick was one. He destroy'd a considerable quantity of arms, ammunition, grain, forrage &c and brought off twenty four head of cattle. I sent the cattle by land to the mouth of

the creek and moved down with the detachment in the boats. Wee got to our camp by eleven o'clock.

British soldier Lt. John Enys, of the 29th British Regiment of Foot, the "Worcestershire Regiment," also kept a journal of the raid:

About the middle of October there were orders given for a party to cross the lake under Major Carlton of our Reg[imen]t, and on the 24th the following party embarked at Isle aux Noix.

You can hardly suppose how quietly all these Yankees take any distresses, so much so that they appear to have lost all sort of feeling. They expressed no sort of surprise or grief at our coming and only said very cooly they did not suppose we should have come so far into their country. One of them appeared a little distressed however when she was told that her husband was to be carried into Canada and that she herself must return to their friends higher up the creek or indeed where she chose, so she did not attempt following her husband which would not be permitted. She said it was very hard to be treated so when they had never done anything against the King's troops which by the bye I believe to be a d-----d lie as from all appearances the house was fitted up as a place of defence to command the passage of the ford.

Our whole party being joined again we proceeded down the creek burning and destroying all we found untill near dark when we encamped at a mile or two's distant from the lower falls (Vergennes). It would be endless to mention every house that was destroyed this day, nor could I do it if I was inclined as I do not know the number. During this days march our guide misled us again, tho not so materialy as before.

I must here also mention a circumstance of generosity in one of the upper country Indians who have very little intercourse with white people and are supposed to be more barbarous and cruel than the Canadian Indians. I observed this young man among the other Indians more active than common in striping one of the houses, in which he was very successful, having got a great quantity of different things. I supposed at first he meant them for himself as all the rest did but to my great surprise saw when he found he could get no more that he collected all he had got together and gave them to the poor woman to whom they belonged nor would he suffer any of the other Indians to take them from her tho they would have been very glad to have done it.

During our stay here one Mr. Jones of the Royalists was sent to destroy a small village called Monkton a short distance from hence and to endeavor to bring off a man called [Winthrop] Hayet who spoke the Indian language very well and who had been very often sent as an emissary to the Canadian Indians.

A little before dusk Mr. Jones returned from Monkton having executed his orders fully. No sooner was he returned than the whole embarked and went down to the bottom of the creek where we encamped that night after having sent all the prisoners on board of the ships which were lying off the mouth of the creek.

Early next morning we began to pass the cattle across the lake which were very numerous so that it was not finished untill 4 o'clock in the afternoon when the whole embarked again to return to Canada. Capt. Ross and his party of the 31st Reg[imen]t crossed the lake to burn two or three houses in and near the River Boquet, at which place he was also to wait untill the cattle had passed him.

The Carlton Schooner burnt 3 or 4 houses on the east side of the lake which had been evacuated for some time... It was not before next morning we found out where we were which we found to be on a small island at the upper end of Grand Isle. We lay in this place untill past twelve o'clock that day supposing the lake to be too rough for a boat about which time we saw a boat of savages under sail in the middle of the lake. On this the major resolved to proceed and when we had got out in the lake we could see some more boats behind us. The wind continued to blow very hard all day, so that some of our boats got into Point au Fer in very good time that evening, but that was not the case with me for before I reached the Point it was dark and rained as if heaven and earth were coming together.

Esther Bishop, Rachel Bishop's daughter-in-law and wife of John Bishop, Jr. made the following statement on January 10, 1851 as part of Napthala's pension application:

I am eighty six years old, and lived in the town of Rutland in the State of Vermont from the eighth to the twentieth (8th to 20th) year of my age and during the whole of the Revolutionary war. I lived about two miles from the fort (Ranger) in said Rutland...I am a sister of Rebecca Bishop who was married to Napthala Bishop. Napthala Bishop was while I lived in Rutland a drummer in the fort ... under Captain Thomas Sawyer and served in that capacity nineteen months and was honorably discharged. Napthala enlisted [after] his father John Bishop and his two oldest brothers John Jr. and Timothy Bishop were taken prisoners by the British and carried off to Quebeck and kept there three years...his older brother... Elijah enlisted and his mother worked for the soldiers where they remained nineteen months.

On September 15, 1782, Claudius Brittel wrote this information in his plea to get released:

"We were captured by Captain Fraser of the 34th regiment on Carlton's expedition on November 8, 1778. We were at our homes, and at our lawful calling, at a place called Weybridge, on the Creek, in the State of Vermont. We being put in prison at Quebec for the space of fourteen months-at the end of which term, myself and son took the oath of Allegiance."

The request was denied.

On March 12, 1835, Claudius Brittel, seventy-four, applied, under the name Claudius Britton, a resident of Pitt Township, Ann Arbor, Michigan, for a Revolutionary War pension:

"...until A.D. 1773 when [he] removed to Weybridge now in the County of Addison & State of Vermont then called the New Hampshire grants where he resided until the fall of A.D. 1778... on the 6th of November A.D. 1778 this deponent & about forty other neighbors were taken prisoners by a Canadian scouting party commanded by Major Carlton & taken to Quebec where he was confined in prison for about three years. Deponent was detained as a prisoner for four years & seven months mostly at Quebec & most of the time in close confinement & was twice confined in the dungeon for attempting to escape. In July 1783 preparations were made for an exchange of prisoners & about 350 prisoners in Canada were exchanged. Deponent signed the Exchange Bill at St. Johns July 14, 1783 & was marched into Vermont & discharged immediately after in the same manner as the other prisoners who were exchanged at the same time. Deponent has no documentary evidence to show that he enlisted, served, or was discharged from the army & does not know any person whose testimony he can procure relative to his service. After deponent was exchanged he removed to & resided in Tinmouth, Rutland County, Vermont until 1812 when he removed to Batavia, Genesee County, New York & resided there until he removed to Ann Arbor, Washtenaw County, Michigan Territory in May 1825.

Brittel's (or Britton's) pension was rejected on the grounds of "no proof of six months service."

Monkton Cannon

When men rejoiced in days of yore
That stamp-acts should appear no more,
They fired their pump instead of cannon,
And shook the very earth we stand on.
But latter years, more full of glory,

Since Whig has fairly conquered Tory,
Pump guns are thrown by in disgrace,
And iron stationed in their place.
The heroes of a certain town,
To please themselves and gain renown,
A cannon made, without a blunder,
To send forth home-made peals of thunder.
Never have such reports been given,
Since Satan cannonaded heaven;
To these reports 'twas merely whistle,
When Queen Anne fired her pocket pistol.
As that, so fame could never say less,
Was fired from Dover unto Calais,
So this, without dispute we know
Was fired from Monkton to North Hero.
This thing was formed, our heroes say,
To usher in our training-day;
But ere their training had arrived,
To try her metal they contrived.
Now courage aids their hearts of steel;
She's mounted straight on wagon-wheels;
In order firm the heroes stand,
'Till the commandant gives command
To load and fire, when at the sound
Hills, dales, and vales all echo round.
What transport fills these sons of Mars;
They shout for joy, and bless their stars;
But oh, how transient is their fun!
They load too deep, and split their gun.
Earth, at the blast, turns shaking Quaker;
Boys curse the cannon and its maker;
What havoc made 'mongst ducks and hens;
The pigs run frightened round their pens;
Young puppies set up hideous yells,
While goslins perished in their shells;
Lake Champlain shakes from shore to shore,
And Camel's Hump was seen no more.

The British hit the area around Monkton, Vermont very hard throughout the war. As one author succinctly and accurately notes: "Few areas in New England...suffered more throughout the Revolution than the countryside along the Otter Creek."

Vermont's Ethan Allen had a thing or two to say to England after the war ended: "Vaunt no more, Old England! Consider you are but an island! and that your power has been continued longer than the exercise of your humanity. Order your broken vanquished battalions to retire from America, the scene of your cruelties. Go home and repent in dust and sackcloth for your aggravated crimes. The cries of bereaved parents, widows and orphans, reach the heavens, and you are abominated by every friend to America. Take your friends the Tories with you, and be gone, and drink deep of the cup of humiliation...Your veteran soldiers are fallen in America, and your glory is departed. Be quiet and pay your debts, especially for the hire of the Hessians."

The Words of Cato in the American Revolution

Some of the most eloquent and famous words penned or spoken by early American historic figures such as George Washington, John Adams, Patrick Henry and Nathan Hale were actually borrowed from an English writer named Joseph Addison.

Addison (1672-1719) appeared in England shortly after Shakespeare, but his words were just as original and entertaining. His writings included some 600 lively and witty essays (think George Will) for publications called the *Tattler* or the *Spectator,* as well as three plays: *Cato-* a tragedy, *Rosamond-*an opera, and *The Drummer-*a comedy. But only *Cato*, first performed in 1713 and later translated into French, German, Latin and Italian met with success. By 1736 *Cato* had made its way across the Atlantic to America. It was incredibly popular in pre-revolutionary days.

In real life, Cato the Younger (to distinguish him from his great-grandfather Cato the Elder) lived from 94 BC to 46 BC. He spent his later life as a Roman statesman fighting the tyranny of Julius Caesar.

The play relates to Cato's struggle against Caesar. Caesar's army eventually surrounds Cato's forces in Utica. No good options remain for Cato; defeat is all around. Woven into the story is a family struggle involving Cato's children. His two sons love the same woman and his daughter has two aggressive suitors—a prince (Juba) and a Roman senator (Sempronious). One writer remarked that Cato's Utica and Caesar's Rome resembled the relationship between America and Europe.

Through it all, the stoic Cato projected honor, determination and integrity. George Washington modeled himself after Cato, perfectly illustrated in these comments from the play that Cato makes to his prospective son-in-law:

A Roman soul is bent on higher views;
To civilize the rude unpolished world,
And lay it under the restraint of laws;
To make man mild, and sociable to man;
To cultivate the wild licentious savage
With wisdom, discipline, and liberal arts
Th' embellishments of life; Virtues like these,
Make human nature shine, reform the soul
And break our fierce barbarians into men.

Washington loved the play, which he called "the very Bible of Republican idealism." He saw it many times and had it performed for his troops at Valley Forge.

In the play, Cato's troops threaten mutiny. George Washington had to deal with a similar threat in Newburgh, New York and according to one writer, succeeded by "essentially...rehashing Cato's speech," including a reference to his hair turning gray (just before pulling out the spectacles): "Behold these locks that are grown white beneath a helmet in your father's battles."

The American founders honored Addison as one writer stated, "for [his] elegance of thought and pertinacious wit; even after the founding era, every young man of substance read [him]." Those who borrowed or were smitten with Addison's words and writing style reads like a who's who of American history.

John Adams wrote of deserving success in a letter to his wife: "We cannot insure success, but we can deserve it." This same expression of deserving success shows up in at least two letters from George Washington: to Nicholas Cooke on October 29, 1775 ("it is not in our power to command success, tho' it is always our duty to deserve it") and to Benedict Arnold on December 5, 1775 ("It is not in the power of any man to command success; but you have done more— you have deserved it.") Read *Cato* the play, where it says: "Tis not in mortals to command success, but we'll do more, Sempronius, we'll deserve it."

No one knows for sure what young Nathan Hale said before he was hanged by the British in New York City in 1776, but it was something like, "I regret that I only have one life to give for my country." In Act IV Cato says: "what pity is it that we can die but once to serve our country!"

Patrick Henry's stirring speech at Saint John's Church in Richmond, Virginia culminated with "Give me liberty or give me death!" a line similar to Cato's "it is not now a time to talk of aught, but chains or conquest, liberty or death."

Early American historian and novelist Washington Irving copied the style of Addison's essays. Ben Franklin claimed in his autobiography that these lines from Cato were the motto for his book:

Here will I hold; if there is a power above us,
(And that there is, all nature cries aloud
Thro' all her works) he must delight in Virtue,
And that which he delights in must be happy.

Thomas Paine quoted from Addison in the *Age of Reason*, as did Thomas Jefferson:

Oh liberty! Thou goddess heav'nly bright
Profuse of bliss, and pregnant with delight,
Eternal pleasures in thy presence reign,
And smiling plenty leads thy wanton train;
Eas'd of her load subjection grows more light,
And poverty looks cheerful in thy sight;
Thou mak'st the gloomy face of nature gay
Giv'st beauty to the sun, and pleasure to the day.

This line from Addison's *Cato* was oft-repeated by the leaders and citizens: "When vice prevails and impious men bear sway, the post of honour is a private station." Washington used something very close to this line in a letter to David Humphreys on June 12, 1796.

Washington also talked an officer, John Thomas, out of resigning in part with this line from *Cato*. In their struggle, "surely every post ought to be deemed honorable in which a man can serve his country."

Voltaire proclaimed that Addison was "the first English writer who composed a regular tragedy and infused a spirit of elegance through every part of it." (And this was after Shakespeare.) When Addison died, Ben Franklin printed this notice in his *Poor Richard's Almanac*:

> "The 19th of this month, 1719, died the celebrated Joseph Addison, Esq; aged 47, whose writings have contributed more to the improvement of the minds of the British nation, and polishing their manners, than those of all other English pen whatever."

Most Americans have heard of the other English writer, William Shakespeare, but sadly, the years have buried Addison's contribution to history.

The Presidential
Cheese Caper of 1802

New Year's Day, 1802 in the new nation's capital saw the beginning of the first full year of Thomas Jefferson's presidency. It also saw, courtesy of a Baptist Congregation in Cheshire, Massachusetts, a surprising offering to Jefferson for his support of religious liberty. The gift measured four feet in diameter, fifteen inches high, weighed 1,235 pounds and was delivered in a wagon pulled by five horses. It was a wheel of cheese.

Jefferson spent the next several months giving out pieces of the gift to friends and supporters. Incredibly it was still around three years later when a senator noted that on Jefferson's table were "two bottle of water brought from the river Mississippi, and a quantity of the Mammoth Cheese." Not surprisingly, he added the cheese was "far from good."

Jefferson's enemies delighted in ridiculing this odd gift. One Federalist newspaper gleefully printed this poem entitled, *Reflections of Mr. Jefferson, over the Mammoth Cheese*:

In this great cheese, I see myself portray'd,
My life and fortunes in this useless mass,
I curse the hands, by which the thing was made,
To them a cheese, to me a looking-glass.

Once I was pure—alas, that happy hour,
E'en as the milk, from which this monster came,
Till turn'd by philosophic rennet sour,
I barter'd virtue for an empty name.

Then press'd by doctrines from the Gallic school,
A harden'd mass of nameless stuff I stood,
Where crude confusion mindless without rule,
And countless seeds of foul corruption bud.

E'en the round form this work of art displays,
Marks the uncertain, endless path I tread,
Where truth is lost in falsehood's dreary maze,
And vice in circles whirls the giddy head.

Delusive view! Where light is cast aside,
And principles surrender'd for mere words,
Ah me, how lost to just and noble pride,
I am indeed become a man of curds.

Like to this cheese, my outside, smooth and round,
Presents an aspect kind and lasting too;
When nought but rottenness within is found,
And all my seeming rests on nothing true.

Fair to the view, I catch admiring eyes.
The nation wonders, and the world applaud.
When spread beyond my just and nat'ral size,
I seem to them an earthly demigod.

Go, hated Mentor, blast no more my sight,
I would forget myself, and heaven defy,
Inur'd to darkness, I detest the light,
Would be a suicide, but dare not die.

The Impeachment of a Supreme Court Justice

The recent criticism of the Supreme Court, particularly Justice Anthony Kennedy's consideration of world opinion in juvenile death penalty cases is tame compared to past reactions. In 1970, Congressman and future President of the United States, Gerald Ford, on behalf of one hundred and nine members of the House of Representatives proposed the impeachment of Supreme Court Justice William O. Douglas. Citing an impeachable offense to be whatever the House considered it to be, Ford's proposal was in retaliation to the Senate's rejection of two of President Richard Nixon's nominees to the Supreme Court.

This year marks the bicentennial of the most remarkable of judicial events-when the highway of American history detoured somewhere between political mayhem and constitutional dynamite: the impeachment of Supreme Court Justice Samuel Chase.

Born April 17, 1741, in Somerset County, Maryland, Samuel Chase was a delegate to the Continental Congress in 1774 and a signer of the Declaration of Independence two years later. "Old Bacon Face" left Congress and government service in 1778, disgraced for using privileged information obtained as a member of Congress to enrich himself in the flour market. He resumed his law practice and did not return to public life until President Washington nominated him to the Supreme Court in 1796.

Usually described in terms like "abrasive, arrogant and overbearing," Chase found an unusually favorable endorsement from fellow justice Joseph Story, who wrote: "Chase abounds with good humor [and] amuses you extremely by his anecdotes and pleasantry. His first approach is formidable, but all difficulty vanishes when you understand him…I like him hugely."

Like President John Adams and other Federalists, Chase believed in a strong central government, a federal standing army and a bitter hatred of Republicans and the Republican press. Chase stated: "There is nothing we should dread more than the licentiousness of the press." He further opined that the press served as a "certain means of bringing about the destruction of the government."

Another party hack lent his fuel to the fire against the press: "All they contained was misrepresentation, slander and falsehood, and they propagated lies and liars, as a hot day breeds maggots or mosquitoes."

Predictably, the Republicans had their opposing insults: "I would sooner have my wounds dressed by a dog than by a Democrat. A dog is in reality a much more respectable character than a Democrat. If a dog was man's best friend, a Democrat was his worst enemy-a treacherous, malignant, hypocritical biped…It was better to be married to a felon or a hangman than to a Democrat."

When Thomas Jefferson and his Republican Party won the presidency and both Houses of Congress in 1800, the Federalist Party started its own death march. Jefferson's victorious words soothed with eloquence but his emotions seethed with contempt. And it included an all-time classic sound bite:

"Let us, then, fellow citizens, unite with one heart and one mind. Let us restore to social intercourse that harmony and affection without which liberty and even life itself are but dreary things…But every difference of opinion is not a difference of principal. We have called by different names brethren of the same principle…We are all Republicans, we are all Federalists."

But nothing was further from his real desire: "I shall take no other revenge than...to sink federalism into an abyss from which there shall be no resurrection for it;" he wished for "nothing but their eternal hatred." Jefferson's victory started a twenty-four year "Republican Ascendancy" accomplished, according to Jefferson by "keep(ing) the people on our side, by keeping ourselves in the right."

Jefferson's venom stemmed largely from the Judiciary Act of 1801, created by the Federalist lame-duck Congress at President Adams' request. It established sixteen new circuit judge positions, which were filled by Adams on his last night in office. It also provided for one less Supreme Court justice (five rather than six), which meant two justices had to retire before Jefferson could appoint one. In addition, in the period between the Federalists' election-day defeat and Jefferson's inauguration, a Supreme Court justice resigned and was immediately replaced by Adams in the person of ultra-Federalist John Marshall. Adams did not give Jefferson, the incoming president whose party had just won both houses of Congress, any input in the matter.

The livid Jefferson called these judicial moves an "outrage on decency" and later wrote in a letter to Abigail Adams, "I can say with truth that one act of Mr. Adams' life, and only one, gave me a moment's personal displeasure. I did consider his last appointments to office as personally unkind. They were from among my most ardent political enemies, from whom no faithful cooperation could ever be expected... It seemed but common justice to leave a successor free to act by instruments of his own choice."

It was no secret that the Judiciary Act was enacted to reward Federalist patronage and as a last-ditch effort to retain some political power. Even an ardent Federalist acknowledged:

"That the leaders of the federal party may use this opportunity to provide for friends and adherents is, I think, probable, and if they were my enemies I should not condemn them for it... They (Federalists) are about to experience a heavy gale of adverse wind. Can they be blamed for casting many anchors to hold their ship through the storm?"

The boiling emotion over the bitterly controversial Sedition Acts, approved into law in 1798 by President Adams and the Federalists along a party-line vote, also created intense enmity. The Acts, which proved James Madison's point that "wise men will not always be at the helm" made it illegal to:

> "...write, print, utter or publish...any false, scandalous and malicious writings against the government of the United States, or either house of the Congress of the United States, or the President of the United States, with the intent to defame...or to bring them...into contempt or disrepute; or to excite against them, or either or any of them, the hatred of the good people of the United States."

Ironically, the Acts were signed into law on July 14th, the anniversary of the storming of the Bastille-the start of the French Revolution. Federalists had a 58-48 majority in the House and a 20-12 majority in the Senate. Most of the antipathy towards Federalists was directed at Adams's home State of Massachusetts, described as: "more degenerated from the love and the very principals of true liberty than any one of the Union."

Only two members from States south of the Potomac River voted in favor. Virginia, strongly opposed to the Sedition Acts, was respected by many States as "the head of a respectable opposition to the most diabolical laws that were ever attempted to be imposed on a free and enlightened people." To Federalists, Virginia was a source of endless problems. Alexander Hamilton laid out his plan to combat the Virginians: "What, my dear sir, are you going to do with Virginia? This is a very serious business...When a clever force has been collected, let them be drawn toward Virginia, for which there is an obvious pretext-& then let measures be taken to act upon the [Sedition] laws & put Virginia to the test of resistance."

A few months later, Chase was in Virginia ordering an arrest under the Sedition Acts and commenting that he "would teach the lawyers of Virginia the difference between the liberty and the licentiousness of the press."

In denouncing the Acts, Jefferson wrote:

"I wish it were possible to obtain a single amendment to our Constitution...I should be for resolving the alien and sedition laws to be against the Constitution and merely void...The English, though charmed with our making their enemies our enemies, yet blush and weep over our sedition law."

A Virginia newspaper predicted the impending battle of the judiciary in this poem published a month before Jefferson's inauguration:

"Now hark ye, sweet Liberty boys,
For these are the days of our glory;
Come on, then, our true-hearted joys,
The aristocrats all fly before ye;
The magistrates, jury and courts,
They stand in the way of our thriving;
They give people little support,
Who have nothing to lose or keep by them,
And so to the Devil we'll pitch them."

Patrick Henry did not overemphasize the Republicans' anger in his response when asked whether the Alien and Sedition Acts were constitutional: "They may be right-they may be wrong. But this much I know...you are progressing to civil war, and when you reach the field, who will you meet-Washington-the father of his country, and you will see when you face him your steel will turn."

Using the Sedition Acts as a political weapon, "men were prosecuted...for offenses as diverse and as trivial as circulating a petition for its repeal, erecting a liberty pole, and expressing a drunken wish that a cannon ball had struck the President [Adams] in the behind."

Federalists argued the Sedition Acts were necessary. The leading Federalist journal, Philadelphia's *Gazette of the United States*, coined the expression: "He that is not for us, is against us." As for newspapers, Jefferson certainly didn't care much for them as evident in this comment: "Advertisements contain the only truth to be relied on in a newspaper."

Newspapers and critics frequently took Jefferson's words out of context with the intention of trying to discredit him. To stymie the enemy press, he often ended up sending messages through friends and supporters rather than writing things down. In a letter a year after becoming president, Jefferson wrote: "Our opponents are so disposed to make a malignant use of whatever comes from me, to torture every word into meanings never meant in order to gratify their own passions and principles, that I must ask the favor of you to communicate verbally the sentiments of this letter to those who forwarded their addresses through you, not permitting the letter or any copy to go out of your hands."

Surprisingly, signing the Alien and Sedition Acts might have actually cost Adams his bid for reelection. And years later he realized it. Three months after his successor was sworn in, the *Palladium Newspaper* (in Frankfort, Kentucky) reported this bit of self-analysis by the former president:

"When President Adams sat to have his likeness taken... he happened to cast his eye upon the portrait of General Washington, which hung in the room; the likeness of Washington was drawn with the mouth closed, that of Adams a little open. Mr. Adams observed that if his lips had, like General Washington's, been kept close, and his pen as inactive, there would have been no danger of his becoming unpopular."

Jefferson, who overturned the Acts in 1801, had earlier written: "A little patience, and we shall see the reign of witches pass over, their spells dissolved, and the people recovering their true sight, restoring their government to its true principles." Jefferson believed he would "restore our judiciary to what it was while justice & not federalism was its object." Once Jefferson took over, Federalists complained "the Constitution was no more." They believed Jefferson was "determined at all events to destroy the Independence of the Judiciary & bring all the powers of Government into the House of Representatives."

Its short tenure resulted in the arrests of approximately twenty-five well-known Republicans, of which fifteen were indicted. All ten who were eventually brought to trial were convicted in "travesties of justice dominated by judges who saw treason behind every expression of Republican sentiments." Jefferson complained: "The Federalists have retired into the judiciary as a stronghold...and from that battery all the works of Republicanism are to be beaten down and erased."

Once sworn in, Jefferson forced a hard march of brutal political warfare. "The judges were antidemocratic, many were arrogant, many were snobs, all were Federalists. Those were reasons enough. The Republican regiments advanced to the attack." First target: the out of control judiciary exemplified by "Chase's bloody circuit" and the deluge of Federalists at all levels of the judiciary. Indeed when Jefferson took office there was not one Republican judge in the entire federal judiciary.

Chase was "the most formidable Federalist presence on the Supreme Court...a white-manned giant who preferred to play Jehovah with all Jeffersonians who had the misfortune to land in his courtroom." His conduct from the bench showed "oppressive and disgusting partisanship."

Jefferson and the Republicans had a long line of deeds to avenge which had been created by Federalist judges, uniquely described by Jefferson as "objects of national fear." His motives were political; he had commented previously when he was vice-president that: "History shows, that in England, impeachment has been an engine more of passion than of justice." It was left to party flamethrower John Randolph, radical to the temperate Jefferson, to carry out judicial revenge.

First Up: New Hampshire Chief Justice John Pickering, who had ranted, raved and shouted profanities during an intoxicated performance from the bench. Many believed that Pickering was insane. Pickering was the first federal judge to be impeached and convicted. The votes for conviction in the Senate were along a party-line vote. On the same day that the Senate convicted Pickering the House passed Congressman John Randolph's resolution to impeach Samuel Chase.

It was Chase's controversial rulings in lower court trials that earned the enmity of Jefferson and formed the basis for the eight articles of impeachment. Indeed, "as a trial judge on circuit, Chase was a holy terror, and when it came to enforcing the Sedition Act, he had no peer." The justices dreaded the time consuming, dangerous and laborious circuit riding. The Federalists had just voted to end the practice when the Republicans under the newly elected President Jefferson restored it.

In 1803, Chase delivered a charge to a Baltimore grand jury, a charge in which he accused the Republicans of mobocracy, abolishing federal judgeships, and threatening the court's independence. But perhaps worst of all, he campaigned openly for Adams in the election of 1800.

Early public notice of the pending impeachment against Chase appeared in the *National Intelligencer & Washington Advertiser* on January 11, 1804: "Wash City-committee to enquire into official conduct of Saml Chase & Richd Peters are: J. Randolph, Nicholas, J. Clay, Early, R. Griswold, Huger & Boyle."

Randolph is John Randolph of Roanoke, Virginia, Jefferson's eccentric cousin, who carried "the wickedest tongue that ever hung in the head of an American Congressman, or at any rate, in the head of one who had both the courage and wit to use it." In an infamous event in Northern Virginia twenty-one years later, Randolph faced Henry Clay with loaded pistols in a duel on the fields of Arlington, Virginia. Randolph was reported to have said of Clay: "He is a man of splendid abilities, but utterly corrupt. Like rotten mackerel by moonlight, he shines and stinks." Randolph ranted with a voice that was:

"A shrill scream when he was giving vent to his turgid philippics. As an orator, he was more splendid than solid... He was noted for his keen retorts, reckless wit and skill in debate. His tall, slender, cadaverous form; his shrill, piping voice; and his long skinny fingers pointing at the object of his invective-made him a conspicuous speaker. For thirty years, he was the political meteor of Congress."

Griswold was Connecticut Federalist Congressman Roger Griswold, famous for clubbing opposing Congressman Mathew Lyon of Vermont on the floor of the Capitol with a hickory walking stick, leaving him with blood running down his face. Lyon had earlier spat on Griswold because Griswold's attack of Lyon's Revolutionary War military record. 'Spitting Matt the Democrat' went on to become the first person indicted under the Sedition Act for writing that Adams had an "unbounded thirst for ridiculous pomp, foolish adulation, and selfish avarice." He then became the first and probably only Congressman to win reelection from a prison cell, described as "the common receptacle for horse-thieves."

The House of Representatives approved each article of impeachment on December 3rd and 4th, 1804. Articles three and four passed with the largest margin at 83-34; article five with the slimmest at 72-45.

The charges against Chase were succinctly summarized 170 years later by the Committee on the Judiciary, House of Representatives, Ninety-Third Congress, during the consideration of impeachment against President Nixon:

"In 1804 the House impeached Samuel Chase, a justice of the United States Supreme Court, on the ground that he had been guilty of certain misconduct to the prejudice of the defendants in the trials of John Fries for treason and James Thompson Callendar for breach of the sedition laws; that he had improperly attempted to induce a grand jury in Delaware to find an indictment against the editor of a newspaper for breach of the sedition laws; and for addressing an intemperate and inflammatory harangue to a jury in the State of Maryland."

The thirty-four senators (Vermont, Kentucky, Tennessee and Ohio had joined the original thirteen States) had to determine if Chase had violated his oath:

"I do solemnly swear, that I will administer justice without respect to persons, and do equal right to the poor and the rich, and that I will faithfully and impartially perform all the duties incumbent on me as a judge of the Supreme Court, according to the best of my abilities and understanding, agreeably to the Constitution and laws of the United States."

One trial related to fifty-year old John Fries, who had created a disturbance in Bethlehem, Pennsylvania in March 1799. Fries led an armed group of anti-tax resisters from Bucks and Montgomery Counties to force federal officials to release protestors who had been arrested. The protest was the result of a Congressional Act established on July 4, 1798, the twenty-second anniversary of the Declaration of Independence, to collect taxes on land, dwelling houses and slaves. No shots were fired, no one was killed, and the disturbance was quickly halted.

One of the few people injured in events related to Fries's Rebellion, was Jacob Schneider, who published the *Readinger Adler*, a German-language pro-Republican newspaper. The Federalist troops made a point to travel through Reading, Pennsylvania after suppressing the uprising. Schneider criticized the hard tactics used by troops in quelling the uprising as well as terrorizing the German people who lived in the area. For his complaints, the captain in charge quickly held a trial, finding Schneider guilty and sentenced him to twenty-five lashes in the public town square.

Fries, on the other hand, was punished for disturbing the peace of tax revenue so dear to Chase and his ilk. He was convicted in Chase's court of treason and sentenced to hang. Chase lectured Fries that:

"...It cannot escape observation, that the ignorant and uninformed are taught to complain of taxes, which are necessary for the support of government, and yet they permit themselves to be seduced into insurrections which have so enormously increased the public burthens, of which their contributions can scarcely be calculated...If you had reflected, you would have seen that your attempt was as weak as it was wicked. It was the height of folly in you to suppose that the great body of our citizens...would not rise up as one man to oppose and crush so ill-founded, so unprovoked an attempt to disturb the public peace and tranquility. If you could see in a proper light your own folly and wickedness, you ought now to bless God that your insurrection was so happily and speedily quelled…The annual necessary expenditures for the support of any extensive government like ours must be great; and the sum required can only be obtained by taxes or loans…You ought to consider the consequences that would have flowed from the insurrection, which you incited, encouraged and promoted….Violence, oppression and rapine, destruction, waste, and murder…A severe example should be made to deter others from the commission of like crimes in the future. You have forfeited your life to justice…The judgment of the law is, and the court doth award, that you be hanged by the neck until dead."

Fries's petition for a pardon originally fell on deaf ears. President Adams's secretary of the treasury, urging denial, stated that Fries and the entire State of Pennsylvania were "the most villainous compound of heterogeneous matter conceivable." Adams's secretary of state also argued against a pardon:

"Painful is the idea of taking the life of a man… I feel a calm and solid satisfaction that an opportunity is now presented in executing the justice of the law, to crush that spirit, which, if not overthrown and destroyed, may proceed in its career and overturn the government."

To his credit, President Adams ignored his advisors and spared Fries's life. Fellow Federalist Alexander Hamilton was outraged at Adams for the pardon:

"…This particular situation of Pennsylvania, the singular posture of human affairs, in which there is so strong a tendency to the disorganization of the government, the turbulent and malignant humours which exist, and are so industriously nourished throughout the United States; everything loudly demanded that the executive should have acted with exemplary vigour, and should have given a striking demonstration, that punishment would be the lot of the violent opposers of the laws...It is by temporizings like these, that men at the head of affairs, lose the respect both of friends and foes."

Hamilton put out a twenty-thousand word pamphlet urging Federalists to abandon Adams. "I will never more be responsible for him by my direct support even though the consequence should be the election of Jefferson...If we must have an enemy at the head of the government let it be one... for whom we are not responsible."

The other articles against Chase related to his conduct during the trial of James Callendar, a Richmond-based journalist whose temerity in criticizing Adams in his book *The Prospect Before Us* led to his conviction for sedition. Callendar, a Scot from Edinburgh, born in 1758, "had acquired enough education to become a vigorous writer. In 1793 he showed his skill in an antigovernment pamphlet that landed him in a king's court, charged with sedition. He fled to America and began to cover Congressional debates. Like any refugee from royal tyranny, he was automatically befriended by James Madison and Thomas Jefferson."

Callendar, muck-racker extradoire, had in 1797 ironically embraced the freedom of the press in America, when he gleefully wrote that it is: "the happy privilege of an American that he may prattle and print, in what he pleases, and without any one to make him afraid." Callendar had an army of hostile enemies who didn't hide their feelings: "A little reptile...a dirty, little toper with shaved head and greasy jacket...the scum of party filth" that "deserved the benefit of the gallows," Callendar had once been physically removed from the halls of Congress because "he was covered with lice and filth."

Grooming issues aside, what was Callendar's seditious crime, returned as a guilty verdict by the jury in a one-day trial? He was charged with two counts of sedition, each consisting of twenty distinct charges, or sets or words. One of the twenty charges consisted entirely of having made this remark: "He (President Adams) was a professed aristocrat; he proved faithful and serviceable to the British interest."

Callendar wrote a plethora of vivid descriptions such as opining that Adams "has never opened his lips, or lifted his pen without threatening and scolding; the grand object of his administration has been to exasperate the rage of contending parties, to calumniate and destroy every man who differs from his opinions." Adams created "a French war, an American navy, a large standing army, an additional load of taxes, and all the other symptoms and consequences of debt and despotism." In a more personal attack just to make sure his feelings were clear, he called Adams:

"A repulsive pedant... a gross hypocrite...in his private life, one of the most egregious fools upon the continent...that strange compound of ignorance and ferocity, of deceit, of weakness... a hideous hermaphroditical character who has neither the force and firmness of a man, nor the gentleness and sensibility of a woman...The reign of Mr. Adams has hitherto been on a continued tempest of malignant passions.

The historian will search for those occult causes that induced her to exalt an individual who has neither that innocence of sensibility which incites it to love, nor that omnipotence of intellect which commands us to admire. He will ask why the United States will degrade themselves to the choice of a wretch whose soul came blasted from the hand of nature, of a wretch that has neither the science of a magistrate, the politeness of a courtier, nor the courage of a man?"

During the trial, Chase angered and humiliated Callendar's defense attorneys so much as to cause them to cease representing Callendar during the trial. The "sarcastic contempt" which Chase showed defense counsel and the interruptions of the sardonic old justice were in a very high degree imperative, satirical and witty...and extremely well calculated to abash and disconcert counsel." Defense counsel Hay testified that he was "more frequently interrupted by Judge Chase on that trial, than I have ever been interrupted during the sixteen years I have practiced at the bar." Defense counsel Nicholas testified: "Not many sentences were uttered by counsel at a time without interruption." The clerk of the court testified: "I have rarely seen a trial where the interruptions were so frequent."

At the time of his conviction for sedition Chase lectured Callendar about "sowing discord among the people," and that an attack on Adams was "an attack upon the people themselves."

For the record, Callendar continued his assault against Adams ("a hoary headed incendiary") after being released from prison and before he was subsequently pardoned by Jefferson. In the end Callendar eventually turned against Jefferson and exposed Jefferson's relationship with his slave, Sally Hemings. Long after his welcome was worn, the ink in the character assassin's pen dry, and the muck he was raking finally hardened, Callendar fell off a ferry in a drunken seizure and drowned in the James River.

One of Chase's witnesses at his impeachment trial was Chief Justice John Marshall, a distant cousin and bitter rival of Jefferson. Jefferson could battle with Marshall politically but not against what Jefferson called his verbal "twistifications." According to Jefferson:

"When conversing with Marshall, I never admit anything. So sure as you admit any position to be good, no matter how remote from the conclusion he seeks to establish, you are gone. So great is his sophistry you must never give him an affirmative answer or you will be forced to grant his conclusion. Why, if he were to ask me if it were daylight or not, I'd reply "Sir, I don't know, I can't tell."

Upon hearing of the charges, Marshall wrote in a personal letter: "I have just received the articles of impeachment against Judge Chase. They are sufficient to alarm the friends of a pure and of course an independent judiciary, if among those who rule our land there be any of that description."

If Chase was Enemy #1 to Jefferson and the Republicans, the ultra-Federalist Marshall was a close second for his famous Marbury v. Madison ruling in 1803, giving him and the Court the power to overrule the efforts of Jefferson's Republican-held Congress. Marshall wrote: "It is, emphatically, the province and duty of the judicial department, to say what the law is."

The most bizarre facet of the Chase impeachment, however, rested in the complex personality of the man presiding over the Senate trial, who at the time was a fugitive from justice for murder in New Jersey, and who, two years later, would be indicted for treason: Aaron Burr. Burr, the Vice President of the United States, and therefore the President of the Senate, had the Constitutional duty to preside over the trial. Burr had killed Alexander Hamilton in a duel in Weehawken, New Jersey on July 11, 1804, and had lost the 1800 election for the presidency to Jefferson by the very slimmest of margins.

One newspaper wit joked: "It was the practice in Courts of Justice to arraign the murderer before the judge, but now we behold the judge before the murderer!"

The trial started on Monday, February 4, 1805. The senators heard testimony during the next three weeks from forty-nine witnesses.

Article One: In the John Fries trial, Chase acted in a manner highly arbitrary, oppressive and unjust.

Article Two: In the James Callendar trial, Chase required John Basset to serve as a juror despite the fact that Basset had already formed an opinion that Callendar's written comments about Adams were defamatory.

Article Three: In the Callendar trial, Chase refused to allow testimony from defense witness John Taylor to be admitted into evidence.

Article Four: In the Callendar trial, Chase's conduct (with numerous examples given) was marked by "manifest injustice, partiality and intemperance."

Article Five: In the Callendar trial, Chase's conduct in having Callendar arrested was contrary to Virginia law.

Article Six: In the Callendar trial, Chase's conduct in bringing Callendar to trial was contrary to Virginia law.

Article Seven: In a Delaware courtroom, Chase "disregarded

the duties of his office, did descend from the dignity of a judge and did stoop to the level of an informer, by refusing to discharge the grand jury."

Article Eight: In a Baltimore trial, Chase made "an intemperate and inflammatory political harangue, with intent to excite the fears and resentment of the said grand jury," in a manner that was "highly indecent, extra-judicial, and tending to prostitute the high judicial character with which he was invested, to the low purpose of an electioneering partisan."

One of the critical points of debate related to the definition of "High crimes and misdemeanors." Must the conduct forming the basis of the impeachment constitute an indictable criminal offense? Also vigorously contested was the "Good behavior" standard required for a judge. House Manager Nicholson:

"The law of good behavior is the law of truth and justice. It is confined to no soil and to no climate. It is written on the heart of man in indelible characters, by the hand of his Creator, and is known and felt by every human being. He who violates it, violates the principals of all law. He abandons the path of rectitude, and by not listening to the warning voice of his conscience, he forsakes man's best and surest guide on this earth."

Cesar Rodney, one of the House Managers pointed out the vagueness of the term good behavior:

"No precise idea can be affixed to it, nor is the language sufficiently technical to constitute a criminal charge...Upon what ocean of uncertainty have we embarked when the plainest language is not understood...Is this tribunal, say they, to erect itself into a court of honor, or assume the chair of chivalry, and form a scale by which decorum and good manners may be nicely graduated?"

Randolph finished his closing argument with this persuasive bit of eloquence:

"It becomes you, then, Mr. President, and Gentlemen of the Senate, to determine, whether a man, whose whole judicial life hath been marked by habitual outrage upon decorum and duty, too inveterate to give the least hope of reformation, interwoven and incorporated with his very nature, shall be arrested in his career, or again be let loose upon society, to prey upon the property, liberty and life of those who will not rally around his political standard. We have performed our duty: we have bound the criminal and dragged him to your alter. The nation expects from you that award which the evidence and the law requires. It remains for you to say whether he shall again become the scourge of an exasperated people, or whether he shall stand as a land-mark and a beacon to the present generation, and a warning to the future, that no talents however great, no age however venerable, no character however sacred, no connexions however influential, shall save that man from the justice of his country, who prostitutes the best gifts of nature and of God, and the power which he is invested for the general good, to the low purposes of an electioneering partizan."

Randolph's political enemies scored his performance predictably poorly:

"...He began his speech of two hours and a half, with as little relation to the subject matter as possible-without order, connections or argument; consisting altogether of the most hackneyed commonplaces of popular declamation, mingled up with panegyrics and invectives upon persons, with a few well-expressed ideas, a few striking figures, much distortion of face and contortion of body, tears, groans and sobs, with occasional pauses for recollection, and continual complaints of having lost his notes."

House Manager Campbell weighed in with his reasons to convict:

"The fountains of justice were corrupted by this poisonous spirit of persecution, that seemed determined to bear down all opposition in order to succeed in a favorite object... The streams of justice that flow from the American bench ought to be as pure as the sunbeams that light up the morning...Mr. President, we, on this important occasion, behold the rights and liberties of the American people (and) hover round this honorable tribunal, about to be established on a firm basis by the decision you will make, or sent afloat on the ocean of uncertainty, to be tossed to and fro by the capricious breath of usurped power and innovation."

Burr was said to have conducted himself and the trial "with the dignity and impartiality of an angel, but with the rigor of a devil."

In order to convict Chase and remove him from office, twenty-three votes, or a 2/3 majority were required. The votes were taken on March 1. Three articles received a majority, with Article Eight getting the largest margin at nineteen to fifteen. Five articles received less than a majority with the biggest defeat on Article Five, which was unanimously defeated. In the end, fifteen senators voted not guilty on every count, including all senators from Massachusetts, New Hampshire, Vermont, New York, Connecticut and Delaware.

Burr announced the acquittal: "There is not a Constitutional majority of votes finding Samuel Chase, Esquire, guilty on any one article." Burr's term as vice president ended three days later.

In the end, Chase was acquitted in the Senate, but pilloried in the press: "Cursed of thy father / Scum of all that's base / Thy sight is odious / and thy name is ---."

A month after leaving the Executive Mansion, Adams remarked on the faults of the Federalists: "No party that ever existed knew itself so little or so vainly overrated its own influence and popularity, as ours. None ever understood so ill, the causes of its own power or so wantonly destroyed them."

The Supreme Court opined on the invalidity of the Sedition Acts in 1964 when it ruled that a newspaper's criticism of government officials is covered under the 1st Amendment even if that criticism is false and defamatory: "Although the Sedition Act was never tested in this Court (the act expired by its term in 1801), the attack upon its validity has carried the day in the court of history...The invalidity of the Act has also been assumed by Justices of this Court."

In a letter to John Adams long after they had left public life, Jefferson wrote: "I like the dreams of the future better than the history of the past."

Part II:
The Civil War

Virginia (Finally)
Joins the Confederacy

When Abraham Lincoln raised his right hand on March 4, 1861 and swore to uphold the Constitution, seven states had already seceded from the Union. Virginia was not one of them. On the subject of secession by Southern States from the Union, consider this relatively unknown quotation of January 12, 1848, made by then Congressman Abraham Lincoln, during a speech criticizing President James Polk for his handling of the Mexican War:

> *"Any people anywhere, being inclined and having the power, have the right to rise up, and shake off the existing government, and form a new one that suits them better. This is a most valuable,-a most sacred right."*

"American history," according to historian Bruce Catton, "has known few events more momentous than the secession of Virginia." The hopes of the Confederacy rested with Virginia, the most populous and economically successful Border State. Specifically, it rested with the State of Presidents joining the Confederacy.

Numerous people commented on the importance of Virginia to the Confederacy, including President Lincoln, who noted: "The course taken in Virginia was the most important." Pulitzer-Prize winning author Margaret Leech wrote in *Reveille in Washington* that Virginia was the most influential of the Border States. Bruce Catton added,

"Without Virginia the Southern Confederacy could not have hoped to win its war for independence; with Virginia the Confederacy's hopes were not half bad."

Henry Adams, historian and grandson of presidents, spoke of the importance of the Old Dominion to the Confederacy's hopes: "The great and decisive struggle rested always in Virginia...and it was evident even to their most enthusiastic supporters that [the Confederate States] were on the high road to ruin unless some change for the better took place. Their only means for effecting this was by getting the assistance of Virginia, which would settle the fact of disunion." Indeed, Virginia was the key and would likely open the door for several other states to join the Confederacy.

As late as April 12, 1861, it appeared that Virginia might not secede.

Many Virginia Unionists spoke out against South Carolina immediately after it seceded in December 1860. Robert Lewis Dabney, who went on to briefly become Confederate General Stonewall Jackson's chief of staff said, "The little impudent vixen [South Carolina] has gone beyond all patience. She is as great a pest as the abolitionists. And if I could have my way, they might whip her to her heart's content, so they would only do it by sea, and not pester us."

When the original seven Southern States formed the Confederate States of America in Montgomery, Alabama in February 1861, Virginia (as well as North Carolina, Arkansas, Tennessee, Kentucky and Missouri) were not included. Not only had these states not joined the CSA, they had each taken affirmative steps to indicate they would not join.

On February 4, 1861, the same day the Gulf States first met in Montgomery, two critical things occurred to reveal Virginia's hand. First, a month-long "Peace Convention" began in Washington. Brokered by Virginia and sponsored by former President John Tyler of Virginia, the convention was attended by 131 delegates from twenty-one states. It is not an unreasonable question: Would a state planning to secede organize and host such a conference?

Secondly, on February 4th, delegates to a Virginia convention considering secession elected 106 moderates and only 46 secessionists.

These clear anti-secessionist actions of February 4 led a Charleston, South Carolina newspaper to report, "Virginia will never secede now." A delegate from the western portion of Virginia wrote to Secretary of State Seward: "We have scarcely left a vestige of secession in Western Virginia and very little indeed in any part of the state. The Gulf Confederacy can count Virginia out of their little family arrangement—she will never join them."

Diplomat William Thayer reported that Seward, "is jubilant over the elections in Virginia and Tennessee. He regards them as substantial Union victories, and still maintains that a continued attitude of conciliation will save the Border States."

A *New York Tribune* reporter remarked: "As to Virginia seceding, that need not be thought of in any event. There are 120 men in the Convention who will vote to remain with the North, thirty-two who prefer the Southern Confederacy." Gideon Welles, Secretary of the United States Navy, wrote that for more than a month after Lincoln's inauguration, "President Lincoln indulged the hope, I may say felt a strong confidence, that Virginia would not...secede...It was notorious that a great majority of the people [of Virginia] were opposed to all disunion sentiments. These last, though vastly more numerous than the fire-eaters, were passive and calm in their movements, while the secession element was positive, violent and active."

President Lincoln opined in July 1861 that Virginia and the other Border States were not set on seceding: "It may well be questioned whether there is to-day a majority of the legally qualified voters of any state, except perhaps South Carolina, in favor of disunion. There is much reason to believe that the Union men are the majority in many, if not in every other one, of the so-called seceded states."

In addition to Virginia, other Border States quickly indicated their aversion to disunion: Before February ended, Arkansas, Tennessee, Missouri and North Carolina had each voted against secession.

The March 21, 1861 edition of the *Commercial Advertiser* included this poem, entitled *Virginia to the North*:

> *Thus speaks the sovereign Old Dominion*
> *To Northern States her frank opinion;*

Move not a finger: 'tis coercion,
The signal for our prompt dispersion.
Wait, till I make my full decision,
Be it for Union or division.
If I declare my ultimatum,
Accept my terms, as I shall state 'em.
Then—I'll remain, while I'm inclined to,
Seceding when I have a mind to.

On March 4, Lincoln was sworn in. None of these states had yet seceded.

On April 4, delegates in Virginia voted; again they voted no, this time 89-45.

On April 12, the guns fired on Fort Sumter. Still, none of these states had yet seceded.

On April 14, Fort Sumter was surrendered to South Carolina Confederates. The states had not seceded.

From February 4 and April 14, 1861, there were seventy days (it was not a leap year)—far more than enough opportunity and time to secede. But it had not happened.

Roger Pryor of Virginia presciently warned what it would take to get Virginia into the Confederacy: "I will tell you, gentlemen, what will put Virginia in the Southern Confederacy in less than an hour by Shrewsbury clock—strike a blow."

On April 15, that blow was struck in the form of a presidential call up of 75,000 troops to prevent the Southern States from leaving the Union. (For the record, it was not a draft; he called up the militia.) By forcing each state to furnish a proportionate share of troops (Virginia was to provide three regiments made up of 2,340 men), the Old Dominion had to make the decision it had desperately sought to avert.

For seventy days (115 if you start the count from when South Carolina seceded in December 1860), all signs pointed to at least a thin possibility of keeping Virginia in the Union.

The proclamation, according to Mr. Catton, "knocked Virginia straight out of the Union." As expected, the reaction to the proclamation was "a blaze of excited indignation." North Carolina Congressman William Smith, a Whig and a strong unionist wrote: "The Union feeling was strong up to the recent proclamation. This War Manifest extinguishes it, and resistance is now on every man's lips…Union men are now such no longer." Another Whig politician made a similar remark in saying he was a strong Union man "up to the time of the proclamation…I then saw that the South had either to submit to abject vassalage or assert her rights at the point of the sword."

The reaction from the Southern States still in the Union was immediate and clear--they would not take up arms against the Southern States of the Confederacy. Virginia Governor John Letcher responded to the proclamation: "…The militia of Virginia will not be furnished…Your object is to subjugate the Southern States [and is] not within the purview of the Constitution [and] will not be complied with. You have chosen to inaugurate Civil War, and having done so, we will meet it in a spirit as determined as the Administration has exhibited toward the South."

Tennessee Governor Isham Harris: "Tennessee will not furnish a single man for the purpose of coercion, but 50,000, if necessary, for the defense of our rights and those of our Southern brethren."

Kentucky Governor Boriah Magoffin: "I say emphatically Kentucky will furnish no troops for the wicked purpose of subduing her sister Southern States."

North Carolina Governor John Ellis: "I regard the levy of troops made by the Administration for the purpose of subjugating the States of the South as in violation of the Constitution and a gross usurpation of power. I can be no party to this wicked violation of the laws of the country…You can get no troops from North Carolina."

Missouri Governor Jackson: "Your requisition…is illegal, unconstitutional and revolutionary…and cannot be complied with. Not one man will the State of Missouri furnish to carry on any such unholy crusade."

Arkansas Governor Rector: "In answer to your requisition for troops from Arkansas to subjugate the Southern States, I have to say that none will be furnished. The demand is only adding insult to injury. The people of this Commonwealth... will defend to the last extremity their honor, lives, and property against Northern mendacity and usurpation."

Finally, on April 17, after spurning the Confederate suitors for so long, Virginia seceded by a vote of 89-55, with ten members absent. Even then, it was close. Had 17 of the 144 votes cast gone the other way, secession would have been voted down yet again. Virginians ratified the secession on May 23. Within a month, Arkansas, Tennessee and North Carolina also seceded.

Mr. Catton summed up the effect the proclamation had in pushing Virginia and some other Border States over the edge: "Lincoln had said that to trade a fort for a state, Sumter for Virginia, might be an excellent bargain, although his efforts to drive such a bargain had been tardy and ineffective. Now both fort and state were gone, and their departure meant that the war would be long and desperate... Once the proclamation was out, Virginia's departure was almost automatic."

Indeed, it appears likely that Lincoln considered letting Fort Sumter go in order to keep Virginia from seceding. He had such a conversation with Virginia Peace Convention delegates William Rives and George W. Summers. Lincoln advisor John Hay wrote in his journal on October 22, 1861 that Lincoln, "promised to evacuate Sumter if they [the Virginia delegates] would break up their [Peace] convention without any row or nonsense."

The Scottish historian Thomas Carlyle made this interesting remark about the psyche of "rebels:" "Men seldom, or rather never for any length of time and deliberately, rebel against anything that does not deserve rebelling against."

The beauty of history is that you can second guess it forever and never know. But one thing is certain: things easily could have taken a much different course than the way they played out. It was not a foregone conclusion that Virginia would secede from the Union.

When the war finally started, it came to Alexandria, Virginia from Washington in the form of the Union Army on four paths: by steamer down the Potomac River, by the Georgetown Aqueduct, and over the Long Bridge and the Chain Bridge. A participant later recalled the event:

"The command marched in column of platoons down Fourteenth Street, and crossed the Long Bridge by the flank-in-route step. It was a beautiful moonlight night and the moonbeams glittered brightly on the flashing muskets as the regiment silently advanced across the bridge."

Lincoln's advisor and future secretary of state John Hay painted this picture: "Most conspicuous of all was the endless stream of volunteers, who flowed in at first by companies and battalions, next by thousands and tens of thousands, and so on up to hundreds of thousands—infantry, cavalry, artillery. You can still hear the incessant tramp of the foot-soldiers and the clatter of the horse, with the roll of drum and rumble of cannon, and the shrill, saucy call of the fifes; on they go over the bridges into Virginia, and many never come back."

One unidentified wit poetically laid out the Union Army's plans:

Emancipation without deportation
Sequestration without litigation
Condemnation without mitigation
Extermination without procrastination
Confiscation without botheration
Damnation without reservation
And no hesitation until
There is a speedy termination
To this Southern Confederation.

The Confederate troops guarding the city hastily retreated. Seemingly overnight, "nearly every prominent hill was crowned with a village of white tents. Every road was a military thoroughfare. The rumble of army wagons, the firing of guns, the marching of troops, the steady tramp of pickets, all bore evidence that the county was dominated by the military. The faces of the leading generals and federal officials became familiar to many residents."

Almost everyone believed the war would be short. Southerners were confident of victory. One Massachusetts soldier noted that Southern newspapers reported one "Southerner could lick five Northern mudsills." This Union man wryly remarked, "it was not so very comfortable to feel that we were to be killed in blocks of five."

An 1861 *New York Times* story titled "Notes of the Rebellion" reported that before the war many Northerners had moved into Fairfax County, increasing real estate values. The story mentioned that at that early point in the war many well known homes were owned by former Northerners, such as Munson's Hill, Upton Hill and Bailey's Cross Roads.

The war years wreaked havoc throughout Northern Virginia. An Alexandria newspaper reported that a shell from a nearby Union fort hit the Hunting Creek home of a man named Samuel Pullman, killing two of his children. The paper also reported:

"The moral condition [of Alexandria] is disgraceful on account of the drunkenness of the soldiers in the street. Every street and square [is] lined with stragglers, a large portion of whom are inebriates…staggering about or lying in the streets and on the door steps. A drunken dog fight occurred among the soldiers near the depot…one man was beaten to death with a large stone….those of our citizens who lived here before the war would hardly know the place."

Even the hospitals treating Union soldiers were laden with squalor. One reporter observed:

"The convalescent camp near Fort Ellsworth should be called Camp Pestilence. The aggregation of filth, dirt, debris and offal is enough to sicken any well man. There are now 14,000 men there in every conceivable state of misery, confusion and dissatisfaction."

The Virginia Historical Society has in its archives a letter from William J. Crossley, a soldier from Rhode Island. In the letter Crossley reported:

"July 17th [1861], we arrived at Fairfax, where some of the smart ones made themselves conspicuous in a few of the houses evacuated by the Confederates, by smashing portraits, pianos, mirrors and other furniture, without cause or provocation."

English novelist Anthony Trollope visited Alexandria in the winter of 1861-62 and observed: "We...saw as melancholy and miserable a town as the mind of man can conceive." Alexandria and its streets were "a reign of terror...crowded with intoxicated soldiery; murder was of almost hourly occurrence, and disturbances, robbery, and rioting were constant. The sidewalks and docks were covered with drunken men, women and children, and quiet citizens were afraid to venture into the streets, and life and property were at the mercy of the maddened throng." Other witnesses commented that:

"Destruction here stares you in the face...Destruction comes with our army and desolation follows it, and these farmers... will find it hard to recognize their possessions when they return to them."

"The streets [are] ...so shockingly filthy that it made me shudder to walk on the pavement...and everybody looking so sad and sorrowfull, and all having a tale of horror and wrong to tell."

"Even in her present aspect of decay and ruin, Virginia is still beautiful, noble in decline. Nature has given here with an unsparing hand, but man has introduced a curse—the serpent has been at work, and this Eden, like that of old, becomes a desert. From any of these hills may be numbered many blackened chimneys that rise above hearths now cold— warmed last by the brand of the destroyer. How sad to look upon one of these ruins; the charred roof-trees, the gardens trampled, the flowers destroyed, the vine and trellis broken down together, and think how sadly sacred every nook of the forsaken home must be in the bitter memory of some exile."

A Connecticut private provided this description of conditions in Alexandria:

"The Government bakery here is the largest in the world. Over 100,000 loaves are baked daily; from 20 to 100,000 loaves are sent to the front by the railroad, so that in many instances it is issued to the soldiers there while it is yet warm from the ovens. There are 250 men employed in this bakery....also the Government storehouses are protected from the "raiders" by strong barricades, which are built by setting large logs in the ground on end, with loop holes for muskets between them. The streets leading to the storehouses are protected by heavy gates, so that if Mosby should make a raid, and succeed in getting into the city, he would find it difficult to destroy the Government stores."

Devilry on Duke Street: The Alexandria Slave Pen

There is a very old three-story brick row house on a busy Alexandria street directly across from a car rental business, adjacent to one of the city's ubiquitous lobbyist associations and a few blocks from Starbucks. Few of the hurried commuters who drive within yards of its front door every day have any idea of its despicable history. Northern Virginia is home to a rich collection of history, good and bad. The most evil of all, the purchase and sale of human beings, occurred on a massive scale at a slave pen located at 1315 Duke Street. Originally built as a private residence, it was converted to a slave auction house in the mid 1820s by John Armfield and Isaac Franklin.

For approximately two decades Franklin ran the New Orleans side of the operations and Armfield managed the Virginia operations. They were so successful that by the mid 1830s they had made a half million dollars and owned three ships-*the Tribune, the Uncas* and *the Isaac Franklin. A*pproximately every two weeks one of the ships made the six-week round trip to New Orleans and back carrying about 160 slaves.

Slaving was a lucrative business, but slavers were held in very low regard as noted by one commentator: "There were none so despised as the slave-trader. The odium descended upon his children and his children's children. Against the legal right to buy and sell slaves for a profit, this public sentiment lifted a strong arm, and rendered forever odious the name of negro-trader."

Armfield was described as "exceedingly strange looking...a queer animal about forty years old, with dark black hair cut round as if he were a Methodist preacher, immense black whiskers, a physiognomy not without one or two tolerable features, but singularly sharp, and not a little piratical and repulsive."

The business closed when the Union Army took control of Alexandria in May 1861. The Union officer who first took command of the city wrote this in his journal:

"I found it (the slave pen) a decent enough, substantial looking building now guarded by our Michigan fellows. There were kept the auctioneer's descriptive book of slaves received and sold, (and) their owners' names. Prices ranged from $50 upward. Some of my officers reported that they had found several slaves, including a man, a 'likely looking $1,800 girl,' and a boy, waiting either to be sold or to be taken away by their respective masters or mistresses. My men set all three prisoners free, and on the appearance of a well-dressed gentleman to 'claim his property,' the negro man, whom he grabbed by the coat collar and attempted to take with him, resisted, and the master was hustled off alone amid the jeers of the Michigan men. That slave took free service and became company cook in Company C. After the war he went to Michigan with Captain Butterworth, at whose home he finally died."

With its proximity to the railroad and the Potomac River, the location was ideal for transporting slaves to cotton and sugar plantations of the Deep South. Behind the walls of the non-descript edifice lay the buried secrets and unanswerable questions of this most-wicked enterprise. How many terrified little girls were ripped from a mother's embrace in that building? How many lives did the auctioneer's hammer shatter? How much sorrow can four walls hold?

During the war the building was used by the provost marshal

as a jail for rebellious Southerners and also as "a place for punishing citizens who did not 'rate' a jail sentence by dunking them." It was reported that a Confederate sympathizer named Billy Brown frequently "jeered at Union troops and yelled hurrahs for the South once too often." These actions did note merit arrest but did result in repeated dunkings in a vat of water in the old slave pen. Mr. Brown wore this penalty as a badge of honor and became a town hero for it.

One Union soldier wrote:

"The Slave Pen…is now used as a military jail. Here drunken soldiers are cured by the hydropathic practice. Soldiers who are found in the city without a pass, and persons convicted of selling liquor to soldiers, are incarcerated here. Near the pen are the Contraband Quarters which are long wood buildings erected by the Government for homes for contrabands, most of whom pay rent. The number cared for in the city is about 6,000, only 200 of whom are entirely dependent. A large proportion of the men are employed by the Government as teamsters, and are loading and unloading ships, cars, & c., for which they receive $20 per month and rations. Schools are provided for the children—the number of scholars being about 1,000. Most of the adults display a strong desire to learn to read and write, and may be seen busily studying their spelling books when through their work. There are five colored churches in this city, and it is estimated that more colored people attend divine service than whites."

After the war, a man named Solom Stover, who had purchased the building in June 1862, filed for $7,400 in reimbursement with the Southern Claims Commission for rental of the prison pen to the Union Army.

Named 'L'Ouverture Hospital after the war, the building later served as an early location of the Alexandria Hospital. Finally, from the 1880s through the 1980s, it was just one of many unremarkable Alexandria row houses covered by decades of decay.

All that changed in 1996 when it became headquarters for the

Northern Virginia Urban League. Now renamed the Freedom House, it is home to well-furnished offices, but the basement of the building was left in its original condition, metal bars still intact. The Urban League has obtained funding to build a world-class museum to reflect and remember this "most peculiar institution."

The museum will feature the stories and achievements of some of its victims, including Lewis Henry Bailey, to whom the building has been dedicated. Bailey was sold into slavery in Texas and eventually walked all the way back to Washington, where he incredibly managed to establish two schools and five churches.

The sad story of Solomon Northup will also be documented. Northup, from Saratoga, New York, enjoyed his freedom for more than thirty years before being kidnapped and sold into slavery, where he spent twelve long years. Afterwards Northup penned a journal about this nightmare.

He was born a free black in 1808 in Essex County, New York. At the age of thirty-three, he lived with his wife and children in Saratoga Springs, New York. He was quite a proficient violinist. One day two men casually approached him on the street and offered him a job playing his violin for a couple days in Washington. They would pay generously and provide return fare after the gig. It would be a short lucrative trip.

He agreed. During the journey he found himself feeling dizzy and ill, probably from laudanum secretly slipped in his drink. He woke up in chains, beaten and soon sold into slavery for $900. He was assigned the name "Platt" which he would be called for the next twelve years. Early in the odyssey, he was held temporarily near the Capitol where he reflected on the cruel juxtaposition in this eerie description:

"Its outside presented only the appearance of a quiet private residence. A stranger looking at it, would never have dreamed of its execrable uses. Strange as it may seem, within plain sight of this same house, looking down from its commanding height upon it, was the Capitol. The voices of patriotic representatives boasting of freedom and equality, and the rattling of a poor slave's chains, almost commingled. A slave pen within the very shadow of the Capitol!"

He spelled out some events in the slave's life during cotton-picking season:

"When a new hand, one unaccustomed to the business is sent for the first time into the field, he is whipped up smartly, and made for that day to pick as fast as he can possibly. At night it is weighed, so that his capability in cotton picking is known. He must bring in the same weight each night following. If it falls short, it is considered evidence that he has been laggard, and a greater or less number of lashes is the penalty.

An ordinary day's work is considered two hundred pounds. A slave who is accustomed to picking, is punished, if he or she brings in a less quantity than that. There is a great difference among them in regards this kind of labor. Some of them seem to have a natural knack, or quickness, which enables them to pick with great celerity, and with both hands, while others, with whatever practice or industry, are utterly unable to come up to the ordinary standard...Each one therefore is tasked according to his picking abilities, none, however, to come short of two hundred weight....The cotton grows from five to seven feet high, each stalk having a great many branches, shooting out in all directions, and lapping each other above the water furrow. There are few sights more pleasant to the eye, than a wide cotton field when it is in the bloom. It presents an appearance of purity, like an immaculate expanse of light, new-fallen snow.

Sometimes the slave picks down one side of a row, and back up on the other, but more usually, there is one on either side, gathering all that has blossomed, leaving the unopened bolls for a succeeding picking...It is necessary to be extremely careful the first time going through the field, in order not to break the branches off the stalks. The cotton will not bloom upon a broken branch. Epps [Northup's owner at the time] never failed to inflict the severest chastisement on the unlucky servant who, either carelessly or unavoidably, was guilty in the least degree in this respect.

The hands are required to be in the cotton fields as soon as it is light in the morning, and, with the exception of ten or fifteen minutes, which is given at noon to swallow their allowance of cold bacon, they are not permitted to be a moment idle until it is too dark to see, and when the moon is full, they often times labor till the middle of the night. They do not dare to stop even at dinner time, nor return to the quarters, however late it be, until the order to halt is given by the driver.

The day's work over in the field, the baskets are 'toted' or in other words, carried to the gin-house, where the cotton is weighed. No matter how fatigued and weary he may be—no matter how much he longs for sleep and rest—a slave never approaches the gin-house with his basket of cotton but with fear. If it falls short in weight—if he has not performed the full task appointed him, he knows that he must suffer. And if he has exceeded it by ten or twenty pounds, in all probability his master will measure the next day's task accordingly. So whether he has too little or too much, his approach to the gin-house is always with fear and trembling. Most frequently they have too little, and therefore they are not anxious to leave the field. After weighing, follow the whippings; and then the baskets are carried to the cotton house, and their contents stored away like hay, all hands being sent in to tramp it down...This done, the labor of the day is not yet ended, by any means. Each one must then attend to his respective chores."

The museum will be asking donors to come forward with artifacts. Perhaps they will obtain a poster similar to the one currently on display in the building, and not uncommon before the war:

WE WILL GIVE CASH for one hundred likely young

Negroes of both sexes, between the ages of 8 and 25 years. Persons who wish to sell would do well to give us a call, as the Negroes are wanted immediately. We will give more than any other purchasers that are in market or may here after come into market.

A picture of the building is frequently included in many Civil War books with the sign "Price, Birch & Co.- Dealers in Slaves" prominently featured above the front door. The photograph shows the main part of the building where auctions were held. Separate rooms on either side held male and female slaves.

Cotton was well adapted to the slave-gang system. The height of the plant was low enough not to hide the workers; they could be kept like an army marching across the wide fields in plowing, hoeing, and picking gangs...The picking lasted from the latter part of August to early January. Women and small children as well as the male hands were used in this operation. Dragging a long sack tied to their waists to deposit the cotton in, they employed both hands to pluck the fleece from the open bolls. Since the bolls ripened unevenly, it was necessary for the field to be picked over at least three times. This unequal ripening was the most important reason for the failure until the 1930s to develop a successful mechanical picker. The yield of cotton was greatly increased after 1815 by the introduction into the lower South of the Mexican variety, whose bolls opened more widely and could be picked more easily than the upland cotton. Consequently the amount of cotton picked by a slave in a day doubled during the ante-bellum period. Full grown hands were required to pick from 150 to 200 pounds of seed cotton per day. The seed cotton was taken to the planter's gin, which was usually driven by mules attached to a long sweep. After ginning, it was pressed into bales by means of a screw and covered with hemp cloth, or bagging, tied by ropes. In the ports it was reduced by steam presses into smaller bulk for shipment to Europe. Three fourths of the world's supply of cotton came from the Southern states, and the remainder from India, Egypt and Brazil... Liverpool determined the world market price for cotton...Slave labor was usually protected from dangerous occupations. Irishmen were employed in posts of danger, such as handling the bounding cotton bales on steamboats as they descended the chutes from river bluffs... The overseer of the Louisiana plantation of Governor Manning of South Carolina [said] that the planters usually employed Irishmen to clear swampy land, for such hard work was "death on n---- and mules." Planters reasoned that it was wiser to hire Irishmen than risk their own slaves in dangerous and unhealthy jobs, for the loss of an $1,800 slave was serious indeed, while the death of an Irishman was a small matter."

President Lincoln provided his opinion of slave dealers in an October 1854 speech:

"He watches your necessities, and crawls up to buy your slave, at a speculating price...You despise him utterly. You do not recognize him as a friend, or even as an honest man. Your children must not play with his; they may rollick freely with the little negroes, but not with the "slave-dealers" children. If you are obliged to deal with him, you try to get through the job without so much as touching him. It is common with you to join hands with the men you meet; but with the slave-dealer you avoid the ceremony—instinctively shrinking from the snaky contact...Kicking, contempt, and death for the slave trader."

The Attempted Slave Insurrection in Fairfax

Virginia had been a cauldron of controversy over slavery for decades before the Civil War. French traveler Alexis de Tocqueville, author of *Democracy in America* remarked in 1835 that "the danger of a conflict between the white and the black inhabitants perpetually haunts the imagination of the Americans like a bad dream." An incident in Fairfax County might have sparked the Civil War in the middle of the 1830s.

John Brown at Harper's Ferry; John Windover at Fairfax. Brown's October 1859 attempt to free slaves resulted in his capture and execution. It sparked the Civil War. Much lesser known was John Windover's earlier attempt in Fairfax, Virginia on September 5, 1833.

During the week that Windover attempted the Fairfax insurrection, there were at least three advertisements in the *Alexandria Gazette* for the recapture of runaway slaves. A $50 reward was offered to anyone who returned Vincent, "a negro boy" of 17 or 18 years old with "no marks recollected except some light spots in his face occasioned by poison." Simon, a "stout made, dark mulatto who limps in his walk" fetched a $40 reward. He was further described as a "tolerable good bricklayer and brickmaker as well as waiter." And "a gentleman from the South wished to purchase forty or fifty slaves, of good character, for his own service." The gentleman did not provide his offering price, but did give details as to what he was looking for: "It is desirable to have a blacksmith, carpenter, coachman, and a man cook."

Slaves were certainly not unusual in Fairfax at that time. One author tabulated that three years earlier, in 1830, there were 3,970 slaves in Fairfax County, representing 44% of the entire population. It was at a time when abolitionists were gaining ground. Fervor on both sides of the slave trade escalated to a boiling point. The British Empire outlawed slavery in all its territories in 1833 and New York City suffered through four violent days of an abolition riot in July 1834. In 1831, William Lloyd Garrison started his abolitionist newspaper *The Liberator* in Boston and Nat Turner led a slave insurrection in Southampton County, Virginia. After Turner's capture and death, the State of Virginia enacted stringent legislation to lessen the potential for future rebellions. Any person expressing the opinion that one man had no right to own another was penalized $500 and imprisoned for one year. Conspiracy to incite an insurrection was considered treason against the state, and the penalty was death.

On a warm Thursday evening in September, outside Allison's Tavern in Fairfax (then known as the Town of Providence), emotions ran hotter than the 87 degree temperature clocked that day. John Windover, a thirty to thirty-five year old, 5'10" white man, described as "stout made, light florid complexion, light hair with very coarse features" had with him a large box believed to contain weapons. He, along with two unidentified men, was seen and heard encouraging a group of nine or ten slaves to rebel. Windover commented, as overheard by white people standing nearby: "If you will only be true, you can all get free."

Windover planned to stay at Allison's Tavern that night, but departed for Alexandria or Washington shortly after talking to the slaves. Allison's Tavern is still standing, at the intersection of Main Street and Old Lee Highway in downtown Fairfax City. He advised others that he had "got the Negros in Prince William County to join (him), and many others." He also told the slaves and a nearby white woman that although they did not know about him at that time, they would in two weeks when he vowed to return. Questioned by authorities after the incident, the slaves reported that Windover gave them money and told them he had plenty of weapons. He asked them to meet him later at a designated place about two miles from the Fairfax Court House.

He returned to Fairfax as promised. An article in the September 20, 1833 edition of the *Alexandria Gazette* reported:

A white man, named Windover, has been arrested and committed to jail in Fairfax County, for trial, on a charge of seditious conduct and improper tampering with some of the blacks of the county. They informed against him themselves.

Before he was indicted, he unsuccessfully attempted to escape by trying to burn the jail. He was subsequently indicted in early 1834 for 'conspiring with Sundry Negroes to make insurrection,' and for 'setting fire to the jail of this county.' He must have learned something about escaping because on April 26, 1834, he slipped out of jail and disappeared into history.

Eighteen years before Windover slipped away from the noose that awaited him in Fairfax County, a white man named George Boxley did the same thing in Spotsylvania County, Virginia. Boxley had been an officer in the War of 1812, and at the time he was charged for fomenting a slave insurrection, he ran a store where he came into contact with neighboring slaves. He was described as thirty to forty years old, slightly over six feet tall, stoop shouldered, thin of face and figure, displaying large whiskers, a sallow complexion, and sparse light or yellow hair. He gave the slaves money and guns and told them he had agents in nearby towns and counties ready to help their cause. The conspiracy came tumbling down when a slave named Lucy, informed her slave master, Ptolemy Powell, about the plot.

Boxley and six slaves were convicted on March 5, 1816 and sentenced to hang. But on May 14, the jailor and Boxley's wife managed to help Boxley escape (which they were indicted for) and despite a $1,000 reward, he was never recaptured.

Fear of insurrections continued up until the Civil War. The *Richmond Dispatch* reported on October 30, 1860 that a man named Dodson was indicted in Pittsylvania Court House, Virginia for "advising and inciting Negros in this state to rebel and make insurrection."

"Dodson was overheard to tell Negros at a late hour of the night, "that the children of Israel were in greater bondage than they (i.e. the negroes) and that they threw off the yoke of slavery by themselves, that the negroes of St. Domingo had overpowered their masters and set themselves free, and that if they would only be determined, and show that they were in earnest, the North would send them help; that there were 500 men in this county who would help them, and that many of the remainder would do nothing against them, and that in a short time they could all be free."

The *Richmond Dispatch* also reported an attempted insurrection in the town of Manchester, Chesterfield County, Virginia in January 1861. The conspirators, who met at the home of a man named Vaughn, consisted mostly of freed slaves, members of the Howlett family. It was reported the conversation included potentially treasonous statements, such as claiming they would all be freed in two months, and that "a vessel laden with silver was now on its way from the North for the use of the colored people." Several of Vaughn's slaves reported the plot to authorities. However, after several hours of testimony it was concluded the comments made at Vaughn's table related to informal news accounts rather than a contemplated insurrection.

Frank Padget:
Virginia's Honored Slave

Seven years before the fall of Fort Sumter, a monument was erected in Virginia to honor the brave deeds of a slave named Frank Padget. January 21ˢᵗ is Frank Padget Day in Glasgow, Virginia.

In the pastoral days before canals and railroads shortened time, a ubiquitous army of river warriors known as bateauxmen, plied the inland waterways to move America's commerce. In tapered flat bottom boats known as bateaux (the singular is bateau), six to eight feet wide and forty to ninety feet long, the bateauman had only his instincts and a wood pole called a tiller to guide these workhorses, hauling as much as eleven hogshead, or 12,000 pounds. It has been estimated that during the boom years 1820 to 1840, somewhere in the vicinity of fifteen hundred of these anonymous men labored mightily to move America.

Along the James River, at a place called Balcony Falls Gorge, lurks the devil, a four mile death-trap filled with rocks, dangerous for bateaux to navigate, even on a good day. It was especially dreadful on January 21, 1854, when havoc and disaster rained down upon Captain Wood and his hearty but hapless passengers heading to their worksites on a canal boat called the Clinton. The towpath line broke and chaos erupted.

Most of the crew members and passengers ended up safely on the towpath. A few however, were left stranded on the 'velvet rocks,' so named for their 'carpet of soft green moss.' They were also left with only a faint glimmer of hope in the form of rescue by a few brave bateauxmen. A group of five, led by Padget, volunteered to save the stranded men from the destruction nature had unleashed. Two trips were made. The first sapped Padget's last ounce of energy; the second stole his final breath.

Except for the heroism that cost him his life, little is known about Padget. His exploits that day were promptly recorded in the local newspaper by Captain Edward Echols, an eyewitness to the event. The account of the incident in the *Lexington (Virginia) Gazette* describes the tragedy:

> "Many persons on shore were affected to tears as they witnessed the scene at this moment…The situation on the rock was dangerous in the highest degree. Away they fly, the man on the rock is motioned to, to jump into the boat, as she passes by, which he understands. He fixes himself so as to jump, the boat arrives, he jumps into her, we all on shore fix our mouths for a shout, but Oh God! Horror of horrors! The boat has struck…in the twinkling of an eye she is wrapped around the rock, crushed like an egg shell…Frank struggled manfully, for a minute, and went down to rise no more… Heaven grant we may not have any more such scenes."

A shorter version of his exploits was soon after etched upon a 900-pound obelisk at the confluence of the James and Maury Rivers:

In Memory of
FRANK PADGET

A coloured slave, who, during a freshet in James' River, in January 1854, ventured and lost his life, by drowning, in the noble effort to save some of his fellow creatures, who, were in the midst of the flood, from death.

A freshet is a flood or overflowing of a river caused by heavy rains. Captain Echols, a businessman and slave-owner, was so moved by Padget's bravery and courage that he arranged and paid for the monument, originally placed along the canal towpath at lock 16, near where the tragedy occurred. The land was subsequently purchased by the Richmond & Allegheny Railroad, and eventually passed to the Chesapeake & Ohio Railroad. For years, the monument rested in anonymity. It was illegal and inconvenient to visit as it was located on private land, approximately thirty miles from the nearest public road.

Padget's story, however, was recently brought back to life by the relocation of the monument from its former site to a public park. The State of Virginia backed the plan and student volunteers provided labor to transfer the Padget Monument to its current location proudly overlooking the James River in Glasgow's Centennial Park. In addition, a Virginia historical marker has been placed near the site.

The bauteauxmen gradually faded away with the coming of canals and railroads. The end of the era was poignantly depicted in *The Amherst County Story*:

> "The river life continued until the coming of the canal. Then one by one the waterman gave up their special craft on the James…Gone were the camps of the bateauman and the sound of music borne at night on the river wind to homes on Amherst hills. Gone the ways of ghostly remembrance are the music and song, the laughter as the brown jug circulated, the beat of the banjo, and the answering Slap Slap of bare feet upon the hard clay. Gone from Virginia."

Decades later, the canals have come and gone and the railroads have seen their heyday. But past really is prologue, and once again the beat of the banjo can be heard as bateauxmen have returned to tame the James. Last year, the James River Bateaux Festival held its 21st anniversary celebration in which numerous bateaux traversed 120 miles in eight days. The festival is held every summer by the Virginia Canals & Navigation Society (VC&NS). If there's a heaven, Captain Echols was smiling because one of the early reproduction bateaux in the festival was named for Virginia's honored slave: The Frank Padget.

Confederate soldiers were also known to pay for and erect a monument to slaves. A Confederate soldier named John Vest, but referred to as "Jack", of Louisa County, Virginia a private in the Richmond Howitzers, took his slave, Alex Kean, with him to war as a cook. Private Vest died in the fall of 1863 and Alex chose to stay on with the soldiers rather than return home to Louisa County and ended up serving through the entire war. Alex Kean died in 1911 and two years later his former comrades erected a monument to, "A man who did his duty both in war and in peace. Well Done, good and faithful servant."

Peyton Anderson:
First Confederate Wounded

Near Fairfax Circle, a couple miles from the court house, Peyton Anderson, a soldier in what became the 6th Virginia Cavalry, became the first Confederate wounded when he was shot in the right arm on May 27, 1861. Anderson and William Lillard were on picket duty at the time, assigned to the Falls Church road with instructions to fire two warning shots and quickly retreat to Fairfax if they sighted Union soldiers. Lillard was captured and the severely wounded Anderson was left for dead. Anderson survived the wound and was subsequently discharged for disability. Injury did not keep him away for long as he later joined Colonel John Mosby's 43rd Cavalry. According to a story about the incident in the Fairfax Herald:

> "One of the officers rushed up, pointed his gun at his [Anderson's] chest, almost touching him, and fired. The ball glanced around the side of his chest and drove through his shoulder, inflicting a very severe and dangerous wound. Hemorrhage was so great that he fainted from loss of blood and the enemy thought he was dead. The men to whom he surrendered cursed and threatened to shoot the officer for shooting a man after he had surrendered and [had] been disarmed."

On May 27, 1927, the United Daughters of the Confederacy

placed a monument near the sight of the incident. The monument was later moved due to road widening and is presently located on Lee Highway in Fairfax City, in front of an EconoLodge Motel. The monument was unveiled "with appropriate exercises" and was "most interesting and largely attended," according to *The Confederate Veteran* Magazine. Those in attendance included Anderson's widow and many of his descendants.

In a letter dated May 27, 1927, on file in the Virginia Room of the Fairfax County Public Library, James Robey, a witness to the event recalled:

"In the early morning of May 27th, 1861, I, as a boy of fourteen years of age was passing the spot where the Flint Hill and Falls Church roads intersect. At this time there were two Confederate pickets stationed there; one lying in the pine woods nearby and the other on his horse on duty, each dressed in civilian clothes with a feather in their hats. I had not gone far down the road before I was met by a squad of cavalry which I counted as boys are want to do, finding twenty-four men and one officer. They were dressed and equipped so finely that I was sure that they were Union soldiers. I was soon to realize this truth, for as they approached the foot of the hill they spurred their horses into a gallop and soon surrounded the two surprised pickets. It was but a moment until a shot rang out followed by a puff of smoke and as I hurried homeward to tell my friends what I had seen I was again passed by the troop of cavalry, who this time had a prisoner. I have since learned that the bullet found its mark in the person of Peyton Anderson, the one in whose honor this memorial is today being dedicated, and it gives me a great pleasure to be able to recall the picture of such an historical event, and to contribute to the success of this occasion."

Had it not been for the fact that he was fighting against Yankees, Anderson could be called a true "Yankee doodle dandy" because he was born, in 1837, on July 4th.

Anderson married Louemma Miller in 1876. After an early morning ceremony, they "began the long drive by buggy to Warrenton where they boarded a train for Philadelphia, Pa., to attend the Centennial Exposition." Peyton died on January 12, 1914: Louemma died in 1951 at age 102. They are both buried in Amissville, Virginia.

The Battle Hymn
of the Republic

Song and poetry takes this story to another part of Fairfax—Upton Hill and Munson Hill, near present-day Seven Corners, where a woman penned her way into history in the February 1862 edition of the *Atlantic Monthly*. Her words have been recited, repeated and sung thousands of times, in many languages for almost a century and a half. Her name was not mentioned or printed in the publication and she was paid five dollars. The magazine's editor provided the title: The Battle Hymn of the Republic.

On November 18, 1861, Julia Ward Howe with her husband Samuel Gridley Howe and a few friends traveled to Falls Church, Virginia to observe a review of General George McClellan's troops. Packed for the outing was "an enormous hamper of fried chicken, Virginia ham, bottles of champagne and other delicacies for a very special picnic." They all sang the song *John Brown's Body* as well as several other popular Civil War marching tunes.

As a side note, John Brown's brother, Frederick Brown, was at the time a civilian U.S. Government employee in Washington. The assistant secretary of the treasury during the Civil War described him as "incompetent and insubordinate...He was a harmless, garrulous old man, who used to obstruct a corridor for hours, pouring out a ceaseless stream of talk upon whomsoever would stoop to listen."

The troops on review must have made an impressive show. They were well-trained and drilled. So much so that according to one soldier in Falls Church at the time:

"The first thing in the morning is drill, then drill, then drill again. Then drill, drill, a little more drill. Then drill, and lastly drill. Between drills, we drill and sometimes stop to eat a little and have a roll-call."

A New York man recounted what a review looked like from the soldier's point of view:

"At evening parade all Washington appears. A regiment of ladies, rather indisposed to beauty, observe us. Sometimes the Dons arrive—Secretaries of State, of War, of Navy,--or military Dons, bestriding prancing steeds, but bestriding them as if 'twas not their habit often of an afternoon.' All which,--the bad teeth, pallid skins, and rustic toilets of the fair, and the very moderate horsemanship of the brave,--privates, standing at ease in the ranks, take note of, not cynically, but as men of the world."

A Wisconsin officer recorded this first-hand account in a letter home:

"On Tuesday we marched out to Bailey's Cross Roads to take part in the grand review....You know it was the largest review of troops ever in America, that 60,000 infantry, 9,000 cavalry, and 130 pieces of artillery passed in review before McClellan...that it took from 11 o'clock A.M. until 4 P.M. to pass the reviewing officer, and that the President, the members of the Cabinet, and all the celebrities, foreign and domestic, were present.

But perhaps you have not seen that General McClellan was so overcome by the lofty pomposity of Drum Major William Whaley of this regiment that he took off his hat when Whaley passed. But sad to relate, Whaley was so overcome by this recognition, which took place while he was indulging in a top-loftical gyration of his baton, that he dropped the baton. From the topmost height of glory he was plunged into the deepest gulf of despair."

Someone much more mortified and scorned than this hapless baton twirler, however, was a colonel of the 49th Pennsylvania Infantry named William Irwin. Irwin's problem involved booze not batons. He was court-martialed for being "so intoxicated as to be unable to perform the duties of commander at the Grand Review at Munson's Hill, Virginia on 21 November 1861." One witness later testified: "He did not seem to know what he was doing. Another witness said: "At the Grand Review, I believe the colonel was intoxicated. His face was red and he had a wild appearance. He rode around a great deal." Irwin was found not guilty of drunkenness, but predictably, he ran into more problems later in the war. In August 1863 he was ordered to the hospital by a board of examiners. One doctor certified Irwin as mentally deranged. At his death in 1886, the superintendent of the Central Kentucky Lunatic Asylum stated the cause was exhaustion… from mental derangement from…pain, loss of sleep and nervous irritation of wounds he had received in the U. S. Army. The army, however, disagreed. They rejected his widow's pension claim on the grounds that the cause of death was not service-related.

On a lighter parade note, one soldier confided an inside secret during the march:

> "We were no exception to the generality of mankind, of liking to see a pretty face, even if it did belong to a woman of 'secesh' sentiments. When the boys at the head of the column discovered a pretty girl, if she was on the right side of the road, "guide right" would be passed along the line; and "guide left" if on the left side of the road. By this ingenious device we were enabled to direct our eyes where we would receive the largest return for our admiration."

Marching and camp life brought all kinds of things for soldiers to think about. Like how could they afford to buy necessities or must-have items and who would carry them on long marches? Frying pans, for instance. These eagerly sought and treasured items were awkward, heavy to carry and cost a lot (about a dollar each).

One group of five entrepreneurial soldiers devised a creative solution to the frying pan dilemma. They established their own joint-stock company, each member paying twenty cents for the initial purchase. "The par value of each was therefore twenty cents."

Each shareholder took turns carrying the pan (for easier carrying the frying pan's handle was often stuck in the barrel of the musket) and was entitled to first use of it for the evening after he had carried it all day.

The entrepreneurials sometimes rented their pan to others outside their partnership, thus "affording means for an occasional dividend among the stockholders." Eventually the stock increased in value to forty cents per share, "so that a man in the Joint Stock Frying Pan Company was looked upon as a man of consequence…being treated with kindness and civility by his comrades, life assumed a roseate hue to the shareholders in this great company, in spite of the deprivations. It was flattering to hear one's self mentioned in terms of praise by some impecunious comrade who wished to occupy one side of it while you were cooking."

Inevitably, however, their stock plunged as soon as they got the orders to move out and leave knapsacks (and everything else) behind.

One soldier gave this amusing description of how utensils and frying pans sometimes changed ownership in the camp:

"Snow-ball battles were sometimes fought with such vigor as to disable the combatants. The result of such a fight was the capture of the defeated party's cooking utensils, and any food that might be contained in them."

Parade jokes, frying pans, and snow-ball fights aside, however, the review had to be abruptly interrupted. But not for batons, booze or women. For Confederates. Many soldiers had to hurry off to defend against a nearby Confederate attack. The Howes, along with a few others, made their way to Washington's Willard Hotel.

By the next morning Howe had written the words to the Battle Hymn of the Republic on the letterhead of the U. S. Sanitary Commission, Washington, Treasury Building. The Sanitary Commission was a forerunner of the Red Cross. (Willard's was the first American hotel to provide writing facilities for its guests in every room.) Howe gave the original draft of the Battle Hymn to a friend, with a notation, 'Willard's Hotel, Julia W. Howe to Charlotte B. Whipple.' The Whipples and the Howes were good friends and had been together at Falls Church. Julia Ward Howe later explained how the words to the song came to her: "As I lay waiting for the dawn, the long lines of the poem began to twine themselves...[and] to my astonishment found that the wished-for lines were arranging themselves in my brain. I lay quite still until the last verse had completed itself in my thoughts, then hastily arose, saying to myself, I shall lose this if I don't write it down immediately."

A witness to the review, Mr. A. J. Bloor of the Sanitary Commission, remarked that Howe was "the instrument for the righting of the wrong and the amelioration of the current conditions of humanity." He went on to creatively characterize the conditions that Ward observed just before writing the Battle Hymn. Her words to the song were discovered "in the midst of the blare and glitter and bedizened simulacra of actual and abhorrent warfare." There are no typos in that quotation.

The song had a magical effect. Tired and hungry soldiers had their spirits lifted by singing the Battle Hymn "as if a heavenly ally were descending with a song of succor, and thereafter the wet, aching marchers thought less...of their wretched selves, thought more of their cause, their families, their country."

Mine eyes have seen the glory of the coming of the Lord;
He is trampling out the vintage where the grapes of wrath are stored;
He hath loosed the fateful lighting of his terrible swift sword;
His truth is marching on.

Howe's daughter may have summarized it best: "In the words of the Battle Hymn we hear not only the voice of the Union Army, but an echo of all the aspiring thoughts and noble deeds of the builders of our great Republic."

At the time Howe was writing the Battle Hymn of the Republic, a Union officer nearby in Fairfax was court-martialed for misconduct. But it was not just any officer…

Colonel James E. Kerrigan of the 25th New York Volunteers was charged with allowing his regiment on October 14 and 15, 1861 at Hall's Hill in Virginia to "suffer and permit the privates… and the non-commissioned officers…to engage in loud and unseemly dispute and brawls, to use disorderly language, and to make noisy disturbances." He was also charged with being drunk on a march, and from July 25-October 1, 1861, leaving his regimental camp in Fairfax County, Virginia to "visit and communicate with the enemy in said county." A member of the 25th New York testified that one man hit another over the head with a pistol and Kerrigan did nothing about it. In addition, "there was much drunkenness, and gambling on dog fights." Kerrigan led a group of New Yorkers whose real sentiment was just as much Confederate as Union. They acted surly and weren't motivated to do much at all. In fact, earlier in the war, when the regiment marched in front of President Lincoln on August 26, 1861, Kerrigan's unit refused to "give a cheer for the president and the Union….Despite warnings that such embarrassing displays would not be tolerated in the future, Kerrigan and his men continued to treat their superiors with disdain."

Kerrigan was found guilty of twelve of the forty-two charges. But remarkably it appears he was allowed to resign. The reason is obvious. At the very time all this was going on, he was a member of the United States Congress! You can imagine the letters on his behalf that came into the Union Army and to President Lincoln.

After he left the army and went back to Congress, Kerrigan eventually was arrested on the House floor when he continued to speak, after debate had ended, against a bill to fund the abolition of slavery in Missouri.

James Kerrigan served as an officer in the Union Army from May 19, 1861 to February 21, 1862, and as an elected Democrat to the 37th Congress from March 4, 1861 to March 3, 1863.

Professor Lowe's Flying Machine

Near the sight of the Grand Review the skies over Northern Virginia became home to revolutionary technological warfare. On June 11, 1861 Professor Joseph Henry, director of the Smithsonian Institution invited Professor Thaddeus Lowe, a twenty-nine-year-old Ohio "aeronaut" to make a presentation before President Lincoln to explain how using balloons could help win the war.

Shortly after this meeting Lowe made several ascents, from the area of today's Washington's Federal Triangle. With a cable running from the White House (then called the Executive Mansion) to the balloon in the sky (equipment and cable loaned by the American Telegraph Company), Lowe telegrammed the president:

> "This point of observation commands an area nearly fifteen miles in diameter. The city, with its girdle of encampments, presents a superb scene. I take great pleasure in sending you this first dispatch ever telegrammed from an aerial station, and in acknowledging indebtness to your encouragement, for the opportunity of demonstrating the availability of the science of aeronautics in the military service of the country."

A week later from the Upton Hill area of Fairfax County, Lowe ascended several times to about 500 feet. (A newspaper correspondent believed he actually ascended only 200 feet).

During a July 24, 1861 flight, Lowe was fired upon by Union troops who mistakenly thought the balloon (named the Union) was a rebel balloon. He followed this close call with a stinging rebuke to the War Department by insisting all Union officers be advised not to shoot at any balloons—they were all "friendly"-- because the Confederates had no such thing in their arsenal.

Confederates "expressed their dislike by pot-shooting at the balloon with its large portrait of George Washington bulging on its side whenever it went up...The Yankees hoisted a balloon this evening just across the river. Our batteries commenced throwing bombs at it." Although the shots missed, this proved to be the first use of anti-aircraft fire. (According to a post-war recollection of Confederate General James Longstreet, Southern women donated their finest silk dresses to make a balloon in the summer of 1862. But the federals quickly captured it, "and with it the last silk dress in the Confederacy... This capture was the meanest trick of the war," Longstreet lamented, "and one that I have never yet forgiven.")

On September 24, 1861, Lowe ascended from Fort Corcoran. Using a white flag, he directed the aerial bombardment of Falls Church for Union troops firing from Fort Ethan Allen near the Chain Bridge. The instructions given to Lowe were basic and brief: "If we fire to the right of Falls Church, let a white flag be raised in the balloon; if to the left, let it be lowered; if over let it be shown stationary; if under, let it be waved occasionally." The signals were met with rave reviews. The artillery battery commander wrote:

"The signals from the balloon have enabled my gunners to hit with a fine degree of accuracy an unseen and dispersed target area. This demonstration will revolutionize the art of gunnery."

Several soldiers went up with Lowe or his assistant William Paulin. The first to join Lowe and Paulin may have been Daniel Sickles. A soldier of the 26th Pennsylvania Infantry named William Small went up on December 8, 1861 and drew a detailed map of the terrain opposite General Hooker's camp. The map covered approximately seven miles of ground.

Count Ferdinand von Zeppelin made several balloon rides. The German officer had taken a leave of absence to come to America to observe the war. Some of his experiences included observing war action at Fairfax Court House and meeting President Lincoln. After seeing the balloon's benefits, he began formulating plans which culminated years later in the world's first guided dirigible.

Mathew Brady also made a trip, perhaps giving Paulin the idea to start a personal photographic business—(which resulted in his getting fired from the balloon crew.) Lowe took General Fitz John Porter up many times. An observer noted:

"It was a weird spectacle,--that frail, fading oval, gliding against the sky, floating in the serene azure, the little vessel swinging silently beneath…its course was fitfully direct, and the wind seemed to veer often, as if contrary currents, conscious of the opportunity, were struggling for the possession of the daring navigator…had he been reconnoitering from a secure perch at the tip of the moon, he could not have been more vigilant… Both armies in solemn silence were gazing aloft, while the imperturbable mariner continued to spy out the land."

The secretary of war instructed Lowe to build four more balloons and by the end of November the Union had five balloons at its disposal (named Eagle, Constitution, Washington, Intrepid and Union). Lowe was indeed the first American "spy in the sky."

A resident of Virginia's Tidewater observed the balloon and noted the novelty of it:

"Every night the Yankees sent up a balloon (called the Intrepid) in front of our house to try to see what was going on in Richmond. General Low[e] was the man who ascended in the balloon, and he told many wonderful things that he saw going on in Richmond—such as people going to church, the evacuation of Richmond (in 1862), wagon trains crossing Mayo's bridge, etc. There was an old lady, Mrs. Woody, who lived three or four miles from us, and a balloon was sent up from her house too. When they were telling her what they had seen she replied, "Yes, Moses also viewed the promised land, but he never entered." That night the church which she attended and which was on a corner of her place was burned by the Yankees."

Lowe, who had been made a colonel by President Lincoln, left the army in May 1863 after his position was subordinated to the chief army engineer.

Lowe's expedition, however, did not represent, by any means, man's first balloon-travel into space. That historic claim belongs to the Montgolfier brothers of France. On November 21, 1783 their seventy-five foot tall craft (and forty-nine feet in diameter) stayed afloat for twenty-five minutes and ascended to 280 feet before safely landing. A couple months earlier in a public demonstration before King Louis XVI and Marie Antoinette, the brothers sent into space a balloon carrying a sheep, rooster and a duck.

A competing hydrogen balloon also went up above Paris in 1783. Competition ran thicker than scientific cooperation and the Montgolfiers brothers were denied admittance. This unmanned balloon, named the "the Globe," rose to 3,000 feet and landed safely after forty-five minutes. Air turned out to be safer than land for this balloon as peasants, so "terrified by this strange contraption, destroyed it with pitchforks."

In addition to Lowe, several other aeronauts tried to convince the government of the benefit of using balloons in warfare. James Allen, who enlisted in Providence, Rhode Island, had made a successful flight in a balloon in 1856. John Wise, of Lancaster, Pennsylvania, had flown as early as 1835 and John LaMountain flew in a balloon in the spring of 1861 from St. Louis, Missouri to upstate New York. These three men competed with each other and Lowe for the rights to be the Union's Balloon Czar. In the end, Lowe may have won the competition simply because he had more influential and powerful political connections.

Northern Slave Traders

Dealing in slavery became a capital crime in 1820-- the sentence was execution. Forty-two years later, in February 1862, the first and only slaver was executed in the United States. Captain Nathaniel Gordon had been nabbed on August 8, 1860, as his ship, the *Erie* tried to smuggle 900 slaves from the Congo to Cuba. Gordon had traded whiskey for his human cargo, and he claimed (as many slave-traders did) that he had previously sold the vessel and was merely a passenger.

He had been apprehended by one of the eight American vessels patrolling African waters. These eight ships represented America's effort to fulfill the 1842 Webster-Ashburton Treaty, an agreement calling for Britain and America to work in "concert and cooperation" to apprehend slavers. For almost four decades the American contribution to this African Squadron was minuscule. That changed, however, in 1860 when Secretary of the Navy Issac Toucey called for aggressive action by the squadron. Ironically, Toucey, a former Connecticut senator had been criticized for his perceived Southern sympathies and had been hanged in effigy with a note pinned to the chest reading: "Toucey the traitor."

By the time Gordon went to trial in New York, seven of the eight vessels had been transferred to the navy's use for the Civil War.

The trial occurred in New York City, a city exquisitely familiar with the lucrative rewards of the slave trade.

Slavery and cotton created New York. The gilded towers of Gotham's affluence--veritable skyscrapers of white gold--were built with bales of cotton dollars over decades of slavery. New Yorkers and New Englanders climbed this edifice of high finance to the top floor, all the way up to the Civil War, determined at every step to strike their perfect heels against marble floors and tap fourteen carat fingers against gold banisters just loudly enough to conceal the distant cries of slavery.

The heart of the slave beast pulsated in the North, its tentacles controlling, as one historian aptly put it, almost every aspect from "plantation to market." Responsibility for slavery rested as much with Northerners as Southerners, a point commented upon by many, including President Lincoln, who said in 1854, "When Southern people tell us they are no more responsible for the origin of slavery, than we; I acknowledge the fact."

Northern cities, principally New York, benefitted in two distinct ways: 1) They collected tremendous fees and taxes for crops picked by slaves and exported to Europe and other foreign locations, and 2) they sent out slaving vessels to capture slaves from Africa and deliver them into slavery. Many Northerners--none with an iota of pro-Southern blood--including Frederick Douglas, W. E. B. DuBois, Horace Greeley, Ralph Waldo Emerson, Charles Sumner and Harriet Beecher Stowe, remarked about New York City as the center of the slave trade.

Cotton was king, but as one historian noted, "he was a puppet monarch" controlled by New York bankers and merchants.

"The physical existence [of New York City] depended upon… the continuance of slave labor and the prosperity of the slave master." The Mayor of New York wrote that as the Civil War started.

Horace Greeley proclaimed New York City, "the nest of slave pirates" and W. E. B. Dubois called the city, "the principal port of the world" for slavery. The 34th Congress of the United States (1855—1857) reported: "Almost all the slave expeditions for some time past have been fitted out in the United States, chiefly at New York." The United States attorney said the city was, "the head and front of the slave trade," and the Marshal for New York called the city, "the principal depot for vessels in this [slave] traffic." A government investigator remarked that most of the money invested in the slave trade had been invested by New Yorkers.

The city's newspapers echoed the same theme. *The New York Times* complained that New Yorkers had lost "their sense of the wickedness of the [slave] trade...New York has been most deeply engaged in the traffic. Her merchants have largely profited by its blood-stained gains." *The Christian Intelligencer* stated, "New York has long enough borne the disgrace of being the greatest depot of the slave trade in the world. Here scores of ships have been fitted out yearly on the negro stealing business." The *Continental Monthly* reported in 1862: "The number of persons engaged in the slave-trade...exceed our powers of calculation. The City of New York has been until late the principal port of the world for this infamous commerce...The impunity which has attended these men [engaged in the slave business] is notorious." It is interesting to note that the same article went on to identify the 2nd and 3rd largest American slave ports, and they were not located in the South--they were Portland, Maine and Boston. *The New York Tribune* reported: "The hideous truth is that not Charleston, not Savannah, no Southern port, but New York City itself became the greatest slave-trading mart in the world." That quote, as well as the next one, comes from a book that won the Pulitzer Prize in 1951.

William Seward, President Lincoln's secretary of state, claimed that when, as senator from New York, he tried to tighten anti-slavery laws, the most intense pressure against him came "not so much from the slave states as from commercial interests of New York."

The North, primarily New York, had a hand in every aspect of the rice, tobacco and cotton harvested from Southern plantations. Northern banks lent the money for plantation owners to buy equipment and slaves (many slaves were bought on credit). Northern businesses set the price for the commodities, leaving, as W. E. B. DuBois acknowledged, "narrow margins of profit for the planter."

Southern cotton exported to Europe did not typically go from Southern ports to Europe. It went from Southern ports to Northern ports to Europe. By controlling the purse strings of slavery, Northerners could tie up Southerners with such a cumbersome and unprofitable arrangement. After unloading the cotton in Europe, these ships were then filled with European goods for transport back to the South. In this manner, New Yorkers cornered the lucrative financial angle of the slavery triangle, fleecing astronomical fees and taxes, widely believed to be nearly forty cents on every cotton dollar.

Massachusetts Senator Charles Sumner used the expression "the lords of the lash and the lords of the loom" to compare Southern planters with the "traffickers of New England." Ralph Waldo Emerson remarked what everyone already knew: "The cotton thread is the Union."

By 1860, New England was home to 472 cotton mills; there were textile mills elsewhere but most were concentrated in the North. In 1860, nearly 50% of all textiles produced in the United States came from mills located only in Massachusetts and Rhode Island.

The North so greatly craved its slave profits that a New York newspaper reported, two weeks before the fall of Fort Sumter, that Rhode Island might secede to get the cotton revenue that New York stood to lose if the South seceded: "That plucky little state [Rhode Island] will at once abandon the old hulk of the Union, offering at once a commercial depot and a summer residence for Southerners. The estimated value of the [cotton] traffic thus directed from New York may be set down at $50,000,000 annually."

So critical were these phenomenal revenues from Southern crops that Frederick Douglas told a Boston audience in 1865 that slavery had been the impetus for the Civil War for both sides, but for reasons that seem so strange that you will want to reread this quotation and may believe it's a typo: "The South was fighting to take slavery out of the Union, and the North fighting to keep it in the Union." Check it out yourself: page 61 of *Black Reconstruction in America, 1860-1880*, by W.E.B. DuBois. Mr. DuBois, who would head any short list of Americans least likely to be called apologists for the South, attributed this remark to Mr. Frederick Douglas, another person on the same list.

Cotton, rice and tobacco represented the vast majority of all exports from the United States, accounting for 66% of all exports ($185 million of $279 million) in 1858. The following year the figure was a whopping 71% ($198/$278 million). Those exports translated to incredible fees and taxes to the North as shown in a comparison of customs revenue.

For a one year period shortly before the Civil War--June 1858 to June 1859-- the New Orleans Custom House led the South with $2,120,058.76. The amounts drop precipitously from there, with Charleston ($299,339.43) and Mobile ($118,027.99) next. Compare that to Northern custom houses, headed by New York at $35 million! ($ 35,155,452.75 to be exact). And a massive amount of the exports going out of New York were from southern plantations. Next on the Northern list were Boston ($ 5,133,414.55) and Philadelphia ($2,262,349.57). As an indication of how dominant southern crops were to the world market, consider this: Of all imports coming into Great Britain in the year 1858, almost 79% came from Southern States ($732,403,840 of $931,847,056).

But Northerners did not just extract great sums of money from slaves working on Southern plantations. New York City also served as the center for the international slavery trade.

Northern crews sailing on Northern vessels from Northern ports, supplied by Northern merchants, funded by Northern money and insured by Northern businesses swept across the sea, banishing thousands of Africans to enslavement in places like Cuba or Brazil. A vast and insidious network of Northern mercenaries--ship fitters, suppliers, recruiters, merchants, shippers, auctioneers, bankers, brokers, insurers, and bribed custom agents to name just a few-- assiduously oiled the heinous engine of slavery, riding the peculiar institution for decades while collecting staggering sums—legally and illegally, directly and indirectly--for their role in outfitting vessels and sending them to Africa.

Because of the movie, we have all heard the story of the *Amistad*; but the *Amistad* was not an isolated incident. The plundering promenade across the Atlantic occurred with dreadful regularity. And the vast majority of slaving vessels like the *Amistad* sailed from New York and New England. The practice went on from 1820, when international slave trafficking became illegal and punishable by death under President Monroe of Virginia, up to, and even into the Civil War.

The trade was so overtly conducted that New York newspapers carried the names of ships departing on slave voyages. W. E. B. DuBois reported that during an 18-month period in 1859-1860, New York harbors fitted out eighty-five vessels, transporting between 30,000-60,000 slaves annually. Count slowly to eighty five. Imagine each number represents a single ship with hundreds of slaves aboard. And that was only for one eighteen-month period. And only New York. Who knows how many went out of Portland, Maine, Boston, Newport, Philadelphia, and other Northern locations?

Here is a partial list of some of the captured Northern slaving vessels, in the 1850s alone: New Yorkers sent out the *Martha* (with 1,800 slaves), the *Advance, Rachel P. Brown, Silenus* (carrying 900 slaves), *Glamorgan* (captured when it was about to deliver 700 slaves), *Julia Moulton, Orion* (captured with 800 slaves) *Peerless* (which landed 350 slaves in Cuba), *Eliza Jane, Cortes, Haidee* (1,100 slaves), the *J. Harris* (550 slaves), *Wildfire* (507 slaves), the *Charlotte,* and the most infamous of all, the *Wanderer.* In November 1858, the *Wanderer* landed 413 slaves onto Jekyll Island, Georgia. Edgar Farnum, instrumental in delivering those slaves to Georgia, went on to become a Civil War Union Army brigadier general. After the war, he was appointed the coveted position as New York City's Inspector of Customs. Other Northern ports sent out the *Lucy Ann* (carrying 547 slaves), *Camargo* (landed 500 slaves in Brazil), the *Grey Eagle, Mary E. Smith* (captured with 387 slaves on board), the *Jos. H. Record, Jasper, Oregon, William G. Lewis* (411 slaves), *Onward,* and the *Charles.*

Incredibly, it didn't stop there. In the early 1860s, captured Northern slaving vessels included the *Bonito* (with 750 slaves), *Thomas Watson,* the *Nightingale* (961 slaves), *Merchant, Falmouth, Storm King* (620 slaves, half of them children) *Cora* (705 slaves), *Splendide* (300 slaves), the *Ocilla,* and the *Erie.*

These are only a sample of the known slaving expeditions. Most expeditions were never captured or discovered, often because the slaving vessels were burned after delivering its slaves to its destination. Profits were so great that the intentional loss of a ship was just minor cost of doing business. The *New Orleans Picayune* reported on July 27, 1860 about one such "unconfirmed" slaving vessel:

> "It is believed that the slaver lately burned off the coast of Cuba, whose crew were in a few days since brought into Key West, was the bark Sultana, Capt. Bowen, which cleared at New York, the 26th of January, for Rio Zaire and a market. She was sold in December, 1859 for $15,000, to a foreign firm in New York, for a Havana house. She was fitted out [in New York City] at the foot of Fourth street, East River. It is said that she landed some 1,200 to 1,300 negroes in Cuba before she was burned."

Southerners railed vehemently against the temerity of Northerners criticizing them for slavery while many Northern cities were so heavily involved in the slave trade. One Southerner summed up this hypocrisy:

> *"Who conducts our commerce, builds for us our ships, and navigates them on the high seas? The North! Who spins and weaves, for our domestic use (and grows rich doing it)? The North! Who supplies the material and the engineers for our railroads where we have any? ... The North! Is there a bale of cotton to leave our ports for Liverpool, shall not a Northern ship transport it? Is there a package of broadcloths or a chest of tea to be landed at our warehouses? There is a tribute, first to Boston or New York!"*

Consider this concluding and conclusive juxtaposition: In 1864, residents of New York City did not deliver the votes to President Lincoln (he lost the city by more than a 2:1 margin); however, ninety miles from the United States, some of its citizens delivered slaves to Cuba aboard the *Huntress*.

An Englishman named William Cowper (1731-1800) wrote this poem, called The Guinea Captain:

> *Lives there a savage ruder than the slave?*
> *Cruel as death, insatiate as the grave,*

False as the winds that round his vessel blow,
Remorseless as the gulf that yawns below,
Is he who toils upon the wafting flood,
A Christian broker in the trade of blood!
Boisterous in speech, in action prompt and bold,
He buys, he sells, he steals, he kills—for gold!
At noon, when sky and ocean, calm and clear,
Bend round his bark, one blue, unbroken sphere;
When dancing dolphins sparkle through the brine,
And sunbeam circles o'er the waters shine;
He sees no beauty in the heaven serene,
No soul-enchanting sweetness in the scene—
But, darkly scowling at the glorious day,
Curses the winds that loiter on their way!
When, swoll'n with hurricanes, the billows rise,
To meet the lightning midway from the skies;
When, from the burden'd hold, his shrieking slaves
Are cast at midnight, to the hungry waves,--
Not for his victims, strangled in the deeps,
Not for his crimes, the harden'd pirate weeps;
But, grimly smiling, when the storm is o'er,
Counts his sure gains, and hurries back for more!

Blenker's Germans

Back along the Little River Turnpike the Confederate pickets moved west toward the court house in late summer 1861. Union pickets moved in to replace them. General Philip Kearney's pickets were posted near Padgett's Tavern. Slightly west of the tavern, General Louis Blenker and his German troops from the 45th New York stood guard.

Germans made up the highest continent of immigrants in the Union army. One historian calculated there were sixty "German" units in the Union Army, primarily from New York, Ohio and Missouri. Cartoonist Thomas Nast (born in Germany) of *Harper's Weekly* drew such inspiring cartoons for Union recruitment posters that Lincoln referred to him as "our best recruiting sergeant." Years after the war President Theodore Roosevelt opined "it would be difficult to paint in too strong colors...the attitude of the American citizens of German birth...toward the cause of the Union."

One journalist estimated there were at least 20,000 German soldiers in the November 1861 Grand Review in Falls Church, Virginia.

Many had come to America several years earlier after an unsuccessful 1848 revolution in Europe and Germany. A St. Paul, Minnesota newspaper proclaimed, "We Germans...are prepared to defend our American home as the blessed place of freedom." Secretary of State William Seward echoed the same sentiment when he proclaimed that the German spirit of tolerance and freedom fought oppression everywhere.

Some joined the army "from the same motives which brought Von Kalb and Steuben in the first revolution, an opportunity to find distinction and to serve the cause of the United States, which they regard as the right cause."

Robert E. Lee was alleged to have said, "Take the Dutch out of the Union army and we could have whipped the Yankees easily." Of all immigrants groups the Germans represented, one writer noted, "the most reliable and consistent supporters of the Union cause."

German soldiers, as well as their votes were critical to Lincoln. It has been reported that shortly before the 1860 presidential election, Lincoln secretly purchased a German-American newspaper, *the Illinois Staats-Anzeiger*, with an understanding that by keeping the former owner (Dr. Heinrich Canisius) as editor, the paper would support Lincoln and his fellow Republicans in the 1860 election. Whether this is true really didn't matter for purposes of the election. The paper probably would have supported Lincoln anyway—of the 265 German-language papers in America in 1860, only three (all published in the South) supported secession.

According to the May 20, 1861 edition of the *New York Tribune*, sixteen brothers originally from Durkheim, Germany, all fought together in the same Ohio regiment. The Finch family (along with their three daughters) had moved from Germany to Dayton, Ohio before the war. The parents had subsequently moved to New York. The article mentioned the entire family had reunited in Philadelphia, and if time permitted, were going to be entertained by a group of Germans in Philadelphia. However, efforts by the author have revealed no such family of Union soldiers.

General Blenker fled Germany after the unsuccessful 1848 revolution. Blenker had been a non-commissioned officer in the German contingent serving under King Otho of Greece. Secretary of State William Seward wanted the war to be 'a people's war' by gathering officers from all over the world; in Blenker's camp he got it. This polyglot collection, according to McClellan, consisted of soldiers from:

"all known and unknown lands, from all possible and impossible armies: Zouaves from Algiers, men of the Foreign Legion, Zephyrs, Cossacks, Garibaldians of the deepest rye, English deserters, Sepoys, Turcos, Croats, Swiss, beer-drinkers from Bavaria, stout men from North Germany, and no doubt Chinese, Esquimaux, and detachments from the army of the grand Duchess of Gerolstein."

(Baron Gerolt was the Prussian Minister to Washington during the war.)

The Blenker camp, according to McClellan, looked like a "circus or opera." Soldiers were dressed in uniforms "as varied and brilliant as the colors of the rainbow." Seeing them was one thing, communicating another. McClellan recalled entering an outpost of Blenker's pickets:

"In reply to their challenge I tried English, French, Spanish, Italian, German, Indian, a little Russian and Turkish; all in vain, for nothing at my disposal made the slightest impression upon them, and I inferred that they were perhaps gypsies or Esquimaux or Chinese."

On December 2, 1861, with little resistance, rebel cavalry charged through Blenker's barricades. The Union troops mistakenly believed the attacking Confederate cavalry were Union. In the melee, the Rebels killed one and took fourteen prisoners. Union General Kearney's troops angrily criticized the Germans of drunkenness and failure to fire at the enemy.

Blenker subsequently transferred to Fremont's Mountain Department where his military resume consisted of falling off his horse and being involved in the Union defeat at the Battle of Cross Keys.

Two weeks before this, another German officer had his own problems. Colonel Emil von Schoenig of the German Rangers (later the 52nd New York Infantry), assigned to defend the capital, was posted at Camp California near Alexandria. Simply put he was incompetent. This "obvious lack of military capacity" led to an inquiry. The court found, among other things, the 'von' was a pretentious fraud and his claimed experience in the Prussian Army was untrue. Furthermore, the colonel was so "notorious" that even his friends back home in the New York German Society had disowned him. "He is a fraud," concluded the review. "His "deficient knowledge of tactics and his lack of grasp of English language wholly unfit him for the command of a regiment. Further, we are of the opinion that he knows nothing of Prussian tactics either. He uses sickness as an excuse. We recommend that he be mustered out as totally incompetent."

Despite their valiant efforts (eighty-two German-American Civil War soldiers received the highest military recognition: the Medal of Honor), the Germans were criticized by many. General McClellan said "few were of the slightest use to us, and I think the reason why the German regiments so seldom turned out well was that their officers were so often men without character."

Vice Crackdown

Across the Potomac in the City of Washington, a lurid spectacle was taking place involving the trial of a former Union officer and a madam for running a prostitution business. Washington swarmed with what newspapers at the time euphemistically referred to as Cyprians, fallen angels, daughters of eve, and gay young ducks. The *Washington Star* complained that uniformed soldiers could be seen at all hours "gallanting with the painted Jezebels with which the city is stocked." Stocked indeed. The Union army provost marshal calculated the nation's capital was home to four hundred and fifty bawdy houses. And that number represented only those which were registered. The *Star* reported five thousand "jezebels" plied their trade and wares in Washington bordellos with names like the Ironclad, the Monitor, Headquarters USA, the Devil's Own, the Wolf's Den (kept by Mrs. Wolf), the Haystack (kept by Mrs. Hay), the Cottage by the Sea, and the Blue Goose.

Alexandria was reported to have about 2,500 jezebels of its own. This soldier's letter to his wife agreed there were too many:

> "I would rather be farther off from town. It is said that one house of every ten is a bawdy house—it is a perfect Sodom. The result will be that in a week or two, there will be an increase of sickness in camp."

A U. S. Sanitary Commission officer also noted the problem in a letter, but felt impelled to provide a few more details:

"But now the evils of this place. There is a whole city of whores. Yes father, a whole city...Of course, it was all built with Army supplies and by the very men for free that they have extracted their sinful wages from...At pay time the lines before these houses are appalling and men often fight each other for a place. The average charge is three dollars and on paydays some make as much as $250 to $300. Though between pay periods, it is said that they will take their time and do many special things and charge accordingly. Some of these hussies, during their indisposed periods sell their services to the men to write letters for them to their loved ones back home. How foul. A mother, wife or sweetheart receiving a mistle penned by these soiled hands. I have not been able to reach [General] Grant to protest these matters."

The conditions were ripe for underworld characters from all over the country to invade the city: "The capital continued to swarm with underworld characters from all parts of the Union...Pickpockets flourished...while gambling halls, illicit liquor houses and brothels were... fearfully on the increase. Landlords winked at the boarding houses which soon spread through all parts of the city...Entire blocks on the south side of Pennsylvania Avenue were devoted to the business... Poisonous tanglefoot whiskey, [was] illicitly dispensed, lead[ing] to "brawls, shootings, stabbings and riots...Night after night, among the thieves, the bullies and the roistering soldiers, the drabs bedizened the police courts." Pulitzer prize-winning author Margaret Leech colorfully summed it up in *Reveille in Washington*: "On scrofulous hillsides...and in a scramble of mean passages...pleasure was dispensed in bare and dirty rooms."

The freshly-minted Washington police began a vice crackdown in the fall of 1863. Twenty indictments were handed down in a single day against brothel owners. Miss Maude Roberts and Mr. H. C. Burtenett were charged with running a bawdy house near the Executive Mansion. Burtenett had been a lieutenant–colonel in a New York regiment and later a major on Fremont's staff. With "reprehensible gusto," polite society followed the sensational events. The jury found both defendants guilty in ten minutes, the lady ordered to pay $50 and the former major fined $500 and imprisoned for a month. President Lincoln pardoned the major four months later.

Some Californians--aka: the Second Massachusetts Cavalry, fight in Fairfax

Many people in many places won the Civil War, including the 17,000 Californians who enlisted in the Union Army. After helping Abraham Lincoln win the presidency in 1860, the Golden State spent the next four years helping him win the war. Admitted to the Union as a free-soil state in 1850, most of its citizens did not feel they had a dog in the fight when the war started eleven years later. "Everyone feels," one observer noted, "neither the separation of the states nor the maintenance of the union would affect [Californians] very directly." The governor of California added he wouldn't "concern himself with a quarrel in…which he had no part and from which he had nothing to gain."

News of the war reached California partly through the telegraph (completed in the fall of 1861) and by the Pony Express (official name: the Central Overland California & Pike's Peak Express Company). The ill-fated business delivered mail and newspapers (for $5 per half-ounce) from St. Joseph, Missouri to Sacramento in 10 ½ days. (The typical overland trail took three weeks or more.)

Abraham's Lincoln's first inaugural message raced across country in the record time of 7 ½ days. Altogether, Express riders (paid the lofty sum of $125 a month for this dangerous work) made about 300 cross-country trips and carried about 35,000 pieces of mail before the express went under, overtaken by the telegraph.

Many California soldiers wanted to go east to fight Confederates, but most spent the war lodged between the Missouri River and the Pacific Ocean doing the critical yet unheralded work of fighting hostile Indians to secure the overland and stage trails.

With the constant threat at sea of Confederate raiders and privateers (approximately 100 ships sank off the coast of California during the war), keeping the overland trail open was critical, but not easy. It involved, according to one veteran, "months and years of living on the outer fringes of civilization, of weeks–long marches through barren mountains or waterless deserts, and of protracted campaigns against wily and ruthless Indians." Those Indians were especially fierce and ruthless (even the traditionally friendly ones) when the war started because they were hungry and desperate. An unusually harsh summer had just occurred, preventing corn from growing and driving many animals from the usual hunting grounds.

Keeping the state from becoming a Confederate stronghold was no mean feat. One secessionist group had planned to seize control of California to hand over to the Confederacy. The depreciated war-time paper currency made gold and silver, and the land it rested in-- California and Nevada--exceptionally desirable. The Comstock Lode in the Nevada Territory had been discovered two years before the war. The Golden State had a healthy contingent of ardent secessionists, but those in neighboring Nevada were even more so, often referred to as a "hotbed of treason."

A secessionist (and former Kentuckian) named Asbury Harpending almost pulled off a plan to seize Pacific steamers loaded with gold and silver headed east to help the Union cause. Harpending claimed Jefferson Davis had personally approved the plan to have armed ships waiting to attack off the San Francisco coast. He bought weapons (through a Mexican claiming he needed them to protect his business from Indians), signed up ambitious recruits, purchased a ship (the *Chapman*), and procured the services of a lady to help conceal his plans (Mrs. Charles Fairfax, a niece of John Calhoun). Mrs. Fairfax later complained she had to "sit up all night sewing the wretched papers" in her dress. Harpending's plan faltered only because he could not find a loyal and experienced navigator. The one he finally hired, William Law, notified authorities of the plan, leading to Harpending's arrest and conviction for treason in March 1863.

To make the trip east, Pacific mail vessels steamed to Panama, where passengers disembarked and then traveled via train across the country to the Isthmus. From there they took another steamer to New York. First class cabin rates: about $200; steerage: about $80.

During the war, rumors of Confederate ships off the west coast with plans to shell San Francisco were frequently retold. Having a foreign force of soldiers to defend the city may have been one reason the city heartily welcomed a fleet of five Russian ships carrying over a thousand men which showed up unexpectedly in October 1863. Another reason for the smooth Russian reception was the rocky relationship that existed between America and Western Europe. (Johnny Bull scowled in America's doghouse where it had been impounded for its conduct in the Trent Affair as well as for outfitting and manning Confederate privateers. France had earned America's hostility for its blatant violation of the Monroe Doctrine by planting a puppet government in Mexico as well as for its non-support of the Union army.) Six months later, in April 1864, the Russians left. Whether their presence prevented a Confederate strike is not known, but is not an absurd notion.

Early in the war, California soldiers almost got their wish to fight Confederates with a planned attack in Texas. As a diversionary tactic, it was believed the plan would force Confederates to abandon their attacks against Arizona and New Mexico. The plan envisioned soldiers traveling by sea to Mexico where they would then march to Texas. But clear thinking soon prevailed to question the wisdom of the plan. The plan was officially scrapped after the Confederate's unofficial ambassador to Mexico got wind of it and demanded Mexican officials retract their agreement to allow Union soldiers to traverse through their country.

But in the end, some Californians finally did go east to fight Confederates. Necessity is the mother of invention: Massachusetts badly needed enlistments and Oregon Senator Edward Baker offered to raise (and lead) enlistments of California men to fill Massachusetts's draft quotas if the Bay State paid for their training and transportation. President Lincoln and Baker were good friends; in fact, Lincoln had named his second son after Baker.

In April 1861, Baker led a movement by handing out circulars in Manhattan calling for men from the west coast to enlist. Within four days more than 600 had volunteered and by early May, almost nine companies had been filled, mostly by California residents. Many Pennsylvanians also enlisted. The regiment--the 71st Pennsylvania--was informally called the California Regiment.

Senator (and Colonel) Baker, a veteran of the Black Hawk and Mexican Wars, died at the Battle of Ball's Bluff in October 1861; Eddy Lincoln, a child of three, died in Illinois in 1850.

In late 1862, a hundred California soldiers were sent to Boston aboard the *Golden Age*, where they became Company A of the Second Massachusetts Cavalry. A few months later four hundred more Golden State soldiers traveled aboard the *Constitution* and ended up fighting Colonel Mosby and his Rangers. One commented that they "hunted [Mosby and other Confederates] summer and winter, day and night, mounted and dismounted, together and in squads...on every road and in almost every house in Loudoun, Fairfax, Prince William and Fauquier Counties." Together the battalion took part in more than fifty engagements.

The Second Massachusetts Cavalry was sent to Vienna, Virginia to maintain security and conduct operations against Mosby. This highly literate group included some colorful characters.

The brigade commander was a nephew of the famous poet James Russell Lowell. "Partial to literature" the cavalrymen borrowed works by Dickens, Longfellow and others from the camp library. Herman Melville, one of America's greatest writers accompanied members of the brigade for three days as a civilian. In *The Scout Toward Aldie,* the novelist who wrote about hunting a whale named Moby, wrote a poem about chasing a ghost named Mosby:

"The sun is gold, and the world is green,
Opal the vapors of morning roll;

The champing horses lightly prance—
Full of caprice, and the riders too
Curving in many a caricole.

How strong the feel on their horses free,
Tingles the tendoned thigh with life;
Their cavalry-jackets make boys of all—
With golden breasts like the oriole;
The chat, the jest, and laugh are rife...

The weary troop that wended now—
Hardly it seemed the same that pricked
Forth to the forest from the camp;
Foot-sore horses, jaded men;
Every backbone felt as nicked,
Each eye dim as a sick-room lamp,
All faces stamped with Mosby's stamp."

Melville spent the following two years writing poems about the war, publishing them in 1866 under the title *Battle-Pieces and Aspects of War*.

One of the men in the Second Massachusetts cavalry was Elhanan Winchester Wakefield, who had moved from Ohio to California, fighting Indians in the Black Hills of the Dakotas and riding in the Pony Express along the way. After his unit was transferred to Vienna, Virginia, he was in injured in 1864.

Shortly after his discharge from the war injury in March 1865, he met his future wife along the Little River Turnpike in Fairfax, near where he had been stationed before his injury. Legend has it that as he passed the home of twenty-three year old Mary Rebecca Tennison, he was so smitten by her singing that he immediately introduced himself by telling her someday they would be married. On September 5, 1865, they were. Two years later he bought from his mother-in-law the twenty-two acre property which became Wakefield Chapel.

One Fairfax incident of the Second Massachusetts Cavalry involved Private William "Pony" Ormsby, a soldier of the Second Massachusetts who deserted on January 24, 1864 and afterward showed up as a member of Colonel John S. Mosby's Rangers. (Ormsby's desertion was rumored to have been caused by "the blandishments of a Southern beauty.") He was captured. Most unfortunate for Pony was the fact that the Second Massachusetts at that time was suffering from a high desertion rate. In addition there had been a couple recent raids against them by Mosby which were believed to have been accomplished with inside knowledge about the camp of the Second Massachusetts. Commander Lowell believed Ormsby had divulged secret information to Mosby.

Ormsby claimed he had skipped out of camp to make a trip home to New York to see his parents and that on the way he stopped and had a few drinks near Aldie, Virginia.

A month earlier Ormsby had been punished, unusually harshly believed his fellow soldiers, for an incident involving the sale of his cavalry horse. On a three-day pass to visit his brother in Arlington, Virginia, Ormsby came back to camp with a broken-down horse. A not uncommon scheme used by cavalrymen at the time to make a few dollars involved trading their government horse to a local townsman for cash and an older broken down horse.

At his trial in December 1863 for this horse-trading charge, he admitted he had traded his horse and received fifteen dollars, but claimed he did so because his horse had a badly injured foot and a cold and could not make the trip back to camp. Ormsby decided that in order to get back to camp by the required time, he had to make the trade. For this he was docked three months pay and assigned one month of extra duty.

President Lincoln often pardoned soldiers for offenses that he did not consider malicious. For Ormsby, however, a camp trial convened within two hours of bringing him in and three hours later he was found guilty. The commander wanted to make an example to his men of the ill-consequences of deserting. Facing a firing squad, Ormsby became the example. A brief telegram of February 7, 1864 revealed his fate:

"I have the honor to report all quiet. The deserter (Ormsby) from the Second Massachusetts Cavalry, captured in arms against the United States, was convicted by drum-head court-martial and shot at 12 this noon."

Twenty years later, Herman Melville started a novella called *Billy Budd* (found and published in 1924) with a scene eerily reminiscent of Ormsby's conduct at his own execution. Immediately before the firing squad Ormsby was asked if he had any last words. He told the regiment, which had been gathered to witness the execution, that it was right he should die for deserting and proclaimed that he believed the Union should and would win the war. "He believed that soon the Stars and Stripes would once again float over the entire nation. With that he said good-bye." Ormsby is buried at Arlington National Cemetery.

Among the soldiers of the Second Massachusetts witnessing this execution was Charles Binns, a man who had earlier deserted from Mosby's Partisan Rangers. Lucky for him he had not been recaptured by Mosby. In his new unit, Binns had superbly led his comrades in the Second Massachusetts on several successful missions against Mosby. Stealth worked, as did "the application to their heads of a loaded revolver [which] caused them to deliver up their firearms and themselves without making any disturbance."

As successful as Mosby was, he had his critics, even within the Confederacy. The father of a Confederate soldier made the following remarks upon hearing that his son had been transferred from Stuart's staff to Mosby's:

"I do not respect the service in which Mosby was engaged. Its object was mercenary rather than patriotic. A number of adventurous men, and I feared men of desperate or doubtful characters, had united under Mosby for the purpose of making raids upon the enemy. In order to encourage them and to make them active, vigilant and dangerous, the Government allowed them the privilege, the extraordinary privilege, of retaining and converting to their own use all property they captured from the enemy. In the capture of horses, arms, etc., their profits were great and excited the cupidity of many with whom a love of country and genuine patriotism are secondary consideration."

Edward "Ned" Carter Turner, the man who made these comments next made this scathing criticism of his fellow Southerners who took the nation to war:

"Led blindly into a war from which under the most favorable circumstances thou hadst nothing to expect but ruin, thy people butchered, thy property squandered, thy territory wasted, thy alters profaned, history must necessarily record the folly, and thy children yet unborn read the humiliating fact that thou allowed thyself to be made a cat's paw of by others who to save themselves, plotted and accomplished thy ruin."

Colonel John S. Mosby

Union General Philip Sheridan: "Mosby has annoyed me considerably."

One partisan ranger stated that each man received more than $2,100 after a raid which netted $170,000.

> "As a Command we had no knowledge of the first principle of cavalry drill, and could not have formed a straight line had there ever been any need for doing so. We did not know the bugle calls, and very rarely had roll-call...two things were impressed upon us well, however; to obey orders and to fight."

But to call them greedy or mean-spirited was not accurate. Mosby wouldn't allow any of his men to commit a crime or do anything malicious to non-combatants. One of his men who had maliciously turned over a farmer's milk cans was immediately transferred out. One of Mosby's Rangers later told of how they made a point to repay local farmers after a raid for their hospitality and to reimburse them for their livestock and supplies. In one raid that netted about 250 cattle from General Sheridan's supply train, Mosby gave about half to nearby farmers.

In his memoirs, Mosby recalled passing a house in Fairfax during the war, with a dog outside barking. Mosby heard a man from the house yelling Mosby! So Colonel Mosby stopped and asked him what he wanted. The surprised man said he had been yelling at his dog to stop barking. At about this same time, Mosby learned that a negro baby boy had been named Mosby. In his memoirs he wrote: 'So I have had the distinction of having had negro babies and dogs named after me."

Forty-five years after the war a Vermont soldier sent a letter to Mosby complimenting him for his exemplary behavior during one of his raids:

"...Your treatment and (that of) your men to us on that occasion has always been gladly remembered by us all –in every respect courteous. And you kindly gave us our horses to ride from Upperville to Culpeper Court House, which was an act of the highest type of a man, and should bury deep forever the name of a "guerilla" and substitute "to picket line a bad disturber."

Both Civil War armies made liberal use of Fairfax roads, particularly Colonel Mosby, whose rangers fomented fear and rattled the opposition at will, sometimes while singing:

"When I can shoot my rifle clear
At Yankees on the roads,
I'll bid farewell to rags and tags
And live on sutler's loads.

He who has good buttermilk aplenty
And gives the soldiers none,
He shan't have any of our buttermilk
When his buttermilk is gone."

Mosby, who said "deception is the ethics of war," struck terror everywhere he went in Northern Virginia, as cleverly described in this brief sketch of the Gray Ghost's legend:

"The very name was enough to strike terror into the hearts of Union soldiers. Mosby was everywhere. Mosby destroyed railroad tracks. Mosby robbed sutlers and paymasters. Mosby captured pickets and shot down stragglers. Mosby, with a price on his head, crossed Long Bridge to Washington in the full light of day, hobnobbed with Union officers at the bar of a crowded hotel, slept in bed next to one of them, and returned unharmed to Virginia. Mosby stopped ladies on their way to Washington and sent a lock of his hair to President Lincoln. Mosby captured Union generals in their beds at two in the morning. Mosby was everywhere."

Confederate General Stuart said of Mosby's achievements: "His sleepless vigilance and unceasing activity have done the enemy great damage. He keeps a large force of the enemy's cavalry continually employed in Fairfax in the vain attempt to suppress his inroads. His exploits are not surpassed in daring and enterprise by those of *petite guerre* in any age."

There were several skirmishes in Annandale during the war and most seem to have involved Mosby. On October 18, 1863, the Grey Ghost reported to have routed the enemy in a sharp skirmish, capturing a captain, six or seven other soldiers and an unknown number of horses. Four days later, he encountered a detachment of a California battalion near the Little River Turnpike, three miles east of Fairfax Court House, reportedly killing one Union soldier and capturing three more. Mosby also was credited with capturing a nineteen-wagon Union supply train near Padget's Tavern.

On August 24, 1864, Mosby and his men attacked, but this time without his usual success, the stockade at Annandale. After several advances, he eventually retreated back to Fairfax Courthouse, having captured three Union soldiers. One account has it that the last casualty of the war occurred in Annandale, probably near a fort that was located at where the Little River Turnpike intersects Hummer Road. One lifetime Fairfax resident recalled that:

"Mosby had had a skirmish near Gooding's Tavern located on Little River Turnpike at Pickett Road (formerly Old Schuerman Road), where the shopping center is now. They had a yard where they put up cattle and turkeys and sheep overnight. They had corrals and pens where they could be watered and fed to be ready for the next day's trip on into Alexandria…Gooding's Tavern was the first one built after the construction of Little River Turnpike. It was quite a place. If you were driving 100 head of cattle, they had pens to put them up for the night before the last leg of the trip to the slaughter houses in Alexandria."

A poem called *How We Rode From Annandale* recalls some memories for some of Mosby's Rangers:

As we rode by Annandale
The moon was shining pale,
And the wind,
Like a panther on the track
With a blood-hound at his back,
Under the cloud-rack
Came behind.
"Form fours!" the General said,
"Draw saber!" And ahead,
At the word,
The column, in the night,
Took the gallop, past a light
In a window—eyes as bright
As one's sword!
What a ride! My heart is cold,
Now when twenty years have rolled
Into the past,
As I think of that wild dash
In the night 'mid the flash
Of the rifles. It was rash,
But we went fast!
This is all about the raid
On Buford, that we made
Long ago;
How we waked the Second Corps,
And came away before
We accomplished any more
Against the foe.

Edwin Stoughton:
The Luckless Sleeper in Fairfax

General Edwin H. Stoughton certainly wished he had never heard of Fairfax. In 1863, Stoughton, a twenty-five-year old bachelor, found himself the youngest-ever brigadier general in the Union Army. In charge of the 2nd Vermont Brigade, he chose a house on Main Street owned by Dr. William Gunnell as his Fairfax headquarters.

To celebrate a visit from his mother and sister, Stoughton had a champagne party at his headquarters on Sunday, March 8, 1863. Snow was lightly falling when the party ended and the guests departed about midnight. He had no way of knowing that events in the next three hours would cause him to be referred to as the "luckless sleeper at Fairfax" by the *Baltimore American* newspaper. Several miles away, the "Affair at Fairfax Courthouse" was just getting started by John S. Mosby who, along with twenty-nine Confederate Rangers, had recently departed from Aldie, Virginia to "do their deviltry" in Fairfax.

In his memoirs, Mosby gave his rationale for undertaking the raid: "I had no reputation to lose…and I remembered the motto: adventures to the adventurous." The real target was Sir Percy Wyndham, the commanding officer of the 1st New Jersey Cavalry. A professional British soldier who had fought in Europe, Wyndham had earned the Confederate's wrath by calling Mosby a horse-thief. Mosby's clever retort clarified that he wasn't a common thief, but rather had to overcome armed enemy soldiers to get to the horses: "All the horses had riders and…each rider had a saber and two pistols."

Because of its critical location, Fairfax Courthouse was heavily guarded by Union troops. At about 2 a.m. on March 9th, Mosby secretly made his way into Fairfax Courthouse. Wyndham was out of town, but not Stoughton. Mosby entered the house, went upstairs to Stoughton's room. Mosby later narrated what happened next:

"When a light was struck we saw lying on the bed before us the man of war. He was buried in deep sleep, and seemed to be dreaming in all the fancied security of the Turk on the night when Marco Bozzarris with his band burst on his camp from the forest shades…He was turned over on his side snoring like one of the seven sleepers…So I just pulled up his shirt and gave him a spank. Its effect was electric. I leaned over and said to him, General, did you ever hear of Mosby? Yes, he quickly answered, have you caught him? No, I am Mosby –he has caught you."

To add to the psychological warfare, Mosby took a piece of coal out of the fireplace and wrote 'Mosby' on the wall.

Mosby and his men spent about an hour inside enemy territory rounding up their bounty before departing with Stoughton, thirty-two men and fifty-eight horses. The *Alexandria Gazette* reported afterwards that "the night was dark and rainy, but these guerillas dashed to and fro in a reckless manner."

The only known written reference President Lincoln made to this incident was to request that a colonel from a Pennsylvania regiment "take the place of the Gen. caught at Fairfax last night." The president was reported to have said, according to the March 11, 1863 *New York Times:* "I can make a much better brigadier in five minutes, but the horses cost $125 apiece."

(The value of horses aside, at least one Northerner, however, was more concerned of raids upon the federal treasury by Northern congressmen than Confederates. New York newspaperman Horace Greeley wrote to Ohio Senator John Sherman in February 1865:

"I fear more the raids of [Pennsylvania Congressman] Thad[deus] Stevens on the treasury than those of Mosby on our lines.")

Stoughton enjoyed the company of Antonia Ford, a young woman who lived nearby on Chain Bridge Road. Ford and her father were widely believed to be spies for the Confederacy as indicated in these prescient lines from a Union soldier's letter:

> "There is a woman living in the town by the name of Ford, not married, who has been of great service to General Stuart in giving information…I understand that she and Stoughton are very intimate. If he gets picked up some night, he may thank her for it. Her father lives here, and is known to harbor and give all the aid he can to the Rebs, and this in this little hole of Fairfax, under the nose of the provost-marshal, who is always full of bad whiskey."

Antonia Ford was arrested a week later. A Union soldier she had met and befriended before her imprisonment in Washington worked hard to get her released. Major Joseph Clapp Willard (co-owner of the Washington hotel with his brother) had been an aide to Union General Irwin McDowell. Later Willard transferred to the Capitol prison staff, apparently to be near Antonia Ford and to help secure her release. Legend has it that Ford, who listed her occupation in the 1860 census as "Lady," had earned the trust of the Confederate army by warning them before the First Battle of Bull Run that the Union army was about to attack. The same person who wrote the letter warning about Ford and her father wrote another letter to the *New York Times*:

> "…and Misses Ford have more to do with the Stuart raid than the Government is aware of. They are 'rebel majors' in disguise. They pass unchallenged by our sentries. They mingle in our camps of officers. They are the Delilahs who betray our Sampsons."

In response to these attacks on Stoughton's integrity, an uncle of the officer offered $250 to the *New York Times* to release the author's identity (the paper refused).

On March 1, 1864, shortly after Ford's release from prison, Willard resigned from the Union Army. Nine days later, in Washington DC, the former Union officer and the Confederate spy married. When asked later why a staunch Confederate such as herself would marry a former Union officer, Mrs. Antonia Ford Willard replied: "I knew I could not revenge myself on the whole nation, but felt very capable of tormenting one Yankee to death, so I took the Major."

Stoughton left the army two months later and died in 1868. A year before he died and in an effort to clear Antonia Ford's reputation as well as his own, he wrote a letter to Colonel Mosby which included the following:

"Inasmuch as I have never in any public manner contradicted the slanderous report concerning my capture & as the public generally seem to not only give it credit but look on it as a justification to implicate me in any disreputable transaction, I have concluded with the advice of my friends to obtain from you a letter stating the truth—which I know you will gladly give me not only as an act of justice to me, but to contradict the shameful aspersion cast upon the reputation of a young lady.

As I recollect the circumstances you entered my room & with about four other men presented pistols to my head—you asking me, "is this Gen. Stoughton." I replied, "Yes, what do you want," you said, "You are my prisoner," said I, "The hell I am"—you said, "Jackson is at Centreville & Stuart is in possession of all your camps. You may have heard of Capt. Mosby—I am Mosby." I said "Oh yes, I have heard of him— but Jackson is not at Centreville—nor could Stuart be in possession of the camps about here without my hearing of it. I think you are a raiding party & a small party at that" & while I was saying this you took a piece of coal from the fireplace & wrote your name on the wall. This is to my recollection the <u>exact</u> <u>conversation</u>. Am I not right? The language attributed to me by several_____ newspaper columns—of alluding to Capt. Mosby—in these terms—when asked if I knew him— "Oh yes, we have caught the son of a bitch" etc. you well know never was used by me—on that or any other occasion."

Frank Moore of the Rebellion Record wishes an accurate account of this transaction & as evil disposed persons have injured me—by circulating erroneous reports...I take the liberty to ask you...was Miss Ford at all instrumental in getting me captured?"

To his dying day at the age of eighty-one Mosby maintained Antonia Ford did not help him during his wartime escapades. She was, Mosby claimed, "innocent as Abraham Lincoln." The evidence indicates otherwise. On October 7, 1861, General Stuart had issued a notice which included the following:

"To whom it may concern:

Know ye: that reposing special confidence in the patriotism, fidelity and ability of Miss Antonia Ford, I, James E. B. Stuart, by virtue of the power vested in me, as Brigadier General in the Provisional Army of the Confederate States of America, do hereby appoint and commission her my honorary aide-de-camp, to rank as such from this date. She will be obeyed, respected and admired by all lovers of a noble nature."

To remind you the Civil War wasn't that long ago, consider this: A Union soldier who witnessed the event visited the house-in 1940! The church rector recounted his discussion with the well-aged veteran, who had been driven by his daughter from Syracuse, New York:

"My spokesman said he remembered being asleep (or very drowsy) when a group of the enemy approached; that he was not aware of his duty, but was quickly disarmed and commanded to give the signal to open the front door. This was done reasonably soon. He said he remembered distinctly the officer, whom, he later discovered was Mosby, seizing the inner guard by the shoulders and demanding to be taken to Stoughton's bedroom…He told me this was the first time he had visited Fairfax since the night of Mosby's raid. His daughter remarked that her father loved to tell the story in detail."

Two first-person accounts of this incident are on file at the Virginia Room of the Fairfax County Public Library. They were each written in 1928.

In one letter a Fairfax minister named Pendleton recounted a post-war visit by Mosby to the "Stoughton capture house" where Pendleton was living at the time:

"He [Mosby] went over the place with me, showed me exactly where General Stoughton was lying and told me the story of the raid with his own lips…Col. Mosby told me that after capturing General Stoughton his men hurried on to other houses, where they had reason to believe other officers whose "company" they desired were stationed. I know that they were particularly anxious to capture Col. Percy Wyndham, who had boasted that he would capture and hang Mosby, but unfortunately Col. Wyndham had gone to Washington for the night, and they captured only his uniform, which they carried off in triumph.

With regard to Ames (Mosby's scout, a former Union soldier] it is my recollection that Col. Mosby clearly indicated that he relied upon Ames' knowledge of the place…Ames deserted [from the Union Army], so I have always understood, as a result of the Emancipation Proclamation.

Col. Mosby told me that when they knocked on the door a man put his head out of an upstairs window and asked "Who's there?" Their reply was "Fifth New York Cavalry with dispatches for General Stoughton." I gather that Ames had belonged to the Fifth New York Cavalry."

In a personal note at the end of the letter, Pendleton recalled: "It seems a long time ago that we were in Fairfax together…the little town will always be dear to me and indelibly impressed upon my memory…"

A letter from Katherine Willis gave a little background of Antonia Ford's roots in espionage:

"It is said that Antonia was very beautiful, popular with the southern officers stationed at Fairfax, and a Southern belle. Her oldest brother, Charlie, was in Jeb Stuart's command. He was in the artillery and stationed at Falls Church, Virginia. Just before the advance…in the first battle of Bull Run he applied for leave, being very anxious to go home; but it was refused him. Stuart told him he could grant no leave at that time, but he said, "I will send you up on a mission; I will make your sister, Antonia, a commissioned officer." Charlie got his leave and Antonia was made a lieutenant in the Confederate Army—this for meritorious service to Stuart and Mosby. If there was any paper connected with this it was never seen by those close to the family.

"My aunt, Miss Sallie Gunnell, who is her seventies now recalls the night Antonia Ford paid a farewell visit to my grandmother…She said "Mrs. Gunnell, I have come to bid you good-bye; I am going on a little trip." Colonel Willard waited on the porch and he was not in uniform. Early the next morning Mr. Ford's carriage made its way down the little river turnpike. Just beyond the Old Broadwater estate one of Mosby's sentries stepped out of the bushes and said, "Halt. Who goes there?" The answer came, "Ford of Fairfax: I am taking my daughter to Washington to see a doctor." The sentry said, "Pass on." It was not known that Colonel Willard sat in the back of the carriage with Miss Ford and her mother."

Indeed much of the Civil War occurred in and around Fairfax, many veterans visited after the war. One later recalled:

"For years and years after the war was over you have no idea of the number of ex-Union soldiers who came out on the trolley to visit Fairfax and the site of their earlier war experiences. Fairfax was the hub of all the troop movements through to Manassas, the Rappahannock and the Rapidan Rivers, to Culpeper and down that way. Fairfax was the route they all used. Everyone that knew anything knew Fairfax Court House and they all wanted to get out to see it. When they came out on the cars they would hire a horse and buggy to drive up to Bull Run, maybe, because there were two battles fought there and there were a lot of men that could have been there. That's what they used to do."

The Gunnell House is now owned by the Truro Church and is used as an administrative building.

Catastrophe on the Potomac

On a perfectly clear summer evening long ago when steamboats roamed the waterways, a mid-river collision occurred and the tranquil Potomac stole the last breaths of seventy-three soldiers, three soldiers' wives and a six-year-old boy named Arthur. Scattered throughout the soil of Northern Virginia rest the bones of many soldiers whose souls were taken by disease or lead during the tumultuous Civil War. But the waters of the Potomac River amassed its own sorrowful collection of grave unknowns.

The *George Peabody*, assessed at $125,000 and leased to the Union Army for $650 per day, headed south from Aquia, Virginia on August 13, 1862 to pour fresh troops into the bloody battle stew of war. The "very old and hardly sea-worthy" *West Point* was heading north to Alexandria from Newport News with 258 wounded soldiers, three soldiers' wives, and little Arthur Dort, proudly bringing his wounded-warrior father safely home. At $500 for each and every nautical day, the army had leased *West Point* two months earlier "with the privilege of sending her to any port or place in the United States, the Gulf of Mexico or the West Indies." The contract specifically excluded the government from responsibility for collisions at sea or in port.

A Sanitary Commission volunteer described helping the wounded from the Virginia Peninsula in 1862:

"The first thing wounded men want is lemonade and ice. The poor fellows are led or carried on board, and stowed side by side as close as can be. They are utterly broken down…All are without food for one day, some for two days."

"Dreadful Disaster on the Potomac!" screamed the tragic headlines of the collision of two government-leased steamers along the most fluid of military highways.

Surprisingly, many aboard did not immediately comprehend the impending doom following the collision: "At first it was supposed that a party of soldiers were bathing in the river from some transport and that the noise was their joyous exclamations." But reality soon struck: "The water was full of struggling humanity, and such cries for help may I never hear again!"

"The air was rent with cries, exhortations and prayers," recounted a survivor. "The boats were lowered away, but in the confusion the ladies, who were to have been placed in them first, could not be found, or else the frantic men gave them little heed. Some… frantically clung to the wood work until the vessel was at last engulfed."

"The scene which followed cannot be described…Escape seemed hopeless…Mrs. Dort, in great distress, had called me from the lower cabin to her berth, to help dress her boy. I rendered the requested aid and helped her and the child upon the hurricane deck… we were all the time floating down the river, and as the forward part of the boat was now under water, we all tried to get upon the hurricane deck. This broke down under such a weight, and nearly all were plunged into the water. Many floated off and sank; others secured broken boards and pieces of the wreck, and floated as long as they could hold on… I heard the surgeon tell the ladies he would do his best to save them, and I think he did, for as he was drowned and was found two days later far down the river with one of the ladies holding fast to him, it is evident that he kept his promise."

Seventy-seven people perished when the *West Point* sank at approximately 8:05 p.m. in twenty-four feet of water a mile from the Maryland shore. Those rescued "near death's door" were sent to recuperate at Fairfax Seminary Hospital. One newspaper summed up the catastrophe: "The scene of this terrible tragedy is likely to be ghost-haunted for all coming time."

Many survivors believed the collision was intentional and that the captain and pilot, who had immediately deserted the sinking ship, must have been Rebels. Perhaps the accident was due to corrupt contractors. Or more precisely, what the contractors were responsible for: "Mismanagement and corruption, of insufficient crews and incompetent officers; of defective machinery and rotting timber; of lack of proper inspection and safeguards."

Pervasive and shocking best described fraud in Civil War expenditures, including for the rental or purchase of steamships. One expert testified to a Congressional committee that the government had been defrauded of $ 25 million to charter and buy vessels, with details to "amaze and sicken a committee accustomed to ordinary political corruption." In one of these schemes, commonly referred to at the time as "dead-horse claims," a judge denounced a contractor for "unconscionable and exorbitant rates of transportation" and the "injustice and extortion" of his claim. The steamship *Illinois* was leased for a few years to the government at a total rental cost of $ 370,000. Yet the total value of the steamer, cost of construction and equipment included, was appraised at less than $ 260,000.

Cornelius Vanderbilt rented and sold ships in "shockingly bad condition," which "in perfectly smooth weather, with a calm sea, the planks were ripped out of her, and exhibited to the gaze of the indignant soldiers on board, showing her timbers were rotten." The investigating committee later had in their possession a "large sample of one of the beams of the vessel to show that it has not the slightest capacity to hold a nail." An expert testifying about the rotten ships palmed off on the government had this to say:

Q: *Did [Marshall O.] Roberts sell or charter any other boats to the Government?*

A: *Yes sir. He sold the Winfield Scott and the Union to the Government.*

Q: *For how much?*

A: *One hundred thousand dollars each, and one was totally lost and the other condemned a few days after they went to sea.*

Most of the vessels were of such scandalous construction that foreign capitalists would not buy them at any price. Safe passages on these death traps may have been due more to luck than anything else. On the Potomac River on August 13, 1862, luck simply ran out for the crew and passengers of the *West Point*.

Shipwrecks and the Blockade

W hen the war started, both Confederate and Union governments were ill-prepared for action at sea.

The Confederates had no navy. To help their cause, they authorized letters of marquee for privateers. (The practice had been outlawed internationally in 1856, but the Confederates justified their action because the United States had not been a signatory to the declaration.) During the war, approximately a dozen privateers captured or destroyed sixty Union vessels. In addition, the Confederate Government sent a buyer to Britain, culminating in the acquisition of eighteen cruisers, including the *Alabama,* the *Shenandoah*, the *Sumter,* the *Georgia,* the *Florida* and the *Tallahassee.*

The Union, on the other hand, had a Navy at the beginning of the war, albeit a remarkably anemic one. They built their navy by construction, one type of gunboat so quickly as to be nicknamed ninety-day gunboats. In addition, the Union purchased "everything afloat that could be made of service." Secretary of the Navy Gideon Welles complained in his diary about how all his decisions were subject to constant criticism:

> "... the sensationalists will get up exciting alarms and terrify the public into distrust and denunciation of the Navy Department...All failures...[are] imputed to the Navy, though entirely blameless, and though the fault, if any, is with the military...There is constant caprice in regard to the

Navy. Those who know least clamor most. If I go forward and build large and expensive vessels, I shall be blamed for extravagance…on the other hand, if I should not build, I shall be denounced for being unprepared."

For his part, Welles knew how difficult it would be to enforce a 3,500-mile blockade along American shores from Alexandria, Virginia to the Rio Grande. Approximately 8,000 violations of the blockade brought in some 600,000 small arms and 550,000 pairs of shoes, among other things. With impunity, Northern states shipped many goods to the Confederacy, via blockade runners. Chances of getting caught by blockade runners in the South were estimated at one in ten at the start of the war; by 1864 it was one in three. So many goods from Northern States came through to the South that Union General William Sherman complained the Confederacy got more goods from Cincinnati than from Charleston, South Carolina. Secretary Welles made a similar complaint when he remarked it was unsettling that the Union was "clothing, mounting and subsisting not only our troops but the Rebels also."

It was widely known that England had helped the Confederacy build and equip vessels. In 1865 President Lincoln remarked that after the Civil War ended, "we could call [on Britain] to account for the embarrassments she had inflicted on us." Secretary Welles warned there would be "a day of reckoning with Great Britain for these wrongs, and I sometimes think I care not how soon nor in what manner that reckoning comes… It is pretty evident that a devastating and villainous war is to be waged on our commerce by English capital and English men under the Rebel flag with the connivance of the English Government, which…is intended to sweep our commerce from the ocean." Secretary of State Seward complained that Confederate raiders were "built, manned armed, equipped, and fitted out in British ports and…harbored, sheltered, provided, and furnished…in British ports."

Upon entering Alexandria aboard a steamer in March 1862, Elisha Hunt Rhodes saw at least a hundred other steamers, a day with such ideal conditions it was easy to forget there was a war on: "The weather is warm and the scene delightful. The ships are gaily decorated with flags, and it looks more like a pleasure cruise excursion than an army looking for an enemy."

The *West Point* was not the only vessel to sink as a result of a collision during the Civil War. The book *Civil War Shipwrecks* by W. Craig Gaines provides information about at least forty-three other Civil War collisions as well as more than two thousand vessels that, during or immediately following the Civil War, were sunk, scuttled, burned, grounded, lost, capsized, missing, blown up, or made unusable without salvage and substantial repairs. They sank all over the world, including the Australian shore, Brazil, the Bering Sea, in European waters and eleven in Chinese waters alone.

They carried items ranging from twenty demijohns (containers of three to ten, usually five gallons, wrapped in wicker) of liquor. The *Mary Lou* carried whiskey: two thousand barrels and ten thousand bottles of it; the *Ruth* $2.6 million in new government greenbacks to be used as payroll for the army of General Grant; the *Golden Gate* at least $1.5 million in gold and money and possibly as much as $3.5 million; the *Princeza* $140,000 in gold; and the *John J. Roe* 165 horses.

The *Condor* went down on its way to the Confederacy from England with famed Confederate spy Rose O'Neal Greenhow and eight hundred gold sovereigns (book royalty payments) sewn into her petticoat. It had run a blockade off Wilmington, North Carolina and hit a sandbar in the darkness. Greenhow and two Confederates agents were getting into smaller boats to go ashore when a wave overturned their craft. Weighted down with the sovereigns, Greenhow drowned. Her body washed ashore the next day and was buried in Wilmington with the honors of war.

Many were caused by defective ships: the *Eclipse's* boiler exploded. This didn't come as a surprise to the captain who had previously reported the problem and asked that it get fixed. The wickedly overloaded *Sultana* probably cost more than 1,500 lives and ill-fated *Brother Jonathon* had the same deadly overload. One of its fatalities was an army paymaster who had a premonition he would die on the voyage. The commander of the *Vesta* (which was carrying a new uniform from Britain for Robert E. Lee) was determined "falling down drunk," and the *Chippewa* caught fire because a drunken deck hand knocked over a candle after he had been tapping some whiskey barrels.

An officer of the *America* sold rescued cotton bales (claimed as destroyed) for personal profit. Discoverers of some of these ships included historian Edwin Bearss (*U.S.S. Cairo*) and a group of Navy divers, who found the *Modern Greece* during a recreational dive. All crewmembers of the *City of New York* survived by hanging on the rigging for forty-two hours. The crewmembers of the *Blanco* weren't so lucky. They were rumored to have been killed by Indians near Oregon where items from their vessel were later found.

The *Explorer,* taken apart and carried by mules across Panama, was later reassembled and put back into service on the Pacific side of Central America. One of the first three ships in the United States Navy is included in this collection of wrecks. The *U. S. S. Constitution,* commissioned in 1798 had been abandoned by the United States. Confederates however, took it and intentionally sank it to obstruct a channel leading to the Gosport Navy Yard.

Many ships sank after being rammed. One participant of a ramming of steamers stated: "The battle of Memphis was, in many respects, one of the most remarkable naval victories on record. For two unarmed, frail, wooden river steam boats, with barely men enough on board to handle the machinery and keep the furnace fires burning, to rush to the front, between two hostile fleets, and *into* the enemy's advancing line of eight iron-clad, heavily armed, and fully manned steam-rams, sinking one, disabling and capturing three and carrying consternation to the others, was a sight never before witnessed."

At the conclusion of the war the United States entered a protracted dialogue with Great Britain to obtain compensation caused by England's assistance to the Confederacy, thereby extending the war.

The claims were eventually bundled together as the "Alabama Claims." After twenty-two months at sea, the CSS Alabama (built and launched by the British) seized sixty-four Union merchant ships, destroyed most of them and took 2,000 prisoners. It eventually sank in a gunfight against the USS Kearsarge off the coast of Cherbourg, France in June 1864. (Cherbourg lays claim to being the only official

Civil War site outside the United States.) Two Confederates and one Union soldier who later died as a result of this encounter are buried in a Cherbourg cemetery.

The Alabama claims were submitted to arbitration before a five-member international tribunal consisting of appointees of the president of the United States, the queen of England, the emperor of Brazil, the king of Italy, and the president of the Swiss confederation.

Sometime after September 1872, the tribunal made its decision (with vigorous dissent by the British member) and Great Britain paid the United States the entire amount ruled upon: $15 million in direct damages.

The following portion of a letter dated January 15, 1866 from Sir Frederick Bruce, then British representative at Washington to the foreign secretary in the administration of Lord John Russell, provides a glimpse of the British view of Virginians. The Virginia Historical Society printed this letter in its July 1961 edition of *The Virginia Magazine of History and Biography:*

"The Virginians, I take it, are different from the men of any other State. They are even prouder of their Virginia than the natives of all or almost all other States are of their own States. Virginia has a history: she has had her proportion of great men, Washington, Patrick Henry, Thomas Jefferson, Henry Clay, Mason & many others. When the war commenced, there was a strong Union party in Virginia, a party, as I believe, composed of the best men, not the politicians (odious name), but the good sense, the thinking men, including a great number of the gentlemen of the state. Robert Lee & his family were of that class. His son Fitzhugh told me so himself. He said that for his part he considered the Union to be a great thing, and he had been its strong advocate.

But when the President issued the Proclamation calling for a contingent, then the State rose, & flew to arms, and neither he nor his father could forsake the State. She was paramount to everything. She might be right or she might be wrong, but where she went one way, & the Unionists the other, the first duty of her sons was to side with her. They therefore had drawn the sword, reluctantly indeed, but because they thought they were obliged to do so, & when once in it, of course they did everything in their power to gain the victory…I have been asked by several men, more in sorrow than in anger, why we did not take part with the Confederacy. "If England & France wished to break down the United States, why did they miss the opportunity? We cannot understand it. We expected you to join us & to help us."

"It is because you do not understand England that our neutrality astonishes you," I answered. "There is no doubt that nine-tenths of the gentlemen of England sympathized with you, & many were for joining you. But it was clear from the first that England would not stir. There is an enormous commercial party with us who are totally opposed to war, & and who have great influence, & then there was the unfortunate question of slavery. England, after the policy she has pursued & with her own outspoken sentiments on this question could not join the Confederacy, the cornerstone of which was stated to be the institution of slavery. "But we would have given up slavery."

"You Virginians might have done so, but the Confederacy would not." As far as the Virginians are concerned I believe the majority are glad that slavery is dead."

Corruption in the Civil War

"There is no kind of dishonesty into which otherwise good people more easily and frequently fall than that of defrauding the government."

Benjamin Franklin

Lincoln's famous comment after the Stoughton raid about the value of horses is indicative of the massive amount of Civil War expenditures. Many of those expenses were fraudulent.

If money is the sinews of war, as Cicero wrote, then fraud schemes such as bid-rigging, bribery and embezzlement are the cancers that thwart victory. Recent allegations of fraudulent expenditures in the Iraq War are no match for those during the Civil War, when corrupt contractors "shamelessly hurried to the assault on the Treasury, like a cloud of locusts."

The massive fraud fueled the controversial and unpopular war. People were horrified and furious to hear the extent of the greed, usually at the soldiers' expense.

In the words of Colonel Henry S. Olcott, a Union officer assigned to ferret out fraud:

"Men there were by the hundred thousand, ready to take the field; but, to uniform them, cloth had to be woven, leather tanned, shoes, clothing, and caps manufactured. The canvas to shelter them had to be converted from the growing crop

185

into fabrics. To arm them the warehouses and armories of Europe, as well as of this country, had to be ransacked. All considerations of business caution had to be subordinated to the imperious necessity for haste. If it was the golden hour of patriotism, so was it equally that of greed, and, as money was poured by the million, by the frugal, into the lap of the government, so was there a yellow Pactolus diverted by myriad streamlets into the pockets of scoundrels and robbers—official and otherwise. The public necessity was their opportunity, and they made use of it."

(The Pactolus River in Turkey was famous in ancient times for the particles of gold in its sands, which legend has was due to Midas having bathed there.)

All manner and means of fraud occurred during the war, the government stuck "paying ruinous prices." In the East and North most expenses were for manufactured items; in the West and Southwest: animals, forage and transportation.

The U. S. Government purchased an incredible array of goods, including food, clothes and medicine. The volume was equally staggering as shown by this sample of a few 1863 purchases: 8,000,000 flannel shirts and trousers, 7,000,000 pair of stockings, 325,000 mess pans, 207,000 camp kettles, 13,000 drums and 14,830 fifes. For a six month period in 1861, 1,903,000 arms were purchased.

"The problem of the war was not men, but money," wrote Ohio Senator John Sherman (the general's brother), noting that annual war expenditures had reached nearly $1 billion. According to Colonel Olcott, that money was spent with "no organized system for the prevention and punishment of frauds." These massive expenditures raised international alarm and concern for America's future. A London newspaper warned: "National bankruptcy is not an agreeable prospect, but it is the only one presented by the existing state of American finance. Never before was the world dazzled by... more reckless extravagance. Never before did a flourishing and prosperous state make such gigantic strides toward effecting its own ruin."

According to Assistant Secretary of Treasury Maunsell Field, however, President Lincoln knew things would eventually improve. Lincoln was visited by a delegation of bank presidents "at one of the gloomiest periods of the war, when depression and ...discouragement prevailed" and was asked whether his confidence in the future was shaken. In response, he recounted a fearful personal anecdote which had occurred years before, and concluded by saying: "The world did not come to an end then, nor will the Union now!"

All types of corruption occurred. There were bounty jumpers who, after collecting a fee for enlisting, put on a disguise or went to another location to reenlist again and by so doing collected another bounty. One peripatetic scammer enlisted multiple times on a single New York trip, collecting bounties of several hundred dollars each at Albany, Troy, Utica, Buffalo and Elmira.

Counterfeit currency was freely passed, and good luck to those honest bidders who tried to buy something at government auction. Conspirators colluded to drive away competition by aggressively bidding so high that prices became outrageous. By doing so, unaware honest bidders would not dare attend another auction. Smuggling was big business. Stephen Vincent Benet's Pulitzer Prize-winning poem *John Brown's Body*, included this verse:

"Shadows sliding without a light,
Through the dark of the moon, in the dead of the night,
Hoops for the belle and guns for the fighter,
Guncotton, opium, bombs and tea.
Fashionplates, quinine and history."

Sutlers often sold defective items to soldiers at enormously inflated prices, including watches that wouldn't keep time a few days after the purchase and coffee that was a "compound of roasted peas, of licorice, and a variety of other substances, with just enough to give it a taste and aroma of coffee." More dangerous was spoiled food that sickened or killed, leading one scribe to write: "In every regiment more than one death could primarily be attributed to certain articles in the sutler's tent."

Quartermasters often withheld a significant portion of goods requisitioned. For example, the quartermaster might distribute only 70 pounds of a 100 pound meat requisition claiming supplies were so short that everyone had to take a partial order. Of course in his account books he claimed the entire requisition had been distributed, thereby giving himself the remaining 30 pounds to sell for personal profit. The soldier collecting the partial requisitioned items would invariably complain that his regiment often received half-rations, and then asked, or at least wondered when back rations would be distributed to make up for shortages. Not surprisingly, the words "no back rations" were often heard.

The most egregious schemes may have been those of fraudulent inferiority. In the parlance of today's law enforcement it's called product substitution. Blankets sold as woolen were made of mystery materials; the only thing certain is they didn't keep soldiers warm or dry. Tents made of cheap materials were considered valueless, leading soldiers to testify they could better keep dry out of them than under. A contractor named Charles C. Roberts sold 50,000 knapsacks and 50,000 haversacks to the government, every single one, according to an expert, was "a fraud upon the government, for they were not linen, they were shoddy."

Everything manufactured was shoddy. The word could not be used often enough. The *New York Herald* reported: "The world has seen its iron age, its silver age, its golden age, and its bronze age. This is the age of shoddy."

Another contractor charged for nursing and subsisting three hundred and fifty men from the steamer *Cosmopolitan* when in fact records revealed that only ninety-seven men were cared for.

Hats quickly dissolved in the rain and shoes fell apart, often in a matter of weeks. A Congressional committee concluded the manufacturers sold five million pairs of shoes to the Union Army from 1861 to 1862, of which the government reported they had been defrauded by at least $3 million: "Shoes which were so bad that they could not be sold privately had been palmed off upon the government."

Forage for horses and mules was diluted by a dishonest mixture of oats and Indian corn. A common fraud was the sale of "doctored-up horses" with a dangerous result on cavalry movements. A case of this sort ended up in court where a judge stated that "frauds were constantly perpetrated…It is well known that horses may be prepared and fixed up to appear bright and smart for a few hours."

Guns, which didn't shoot, and powder which didn't explode caused more danger to the men using them than the enemy. In one instance, the War Department sold a large quantity of condemned carbines for a nominal sum to get rid of them, unwittingly (and fraudulently) bought the same ones back (at $15 each), sold them again at $3.50 each to get rid of them, and unwittingly and fraudulently bought them back again (for $22 each.)

Another "dishonest parasite" profited immensely through fraud in oil contracts. "Without having bought a gallon of 'the best wintry strained sperm oil,' such as his contracts called for (and despite his taking the same at one dollar per gallon, when the market price stood at two dollars), he had realized a profit of $117,000 on the year's transactions!"

In June 1861, the journalist Whitelaw Reid reported that the pantaloons of the Ohio soldiers were all in rags after a week's service. Sending a sample of the cloth, Reid urged the folks back home to "put it up in the counting room and let Ohioans see how Ohio troops in the field are clothed…As you will see…the material is not strong enough to hold the stitches, and with the utmost care "rips" of an inch or more are caused by every rapid movement. It is an outrage to allow the troops to remain in this condition a day longer than is absolutely necessary to get clothes here."

The poem *Dedicated to Knavish Speculators who have Robbed the State* was published during the war in the *Philadelphia Intelligencer*:

"The world is flush of rogues and knaves,
Who sham the patriotic,
And hope to keep the people slaves,
By scheme and plan Quixotic;

While some are boasting what they'll do
In 'fuss and feathers' dressy,
Let honest men prepare again,
To give the traitors "Jessie."

From top to toe, from head to foot,
Our politics are rotten;
And those we pay are bribed to boot,
While justice is forgotten!

For every one that gets a chance
To serve the State, is stealing,
And honest men must pay again
For scoundrels' double-dealing.

In court and camp it's all the same,
From judge to quartermaster;
The devil takes the one that's lame—
He should have robbed them faster!

For pork or progress, blankets, brief,
The roguery's defended,
And honest men are told again,
The system can't be mended."

Secretary of the Navy Gideon Welles held nothing back in his diary when expressing his feelings of General Dix and Senator Hale, two men he held in very low regard for their fraudulent ways:

"General Dix is pressing schemes in regard to the blockade… which are corrupt and demoralizing. Dix himself is not selling licenses, but the scoundrels who surround him are, and he can hardly be ignorant of the fact. The gang of rotten officers on his staff have sent him here. One of the worst has his special confidence, and Dix is under the influence of this cunning, bad man. He has plundering thieves about him— some, I fear, as destitute of position as honesty."

"A charge of bribery against a Senator has resulted in [New Hampshire Senator] John P. Hale's admission that he is the man referred to, acknowledging he took the money, but that it was a *fee*, not a *bribe*. 'Strange such a difference there should be twixt tweedle-dum and tweedle-dee.' This loud-mouthed paragon, whose boisterous professions of purity, and whose immense indignation against a corrupt world were so great that he delighted to misrepresent and belie them in order that his virtuous light might shine distinctly, is beginning to be exposed and rightly understood.

But the whole is not told and never will be; he is a mass of corruption...How little do the outside public know of the intrigues of Congressional demagogues, who, under the guise of great public economists, are engaged in speculating schemes and fraudulent contrivances to benefit themselves, pecuniarily! John P. Hale, who is eminently conspicuous in this class of professed servants and guardians of the public treasury, has been whitewashed for his three-thousand-dollar retainer. The committee excuse him, but propose a law...on any one who shall again commit the offense."

According to one journalist's 1886 memoirs, many women engaged in disgraceful schemes of plundering the Treasury by gaining favor with Congressmen controlling government spending: "The most active advocates of these swindles...were the lady lobbyists... the widows of officers of the army or navy, others the daughters of Congressmen, and others had drifted from home localities where they had found themselves the subjects of scandalous comments." Some became quite successful-- after all, "who could blame the Congressman for leaving the bad cooking of his hotel or boarding-house...to walk into the parlor web which the adroit spider lobbyist had cunningly woven for him?"

Edmund Burke said the only thing necessary for evil to occur was for good men to remain silent. During the Civil War, a lot of good men stood silent, or at least looked the other way.

All it took was a scheme and someone to approve a false invoice or phantom delivery. With huge illegal gains, cooperation was purchased pretty cheap: "Presents of horses, carriages, jewelry, wines, cigars, and friendly help toward promotion" were passed "under a politer name than bribery." Another writer opined: "A little money, a good deal of soft talk, unlimited liquor, and, occasionally, some pressure from superiors, went a long way."

A man named Henry Clay Dean colorfully summarized in 1869 the enormous extent of the fraud. Dean, a lecturer, lawyer and writer, called his Missouri home "Rebel Cove," and his masterful skills in oration led to his nickname: the Orator of Rebel Cove.

"The quartermaster cheated the government in his official returns. He cheated the farmer and planter of whom he bought his provisions, in the weights, measures, exaction of his price, and if possible, plundered it under the pretext of confiscation. He finally cheated the soldier in the issue of his rations, and murdered both prisoners and soldiers, by the substitution of deleterious compositions for wholesome food and poisonous drugs for medicines. His official life was a perpetual series of cheats and frauds, impositions and oppressions. The sutler exceeded, if possible, the villainies of the quartermaster, availing himself of the soldier's necessity and absence from stores and supplies; would charge him a thousand per cent upon the market value of the necessities of camp life, tempt his last farthing by shamefully perverting his appetite with villainous rum, and filch it from his pocket, which was due to his destitute family at home. The contractor, who supplied the immediate wants of the army, received his contract as a personal and political favor, often with the distinct understanding that he might rob the government at discretion. Without compunction he furnished the government with shoddy clothes, ill-made shoes, and such rations as were refused at the regular markets, and entered into the general system of robbery and murder. The war was made the occasion and the apology for every imaginable species of fraud."

Many people took note of the problem but were ill prepared to stop it. Secretary of Treasury Salmon Chase defensively noted in his diary: "It is impossible for me to look after all the acts of all the agents of the department...But whenever informed of any delinquency, I institute proper investigation, and...take proper measures..."

A Congressional committee investigating this "colossal graft" produced a scathing 1,109 page report, condemning "such prostitution of public confidence to purposes of individual aggrandizement." The Congressman leading another committee had this to say: "The starving, penniless man who steals a loaf of bread to save life you incarcerate in a dungeon; but the army of magnificent highwaymen who steal by tens of thousands from the people, go unwhipped of justice and are suffered to enjoy the fruits of their crimes."

Secretary of War Edwin Stanton commended Colonel Olcott after the conviction of a man named Kohnstamm who submitted $300,000 in fraudulent invoices: "It is as important to the government as the winning of a battle." Following a four-day trial, Kohnstamm was convicted in twenty minutes.

The chairman of the House of Representatives made this opening remark about the extent of the fraud:

"In the early history of the war it was claimed that frauds and peculations were unavoidable; that the cupidity of the avaricious would take advantage of the necessities of the nation, and for a time must revel and grow rich amidst the groans and griefs of the people; that pressing wants must yield to the extortion of the base; that when the capital was threatened, railroad communication cut off, the most exorbitant prices could safely be demanded for steam and sailing vessels; that when our arsenals had been robbed of arms, gold could not be weighed against cannon and muskets; that the government must be excused if it suffered itself to be overreached. Yet, after the lapse of two years, we find the same system of extortion prevailing, and robbery has grown more unblushing in its exactions as it feels secure in its immunity from punishment, and that species of fraud, which shocked the nation in the spring of 1861 has been increasing... The freedom from punishment by which the first greedy and rapacious horde were suffered to run at large with ill-gotten gains seems to have demoralized too many of those who deal with the government."

President Lincoln got Congress to pass the False Claims Act in March 1863. By combining this new 'Lincoln's Law,' with the already existing financial rewards for reporting corruption, it was hoped that more allegations of fraud would be brought to the government. The process of collecting from the government a percentage of funds recovered for reporting fraud is known as 'Qui Tam' and had been around before the Civil War, the first recorded use in 1755. Qui Tam is short for a longer Latin phrase meaning something to the effect of: "He as well for the Lord the King as for himself sues."

Combating fraud had been remarked upon by the philosopher Thomas Hobbes, who wrote that the most critical elements of war were force and fraud. You lose with too little of one or too much of the other.

In the end, defeating Confederates proved easier than stopping fraud. It was a decisive victory for the corrupt band of contractors. A Congressional committee summed it up this way: "The leniency of the government…is a marvel which the present cannot appreciate, and history will never explain."

Colonel Olcott estimated that twenty to twenty-five percent of the entire expenditures of the federal government during the Civil War, or approximately $700 million, were tainted with fraud. Surprisingly however, he believed there was something worse than this "carnival of fraud." America could recover from theft and embezzlement of enormous amounts because of its "boundless resources and unprecedented recuperative methods." More pernicious, according to Olcott, was that "every dollar of this ill-spent treasure contributed toward a demoralization of the people, and the sapping of ancient virtues." In this verse, Stephen Vincent Benet shared his view of those making money on the war:

"And, should war and hell have the same dimensions,
both have been paved with the best intentions
and both are as full of profiteers."

Civil War Pensions

Pensions for military veterans have been around a long time. In 1592 England provided assistance "for reliefe of Soldiours" who had served in the Spanish Armada. Across the Atlantic, the Colonies helped those injured while fighting Indians-Virginia in 1624 and the Plymouth Colony in 1636.

Prior to the Civil War, the United States had allowed 143,644 total pensions for veterans of Indian Wars, the American Revolution (total pensions: $46.2 million), and the War of 1812. (Mexican War pensions were not approved until 1887.)

The Civil War resulted in about a million pensions, approved largely because of remarks like this from the Record of the 48th Congress:

> "These soldiers are not paupers asking for alms; they are heroes, honorable men; demanding their rights. It would be a burning shame if the government should permit any soldier of the Union Army ever to go to the poor house…thousands of men who served faithfully are beginning to look with anxiety to the future, and are wondering whether their last days are to be spent in hunger and poverty in sight of the capitol of the nation that was saved by their valor. There are children whose fathers lie upon the field of battle; there are widows whose husbands went down to death in the strength of their manhood who are struggling with want. These are common

statements, but everybody knows them to be true...many of the best and most meritorious soldiers after the war...desired to be independent, and although suffering from wounds and disability arising in the service they were loath to seek assistance. As years roll by they are reluctantly forced to the conclusion that they must apply for aid."

Civil War pensions increased over the years and payments for specified disabilities also steadily increased; for example, the loss of a leg at the hip joint went from $15 in 1866 to $24 (1872) to $37.50 (1879) to $45 (1886) and finally to $55 (1903).

An 1888 list of disabilities revealed, not surprisingly, gunshot wounds and chronic diarrhea leading the list of most common reasons for pensions. Ulcers, muscular diseases of the foot and double hernias ranked at the bottom. Making the medical determinations were 1,237 examining boards, consisting of three members each.

An army of government clerks maintained and organized the index cards containing all this military information. These weighty records caused the floor of Ford's Theatre (where they were stored at the time) to collapse in June 1893, killing twenty-two government workers.

The pension issue inevitably became a huge financial bonanza, built on the politics of patronage. One pension commissioner called the bureau an "avowedly political machine." This machine reached top speeds in 1881 when its powerful veteran constituency-the Grand Army of the Republic-officially started lobbying Congress. The French traveler DeToqueville said America was a nation of joiners, and the GAR was no exception. By 1890, there were 7,178 GAR posts with 427,981 members, each representing a vote to pay more pension money to veterans, widows and family members.

Currying GAR support counted heavily at the polls. General Benjamin Butler told GAR members in 1890 that acting together they could "make politicians dance like peas on a hot shovel." It was politically easy to support pension legislation. One pension secretary stated every claimant would get "a favorable recommendation." Sure enough, when a pension employee reviewed 250 consecutive claims in the 1890s, he found every single request had been approved.

This liberalization of pension laws cast a wide net. In 1902, with the U. S. population at 76 million, 999,446 people were on the pension rolls, a national average of one pensioner for every 76 citizens. Maine, Kansas, Indiana and Vermont topped the list, each averaging about one for every 36 people. One historian estimated there were 1.3 million Civil War veterans living in 1890.

These pensions came with three certainties: change (in rules) staggering sums, and rampant fraud.

Changes in rules: Mothers and sisters of deceased soldiers became eligible to collect pensions by an act in 1862; brothers and fathers were added in 1866.

Before 1873, a parent was eligible for a pension if their son had supported them when he was alive. A law in March 1873 expanded this to allow a parent to collect merely if their son had indicated "a willingness or desire" to provide support. The law was expanded again in 1890 to allow a pension to a parent who simply needed the money, with no requirement to show the son provided, or intended to provide support. Veterans were entitled to pensions in 1890 if they had served 90 days and were unable to perform manual labor, regardless of the cause of the disability.

Staggering sums: In 1895 the pension bill totaled $140 million, representing more than a third of the entire federal budget. For the thirty years from the end of the war to 1895, the total pension tally exceeded $1.6 billion. That's billion nineteenth century dollars, with no adjustment for inflation. By the time America entered World War I in 1917, over $5 billion had been paid out. The payments continued for several decades--a few Union veterans were still living in the 1950s; the last may have been Albert H. Woolson, who died in August 1956. (It is widely believed the last Confederate veteran was Walter W. Williams, who died on December 19, 1959.)

Rampant fraud: The entire system was rife with fraud and everyone knew it. One pension officer estimated 30% of all pensions resulted from fraud. Another called the system "an open door to the treasury for the perpetration of fraud."

The president of Harvard University labeled the system "a hideous wrong...prostituted and degraded...a crime against all honest soldiers." The *New York Sun* editorialized the pension schemes—"the chimera of madmen"-- had "assumed the proportions of legislative insanity." One senator bellowed the pension act "was conceived in sin and brought forth in iniquity. It is a fraud upon the America people, and a standing monument to the ignorance, selfishness and cowardice of the American Congress."

In 1874 special agents of the pension bureau investigated 1,263 claims and found nearly 40% to be fraudulent. Between 1876-1879, 5,131 claims were investigated, of which 28% were determined fraudulent.

Pension agents and attorneys came under bitter abuse for their perceived and actual misdeeds. One congressman called them "vampires who suck the very life-blood of the poor dependent pensioners...parasites who prey upon the penniless widow and orphan...the most infamous gang of cut-throats who ever lived." Another congressman remarked they were "the friends of the soldiers as the vultures are the friends of dead bodies—because they fatten and feed upon them." Special vitriol was aimed at one George E. Lemon, pension attorney and owner of two ardent pro-veteran newspapers, whose firm handled more than 125,000 pension claims.

Widow pensions were occasionally targeted for suspected abuses. In November 1868, the pension commissioner requested discretionary power to review pensions received by war widows who cohabitated out of wedlock, refusing to get married for fear of losing their pensions. "Others," he opined, "lived openly in prostitution for the same object." Congress denied the request, advising it was not the government's role to regulate "the morality of its citizens."

In 1877 a Philadelphia widow was investigated for collecting a pension even after she had remarried (this was not allowed). She admitted to the Bureau of Pensions special agent that she was living with a man, but she claimed he was strictly a tenant who paid rent for room and board and was married to another woman (who he visited twice a week).

(But by 1882, Congress enacted measures to terminate pensions of war widows who cohabitated.)

The federal government did not pay any Confederate pensions but from time to time had discussions to do so. The eleven states of the Confederacy paid pensions to Confederate soldiers, with Georgia paying the most per year, followed by Alabama.

The Bogus Proclamation
of 1864

In addition to contractors perpetuating a cycle of corruption, a few newspapermen spun some pretty incredible tales.

In May 1864, a simple yet dangerous hoax, perpetrated in the name of greed led President Lincoln to order the arrest of two editors and the suppression of their newspapers. For all the trampling of civil liberties by the Lincoln Administration and the Union Army, this was the only known instance when the president signed such an order: "You are…commanded…to arrest and imprison…the editors, proprietors and publishers of the aforesaid newspapers…and you will hold [them]…until they can be brought to trial before a military commission…You will also take possession by military force, of the… "New York World," and "Journal of Commerce," and…prevent any further publication therefrom."

Using his extensive knowledge of the newspaper business and the recently formed New York Associated Press (NYAP), veteran newsman Joseph Howard Jr. of the *Brooklyn Daily Eagle*, and fellow *Eagle* reporter Frank Mallison prepared and had hand-delivered to the New York newspapers (through a copyboy at about 3:30 a.m. on May 18th) a fictitious proclamation purportedly signed by Lincoln. It was later described by Secretary of War Edwin Stanton as "admirably calculated to deceive" and by the *Telegraph Age Journal* as "the work of a skilled hand." The proclamation stated among other things, that the government was going forward with a draft of 400,000 new soldiers.

Less than a year earlier, the "draft riots" engulfed New York City in terror and destruction. People did not approve of the war and might not accept another large-scale draft. Howard hoped, and reasonably expected, that his bogus proclamation would enflame the citizenry, panic the stock markets and cause gold prices to skyrocket. It (very briefly) did all three.

The timing was especially sensitive to Lincoln and the Union for three reasons. First: two weeks earlier General Grant had begun the Overland Campaign, the final thrust to Richmond, one dead soldier at a time. The proclamation would signal failure. With the election only six months away (and Lincoln's hope for reelection bleak), Grant simply could not fail.

Second: May 19th was 'steamer day' in New York—the day news traveled to Europe across the Atlantic with the latest war updates. (There were no transatlantic cables until 1866). The proclamation would indicate the war effort was going badly, thereby likely pushing Europeans further away from the Union and closer to the Confederate cause. (To help shape European sentiment, the government had earlier in the war adjusted publication of news to fit the schedules of transatlantic steamers.)

Finally, on the same night that Howard penned the bogus proclamation, President Lincoln actually had written a genuine proclamation, calling for 300,000 new troops. Lincoln, however, put his proclamation away in a desk drawer. Waking up to see a proclamation very much like the one he had put away a few hours earlier must have unnerved him greatly.

Howard, who had previously worked for several New York papers, was the reporter who had claimed back in February 1861 that Lincoln snuck through Baltimore in the middle of the night in a "scotch plaid cap and a very long military cloak." He had annoyed his former editors with clever pranks, including holding the telegraph lines open and filling them with Jesus's genealogy. On another occasion, he violated an order banning reporters from the funeral of Phil Kearny by sneaking in, dressed in a clerical robe.

Two New York papers printed the bogus proclamation. Coincidentally, or not, both were vehemently hostile to the Lincoln Administration. The *New York World,* ten months earlier, had stirred draft riots to deadly results by ridiculing the president's then call-up as "unnecessary and mischievous." The *World,* according to one analyst, was "the most malignant, the most brutal, the most false and scurrilous of all assailants of the president."

The other paper, *the Journal of Commerce,* had been named in a grand jury presentment in August 1861 as disloyal to the government. Its mail privileges had been revoked and later restored only with the paper's reorganization and its editor's resignation.

The draft news caused the markets to open just as Howard expected. Lincoln's advisor John Hay reported the stock exchange was "thrown into violent fever." Gold prices spiked and angry crowds started to form, demanding the proclamation be rescinded.

Union General John A. Dix saved the day and prevented a full blown riot by quickly solving the case. Thinking the scheme might have been set in place by someone looking to make money in the gold spike, he inquired about gold purchasers. (A few days earlier Howard had asked gold merchants of the effect on gold prices with such a proclamation). Dix promptly nabbed Howard, who along with Mallison, quickly confessed.

The other newspapers then ran stories reporting the draft was a hoax, quieting the mob. Samuel Cunard agreed to delay the departure of his steamer (the *Scotia*) to Europe until the matter got straightened out.

The military arrested the owner of the Independent Press, a newer (and less government-connected) competitor of the NYAP. Secretary of War Stanton falsely concluded the Independent had sent the story out over its wires. It turned out, however, the NYAP's wires sent the story out (it got picked up in the *New Orleans Picayune*). Stanton later tried to "soothe the righteous anger" of the Independent by leaking important military news to them.

Also arrested were editors and employees of the two newspapers. Although they were not aware the proclamation was phony, they were imprisoned and not able to publish again for four days. A riot was averted, civil liberties trampled. Secretary of the Navy Gideon Welles, who blamed Secretary of State William Seward for forcing Lincoln's hand, called the seizures "hasty, rash, inconsiderate, and wrong."

The *Journal's* editor later wrote to Lincoln asking (and answering) if he would have suppressed the other (pro-Lincoln) newspapers, like he did the *Journal* and the *World*, if they had unwittingly published the bogus proclamation: "You know you would not. If not, why not? Is there a different law for your opponents and for your supporters?" He claimed the government actions were "a shock to the public mind." Even the *New York Times* seemed to agree, calling the actions analogous to "hanging a man in advance of the trial."

Censure resolutions were offered in the House and Senate shortly after the incident (but did not pass) calling the government's response a "violation of the Constitution, and subversive to the principles of civil liberty."

Not much is known about Mallison. Howard ended up spending three months in jail. He was later elected president of the International League of Press Clubs and became one of the first columnists to be syndicated throughout the country.

At least one merchant tried to capitalize on the excitement of the issue. In an advertisement, it was promised to not be a bogus proclamation that "Golden Bitters—are the best tonic in town!"

As a side note, Congress called a draft shortly after this incident. A draft of July 18, 1864 resulted in 385,163 enlistments.

The egregious misbehavior of the press during the war was legendary. Although placed by many on a mantle of purity (Union General Irwin McDowell suggested war correspondents should wear white uniforms to indicate the purity of their character), the reporting was often egregiously slanted. Many readers understood they could not believe anything published in the newspapers. Henry Adams wrote, "people have become so accustomed to the idea of disbelieving everything that is stated in the American papers that all confidence in us is destroyed."

There were seventeen daily papers in New York City alone when the war started and many of them used their power of the ink to shape whatever opinion they wanted, regardless of facts or truth. Others simply acted as press agents for the military or certain officers within the army, with some reporters accepting money from officers for a positive write up. One reporter shamelessly noted in a letter home that he had received $50 from a Northern artillery officer.

A Congressional committee learned the Lincoln Administration could and did use the wire service to disseminate false information to garner favorable impression of the government and the war effort.

One seasoned telegraph man, who also served as a former congressman from Maine spelled out the power of the press when he said they sent or withheld news as they chose, and thus shaped public sentiment at will. The press, he claimed, had "more power to make and unmake presidents than either party."

President Lincoln well understood the power of the press. Before the war he had written: "Public sentiment is everything. With it, nothing can fail; against it, nothing can succeed. Whoever moulds public sentiment, goes deeper than he who enacts statutes, or pronounces judicial decisions."

Like today's media, the Civil War press often tried to sway public opinion by what they didn't print as well as what they printed. As a penalty against General Meade, reporters conspired to ruin his career because they believed the good general had penalized a reporter too harshly. Earlier, as a penalty for printing secret war information, Meade had placed the reporter backwards on an old horse, a placard marked "Libeler of the Press" tied to his chest and paraded him through camp to the tune of "Rogue's March." When the reporter's fellow journalists heard about this, they got together and agreed to never mention General Meade's name in a dispatch again, perhaps denying the politically ambitious Meade a later successful political career, including election to the presidency.

Shocking Advertisement Leads to Arrest

Many Southerners got roped in during the federal dragnet for the Lincoln assassination conspirators. One of those arrested was a citizen of Cahaba, Alabama. Cahaba was known when the war started, according to one resident, for its culture, wealth, hospitality and secessionist passion. "Political meetings were a nightly occurrence." Cahaba is located about fifty miles southwest of Montgomery, the original capital of the Confederacy and probably the state's most famous contribution to the war effort; a lawyer named George Washington Gayle was its most infamous. Gayle had formerly served as a Democratic state legislature and the United States attorney for the Southern District of Alabama.

Newspapers in the North and South carried some incredibly vicious advertisements and stories attacking President Lincoln and his administration during the war, but Gayle's offer in the December 2, 1864 edition of the *Selma, Alabama Dispatch* had to be the most shocking:

ONE MILLION DOLLARS WANTED
TO HAVE PEACE BY THE 1ˢᵗ OF MARCH

If the citizens of the Southern Confederacy will furnish me with the cash, or good securities for the sum of $ 1,000,000, I will cause the lives of Abraham Lincoln, William H. Seward and

Andrew Johnson to be taken by the 1ˢᵗ of March next. This will give us peace, and satisfy the world that cruel tyrants cannot live in 'a land of liberty.' If this is not accomplished, nothing will be claimed beyond the sum of $50,000 in advance, which is supposed to be necessary to reach and slaughter the three villains. I will give, myself, $1,000 towards this patriotic purpose. Everyone wishing to contribute will address Box X, Cahawba, Alabama.

A citizen of Cahaba named Mrs. Anna Fry chalked up Mr. Gayle's impulsive comments and actions to "outbursts of enthusiasm" that no one who knew him would take seriously, but Secretary of War Edwin Stanton and federal authorities weren't quite so understanding when the advertisement came to their attention after Lincoln's death. They ordered Captain Cocheran of the Union Army to arrest Gayle and take him north to Fort Lafayette Prison in the New York Harbor. (Cocheran later became the postmaster in Selma, Alabama after the war.)

The trial of the Lincoln conspirators ran from May 10 to June 29, 1865 and included testimony from 366 witnesses. Two of those witnesses worked for the *Dispatch*. John Cantlin testified that in December 1864, he worked as a foreman for the newspaper, which had a circulation of about eight hundred. He said the advertisement ran four or five times and had come in from Gayle, in Gayle's handwriting. "Mr. Gayle," Cantlin remarked, "is a lawyer of considerable reputation, and is distinguished, even in Alabama, for his extreme views on the subject of slavery and the rebellion, and as an ardent supporter of the Confederacy."

Dispatch employee Watson D. Graves also testified the handwritten text delivered to the newspaper bore Gayle's handwriting, which Graves recognized, "having seen it frequently in articles we had published before."

Gayle, the ardent secessionist and scion of the South, was indicted on two charges: conspiracy to murder the President of the United

States and giving aid to the Rebellion. On December 21, 1866, the *New York Times* reported:

> "Another interesting case is that of the United States vs. George W. Gayle, charged with complicity in the assassination of Mr. Lincoln. This case is set for Friday next, and some of the most eminent jurists of the State are retained for the defense. Mr. Gayle is a prominent lawyer of Middle Alabama, and resides in Cahawba, Dallas County. During the late war an advertisement appeared in the Selma Dispatch, a newspaper published in the same county, over the signature of Mr. Gayle, as is alleged, offering to be one of a certain number to contribute a certain amount for the assassination of the late President. Such is the charge on which the indictment is founded. The counsel of Mr. Gayle are sanguine of being able to secure a clear acquittal from all participation in the deed that was so generally condemned throughout the South, and is still regarded as a most unfortunate occurrence for the people of the States lately in rebellion."

But the trial never took place. Instead authorities transferred Gayle to a prison at Fort Pulaski outside Savannah, Georgia. Gayle had nothing to do with John Wilkes Booth or the conspiracy. Arresting Gayle (and other Southerners) after the assassination was a political move, according to an author of Alabama history, "to pander to fanatical malignity." Authorities finally released him and on April 27, 1867, President Andrew Johnson pardoned him.

Pardoning Southerners was a major factor leading to Johnson's impeachment in 1868. Perhaps Johnson had a personal reason for issuing this pardon. Mrs. Fry explained that Gayle and Johnson knew each other decades earlier when the future president had worked as a tailor.

Years later, Mrs. Fry published a poem called *Memoirs of Old Cahaba*, which included these verses:

By the side of the river, we sat down and wept,
And sighed for the days that are gone;

And told the story, o'er and o'er,
Of the glory of the dear old town.

Each scene was recalled of youth's golden hours,
Each friend we used to know
Was with us again, from the silent land,
The land of long ago.

And again we heard the songs of the birds,
With the ripple of the waters' flow;
The memories of years, forever lost,
Swept over our hearts once more.

And when in '60 Abe Lincoln elected,
Our hearts the bitterest resentment reflected.
Alabama seceded—the bitter passion is rife,
The North and the South are ready for strife.

Wild with excitement, and meetings at night,
Our town is eager to enter the fight;
And now, in place of party and ball,
Political banquets are given by all.

At one of these banquets, a brilliant ovation,
In speeches the North was condemned as a nation;
And George W. Gayle joined his glass in a toast
With "death and damnation to the whole Yankee host."

And then in an eloquent oration he led,
And offered a reward for Abe Lincoln's head;
One million dollars was the sum he named,
For which he became in the South so famed.

In a flush of secession, a thoughtless boast,
A reckless defiance to the Northern host;
It went out to the world in the weekly edition
Of John Hardy's paper, famed for sedition.

And was copied in all the Northern papers,
Who execrated our Southern traitors;
And George W. Gayle, with our leaders of State,
Became a target for all Yankee hate.

Though utterly ignorant of Booth and his plan
To murder Lincoln, the Northern land
Remembered his words, in the excitement of war,
And arrested him now as a conspirator.

He was cast in prison, at Fortress Monroe,
With John A. Campbell, and Clay,
Where Jeff Davis, our honored President,
In irons and shackles lay,

By command of that monster in human form—
The illustrious Nelson Miles—
Who, with Stanton and others then in power,
Were fiends in mens' disguise.

The planter has gone, with the lordly grace;
His home is in alien hands;
His children are ruined, dead or lost,
Or struggling in foreign lands.

Not a mark is left of the former glory—
Of this land in its beauty and pride;
Not a soul is left to tell the story;
They have all passed away and died.

Mrs. Fry eloquently summarized life and history for the old Town of Cahaba, as well as for each of us:

"But those beautiful scenes are no more. All those noble, grand old people have passed away, and their like will never be seen again...They are gone never to return, and Cahaba, like Rome, must ever remain a Niobe of the nation, a mother bereft of her children, to whom our hearts still cling with living enthusiasm in memory of her departed glory. Though long years have passed and the ruin is now perfect and complete, the site of the old town is still a lovely spot, where the pure, limpid waters gush unceasingly from the artesian wells; where the flowers planted long years ago still bloom in perennial spring in the old-time yards; where the mocking bird still sings in springtime, and the Cherokee roses, full with blossoms; shed their snowy petals along the deserted streets; where the sweet breath of the china blossom is wafted by the night breeze; where the stars still shine in all their brilliant beauty, and the moon rises in its old-time splendor infolding the ruined town in its soft, mellow light."

Civil War Graffiti

Mosby writing his name on General Stoughton's wall during the capture might be the best known Civil War graffiti, but there was a lot more of that kind of thing going on. One soldier wrote in a letter home:

> "I have just been to a village about one and half mile[s] west called Falls Church. It is a small place. There are three churches in the neighborhood but they are all in ruins. One of them is the oldest church in Virginia. It is built of brick, and is the same that Washington was married so the folks say in the village.
>
> The insides are all torn out with nothing left but the pulpit. I went into it just for fun. People carry away pieces of boards and write their names on the walls. Mine is there."

Few examples of Civil War graffiti-the scribblings and doodlings written or carved by soldiers on walls with soot, ashes, pencils or knives—have survived time. Most of the graffiti walls and buildings no longer remain and those not destroyed have been buried under generations of paint and wallpaper.

Luckily, there are at least four buildings in Virginia with the signatures, poems, drawings and trash-talking of soldiers from both sides: The Blenheim House in Fairfax City, the Graffiti House in

Culpeper County, the Massaponax Baptist Church in Spotsylvania County, and the Old Court House in Frederick County.

The Blenheim House, located at 3610 Old Lee Highway in the City of Fairfax, was purchased from private owners in 1999. Its walls have the names of eighty-eight identifiable Civil War soldiers, a drawing of Colonel John S. Mosby, and an excerpt from the Star Spangled Banner. One of the soldier's remarks communicated a message to the homeowners: "Lovely ones, we come to protect and not to injure. The others have destroyed your house-We are guarding it at present from vice."

The Graffiti House, located at 19484 Brandy Road in Brandy Station, was purchased from private owners in 2002. There are thirty-four recognizable names, of which thirty are Confederates. There are also six drawings of women, including one crossing a stream and another smoking a pipe. A Confederate succinctly and happily reported one day's event: "April 16th, 1863, Battle of Beverly's Ford, Yanks Caught Hell." There is also a large picture of a bird, replete with its feathers and captioned "birds of a feather flock together."

Brandy Station Foundation President Bob Luddy will gladly share the stories of all the Graffiti House names, including a tale of John Egbert Farnum of the 70th New York Infantry.

A swashbuckler who had been described in *Harper's Weekly* (October 1858) as a "man of destiny" and in the *Albany Statesman* Newspaper as "the renowned overland rider, whose brilliant career in Texas, California and Nicaragua is familiar to so many of his countrymen," Farnum had been a commander in a mercenary army that conquered parts of Mexico and Central America. The *Wanderer* was the last confirmed ship to have illegally imported slaves to the United States. Farnum and others were involved in the operation of delivering African slaves to Georgia's coast near Jekyll Island (near a present day federal law enforcement training center) on November 28, 1858. He missed the trial and the not-guilty verdicts against his comrades for this illegal enterprise. (This verdict came in eight days before John Brown was executed for his effort at starting a slave insurrection.)

By skipping out to New York, Farnum bought himself some time until he was tracked down and eventually extradited to Savannah, Georgia to stand trial. A journalist who saw him on the street before he was extradited to Georgia said Farnum "struts…with an unholy odor, not of rosemary but of ebony, clinging to his clothes and beard." Before the trial began, a group of his friends tried to break him out of jail. They got into a tussle with the deputy jailer. The jailer's name, incredibly, was Luddy: Peter Luddy. After thirty hours, without food or sleep, the jury came back deadlocked in favor of guilty, ten to two. Farnum was never tried again.

After the trial, Farnum served as an officer in the Union Army, fighting at Fredericksburg, Chancellorsville and Gettysburg before achieving the rank of brigadier general. After the war he was appointed to the lucrative position of New York City's Inspector of Customs. He died at age forty-seven and is buried in Brooklyn's Greenwood Cemetery.

As for the *Wanderer*, it was converted to a Union gunboat and captured two schooners and two sloops during the Civil War. After the war it was sold at auction and eventually sank in 1871 during a storm off the coast of Cuba.

Back to the Graffiti House where the most-prized item is a drawing of a scroll containing the complete roster of sixteen members of Confederate Marylanders in the "Rifle Gun #1 Stuart Horse Artillery." The Graffiti House boasts a 'next-generation wall' with the signatures of about 125 ancestors of soldiers from both sides who fought in the Battle of Brandy Station. Included in this collection of names are four generations of Jeb Stuarts, starting with Jeb Stuart IV.

The Massaponax Baptist Church, located at 5101 Massaponax Church Road in Fredericksburg, was the site of the famous photograph of General Grant sitting outside on church pews, under the trees with his officers. Perhaps while they conferred, the privates were inside writing on the walls: "The Union forever, firm noble and true / And the Flag of the Union, The Red, White and Blue." And nearby: "The Union forever. Who is not for the Union? None but traitors."

The Confederate rants were more vitriolic. They included a drawing of a man hanging from a scaffold with the caption, "Abe

Lincoln dancing on nothing." Another Confederate took a direct attack against a Union soldier named Nepp: "You say your name is Nepp well I would make you one sweet mess if here I should catch you." Included is a sincere wish of a Confederate soldier: "I hope this Sacred place may never again be polluted by Yankee feet." One last oblique comment: "Fools names are like their faces / Always seen in public places."

The Old Court House, located at 20 North Loudoun Street in Winchester, contains the names of hundreds of soldiers, of which twenty-five have been meticulously documented to show when and how they ended up there. Built in the 1840s, the Court House was used as both hospital and prison during the war. The extensive volume of graffiti is no wonder given the town changed hands approximately seventy times during the war.

The Old Court House has a creative curse to the President of the Confederacy: "To Jeff Davis: May he be set afloat in a boat with out a compass or ruder, the boat swallowed by a shark, the shark in the belly of a whale and further may he be locked in Hell with the key lost and set in a northwest corner with a southeast wind blowing ash in his eyes for all ETERNITY."

These walls present a vivid reminder of how close we are to the Civil War. The war was right here and seems in many ways to have taken place recently. They're not just names on a wall but men who shared some of their thoughts. How many letters home were written in the graffiti houses by men recuperating from wounds? How many got their only look at Mosby, Grant, or Lee from one of the graffiti buildings and proudly told their grandchildren fifty years later about the time they ran into Marse Robert?

The Soldier's Home:
Lincoln's Summer Retreat

Like a lighthouse in the Sea of Turmoil, the Soldier's Home, a heavily wooded hilltop retreat located three miles from the White House, brought the Presidential Ship of State safely home to tranquility for three consecutive summers during the Civil War. "How dearly I loved the Soldier's Home," Mary Todd Lincoln wrote of the grounds and 10,000-square foot stucco cottage.

Lincoln initially saw the Soldier's Home-the 19th Century equivalent of Camp David, a few days after his inauguration; his final visit was the day before the assassination. In between, the Lincolns summered at the "place where kings might dwell" for about thirteen of the forty-nine months of his presidency.

The origins of the Home go back to 1827, when the secretary of war recommended the establishment of an Army Asylum. Six years later the need to "care of the superannuated soldier" came up again. Both proposals became as forgotten and neglected as the prospective veterans the home was intended to serve. Eventually Congress established a Military Asylum in 1851 to provide "for the aged and crippled soldiers who have fought their country's battles, and have settled down quietly till the Great Captain calls them up higher." The details of the Soldier's Home were established by a banker, politicians and a poet: a country estate built by George Riggs provided the site, an 1859 Congressional Act bestowed its name and Walt Whitman painted a first-hand image:

"Mr. Lincoln on the saddle generally rides a good-sized, easy-going gray horse, is dress'd in plain black, somewhat rusty and dusty and wears a black stiff hat, and looks about as ordinary in attire &c., as the commonest man...the entirely unornamental cortege as it trots towards Lafayette square arouses no sensation, only some curious stranger stops and gazes...Sometimes one of his sons, a boy of ten or twelve, accompanies him, riding at his right on a pony."

Today's route to the Soldier's Home passes by a Children's' Hospital and the African American Civil War Museum, over a paved road with numerous traffic lights to regulate the thousands of vehicles that traverse daily. Lincoln's path would likely have taken him by taverns, brothels and a contraband camp where runaway slaves enjoyed their freedom. Indeed, it was a much simpler time when an individual toll booth operator decided whether he would charge the President of the United States:

"Mr. President... [I] am please (sic) to see that your family pass over our Seventh St. Turnpike and I have given direction to our toll gather(er) not to detain your carriage or to receive any compensation for its passage."

Lincoln's own words from a poem he wrote in 1846 presciently capture his somber mood during peaceful walks winding past a burial ground next to the Home, established as a National Cemetery after the First Battle of Bull Run:

"Air held his breath; trees all still
Seemed sorrowing angels round,
Whose swelling tears in dew-drops fell
Upon the listening ground.
I range the fields with pensive tread
And pace the hollow rooms,
And feel (companion of the dead)
I'm living in the tombs."

Lincoln rested at the Soldier's Home, but each soldier's death carved anguish on a countenance a portrait painter called "the saddest face I ever painted." But there were productive times too. Lincoln completed the Emancipation Proclamation at the summer residence. An advisor described: "The Tycoon is in fine whack…I have rarely seen him more serene and busy…The most important things he decides & there is no cavil…There is no man in the country, so wise, so gentle and so firm. I believe the hand of God placed him where he is."

But danger and threats lurked all around. A reporter remarked that rebels might kidnap the president, who "we could ill afford to spare just now." One Confederate signed a death threat: "The worst rebel you ever saw." Lincoln dismissed the threats, as did Secretary of War Edwin Stanton, who opined that "assassination is not an American practice." Pennsylvania soldiers were eventually assigned as guards but Lincoln joked he was more likely to get shot by an accidental discharge by one of them than by a Confederate. He did, however, like having the guards around because they provided companionship and could share with him the soldiers' mood and sentiments.

Ninety-nine veterans lived at the Home in 1864; today about 1,100 military veterans reside at the U. S. Soldiers' and Airmen's Home. Military personnel with at least twenty years of service are eligible to live at the Home. The Soldiers Home is financed through deductions, fines and forfeitures from military personnel, not taxes.

Abraham Lincoln's Personal Finances

"Now vere ish my hundred tollars?" Abraham Lincoln asked in a July 4, 1851 letter, joking as to what "the Dutch justice said when he married folks." The man who said he didn't know anything about money and never had enough of it to fret about was inquiring about legal fees due to him after winning a court case. Lamenting his bleak financial means, Lincoln proclaimed he brought nothing with him to the White House and wasn't likely to carry anything out. However, a closer inspection of his finances reveals a well-diversified portfolio surprisingly robust in sophistication and savings. Perhaps he just didn't realize that he had enough money to fret about. Certainly Lincoln's death precluded him from carrying anything out, but his heirs walked away with more than $110,000.

His first earnings came as an eighteen-year-old. Thrilled to receive two silver half-dollars for transporting two men and their trunks from a flat boat to a steamer, the young entrepreneur exclaimed, "I could scarcely believe my eyes as I picked up the money." Many years later, on March 1, 1853, Lincoln deposited $310 to open an account at the Springfield Marine Bank. He eventually had enough money to loan some of it out. In the fifteen year period leading up to the presidency, Lincoln made seventeen loans to various people, at approximately 10% interest, totaling almost $12,000. When the new president arrived in Washington in February 1861, with a net worth of approximately $15,000, he promptly chose a Washington bank to deposit his $25,000 presidential salary.

Established in 1840 by William Corcoran and George Washington Riggs, Riggs & Corcoran Bank, as it was originally known before it became Riggs (now PNC Bank), was already steeped in history by the time the Civil War began. Riggs was the son of Elisha Riggs, who as a young soldier in 1814 "rode madly" Paul Revere-style to the Executive Mansion to warn then-President Madison that the British were on their way to Washington.

Numerous Americans whose names and exploits fill history books had accounts at Riggs, including Winfield Scott, Jefferson Davis (who closed out his account the day after Lincoln was sworn in as president), John Fremont, Henry Clay, Daniel Webster and Generals Grant, McClellan and Sherman. And Tyler too. The first American president with an account at the 'Bank of Presidents,' as it later became known, was John Tyler, of 'Tippecanoe and Tyler too' fame.

Lincoln, America's first Republican president, deposited the sum of $2,083.33-the total amount of his first monthly paycheck--to Washington's Riggs & Company Bank. In an interesting bit of political trivia, Riggs was an ardent Democrat who had served as treasurer for the 1860 Democratic National Committee.

Altogether Lincoln received forty-nine monthly presidential paychecks, then called warrants. Twenty-six were used to purchase government bonds and notes, four were found in his desk after the assassination, eighteen were deposited at Riggs and one went to First National Bank of Washington, widely believed to have been deposited there in error by George Harrington, who handled Lincoln's finances in the last nine months of his life. Lincoln often left the paychecks in his desk drawer undisturbed for several months. At one point Lincoln had seven uncashed paychecks; on another occasion, he had eleven.

There were 234 checks for slightly more than $40,000 written from the Riggs account. Eleven checks were for a special hospital account that Lincoln appears to have established for contributions to help wounded soldiers. The checks do not have an account number, are not pre-numbered and do not have the account holder's name imprinted on them. Only a handful of originals are known to still exist.

"Colored man, with one leg," was the payee written by Lincoln on a five-dollar check dated August 11, 1863, five weeks after the Battle of Gettysburg. The PNC archives has a handwritten letter written by Riggs's granddaughter in 1948 which gives some clues as to the background of the 'colored man with one leg':

> "I spoke to my mother again and she distinctly remembers the old one legged colored man. She says he was a fine looking man with a beard that was turning grey and he always stood on H Street between the Old Freeman House and St. John's Church and Mr. Riggs gave him something every morning as he passed along there on foot from his house to the bank. As a little girl my mother sometimes walked that way with her grandfather."

On March 10, 1862, just nineteen days after his son Willie died, Lincoln wrote a check to son Tad, who at the time was ill and refusing to take his medicine. Called out of an important meeting with a group of border-state senators and representatives to deal with this critical personal family crisis, Lincoln used his legendary skills of persuasion to convince the obstinate nine-year-old to take the medicine. A few minutes later upon leaving Tad's room, the smiling father announced: "It's all right. Tad and I have fixed things up." This transaction netted Lincoln one less crisis and provided Tad with a five dollar check, negotiable only when he got well, payable to "Tad, when he is well enough to present." Apparently Tad got well very quickly or found someone to get him the money; the check was cashed the following day. This check was sold at auction in New York City in 1967 for $5,500.

An uncashed check dated May 4, 1864, in the amount of $2.50 is believed to still exist. The payee, Isaac Heilprin, who sold glasses in his shop, Franklin & Company, located about four blocks from the White House, held onto the check to save Lincoln money because he had read about Mary Todd Lincoln's voracious spending habits. Heilprin wanted to do whatever he could to help the president, who was under tremendous pressure in prosecuting what was then a very unpopular war. Lincoln's account balance was $78.85 when he wrote this check. On the next day, he cashed a check for $800, overdrawing his account by $721.14. By the next month, the account was overdrawn by $2,141.44, and it stayed in the negative until the 9th of July.

On April 28, 1864, Lincoln sent his wife, while she and Tad were in New York, a $50 check. She had requested the money a few days earlier in a letter which included a question from son Tad about the animals left back at the Executive Mansion: "Tad says are the goats well." Along with the money, Lincoln wrote: "Tell Tad the goats and father are very well-especially the goats."

In October 1864 Lincoln paid the United States Government $500 for an expense he wanted to, but was not required to pay. Draftees were eligible to "buy" their way out of service for $500 (originally $300) if they could obtain a substitute to take their place. Although exempt from the draft, Lincoln voluntarily chose to find (and pay) a substitute as a sign of goodwill and patriotism. John Summerfield Staples, a Pennsylvanian, served in the Second District of Columbia Infantry as Lincoln's substitute. He performed duty as a clerk at Camp Sedgewick in Alexandria. Staples died on January 11, 1888, at age forty-three in Stroudsburg, Pennsylvania.

Other checks written by Lincoln include one to the Christian Commission dated November 15, 1864, for $10, and a check dated September 6, 1861, to Master Tad for one gold dollar. Other payees included "Lucy (colored woman)," William, with no last name given, and "Mr. Johns, a sick man."

Apparently the use of descriptions for the payee was not unusual. In fact, for the payee on a check written out to himself, Gideon Welles, Lincoln's Secretary of the Navy, wrote: 'Me.'

A June 10, 1864 incident reveals Lincoln's casual approach to handling his finances. On that day he brought in a plethora of financial assets-bonds, notes, greenbacks (cash), and gold, and left them with Salmon Chase, the secretary of the treasury, to consolidate. In a book published in 1873, Chase's assistant, Maunsell Field, recounted this interesting episode:

"I happened once to be with the Secretary [of the Treasury] when the President, without knocking, and unannounced, as was his habit, entered the room. His rusty black hat was on the back of his head, and he wore, as was his custom, an old gray shawl across his shoulders…I said good-morning to Mr. Lincoln, and then, as was the established etiquette when the President called, withdrew from the office…In less than five minutes I was summoned to return to the Secretary… The President was gone, and there was lying upon one end of Mr. Chase's desk a confused mass of Treasury notes, Demand notes, Seven-thirty notes, and other representatives of value. Mr. Chase told us that this lot of money had just been brought by Mr. Lincoln, who desired to have it converted into bonds…the amount proved to be sixty-eight thousand dollars, which was certainly a large sum for Mr. Lincoln to have saved from his salary in three years. Possibly a good deal of this money may have been anonymous gifts. However, it may be said that there was very clever financing done in the White House in those days, about which the president was supposed to have little or no knowledge. He only knew that the establishment was conducted in a marvelously economical manner. I had it from a Senator, who was appointed chairman of an investigating committee upon the subject at a secret session of the Senate, that a state dinner was paid for out of an appropriation for fertilizer for the grounds connected with the Executive Mansion. How far this "Heathen Chinee" business was carried, it would probably be difficult to ascertain at this distance of time. One thing only is certain, and that is that Mr. Lincoln was personally thoroughly honest."

Mr. Field may have misspoke about the sum of money Lincoln brought in, as another source indicated the pecuniary pile boasted the smaller but still princely sum of $54,515.07.

On the day before he was shot, Lincoln wrote and cashed a check to himself, payable to "Self" for $800. He also, on April 13th, cashed a check for $500 from a Philadelphia lawyer named Eli Kirk Price. It is not known why Price paid Lincoln $500.

To help fund the war, Congress passed legislation which pegged interest rates on bonds at 6%. Treasury notes, which paid 7.3%, were referred to as seven-thirties. In addition, Congress passed the Revenue Act imposing the first income tax, then called an income duty, on Americans. As of September 1, 1862, income became taxable at the rate of 3% for amounts greater than $600 and up to $10,000; 5% for income greater than $10,000; 1 and ½ % for interest income; and 5% for all property of any kind. In June 1864, the rate of tax for income greater than $600 increased to 5%. The pro-tax *New York Herald* had this to say on September 1, 1862, the day the national tax began:

"To-day begins a new era of this country. Beyond a few local and state taxes, which were felt by none but owners of real estate, this country has never been taxed before. We have jogged along quietly and comfortably, and have amused ourselves greatly by laughing at the over taxed people of England, where a man is taxed from the cradle to the grave; where light, heat and water are taxed, and where not only every rich man, but even the poorest peasant, is obliged to pay largely for the privilege of existence and the blessings of bad government....We could have wished, however, that this necessary tax should be more equally imposed than at present, and that the Eastern manufacturers and the Western farmers had been compelled to bear an equal share of the burden with the people of the other states, instead of being almost entirely exempt, and leaving the commercial people of the Middle States to pay an unfair proportion of the debt...The effect of the tax will be to deepen public sentiment. The people will be less ready to excuse the mistakes of our government and our generals...The war will be better conducted, for every man, having to pay his money towards carrying on the war, will insist and assist that it shall be properly prosecuted and speedily and gloriously concluded...every man, woman and child will have a personal interest in the government and in the war, and we may be assured that the government will be more respected and better administered...None value a thing so much as they who pay dearly for it."

Tax on whiskey at the beginning of the war was twenty cents a gallon; it gradually increased to two dollars, but at that high price "frauds and illicit distilling became serious evils." So it was decreased to ninety cents a gallon. Income to the government from internal revenues (which included taxes on alcohol, tobacco, stamps and income) amounted to the following (calendar year ending dates):

June 30, 1863: $37,640,787
June 30, 1864: $117,145,748
June 30, 1865: $211,129,529

The amount to follow is not a typo. The war cost so much (almost one billion a year) that the national debt on October 31, 1865, six months after it ended, was the astronomical figure of $ 2,808,549,437.55. Yes, 2.8 billion. And that's 1865 dollars with no adjustments for inflation or anything else.

Years later, when it was determined the tax did not apply to the president or Supreme Court justices, Lincoln's executor filed a claim which resulted in a $3,555.94 refund check paid in 1872 to Lincoln's heirs.

It is certainly an inexact calculation to determine how the value of money in the 1860s compares to that of today. A relatively easy match would be the presidential salary, which at its current rate of $400,000 is sixteen times greater than during the Civil War. An interesting analysis would be to find an appropriate comparison for what a speaker of Lincoln's stature and notoriety would be paid today. For his historic 1860 speech at New York's Cooper Union, Lincoln received $200.

Lincoln's estate totaled $83,343.70. Through wise investments and management by the executor, the total distributed two years later was $110,974.62. It was evenly divided between Tad, Mary Todd and Robert, each receiving $36,991.54. Tad died on July 15, 1871, with his estate evenly split between Mary Todd and brother Robert. Mary Todd's estate of $84,035 went to son Robert after she died on July 16, 1882.

Abraham Lincoln's Favorite Poem

Abraham Lincoln loved poetry. He loved reading, writing and reciting it, often from memory. He commented that he would have traded almost everything he had to be able to write really good poems. In 1849 as he was challenged by friends to sing a song, the embarrassed Lincoln said: "You fellows are trying to make a fool of me" before adding that he "never sung in his life and never was able to." Instead, he offered to recite a poem. Closing his eyes, he recited from memory:

"Oh, why should the spirit of mortal be proud?
Like a swift-fleeting meteor, a fast-flying cloud,
A flash of the lightning, a break of the wave,
Man passeth from life to his rest in the grave.

The leaves of the oak and the willow shall fade,
Be scattered around, and together be laid;
And the young and the old, and the low and the high,
Shall molder to dust and together shall lie.

The infant a mother attended and loved;
The mother that infant's affection who proved;
The husband that mother and infant who blessed,--
Each, all, are away to their dwellings of rest.

The maid on whose cheek, on whose brow, in whose eye,
Shone beauty and pleasure,--her triumphs are by;
And the memory of those who loved her and praised
Are alike from the minds of the living erased.

The hand of the king that the sceptre hath borne;
The brow of the priest that the mitre hath worn;
The eye of the sage, and the heart of the brave,
Are hidden and lost in the depth of the grave.

The peasant whose lot was to sow and to reap;
The herdsman who climbed with his goats up the steep;
The beggar who wandered in search of his bread,
Have faded away like the grass that we tread.

The saint who enjoyed the communion of heaven;
The sinner who dared to remain unforgiven;
The wise and the foolish, the guilty and just,
Have quietly mingled their bones in the dust.

So the multitude goes, like the flowers or the weed
That withers away to let others succeed;
So the multitude comes, even those we behold,
To repeat every tale that has often been told.

For we are the same our fathers have been;
We see the same sights our fathers have seen;
We drink the same stream, and view the same sun,
And run the same course our fathers have run.

The thoughts we are thinking our fathers would think;
From the death we are shrinking our fathers would shrink;
To the life we are clinging they also would cling;
But it speeds for us all, like a bird on the wing.

They loved, but the story we cannot unfold;
They scorned, but the heart of the haughty is cold;
They grieved, but no wail from their slumbers will come;

They joyed, but the tongue of their gladness is dumb.

They died, ay! they died; and we things that are now,
Who walk on the turf that lies over their brow,
Who make in their dwelling a transient abode,
Meet the things that they met on their pilgrimage road.

Yea! hope and despondency, pleasure and pain,
Mingle together in sunshine and rain;
And the smiles and the tears, the song and the dirge,
Still follow each other, like surge upon surge.

'Tis the wink of an eye, 'tis the draught of a breath,
From the blossom of health to the paleness of death,
From the gilded saloon to the bier and the shroud,--
Oh, why should the spirit of mortal be proud?"

Lincoln recited the lines frequently, including to Francis
Carpenter, a painter who spent several months at the White House.
Lincoln explained to Carpenter that he had carried the poem in his
pocket since cutting it out of a newspaper and said he wished he had
written it: "I would give all I am worth, and go in debt, to be able to
write so fine a piece as I think that is." The poem "Oh, Why Should
the Spirit of Mortal be Proud?" had been written by William Knox, a
Scotsman who died early in the Nineteenth Century.

The Saga of Wilmer and Virginia McLean

Some people think bad luck follows them everywhere. For Wilmer and Virginia McLean, it really did. In what has aptly been called a "coincidence of fantastic dimensions," the Civil War started in the kitchen of the McLean's Manassas, Virginia house in 1861 and ended, four years later, in the parlor of their Appomattox, Virginia home, where they had moved to get away from the war.

Wilmer McLean and Virginia Hooe Mason were married in St. Paul's Episcopal Church in Alexandria on January 19, 1853. The following year they acquired from her father, the 1,200-acre *Yorkshire* Plantation near the Bull Run in Prince William County. From a prior marriage Virginia had two daughters: Maria Beverly Mason and Oscesla "Ocie" Seddonia Mason. Together, Virginia and Wilmer had a son and three daughters: Wilmer Jr., Lucretia "Lula," Nannie and Virginia Beverley "Jennie."

On July 17, 1861, McLean rented the Yorkshire Plantation to the Confederate Army for use as a hospital and the headquarters for General Pierre G. T. Beauregard.

> For rent of two dwelling houses, as Surgeons quarters, one barn, as Hospital and outbuildings as quarters for Hospital attendants, from 17th July 1861 to Dec 31st, 1861, 5 months and 15 days at $150.00 per month-$825.00.

This was not the first known financial transaction between the parties; two weeks earlier McLean had sold a horse to the Confederate quartermaster for $100.

At this point in the Civil War, cadets from the Citadel had fired on the Union ship *Star of the West* preventing it from providing supplies to Fort Sumter; Fort Sumter had been fired upon and surrendered to the Confederate Army; and a few small skirmishes had occurred; however, no major battle had yet taken place, but both sides knew it was imminent.

On July 18, 1861, Union Army cannons trained at the buildings of Yorkshire scored a direct hit on the chimney of McLean's kitchen. In his memoirs, Beauregard recalled the incident:

"A comical effect of this artillery fight (which added a few casualties to both lists) was the destruction of the dinner of myself and staff by a Federal shell that fell into the fireplace of my headquarters at the McLean House."

Edward P. Alexander, Beauregard's chief signal officer was present at Yorkshire and witnessed the event:

"My spy glass showed me everything as clearly as if I were quite close to them & I watched with great interest...They loaded three or four guns, taking quite a time at aiming very carefully & then they fired all three simultaneously & in about five seconds all three arrived shrieking in chorus. One ploughed into the ground close by the house, one smashed into a corn & cob grinding machine standing in the yard & a third... came directly through the kitchen, a large log cabin close by the house in which our headquarters' servants were just dishing up a dinner they had cooked for us. Fortunately not a soul was touched. But there was a general stampede of all the houses hitched about the yard & an ambulance or two standing around & of a good many miscellaneous people... our dinner was ruined by the mud daubing between the logs jarred out as the shell passed through both walls falling into the sliced up meat & dished up vegetables."

A few days later in the aftermath of the First Battle of Bull Run, Yorkshire was used as a hospital and a place to temporarily hold captured soldiers (and a member of Congress). New York Congressman Alfred Ely, who had gone to Manassas to watch the battle (like many others) was captured and eventually held in Richmond's Libby Prison by Confederates as a prisoner of war for six months.

To get far away from the war, McLean and his family left Manassas and settled in the hamlet of Appomattox Court House. In about the summer of 1862, the McLeans purchased the Raine House, an Appomattox residence built in 1848 by Charles Raine, which had been on the market for several years.

Finally almost four years after the First Battle in Manassas, the fighting was just about over: "There is nothing left for me to do but to go and see General Grant, and I would rather die a thousand deaths," lamented General Lee. In the early afternoon of April 9, 1865, Palm Sunday, Lee visited General Grant. Arrangements to use the house had been made earlier that day at about 2:00 a.m. when McLean was approached to help find a suitable venue. Generals Robert E. Lee and Ulysses Grant met in McLean's living room and agreed to the surrender terms that essentially ended the Civil War.

Immediately afterwards there was a "spirited auction" in which many of the house furnishings were taken away, by theft or sale. McLean claimed the furnishings were stolen by Union soldiers; the soldiers claimed they purchased them. Union General Philip H. Sheridan was said to have purchased for $20 in gold the table on which the surrender agreement was signed. Sylvanus Cadwallader of the *New York Herald* reported General George A. Custer paid $25 for another table.

> "Officers then began forcing money into McLean's hands, but McLean threw it back. Suddenly there was a rush, and the furniture was gone. Cane-bottomed chairs were ruthlessly cut to pieces, the cane splits broken into pieces a few inches long, and parceled out among those who swarmed around. Haircloth upholstery was cut from chairs, and sofas were also cut into strips and patches carried away."

The chairs of which Generals Lee and Grant sat on are now at the National Museum of American History. Immediately after the surrender, both chairs were seized by officers under General Custer.

An oval table on which Grant wrote the terms of the agreement ended up afterward with General Custer. Almost fifty years later Custer's wife donated it to the Smithsonian Institution. General Edward Ord took the marble–top table in which Lee signed the surrender. Twenty-tow years later, Ord's wife obtained a letter of authenticity for the table from none other than General Grant's wife. With that certificate, a buyer in Chicago purchased the desk (with its marble slab broken) for $1,000. It is now at the Chicago Historical Society.

According to a post-war recollection of General E. P. Alexander:

"When I first joined the Army of Northern Virginia in 1861, I found a connection of my family, Wilmer McLean living on a fine farm through which ran Bull Run, with a nice farmhouse about opposite the center of our line of battle along that stream. General Beauregard made his headquarters at this house during the first affair between the armies—the so-called battle of Blackburn's Ford, on July 18. The first hostile shot which I ever saw fired was aimed at this house, and about the third or fourth went through its kitchen, where our servants were cooking dinner for the headquarters staff.

I had not seen or heard of McLean for years, when [April 10], the day after the surrender, I met him at Appomattox Courthouse, and asked with some surprise what he was doing there. He replied, with much indignation: "What are you doing here? These armies tore my place on Bull Run all to pieces, and kept running over it backward and forward till no man could live there, so I just sold out and came here, two hundred miles away, hoping I should never see a soldier again. And now, just look around! Not a fence-rail is left on the place, the last guns trampled down all my crops, and Lee surrenders to Grant in my house." McLean was so indignant that I felt bound to apologize for our coming back, and to throw all the blame for it upon the gentlemen on the other side."

According to Wilmer McLean's son-in law: "I have heard Mrs. McLean say frequently that the Union troops not only stole the tables and chairs besides other small furniture, but even took the children's' play things." One of those play things was seven-year-old Lula McLean's rag doll, "lovingly handmade by a doting mother... The younger officers tossed [it] from one to the other, and called [it] the silent witness."

The April 22, 1950 edition of the *Saturday Evening Post* featured a story about the McLean House in Appomattox. The story ended with the sentence: "Where Lula's rag doll is, nobody knows-but dolls have a way of turning up unexpectedly." Sure enough, forty-two years later, in 1992, the doll turned up. It had been taken by a captain on General Sheridan's staff. The doll, along with some original furniture has been donated to Appomattox Court House National Historical Park and is now on display. (Replicas of the rag doll are offered for sale at the gift shop.)

After the furnishings were taken by soldiers, souvenir seekers took everything else from the house, including the bricks. With the surrender, the Confederacy and its currency died and McLean's wealth became an enormous heap of worthless paper.

McLean's "Surrender House" was foreclosed and sold at public auction in 1869 for $3,060. In 1891, Myron Dunlap, a Niagara Falls, New York investor, bought the house and land for $10,000 with the intention of dismantling and rebuilding it for Chicago's 1893 World Columbian Exposition, or as a Washington, DC tourist attraction. The house was disassembled in 1893, but the "Appomattox Surrender House and National War Museum" never rebuilt the house anywhere. The original dismantled parts of the house either rotted in the elements or were taken by souvenir hunters.

General Joshua Chamberlain, who had been in charge of the Appomattox surrender parade in April 1865 visited the house in 1903. He noted it was "torn down and left a dismal heap of ruin."

Congress subsequently appropriated $100,000 in 1930 to acquire the land and rebuild the house. The house was rebuilt at the same location as the former residence by the same firm that had dismantled it -C. W. Hancock & Sons. Flooring and paneling from other old houses were used. The new house opened to the public on April 9, 1949. In attendance at the dedication ceremony were Ulysses S. Grant III and Robert E. Lee IV. Pulitzer Prize winner Dr. Douglas Southall Freeman gave the dedication speech before a crowd of about 20,000.

McLean's Yorkshire house is gone, and unlike the Appomattox house, it has never been rebuilt. What's left of the foundation of the building lies quietly under an unmarked mound of earth and rubble, with several old rusted automobiles in the backyard of a dilapidated house in the Yorkshire subdivision of Manassas. The occupant of the house as well as several neighbors were contacted and asked if they were aware of the historical significance of their neighborhood. One did.

Bobby Williams knew of McLean and mentioned that relic hunters with metal detectors sometimes show up in his yard. He usually gives them permission to use their detectors as long as they bring an extra detector for his thirteen-year old son Beau. Mr. Williams said these hunts often turn up bullets, buckles and other souvenirs.

There is a historical marker next to a CVS Pharmacy along Route 28 in Manassas, erected in 1988, pointing out the significance of the McLean House.

Through his friendship with Colonel John S. Mosby, McLean obtained federal employment after the war as a "gauger" for the Internal Revenue and later as an inspector with the U.S. Bureau of Customs.

McLean assisted the Confederacy and sold goods to them but did not appear to have served in any military capacity. Interestingly however, both E. P. Alexander and John S. Mosby referred to him as Major McLean.

Wilmer McLean and Robert E. Lee probably knew each other as children in Alexandria. October 16, 1824 would have found them eagerly awaiting and cheering the arrival of the famed French General

Lafayette, who visited Alexandria that day during his year-long tour of America.

Virginia was Wilmer McLean's wife. She lived with him at Yorkshire and Appomattox. But she did not just live at Yorkshire. She owned it. Exclusively. She had inherited the property from her father and had a lawyer draft an iron-clad pre-nuptial agreement, signed the day before her marriage to Wilmer to legally maintain the property for her sole and exclusive use and enjoyment. So the Civil War did not start in Wilmer McLean's house at all. It started at Virginia Hooe Mason McLean's house.

> This Indenture made and entered into this 18ᵗʰ day of January 1853...Whereas a marriage is intended to be had and solemnized between the said Virginia B. Mason and the said Wilmer McLean and it has been agreed between them that notwithstanding the happening of such marriage the said Virginia shall thereafter hold, possess and enjoy to her sole and separate use...and subject to her sole disposition all the estate real and personal to which she is entitled in any right whatsoever...[including] a tract of land situated in said County of Prince William called <u>Yorkshire</u> estimated to contain twelve hundred acres.

After the war Wilmer and Virginia McLean moved to Alexandria and lived at the corner of Pitt and Wolfe Streets next to the grounds of Christ Episcopal Church; they were so close in fact that "there was a turnstile between them, so family members could merely step from their garden into the church premises." They are buried in St. Paul's Episcopal Cemetery in Alexandria, Virginia. The June 7, 1882, edition of the *Alexandria Gazette* mentioned Wilmer McLean's death, but not his connection to the war.

On August 11, 1885, Virginia sold her remaining 302 ¾ acres of the Yorkshire property to Robert Portner for $2,700. This is the same Robert Portner who started a brewery in Alexandria early in the war. At Portner's death in 1906, his Manassas estate, "Annaburg," totaled approximately 2,000 acres.

Virginia died on August 26, 1893:

Death of Mrs. McLean- Mrs. Virginia B. McLean, widow of the late Wilmer McLean, formerly of this city, and at whose house the surrender of Gen. Lee at Appomattox, took place, died at Camden, W. Va., on Saturday.

The 27th Michigan Regiment's Fighting Indian

Indians have fought in all American wars. The National Archives magazine *Prologue* recently published a story stating that a group of eleven Delaware Indians served together in the same company during the Revolutionary War. In the War of 1812, more than 1,000 Indians served. The Civil War was no exception.

President Lincoln is reported to have thanked God for Michigan soldiers when he remarked they were born "ready-made" for war. Perhaps the most ready-made were the Indians who comprised Company K of the 1st Michigan Sharpshooters. This full company of Indians was described as "nearly all tall and good looking fellows... the stuff...of which good sharpshooters can be easily made."

It took awhile, however, for the Government to notice and accept the Indians as a fighting force. Early in the war, a Chippewa Indian and Methodist minister named George Copway offered to raise from the Great Lakes Region a regiment of "young men, inured to hardship, fleet as deers (sic), shrewd and cautious." He proposed the men would "not be employed for using the tomahawk or scalping knife upon the people of the South but as scouts and runners for the army."

In time the Indians showed their wartime skills and were highly commended: They were reported to have carried "some of the deadliest rifles in the regiment." They seemed "all the go," and always stirred interest and excitement wherever they went. Although they generally kept to themselves, they were very much respected as "the best skirmishers in the division."

They were characterized as "typical English dudes" who, among other traits, had a unique ability to avoid capture, as expressed by one Confederate: "When driven into the open...they ran like deer. We captured not one of them."

The Indians brought many of their unique customs to the battlefield, including a tradition, noted by a Union soldier, on the subject of death: they pulled their shirts over their faces and chanted their death song as they died "a long way from the cool air and giant whispering pines of Michigan's North Country."

One interesting tale involves Michael White, born and raised on the St. Regis Indian Reservation near Hogansburg, Franklin County, New York. In October 1861, twenty-five Saint Regis Indians enlisted in the 98th New York Infantry, but White was not included. A few years earlier, at about age eighteen, White had left New York and moved to Michigan. It is not known why he made the move but at the time many people from upstate New York moved to Michigan for job opportunities in the iron ore mining industry. Years later a cousin named Jake Billings recalled White's departure from New York:

> "The soldier lived here when he was a boy...and then went off to Montreal and then went over towards Chicago, in Michigan I think, but I do not know what cities he went to... he [later] told me where he had been after he left here and before he enlisted, but I do not remember the name of the place, but it was where they fish and catch herring on Lake Michigan, or somewhere along there...he told me he was with a gang of workmen who were surveying out land in Michigan."

White enlisted on January 26, 1864 in Marquette, Michigan with Company B of Michigan's 27th Infantry Regiment. Sixty years after the war, soldiers from Michigan's Upper Peninsula were honored with a monument, inscribed with this inspiring poem, written by Mrs. De Verrah Myers of Jackson, Michigan:

Columbia ever will know you,

From her glittering towers:
And kisses of love will throw you,
And send you wreaths of flowers.

Ever in the realms of glory,
Shall shine your starry fame;
Angels have heard your story,
God knows all your names.

During the Battle of Weldon Railroad in Virginia in August 1864, White suffered a gunshot wound to the mouth. The injury left him with only four teeth: two molars on the right upper jaw and two incisors on the left lower jaw. He was sent to City Point Hospital to recover where he stayed nine days. Later pension records reveal that he suffered deafness, impaired vision and chronic inflammation of the throat. Predictably, the surgeon determined the soldier's poor health was attributable to the gunshot wound and not "vicious habits." (Pension applications required doctors to address whether the medical impairments resulted from military service or personal behavior.)

After the war, Michael returned to New York's St. Regis Reservation rather than Michigan. He married a woman named Hannah who was about his age and who had grown up with him on the reservation. Several years later, on March 7, 1908, Michael died. Hannah White promptly made a claim to collect his $15 military pension but the government denied the request because no record of the marriage existed.

Difficulties in proving marriages were not uncommon. The subject was addressed by a congressman who said:

"After meeting the soldier, going through a ceremonial marriage with him, and living with him in the ostensible relation of husband and wife for a long period of time, she is called upon after the death to prove whether her husband had ever been married before, and, if so, what had become of the former wife or wives...years ago, in many localities, the records of marriages and deaths were imperfectly kept and in many cases no such records can be found. It has been found that many widows who have lived with their soldier husbands almost for a lifetime, have raised families, and been recognized as the lawful wives of the soldiers during all those years find it now impossible to prove their marriage by record evidence, or to prove…the time of their marriage, many years ago…the Committee believes that where it is shown that an applicant for widow's pension had lived and cohabited with the soldier, and been generally recognized as his wife. For 20 years or more preceding his death such proof should be sufficient to establish the fact that she is his lawful widow, providing, of course, that she has not remarried since his death."

The United States Bureau of Pensions then conducted an investigation to determine if Hannah and Michael White were married. Special Examiner Edward C. Miller was assigned the case.

Miller interviewed several neighbors and family members, taking depositions from each. Each claimed they believed the Whites had been married and never divorced. Documentation, however, could not be found.

Hannah, who could not read or write, provided her statement through an interpreter. She had previously been married to a man named Frank Terrance, who died shortly before her marriage to Michael White: "I do not remember just what year it was that I was married to the soldier [Michael White], but it was just about seven months after my first husband [Frank Terrance] had died, and it was in the month of May." Hannah testified that Michael often left home, sometimes for several months or years. She said he was a basket-maker and often traveled to sell baskets. When she did know where he was, she had her son help out to bring him home: "I often sent my boy to have him come home, but he would not, because he did not like it that I was a Protestant and he was a Catholic."

When asked whether there was ever a divorce she stated, "No, I never knew or heard of any divorce the soldier [Michael White] obtained from me. I do not think he ever had enough money to get one anywhere, as he drank up all the money he could get."

Frank Terrance Jr., Hannah's son and Michael White's step-son was interviewed. Terrance explained what he knew about how his mother and stepfather got married:

"My father [Frank Terrance] died in the fall, and then in the following summer my mother married the soldier, who was generally called Mitchel White, but some called him Michael White. No, I was not present when my mother married Michael White, but I well remember that the day he married her. I was working for John McCabe, who is still living about a mile and a half from Colton, and who then lived next neighbor [sic] to where my father [Terrance] died. Michael White came to me to borrow five dollars, and I loaned him the five dollars and the next day I heard that he had married my mother and they told me they had got married by a Justice of the Peace near there who was also a farmer, but I do not know the name of the Justice...No, there never was any divorce obtained between my step-father and my mother, so far as I know. He would go off and stay away for six months at a time, and he died when he was below Hogansburg away from home a year ago last winter, and was buried in St. Regis Catholic burying ground."

Special Examiner Miller concluded his investigation in June 1909 with a cover letter summarizing the evidence. Despite the lack of documentation of a marriage or divorce, he concluded that, based on witness testimony, Michael and Hannah White were most likely married. In addition, he remarked that common law marriages were "perfectly good" in New York before 1902.

Miller's century-old remarks in the report make for interesting reading. He opined that it would be difficult to locate witnesses with knowledge of Michael White because "the soldier, like many Indians, drank all the liquor he could hold, and was away from home nearly all the time after the first ten years of the marriage."

Furthermore, if any friends could be found they would not be much help: "The memory of Indians as to dates is very poor, and also of names, but they appear to be as a class, very conscientious in regard to their statements, all of which substantially agree." Miller then ruled out the likelihood that White might have told any of his friends from the 27th Michigan about his marriage: "Indians are not talkative, and I doubt if any comrade would have learned anything definite as to the soldier's marriage."

The 27th Michigan Regiment Quells a Race Riot

In March 1863, the 27th Michigan Infantry was sent to Detroit to quell a race riot. In circumstances eerily familiar and destined to repeat itself many times, a riot erupted over the white-hot emotions of race outside a Detroit courtroom. The March 9, 1863 article in the *New York Daily Tribune*, titled "The Great Riot in Detroit" announced: "Thirty-Two Houses Destroyed. 200 People Rendered Houseless. Terrible Scenes of Fiendishness. Innocent Persons Murdered in Cold Blood. Quiet Restored by Military Power." And that was just the headlines. The story reported: "With commendable promptness, at nine o'clock, a detachment of the 27th Michigan, consisting of Companies A, B, C, F, and G, numbering about 400 men, under command of Colonel Fox and Lieut. Colonel Richardson, arrived and reported at headquarters. They were immediately sent to the scene of the riot to disperse the crowd…The 27th was divided into eight patrol squads, properly officered and provided with ammunition." Within hours the rioting had ceased, but for careful measure, "the 27th Regiment will remain in town for several days, or until the excitement dies away, to prevent a fresh outbreak of any disturbance." The riot resulted from a mob of angry whites which wanted to take out their own style of vigilante justice against a black man who was on trial for (unspecified) offenses against a white woman.

The *Detroit Free Press* reported the riot occurred as the defendant, a black man named Faulkner, was being transported back to his jail cell after the trial. Faulkner, "who was claimed to be a negro (and who) ran a saloon on Cadillac square," was the target of the mob hostility largely because of hatred stirred up by a *Free Press* reporter who "wrote the case up in vigorous style, calculated to create sentiment for the girl. It had the desired effect." Fortunately, the 27th Michigan Regiment was able to quell the rioters. Unfortunately, Faulkner was convicted and served time in prison based on evidence that the main witness (the unidentified woman) later recanted.

First Woman on
American Currency

When the final words have been printed in the book of *Firsts for American Women*, many pages will be devoted to famous pathfinders like Sandra Day O'Connor, Jeanette Rankin, Sally Ride and Virginia Dare. In addition, with a chapter of her own, will be a little-known woman named Lucy Petway Holcombe Pickens. Rappers and teens talk today of their desire to acquire "Benjamins," a reference to Benjamin Franklin's image on the face of the $100 bill, but move these folks back fifteen decades, put them in eleven Southern States and their monetary aspirations might have been to get the "Lucys." Lucy, as in Lucy Petway Holcombe Pickens, the first woman to have a facsimile of her face on the obverse of currency with the word America on it.

Lucy was on $100 and $1 bills printed and circulated by the Confederate States of America during the Civil War. Why her image was selected is unclear. It may have been because the CSA Treasury printed its money in Columbia, South Carolina, where at that time, the lovely, charming, Lucy was living. With nicknames like the Rose of Texas and the Queen of the Confederacy (makes you wonder what Jefferson Davis's wife thought of that!), it's no wonder people took notice of her. Varina Davis, perhaps the most likely other woman to be on the currency, was at that time in Richmond, Virginia, two states and 300 miles away. It's likely the decision was made by Christopher Memminger, CSA Secretary of the Treasury, a good friend of Lucy and her husband. Perhaps the CSA Treasurer, Edward Elmore had a role in the decision. Certainly the impulsive Elmore was just erratic enough to put Lucy on the bill instead of Mrs. Davis. Before the war was out, he had challenged and faced a Richmond newspaper editor in a duel.

But that's getting ahead of the story. In August 1851, a decade before the war started, nineteen-year-old Lucy had her heart broken when her true love, William Crittenden of Kentucky, was killed in Cuba in an unsuccessful expedition to free that country from Spanish tyrants. Things down south really went south for Lieutenant Crittenden, who was executed by a barbaric method of slow strangulation. His fifty men fared slightly better-- they were all killed by firing squad.

As this was at about the same time that *Uncle Tom's Cabin* was furiously pumping emotions around the country, Lucy decided to pen a novel about the failed mission, glamorizing its objective and heralding its noble cause. Called the *Free Flag of Cuba,* and penned under the pseudonym H. M. Hardimann, Lucy barely concealed the characters of herself and Crittenden. Whether she made money from it is unknown, but it probably helped through her grief.

Many believed her winning personality as exemplary to the South, but others saw nothing but wily and cunning motives. Famed Southern diarist Mary Boykin Chestnut, Lucy's neighbor in Columbia, South Carolina, confided caustic thoughts about Lucy, including an entry early in the war when she wrote Lucy, "is very clever but affects silly, fine lady airs, for reasons of her own--& it seems to pay." Mary Chestnut clearly reveled in Lucy's faux pas when Lucy complained publicly that Jefferson Davis always sent men originally from the North to command at Charleston. Unbeknownst to Lucy, the Confederate officer standing next to her (General Cooper) and listening intently, had been born in the North. You can almost feel Chestnut's elation when another person in the room casually tells Lucy that General Cooper was born in New York. "Sudden silence," Chestnut added, probably smiling as she wrote the words.

Lucy's marriage at the age of twenty-five to the very powerful and very rich Francis W. Pickens of South Carolina was about moving up the social registry. In the 1860 census, Pickens reported $300,000 worth of assets, not including plantations in Mississippi and Alabama and 300 slaves. That wealth made the fifty-three-year-old Pickens quite a catch. Lucy confided in a letter to her mother that she was marrying Pickens to pay off her father's debts.

Perhaps the reason she was selected to be on the $100 bill was because of how aggressively and energetically she supported the Confederate cause. She worked so tirelessly that a group of South Carolina soldiers called themselves the Holcombe Legion in her honor.

The Confederate Treasury also issued $500 and $1,000 bills. On the $500 bill was Thomas "Stonewall" Jackson; on the $1,000 were John Calhoun and Andrew Jackson. Other Confederate currency bore likenesses of George Washington, George Randolph, Jefferson Davis, Alexander Stephens, Francis Marion, Robert Mercer Taliaferro Hunter, Christopher Memminger, Judah Benjamin (back to the Benjamins!), Clement Clay and John Ward. Numerous Goddesses also appeared on the money including Minerva (Goddess of Peace), Ceres (Agriculture and civilization), Themis (Justice), Tellus (Earth), Proserpina (Vegetation), and Cupid (Love).

Shortly after the war ended, a Major A. S. Jones of Aberdeen, Mississippi traveled with several other Confederate officers to Richmond to arrange transportation home. While in Richmond, the officers chanced into meeting a Miss Anna Rush, a Northerner who happened to be visiting. Miss Rush had a stack of Confederate notes with her which she planned to take home as souvenirs. She distributed the notes to the Confederate officers and asked each to write something on the back. Major Jones wrote the following poem on the back of his note. Miss Rush eventually had it published in the New York Metropolitan Record under the title *Something Too Good To Be Lost*. Years later, Tyler's Quarterly Magazine republished it:

Representing nothing on God's earth now,
And naught in the waters below it,
As the pledge of a nation that's dead and gone,
Keep it, dear friend, and show it.
Show it to those who will lend an ear
To the tale that this paper can tell
Of the liberty born of the patriot's dream,
Of a storm-cradled nation that fell.

Too poor to possess the precious ores,
And too much of a stranger to borrow,
We issued to-day our promise to pay,
And hoped to redeem on the morrow.
But days flew by, weeks became years,
Our coffers were empty still;
Coin was so scarce our treasury'd quake,
If a dollar would drop in the till.

We knew it had scarcely a value in gold,
Yet as gold the soldiers received it;
It looked in our eyes a promise to pay,
And each patriot believed it.
But the faith that was in us was strong indeed,
And our poverty well we discerned;
And these little checks represented the pay
That our suffering veterans earned.

But our boys thought little of prize or pay,
Or of bills that were overdue;
We knew if it bought our bread to-day
'Twas the best our poor country could do.
Keep it, it tells our history over
From the birth of the dream to the last;
Modest and born of the angels' hope,
Like our hope of success it passed.

After the war, Lucy founded the Maxcy Gregg Chapter of the United Daughters of the Confederacy; today the UDC chapter in Denton, Texas is named for her. Even the Daughters of the American Revolution picked up on her efforts-the Washington DC Chapter of the DAR called themselves the Lucy Holcombe Chapter.

Lucy died in August 1899 in Edgefield, South Carolina. A few years before she died, the United States Treasury printed and circulated dollars (silver certificates) bearing the image of Martha Washington.

Confederados in Brazil

Texas fever! Mexico fever! Brazilian fever! Plagued with economic ruin, psychological terror and personal tragedy at the end of the Civil War, many Southerners found themselves, to borrow an expression from Charles Dickens, "standing among the crowded ghosts of many miserable years." They began to discuss the subject of packing up their war-torn lives and emigrating to foreign lands as an antidote for their suffering.

Southern diarist Mary Boykin Chestnut wrote about Confederate officers going to Mexico and Brazil, and Scarlett O'Hara twice considered the idea of fleeing to Latin America in the epic novel *Gone with the Wind*. One Southern girl confided in her diary: "The men are all talking about going to Mexico and Brazil." Another penned the same theme: "There is complete revulsion in public feeling. No more talk about help from France or England, but all about emigration to Mexico or Brazil. We are irretrievably ruined." One man summed it up for many Southerners: "You folks made our lives so impossible in the United States that we had to leave."

Making them feel compelled to leave was the near-certainty of many dismal years well into the future thanks to vitriolic Northerners who seized control of the government after Lincoln's death like Edwin Stanton, James Blaine and Thaddeus Stevens. Bent on retribution, they "waved the bloody shirt" (the continual efforts to stir up pro-Union, anti-Confederate legislation and voting), relentlessly hammering Confederates who were desperately trying to recover from Sherman and four years of war. In 1868, the 14th Amendment to the Constitution made it illegal for former Confederate officers to hold any state or federal position in the United States. It is no wonder so many felt like exiles and strangers in their own homes. Northern carpetbaggers were banging at the door, clamoring to strip away what few remnants remained of their wretched lives.

Those lives of seemingly endless despair motivated many to relocate. So an estimated three million of them abandoned their homes in the former Confederate States. They moved all over, to Texas, out west and even to northern states. And in one of the more shameful episodes of the era, many left the United States altogether, despite the language difficulties, the distance and the expense, never to return.

Many migrated to Mexico, Canada, England (pro-Confederacy during the war), Venezuela, or numerous other foreign locations. But the most popular country of Southern emigration was Brazil. Southerners were energized with the favorable news that Brazil rolled out welcome mats for them, provided cheap land, and for good measure threw in cheering crowds, parties and serenades. It was almost too good to be true, but adventurers such as the scientist Mathew Fontaine Maury had already scouted out Latin America years earlier and had written extensively about its benefits. ("The Amazon," he wrote, "reminds us of the Mississippi…Its climate an everlasting summer and its harvest perennial.") A popular ditty about such a move went:

Oh, give me a ship with a sail and with wheel,
And let me be off to happy Brazil!
Home of the sunbeam—great kingdom of Heat,
With woods ever green and snakes forty feet!
Land of the diamond—bright nation of pearls,
With monkeys aplenty, and Portuguese girls!

Oh, give me a ship with a sail and with wheel,
And let me be off to happy Brazil.
I yearn to feel her perpetual spring,
And shake by the hand Dom Pedro her king,

Kneel at his feet—call him, "My Royal Boss!"
And receive in return, "Welcome, Old Hoss!"

Brazil had officially been neutral during the war but made no secret that it sympathized with the Confederacy. They had harbored and supplied Southern ships (including those running Yankee blockades) and had refused Union demands to treat Southern ships as pirates.

With an open border, Brazilian Emperor Dom Pedro II welcomed the Southerners' technical expertise and determination. He hoped they would make Brazil the major cotton supplier to Britain. He had agents meet with prospective colonizers at offices in New York and Washington. He subsidized passage, made land available very cheap, provided free temporary housing, and accelerated and simplified the naturalization process. In 1866 a group of Brazilians established the International Society of Immigration to encourage legislation for new and beneficial immigration programs. Numerous colonization groups were established to assist the Southerners. Here is a notice from one group:

Emigration to Brazil!

Notice to members of the Pioneer Colony of Major Hastings. Members of the Colony will take notice that the Colony will sail from Mobile, Ala., on the 1st Day of December, next. A commodious sailing ship of ample tonnage with comfortable accommodations for at least 500 passengers will be provided. Heads of families and single persons will pay $30 each; other members of families over 12 will pay $20 each; and children between 2 and 12, $10 each; which payment will be made in gold coin. Families will be allowed one ton, and single persons 200 pounds of freight, free of charge.

The present destination of the Colony is the City of Para, on the Amazon, its ultimate location, on a tributary of that river between five and ten degrees latitude. Length of voyage 2,000 miles, sailing time about three weeks.

Planters should take their farming utensils, mechanics their tools. Families should take tents and all should provide themselves with provisions for about six months.

A former Alabama cotton grower encouraged others in 1868: "Move here and buy land, which you can do on four year's credit, at twenty-two cents per acre, better than I ever saw anywhere in the United States even in the richest portions of Alabama...Bring with you all tools you can, as yours are generally better than can be bought here. Bring all your household furniture except very heavy articles of wood. Bring as many kinds of seed as you can, fig and grape cuttings...With what means you have don't fear to start...If you can bring any number of such families as your own, I can safely guarantee them homes, and plenty of land for which Providence has done more than for any other I have ever seen or heard of. (I have almost forgiven our enemies all their wrongs, on account of the better country to which they forced me.) We have here a beautiful place for our village, in the center of rich land, and on a grand river...This is mid-summer, thermometer at 85 ranging through the year from 95 to 65. We are twenty-five miles from the sea, and have a daily breeze from the Atlantic. There are now about twenty families here, and before you can join us, shall have a steamer on the river."

Nearly all Southern newspapers rallied against the exodus, knowing the loss of citizens (today it is referred to as "brain-drain") to be harmful to society. General Robert E. Lee and former President of the Confederacy Jefferson Davis vociferously urged against it.

Despite these protests by Southern newspapers and leaders and the difficulties of starting new lives, many went to Brazil. They planned to stay and usually did. By 1867, one Brazilian newspaper reported that it seemed like Confederados were living on every block of Rio de Janeiro. Their letters back home to friends and newspapers were positive. Emigrants wrote of a perfect climate, "neither too hot nor cold, and where frost is never known, water as cold as the mountain spring, and so equally distributed as to allow every man to run his plantation machinery from it. Here also everything grows, and grows well." Another wrote, "The war worn soldier, the bereaved parent, the oppressed patriot, the homeless and despoiled, can find refuge from the trials which beset them, and a home not haunted by the eternal remembrance of harrowing scenes of sorrow and death." Although slavery still existed in Brazil at the time, the great majority of Southerners who emigrated were pleased simply to have found comfortable new homes.

They became known as Confederados and quickly gained a reputation for honesty and hard work. They adapted and set up communities, including those known today as Americana and Florida. They have frequent gatherings and celebrations, including some where women dress in antebellum gowns and men in gray uniforms similar to the type worn by their ancestors. Many Brazilians still carry names like Lee, Jefferson and Washington. In fact, the most popular Brazilian singer in 1984 was named Rita Lee. They learned Portuguese but often continued to speak English at home and at gatherings with other Confederados. Georgia Governor Jimmy Carter visited in 1972; both he and his press secretary remarked how the Confederados sounded and seemed just like Southerners.

Recently, Ms. Anne Keene posted an Internet website for people interested in this Brazilian exodus: www.confederates-brazil.com.

Shortly after the Civil War, a Brazilian newspaper printed this poem, with the reasons for making the move:

With what joy our hearts were burning
As we gazed upon the bay,
On a bright and glorious morning,
Just two years ago today!

Round us lay a scene more charming
Than our dreams of Fairyland,
And our breasts with rapture warming
Throbbed with feelings deep and grand.

Thought we of the cause we cherished,
Of its short but glorious reign,
How our heroes fought & perished,
Died for us, alas, in vain!

Then we thought how foul submission
Stained a once untarnished name,
Of our sad oppressed condition,
Of our bitterness and shame.

Then we fondly blessed the nation
Which with pity 'cross the sea'
Looked upon our abject station,
Welcomed us and made us free.

Many changes have come o'er us,
Weeks & months have passed away,
Toils & hardships are before us,
But we'll n'er forget that day.

Still its thrill magnetic feeling,
Onward we our course pursue,
Thus ourselves for action steeling,
We will build our homes anew.

And we bless the glorious nation,
That unto our rescue came,
Saved us from humiliation,
From oppression and from shame.

For the kindness she extended,
In our days of direst ill,
To a people unbefriended,
May God ever bless Brazil!

General William T. Sherman Monument

In October 1903, before the first slab of marble was placed at the Lincoln Memorial and before the 46th star was sewn on the American flag, a fifty-foot monument to commemorate the life of General William T. Sherman was unveiled on Fifteenth Street, a block from the White House. Efforts to erect the monument to the man who made Georgia howl began within months of Sherman's death on February 14, 1891 at age 71. By an Act of Congress, 12,000 copies of *Sherman, A Memorial in Art, Oratory, and Literature* were printed and bound in 1904, providing a full report of the ceremony. The final product, consisting of 410 wonderfully detailed pages, reported the solemnity of the occasion with photographs and text.

Originally announced on March 22, 1895, an open competition offered $90,000 to the winning sculptor. Sculptors based in Chicago, New York, Saint Louis, Washington and Paris submitted twenty-three designs. Carl Rohl-Smith, a fifty-year-old who had moved from his native Denmark to Chicago in the early 1880s won. But before he could finish the project, the Dane's luck ran out during a trip for rest and relaxation back to Denmark. Rohl-Smith fell victim to an illness and died. The project however, had progressed so well by that point that his wife's request to complete it was granted.

On October 15th, Master William Tecumseh Sherman Thorndike, the young grandson of the famed general, performed the honors by pulling the unveiling cord, immediately followed by the firing of seventeen guns "trumpets sounding three flourishes, drums beating three ruffles, and the assemblage cheering vociferously." The assemblage included President Theodore Roosevelt and approximately 1,100 dignitaries and guests invited by members of the Sherman Statue Commission. The statue, Sherman riding his horse, was indeed impressive. The bas-reliefs on each of the monument's four sides suggested an episode in Sherman's life: The March through Georgia, Sherman at the campfire, Missionary Ridge, and facing southward: the Battle of Atlanta.

President Roosevelt spoke boldly of the greatness of Sherman as well as "the men who did the mighty deeds," the heroism of all soldiers. "We need their ruggedness of body, their keen and vigorous minds, and above all their dominant quality of forceful character. Their lives teach us in our own lives to strive after not the thing which is merely pleasant, but the thing which is our duty to do. The life of duty, not the life of mere ease or mere pleasure, that is the kind of life which makes the great man as it makes the great nation."

Another speaker, General Charles Grosvenor of Ohio lamented there was nothing original left to say about Sherman: "When death, the great destroyer, swept him off the stage of action he became the subject of almost universal eulogy...Turn as you will, study as you may, think as you can, and the world would pronounce you a genius if you, by any result of study or accident of the hour, said something new of Sherman. There was no phase of his character, striking or commonplace, lovable or unbeloved, great or small...that has not been discussed elaborately and minutely."

The impressively bound volume listed the day's events, including the parade, the seating assignment for the dignitaries, and a biography of Sherman's life. When he was nine years old, long before he gave Savannah, Georgia to President Lincoln as a Christmas present, the future hero, upon the death of his father, had been sent to live with Senator Ewing of Ohio.

In 1840 he graduated 6th out of forty-three in his West Point class, having missed a higher ranking because of numerous demerits. His legendary military career culminated in the position of Commander of the Army from March 1869 until November 1883.

If Sherman had any interest, he would have easily been elected President of the United States. Numerous party leaders urged him to accept the 1884 presidential nomination. Sherman adamantly declined: "I will not in any event entertain or accept a nomination as the candidate for president by the Chicago Republican convention nor any other convention."

The commemoration book noted some reasons Sherman was so admired: "His brusqueness of manner and bluntness of speech were an incongruous manifestation of a heart as tender as a woman's. The very twinkle of that keen eye put the stamp of gentleness itself upon his words. His wholesome humor again belied the bluntness of the soldier."

Simply put, he understood how to command soldiers and how to win at war. Americans loved General Sherman, and as for his troops, no one loved 'Uncle Billy' more. Even opposing officers liked him. Confederate General Joe Johnston, who surrendered his Army to Sherman two weeks after Appomattox, attended Sherman's funeral. Despite the inclement weather, he refused, as a sign of respect, to wear a hat. The 84-year old Johnston came down almost immediately with a cold and died the following month. There's no way to know, but one could imagine Johnston refusing to wear his hat that day even if he knew the consequences.

Book Review: Black Horse Cavalry, Defend our Beloved Country

By: Lewis Marshall Helm

"What a liar history is," wrote William Henry Fitzhugh Payne, lamenting that "the best & the noblest men of the war will die unknown." Payne, one of the principal founders of Fauquier County's Black Horse Cavalry Troop, then proceeded to assault the legendary reputation of the famed Gray Ghost of the Confederacy, Colonel John S. Mosby: "Raiding and guerilla warfare is but another name for shirking danger & hardship." These refreshingly opinionated and contrarian remarks are among the delightful morsels contained in the fifty-five short vignettes making up *Black Horse Cavalry: Defend our Beloved Country.*

The stories relate chronologically to the Black Horse Cavalry (BHC), "one of the most gallant, serviceable and picturesque contingents of the Army of Northern Virginia" from its inception on the anniversary of the Battle of Waterloo to post-war reunion camp meetings where old veterans reminisced and "where whiskey drowned out the ugly that no one wanted to see."

The stories are sometimes sad, often humorous, and always informative. The BHC, like many regiments in the War Between the States was made up of families and neighbors; at least fifty families had two or more members in the Black Horse. The author has Black Horse Cavalry in his heart and in his ancestry. In narrating its exploits, William Payne wrote, "no family had done more nobly than that of the Helm family." It sent four brothers to the BHC.

Prominently mentioned in the book is Payne, who was, simply put, a character. He got expelled from the Virginia Military Institute (what made him think he could lead a cavalry charge into the ranks of a cadet formation?) He survived several war wounds and imprisonments, most amazingly a gunshot to the face: "The ball which had wounded him had gone through his jaw, broken the bone, knocked out four teeth, and the ball and teeth had passed through the tongue and the ball had knocked out three more teeth on the other side, coming out near the jugular vein." Even more shocking was that while recuperating from the injury, with his jaw wired shut, he managed to capture two Union soldiers and transport them to Confederate guards.

In an unlucky stroke of exceptionally bad timing, he was sent to Washington as a prisoner a few days after the war ended and mistaken there for one of John Wilkes Booth's fellow conspirators. It was always a bad time for a Confederate to get sent as a prisoner to Washington, but especially bad the day after Lincoln died. All the awful battles and carnage of the war were nothing compared to the fury directed at Payne as he was led through Washington: "I am sure that I never passed through a more trying scene during the war. I never faced a more beastly and blood-thirsty set of savages."

The strength of the book rests on its ability to share the personal experiences of the "Terrible Black Horse" through heavy use of a rare treat: unpublished primary source material.

Payne is frequently quoted in the book. He wrote as passionately about the exploits of the BHC as he fought them. He quotes Napoleon and turns the opening sentence of Revolutionary War writer Thomas Paine's *American Crisis*: "I have seen moments when men's souls were tried."

Payne commended Jeb Stuart: "To criticize him is like finding spots on the sun;" complained about the lack of food: "3 crackers and a greasy spot a day," and even took a stab at a poem about the ephemeral nature of history:

"These humble lives which here I trace,
Years cannot change, nor age efface;
They may be read though valued not,
When the one who wrote them is forgot."

With Helm's book, the ones from Virginia who wore the black plume hats and rode the black horses are not forgotten.

Book Review:
Summers with Lincoln

By: James A. Percoco

"There is no new thing to be said of the mountains, or of the sea, or of the stars," observed Homer Hock, the guest speaker at the 1920 Annual Lincoln Dinner. He also remarked (and this was eighty-eight years ago) "there is no new thing to be said of Lincoln." Perhaps not. But there are still clever and informative ways to study the 16th president.

Hop aboard the Clio (the Muse of History) car for a delightful 241-page Lincoln road trip through DC, New Jersey, Ohio, Indiana and Illinois narrated by a Fairfax County high school teacher and featuring guest appearances by a Lincoln-loving Chinese tourist, several of the teacher's students and a group of Lincoln reenactors, proving, once again, that Lincoln is loved worldwide, roadumentaries can be fun as well as educational and Elvis is not the only American superstar with a ton of impersonators.

During the Civil War, Lincoln said if there was a place worse than Hell then he was in it. Today, almost a century and half later, he's everywhere. Roads, banks and schools, stamps, cities and money, a tunnel, an automobile, an insurance company and much more ubiquitously herald his name and image. In the movie *Mr. Smith Goes to Washington*, Jimmy Stewart has a line upon visiting *the* Lincoln Monument where he says, "there he is, just looking straight at you as you come up those steps. Just sitting there like he was waiting for somebody to come along." Of the more than 600 presidential memorials in America, at least 191 are dedicated to the man who (as of next February) came along 200 years ago.

In *Summers with Lincoln: Looking for the Man in the Monuments* James Percoco intrepidly explores the past to share the history of how seven of these monuments got constructed, what they meant to the sculptor and the public at their unveiling and what they mean to us today. Where history, politics and creativity meet is where you can reflect upon these artistic images in bronze. The word monument comes from Latin ('to remind') and means 'thought object' in German. The question of whether there is a right or wrong way to portray these thought objects has provoked intense debate and controversy. What should they look like and what happens when the sculptor's idea doesn't match the public's?

Most artists commanded effusive praise for their aesthetics, but one sculptor received the appreciative equivalent of a sharp poke in the eye. The hostility heaped upon George Grey Barnard for his monument in Cincinnati, Ohio's Lytle Park almost makes the reader cringe. Lincoln's son, Robert Lincoln charged Barnard had a "screw loose" for coming up with such a "grotesque likeness" and "beastly thing." *The New York Times* described the work as "a long-suffering peasant" and the editor of *Art World* characterized it as "a calamity and an atrocity" that made Lincoln look like a "stooped-shouldered, consumptive-chested, chimpanzee-headed, lumpy-footed, giraffe-necked, grimy-fingered clod-hopper." Simply, "a mistake in bronze." The reason for all this? Barnard dared to make his work more real than ideal. "Art, like history," the learned teacher instructs, "is not uncontested ground."

Once you get past questions like the dress and the pose, then the artists had to accurately depict the uniqueness of Lincoln's face, the off-center alignment of his nose and the fact that the right side of his face was more relaxed than the left. One sculptor believed Lincoln knew he looked better from the right side. Whether he knew or cared seems doubtful. When accused of being two-faced, the man whose countenance graces Mt. Rushmore retorted: "If I had another face, do you think I would wear this one?"

An admitted victim of hero-worship, Percoco deserves extra credit for including in this wonderful book something often ignored in Lincoln studies: a recitation of some of the flaws of the lawyer, politician and lobbyist (before the term was coined). As a lawyer Lincoln represented a slave owner trying to get his 'property' back; as a politician he could, as the author noted, "be Machiavellian when he needed to be." As president, he waffled on slavery, originally having no intention whatsoever to abolish it where it already existed. He shut down newspapers, destroyed printing presses and suspended habeas corpus.

We are warned to not elevate Lincoln to God-like status by the author who opines that we have created "a civil religion where Lincoln emerges as one of our venerated saints." He is loved almost everywhere. In the former Soviet Union, Lincoln placed 36th in a poll of the most influential people in history. Even in China, he (and Martin Luther King) are the most highly regarded Americans.

Secretary of War Edwin Stanton proclaimed Lincoln belonged to the ages. Former British Prime Minister David Lloyd George used a few more words to come to a similar conclusion: "He is one of those giant figures, of whom there are very few in history, who lose their nationality in death. They are no longer Greek, or Hebrew, or English, or American; they belong to mankind."

Book Review:
Alexandria Goes to War:
Beyond Robert E. Lee

By George Kundahl

In the book *Alexandria Goes to War: Beyond Robert E. Lee,* George Kundahl masterfully narrates the weal and woe, and some highs and lows of Anne Frobel and fifteen other Alexandrians, primarily from their diaries, letters and books to paint a vivid picture of what their city must have been like during the war.

"Come weal, come woe, my lot is cast with that of Virginia," wrote George Brent of Alexandria, despite knowing secession was "utter folly" and "national suicide."

This was an accomplished group with varied and unique experiences and exploits: Samuel Cooper, whose house and property were seized by the Union Army and ignominiously named Fort Traitor, wrote the military handbook *Concise System of Instructions and Regulations for the Militia and Volunteers of the United States* (popularly known as Cooper's Infantry Tactics).

Custis Lee bested his father by graduating first in his West Point class (Robert E. Lee was second in his). But grades could not buy happiness, and Custis once lamented that he never had any fun in life. As Kundahl keenly points out: "Being heir to an idol must be a weighty burden."

Alexander Hunter, however, who authored the Civil War classic *Johnny Reb and Billy Yank,* knew how to have fun. After escaping from the Old Capitol Prison, Hunter enjoyed watching the play *"Taming of the Shrew"* in Baltimore before returning to the safe soil of the Confederacy. Hunter had one of the best quotes of the war: "[Colonel John S. Mosby] had no magnetism; he was as cold as an iceberg, and to shake hands with him was like having the first symptoms of a congestive chill."

Frank Stringfellow, a probable spy, worked as a dental assistant in Washington for five weeks during the war. On a trip to Alexandria, he took in a play about Mosby called *The Guerilla, or Mosby in 500 Sutler Wagons.* Even disguised like a woman did not prevent Stringfellow, "a beardless youth with a waist like a girl's," from repeated arrests by both Union and Confederate soldiers.

But these are only mild annoyances compared with the tragedy visited upon Wilson Presstman, the commander of the O'Connell Guards, a company comprised mainly of railroad workers, which became Company I of the Seventeenth Virginia Infantry. As he crossed back into Virginia to recover after almost four years of continual soldiering, the railroad man met his "bitterly ironic" end at the front of a train.

Edgar Warfield, the "generally unremarkable" longest surviving Alexandria veteran lived to see the placement of the Confederate Memorial 'Appomattox' before he died at age 92. During the war, Warfield learned of his brother's death after noticing his brother's name inside a wounded soldier's cap, who casually announced that he had taken the cap from a corpse.

Orton Williams, who knew the South would lose the war, but chose to stay with Virginia because he couldn't fight against relatives and friends, was executed by hanging after being captured in a Union camp. Yes, captured *while in a Union camp.* Williams nearly pulled off the incredibly bizarre and amazing ploy of passing himself off as federal inspector general sent from Washington to inspect troops in the West.

Earlier in the war, Williams had got himself into trouble when he killed a fellow Confederate who saluted poorly. The result? A quote of mind-numbing bluntness: "For his ignorance, I pitied him; for his insolence I forgave him; for his insubordination, I slew him."

Alexandria overwhelmingly supported the secession (by a 958-48 vote), but four of the book's subjects had strong reservations, including Robert E. Lee, who "could not see the good of secession." Lee's resignation from the Union Army was said by one of his children to be "like a death in the house."

The Confederate soldiers of Alexandria may have "yielded up their lives, though vainly, upon the alter of Southern Liberty," but their city was forcibly taken. In the end, Union soldiers built numerous forts and batteries in Alexandria, and like really bad tenants, they stayed too long and pretty much destroyed everything. The *New York Herald* wrote: "Many hamlets and towns have been destroyed during the war...but Alexandria has most suffered...Alexandria is filled with like ruined people; they walk as strangers through their ancient streets." But through all the devastation and hardships, Alexandria and its people survived.

At one point after the Battle of Five Forks, General Montgomery Corse had to slow his marching soldiers down in order to maintain a composed and orderly retreat. Perhaps years later his commands were recalled by Alexandrians rebuilding their lives and homes one fencepost at a time, after the surrender and the indignity of the war came crashing down: "Steady men, steady men, remember you are Virginians."

Book Review:
Virginia's Civil War

Edited by Peter Wallenstein and Bertram Wyatt-Brown

In what could be titled the New Historian's Handbook, *Virginia's Civil War* consists of twenty disparate well-documented stories, always informative and sometimes controversial, with a focus on the long-ignored roles that society, gender and religion played in the war.

Several relate to the elevation of white Virginia women to center stage in the Civil War. *Surviving Defeat* narrates the saga of Julia Tyler, just one of many plantation widows faced with the daunting task of surmounting "the trials of genteel penury and diminished social position." With her husband's death she was left with only the memories of a dead Confederate husband who happened to be a former President of the United States. Her views were so staunchly Confederate that a Union soldier believed she deserved the title *Her Secession Ladyship*. Her deceased husband's august political position didn't warrant a federal pension or sympathy, and neither did her unpopular political leanings. She worked relentlessly in her upended world to eventually get Congress to grant her a federal pension.

To Honor Her Noble Sons gives descriptive insight into some of the turn of the century efforts by women's groups "to keep Confederate flames aglow." One group-The United Daughters of the Confederacy, which had 412 chapters and 17,000 members in 1900, espoused among other goals, "to endeavor to have used in all Southern schools only such histories as are just and true."

War Comes Home illustrates how some slaveholding women, relentlessly encouraging their Southern men, were "outright secessionists" and "not necessarily demure bells and shy matrons." They had quite a fight keeping the home and family together without support or assistance. When a Confederate woman complained to a Union general about soldiers' actions, the response was steely and war-like: "He told her he was glad of it, for that the (Confederate) women and children were the very fiends of this war, sending their husbands, fathers and brothers into the army." Twenty-eight women of Harrisonburg, Virginia proposed to raise "a full regiment of ladies," armed and equipped to perform regular service.

Queen Victoria's Refugees cogently reveals the important role that narratives authored by escaped slaves had in diminishing the likelihood of British assistance to the Confederacy. Two slaves made their way to Europe where each of their stories describing the horrors of slavery were published in 1863. Strong Southern sympathies would be hard-matched against these wicked realities of hell.

Contested Unionism describes the investigation that the three-member Southern Claims Commission conducted to determine, among other things, whether Southerner William Pattie's claim for $1,700 wartime property damages should be allowed. In order to be allowed, Pattie's loyalty to the Union had to be deemed "iron-clad," continually from succession to surrender. Obviously living on Southern soil during the war required the suppression of pro-Union sentiment. Like many other Southerners, Pattie told the commission he really had the Union in his heart but knew it was too dangerous to show it. This lively tale discussed some of the testimony obtained by the commission.

Navigating Modernity portrays Seminarian Robert Dabney's difficult struggle to balance the tension between modernity and the scripture. He tried his best and along the way came up with some pithy platitudes: "Prove all things, hold fast to that which is good." On history: "Be sure that the former issues are really dead before you bury them." An epitaph suggested by his son reveals the storm he lived under in this trying time: "He was what he was. Let the Heathens rage."

This book highlights the societal issues of the war rather than soldiers or battles. It would have been much better if the editors had excluded any analysis of soldiers or battles entirely because their single foray into that area proved disastrous.

They delved into a study of General Robert E. Lee, with not one, but four stories, filled with such venom and contempt that you might wonder why they included these hate-filled diatribes to detract from an otherwise unique and highly readable book. "A Hitler... a Stalin...valued his own honor more than the independence of the South...His life was replete with frustration, self-doubt and a feeling of failure...the deracination of Lee from his historical context of rebellion and resistance was all mythic, all historically inaccurate, and all ideologically indispensable...The longer I've contemplated (Lee)... the more I've hated him."

One incident revealing the Lee enmity relates to an actual occurrence in Richmond's St. Paul's Church in June 1865, when a black man was the first to receive communion. At the time this was unheard of. "Gasp. No one moved, except Lee, who walked forward and knelt beside him." The stories in the book use this incident to maliciously criticize Lee. One suggests Lee may have been trying to shame the black man. Another suggests the black man may not have been given the Eucharist, and then points out that it is not known if Lee made any gesture of Christian welcome after the service. Many things could have happened and might have happened but it seems grossly mean-spirited to ascribe malice to Lee's simple quiet deed.

Book Review:
John M. Schofield and the
Politics of Generalship

By Donald B. Connelly

John McAllister Schofield might be the most underrated general of the Civil War. His meticulous and cautious nature earned him praise, victories and the exulted rank of lieutenant general, but his lack of notoriety and élan relegated him to relative anonymity. Having started inauspiciously as a West Point cadet in 1849 as a last-minute replacement, he retired at the pinnacle of his profession, in the heady company of George Washington and Ulysses Grant, as only the 6th lieutenant general in American history. In *John M. Schofield and the Politics of Generalship*, Donald B. Connelly masterfully narrates how the judicious and quiet officer deftly combined intellect, a sense of fairness and political shrewdness to navigate through four and a half decades of political and military minefields.

At West Point, Schofield miraculously averted dismissal after collecting an astounding 196 demerits (maximum allowed: 200) and being court-martialed for disorderly conduct, disobedience of orders and neglect of duty. These deficiencies however, did not interfere with his impressive (Class of 1853) ranking of 7th (of 55 cadets), besting fellow cadets Philip H. Sheridan (35th) and John Bell Hood (44th).

Schofield acknowledged in retrospect that what he needed to learn "was not so much how to command as how to obey."

Schofield spent the early years of the war in Missouri assigned to fight ferocious guerrilla bands. He received the Medal of Honor and commendations for demonstrating "conspicuous courage" and "coolness and equanimity" for his actions at Wilson's Creek, a small but very bloody battle. A newspaper glowingly effused: "a braver soldier does not live." His political assignment to balance Missouri's goal of protecting its borders along with the national government's goal of defeating the Confederacy guaranteed a situation Connelly characterized as "tailor-made for dissension and abuse."

Schofield got some unsolicited advice from someone at a very high level, abundantly experienced at being attacked simultaneously by every side-President Lincoln, who counseled: "It is a difficult role, and so much greater will be the honor if you perform it well. If both factions, or neither, shall abuse you, you will, probably, be about right. Beware of being assailed by one and praised by the other."

Schofield succeeded and in the process drastically reduced the number of guerilla bands from the thousands early in the war to several dozen by 1864. He must have been abused just about enough by all factions to earn Lincoln's praise: "I affirm with confidence that no commander of that department has, in proportion to his means, done better than General Schofield."

Secretary of War Edwin Stanton and General William Sherman also took note of the young general's work. Stanton thought Schofield "earnest, faithful and able;" Sherman remarked that Schofield "did not allow himself to be used by a political faction."

Schofield was next promoted to command of the Army of the Ohio, where his steady and reliable efforts leading the left wing of the Atlanta Campaign built the foundation for a life-long friendship with Sherman. Schofield subsequently performed infallibly in various demanding assignments including fighting guerilla bands in Tennessee and carrying out the duties as Military Commander in Reconstruction Virginia.

The year 1868 found Schofield at 'Ground Zero' in the collision of military, politics and the Constitution: the impeachment of President

Andrew Johnson. As an acceptable alternative for all sides to replace Secretary of War Stanton, Schofield probably had a hand in averting Johnson's removal from the presidency. As Johnson's secretary of war, Schofield's usual steadiness and fairness guided him through the highest level of government where the brawling could not have been nastier.

His self-proclaimed "biggest mistake" was accepting the duties of Commander of West Point in 1876. He was assigned the thorny task of chairing the review of the 1862 court-martial proceedings of Major General Fitz John Porter, who had been convicted and removed from the army after his abysmal performance at Second Bull Run. Coincidentally, Porter was one of two officers who had voted to expel Cadet Schofield from West Point many years earlier. This politically-charged proceeding to restore or destroy reputations included testimony from Joshua Chamberlain and James Longstreet. In the end, Porter averted conviction and Schofield, with calm and customary proficiency, averted another potential disaster.

One episode however, resulted in a highly uncharacteristic stain to Schofield's reputation. On April 6, 1880, Cadet Whittaker, the only black then enrolled at West Point, was found tied, beaten and unconscious on the floor. Instead of doing the right thing, Schofield was derelict in his duties. He shamefully rushed to the judgment that the wounds were self-inflicted as a drastic attempt to avoid academic dismissal. At the time, Whittaker was close to failing a course for the second time.

Schofield, who died in 1906 and is buried in Arlington National Cemetery, made numerous contributions to the army over a stellar forty-six year career. He consistently pushed for reforms to improve the morale and performance of the army, including increasing soldiers' pay and benefits, treating them more fairly and providing more training. These efforts which made the army a more professional organization, and one ready for 20th Century, constituted Schofield's most important achievement.

Researchers, writers and scholars of the Civil War will be most appreciative of Connelly's marvelously researched and documented study of General Schofield's ability to successfully balance conflicting political and military demands.

Book Review:
"Lincoln Unmasked," by Thomas J. DiLorenzo; "Lincoln: A Foreigner's Quest," by Jan Morris

Full disclosure: For many years I have had a picture of Abraham Lincoln by my desk.

Daring to pierce the immaculate rings of purity circling the 16th president for almost seven score and two years, Morris and DiLorenzo make the lonely argument that there is a dark side to the Constellation Abraham Lincoln. While Morris gently tugs at the legend on the "high marble throne" by pointing out flaws in a forgiving manner, DiLorenzo wields a sledgehammer to unapologetically spew malevolent rants at Lincoln and the "professional historians," who penalize and demonize those who dare to say or write anything negative about Lincoln. It's hard to tell which DiLorenzo despises more: Lincoln or the historians and writers he calls the "self-appointed Gatekeepers of the Truth" who have "poisoned the history profession by political correctness."

Morris, who argues we are "almost deranged in our obsession," points out that we have named at least thirty-five cities, twenty-two counties, 125 statues, a luxury car and a tunnel under the Hudson River after the most revered politician in history. And there's more, including the penny and the five dollar bill. The charge here is that perhaps the rural country boy should be remembered more as the wealthy trial lawyer and politician well-versed in manipulation and deceit. Like today's K Street lobbyists, Lincoln's clients included giant corporations and millionaires. That might explain how a new town along a railroad was named after him and how he traveled free in private rail cars often accompanied by an entourage of railroad executives.

The authors argue that Lincoln was not the slave's best friend. According to DiLorenzo, Frederick Douglas said, "the Negro people are only the step-children" of Lincoln, "by force of circumstances and necessity." Civil rights activist William Lloyd Garrison said Lincoln did not have "a drop of anti-slavery blood in his veins." Lincoln made several comments to indicate that he did not consider blacks his equal and in fact favored a colonization plan to remove blacks from the United States. These authors criticize Lincoln for talking out of both sides of his mouth, and opined that the further south he went, "the whiter his principles" became.

The man with the legendary political and persuasive skills talked about a plan for compensated emancipation as other countries had done, but never pressed for it or made it happen. The man who freed the slaves allegedly agreed to provide his formidable and highly-paid legal skills to a slave-holder trying to get his runaway slave forcibly returned to him. Lincoln said he wanted God on his side, but he "had to have Kentucky" for its votes. Lincoln spoke of God quite often, but was his religion just hard-ball politics? To what extent did politics play a role in Nevada's gaining statehood on the eve of Lincoln's reelection? Certainly he got its freshly-minted electoral votes.

Along with shutting down hundreds of Northern newspapers that opposed his views on the Civil War, the Lincoln Administration jailed many political dissenters without due process. When the Supreme Court chief justice said these actions were unconstitutional, Lincoln simply ignored him. More disturbing and lesser-known is the allegation that Lincoln ordered the execution of thirty-nine Indians after an uprising.

Did the Southern States, as the authors claim, have a legitimate right to secede from the Union? The New England States apparently thought so because they had previously threatened to do so in 1804 over the Louisiana Purchase and eight years later over the War of 1812. DiLorenzo points out the Revolutionary War Treaty with Great Britain named each of the states individually and referred to them as "free, sovereign and independent States." According to Federalist Number Thirty-Nine, authored by James Madison, the Father of the Constitution: "Each State…is considered as a sovereign body independent of all others, and only to be bound by its own voluntary act."

The Gatekeepers, according to DiLorenzo, overemphasize slavery and minimize tariffs as causing the war. DiLorenzo quotes from Virginia Senator James Webb's book about the Scots-Irish in America. According to Webb, "Slavery was emphatically not the reason that most individual Southerners fought so long and hard, and at such overwhelming cost. Slavery may have been the catalyst issue from a governmental perspective…but other factors, some cultural and some historical, brought most of the Confederate soldiers to the battlefield."

Furthermore, according to Webb, the Scots-Irish in the Confederacy did not fight to defend and protect the institution of slavery for the miniscule 5% of their population who were slave-owners. Webb opined that "in virtually every major battle of the Civil War, Confederate soldiers who did not own slaves were fighting against a proportion of Union Army soldiers who had not been asked to give theirs up." Confederates fought simply because they were "provoked, intimidated and ultimately invaded."

Two months before the Civil War started, Lincoln told a Northern audience what he believed to be the single most important issue facing their Congressional representatives. It wasn't slavery. It was tariffs.

Three decades earlier, South Carolina nullified a Tariff Act and made $200,000 available to enforce the nullification. Of the 107 'yes' votes in the House of Representatives and 25 votes in the Senate for the Tariff Act, only three and two, respectively, were cast by Southerners.

A 30-year *New York Times* veteran journalist recently asserted that South Carolina's chief complaint with the North dealt with tariffs. In addition, a peer-reviewed academic journal in economics asserted the tariff issue was a much more important cause of the war than most historians currently believe. A foreign newspaper made this point in 1862:

> "The 'Tariff' question, again, enters largely—more largely than is commonly supposed—into the irritated and aggrieved feelings of the Southerners. And it cannot be denied that in this matter they have both a serious injury and an unconstitutional injustice to resent...All Northern products are now protected; and the...Tariff is a very masterpiece of folly and injustice... No wonder then that the citizens of the seceding States should feel for half a century they have sacrificed to enhance the powers and profits of the North; and should conclude, after much futile remonstrance, that only in secession could they hope to find redress."

H. L. Mencken, the famous Baltimore newspaper wit, wrote, "The varnishers and veneerers have been busily converting Abe into a plaster saint...There is an obvious effort to pump all his human weaknesses out of him... Lincoln has become one of the national deities, and a realistic examination of him is thus no longer possible."

Perhaps everyone can agree on Morris's line: "Abraham Lincoln's was a martyrdom waiting to happen." Raising legitimate issues, these books are chock full of criticism but short on objectivity and context. The understanding of President Lincoln deserves a discussion of all relevant issues, even those that are politically incorrect and out of favor. But it also deserves all points be made in a comprehensive, fair and objective manner. Unquestionably, Lincoln was a great man. And although I'll be the first to say he wasn't perfect, the framed picture of Abraham Lincoln stays right where it is, prominently displayed on the wall above my desk.

Part III:
Other Stories

Anti-Immigrant Fury
in World War One

During World War I, a vicious pox of anti-German hysteria spread hate and cowardice through wide swaths of America. Infecting otherwise sensible people with dizzied states of senselessness, honorable folks were left mute, silenced against its toxic venom.

It was a time of cruel attacks against Americans of German descent. Figuratively and literally. An evangelist named William Ashley "Billy" Sunday summed up this frothy zeitgeist of animus: "If Hell could be turned upside down, you will find stamped on its bottom: Made in Germany!" A poster blared out: "Everything in this country that is pro-German is anti-American. Everything that is pro-German must go!"

Teddy Roosevelt railed against "hyphenated Americans." Woodrow Wilson criticized German immigrants who had "poured the disloyalty into the very arteries of our national life," before claiming, "such creatures…must be crushed out." *The Saturday Evening Post,* one of the most popular magazines in America, referred to German-Americans as "the scum of the melting pot." Against powerful voices and forces like that, America's conscience became lost. Only a dreadfully scant handful of intrepid souls mustered the courage to find their larynxes during this shameful episode.

All things German were verboten. German books were widely burned. The United States War Department banned from camp libraries seventy-five books it labeled German propaganda. Librarians throughout the country followed suit. *The New York Times* shamelessly reported, "Any book whatever that comes to us from a German printing press is open to suspicion. The German microbe is hiding somewhere between its covers." A speaker at a peace conference remarked, "Behind the chair of innumerable teachers we have seen the shadow of the spiked helmet." Many schools banned the teaching of the German language.

Theatergoers in Milwaukee were prevented--by the threat of machine guns--from watching the play *Wilhelm Tell*. In many places, the music of German composers such as Bach, Beethoven and Wagner was prohibited. German actors and opera singers found it almost impossible to get work. The Metropolitan Opera refused to perform German operas. German churches around the country began conducting services in English. Approximately 1,200 German-Americans were placed in internment camps, including Carl Muck, the conductor of the Boston Symphony Orchestra, just as he was about to conduct Bach's *Saint Matthew Passion*.

Dogs were targeted too. Owners of German Shepherds were suspect. They became known as 'police dogs,' and in the United Kingdom the breed was renamed Alsatian. In fact, the English Kennel Club did not reauthorize the name German Shepherd again until 1977. Dachshunds became liberty dogs and in many places in the United States, stones were thrown at them. The German Spitz breed temporarily became the America Spitz before officially being renamed American Eskimo dogs.

Many German families anglicized their names. Communities renamed their towns, streets and even institutions—such as Berlin, Maryland to Brunswick, and Berlin, Michigan to Marne. Potsdam, Missouri became known as Pershing and New Orleans's Berlin Street was renamed General Pershing Street for the American officer. Brandenburg, Texas changed its name to Old Glory, and Kiel, Oklahoma became Loyal, OK. Germantown, Texas changed its name to honor a local boy killed in France during the war, perhaps unaware that Schroeder is a German name. New York City's German Hospital and Dispensary changed its name to Lenox Hill Hospital and Germania Life Insurance Company became Guardian Life Insurance Company.

Hamburger was renamed Salisbury steak. Sauerkraut and frankfurters became liberty cabbage and liberty sausage. German measles were called liberty measles. Hasenpfeffer and wiener schnitzel were banned from restaurants and beer halls no longer offered pretzels. It is widely believed that German toast was renamed French toast during this time.

Gangs of vigilantes ransacked the homes of people bearing German names. A mob in Collinsville, Illinois lynched a German immigrant named Robert Prager for suspected disloyalty, despite the fact that Prager had tried to enlist in the American army and seemed loyal to the United States in every way. Prager had been rejected by the army because he was blind in one eye. At their trial, the mob's ringleaders wore red, white and blue ribbons. They were all acquitted. Incredibly, New Hampshire Senator Jacob Gallinger opined that since the mob was "inflamed by strong drink," it seemed to him the solution to this problem was simply to reduce the availability of grain in the manufacture of beer.

Invoking Woodrow Wilson's Espionage Act of 1917, the Department of Justice prosecuted more than two thousand dissenters during the war, including thirty German Americans in South Dakota for sending a petition to the governor asking for reforms in the selective service procedure. A man in Iowa was sentenced to a year in jail for attending a meeting in which disloyal utterances were made, applauding some of the [disloyal] statements and contributing twenty-five cents.

A resident of Latah County, Idaho recalled that some of the town's German-American men who got draft deferments were tarred and feathered. This witness also recalled that a prominent and wealthy shop owner "gathered up everything [from his store] that was made in Germany, and had a big bonfire out in the middle of the street... although he had many good German friends all over the county." In Willard, Ohio, a mob of 200 dragged a couple named Mr. and Mrs. Zuelch to city hall where they were forced to salute and kiss an American flag.

Wisconsin resident John Deml stated that a group of men showed up at his house and demanded he purchase $500 worth of war bonds. Although Deml had earlier purchased bonds, he didn't have enough money at that time to buy more. The mob forcibly dragged him out of his house and mercilessly beat him while stringing a rope around his neck. Miraculously a friend appeared and convinced the mob to leave.

In Oklahoma, a former minister who opposed the sale of war bonds was tarred and feathered. A brewery-worker in California who made pro-German remarks was tarred and feathered and then chained to a brass cannon in a city park. In Texas, six farmers were horsewhipped because they declined to donate to the Red Cross.

Germans everywhere constantly had to prove their loyalty. People were warned to keep an eye out for "gloaters," the name given to people who smiled or expressed approval of German victories in the war. In addition to Germans, pressure was put upon other immigrant groups, including American Indians, to prove they were "100% American" by buying war bonds. The widow and son of Geronimo purchased many of these bonds. A man in Lansing, Michigan was sentenced to ten years in prison for complaining about the pressure to buy war bonds.

Anti-German rumors abounded. Germans were said to be putting ground glass into food, and poison on Red Cross bandages. Flashes of light refracted from a New York apartment along the Hudson River were believed to be signals to German submarines skulking in water below.

Even prohibition forces saw public relations success in bashing Germans. The Great War in Europe played perfectly into their naive nanny-state experiment called prohibition. Anti-saloon pamphlets spewed Germanophobic rants such as: "German brewers in this country...have rendered thousands of men inefficient and are thus crippling the Republic." Another demanded to know, "How can any loyal citizen...vote for a trade that is aiding a pro-German alliance?" "We have German enemies in this country too," asserted anti-saloon league supporters, "and their names are Pabst, Schlitz, Blatz and Miller." Posters proclaimed, "Liquor is the Kaiser's mightiest ally!" The President of Brown University neatly summed up the sentiment: "Prohibition spells Patriotism!"

Ulysses, the Poem

The author asserts author's prerogative and includes this poem for no good reason other than it is his favorite. (Thanks Randy for sharing it with me.) It was written in 1833 by Alfred, Lord Tennyson (1809-1892).

It little profits that an idle king,
By this still hearth, among these barren crags,
Match'd with an aged wife, I mete and dole
Unequal laws unto a savage race,
That hoard, and sleep, and feed, and know not me.
I cannot rest from travel; I will drink
Life to the lees. All times I have enjoy'd
Greatly, have suffer'd greatly, both with those
That loved me, and alone; on shore, and when
Thro' scudding drifts the rainy Hyades
Vexed the dim sea. I am become a name;
For always roaming with a hungry heart
Much have I seen and known,-- cities of men
And manners, climates, councils, governments,
Myself not least, but honor'd of them all,--
And drunk delight of battle with my peers,
Far on the ringing plains of windy Troy.
I am a part of all that I have met;
Yet all experience is an arch wherethro'
Gleams that untravell'd world whose margin fades

For ever and forever when I move.
How dull it is to pause, to make an end,
To rust unburnish'd, not to shine in use!
As tho' to breathe were life! Life piled on life
Were all too little, and of one to me
Little remains; but every hour is saved
From that eternal silence, something more,
A bringer of new things; and vile it were
For some three suns to store and hoard myself,
And this gray spirit yearning in desire
To follow knowledge like a sinking star,
Beyond the utmost bound of human thought.

This is my son, mine own Telemachus,
to whom I leave the sceptre and the isle,--
Well-loved of me, discerning to fulfill
This labor, by slow prudence to make mild
A rugged people, and thro' soft degrees
Subdue them to the useful and the good.
Most blameless is he, centred in the sphere
Of common duties, decent not to fail
In offices of tenderness, and pay
Meet adoration to my household gods,
When I am gone. He works his work, I mine.

There lies the port; the vessel puffs her sail;
There gloom the dark, broad seas. My mariners,
Souls that have toil'd, and wrought, and thought with me,--
That ever with a frolic welcome took
The thunder and the sunshine, and opposed
Free hearts, free foreheads,-- you and I are old;
Old age hath yet his honor and his toil.
Death closes all; but something ere the end,
Some work of noble note, may yet be done,
Not unbecoming men that strove with Gods.
The lights begin to twinkle from the rocks;
The long day wanes; the low moon climbs; the deep
Moans round with many voices. Come, my friends.

'Tis not too late to seek a newer world.
Push off, and sitting well in order smite
The sounding furrows; for my purpose holds
To sail beyond the sunset, and the baths
Of all the western stars, until I die.
It may be that the gulfs will wash us down;
It may be we shall touch the Happy Isles,
And see the great Achilles, whom we knew.

Tho' much is taken, much abides; and tho'
We are not now that strength which in old days
Moved earth and heaven, that which we are, we are,--
One equal temper of heroic hearts,
Made weak by time and fate, but strong in will
To strive, to seek, to find, and not to yield.

The Little River Turnpike

When the Indian trail gets widened, graded, and bridged to a good road, there is a benefactor, there is a missionary, a pacificator, a wealth bringer, a maker of markets, a vent for industry.
Ralph Waldo Emerson

Think Dulles Access Road traversed by four-legged livestock instead of all-wheel drive Jaguars, carriages powered by four real horses rather than 240 factory-assembled ones, and you have a pretty good image of the Little River Turnpike in the 1800s. With roots that predate the United States Constitution, the turnpike is one of the oldest of its kind in America.

As early as 1235 towns in England collected tolls. Henry III granted Oxford the right to levy a toll for all entering the city. Various prices were established for carts and animals including horses, cows, goats and sheep. The first turnpike in which records exist goes back to 1346 in London.

To obtain decent roads to transport their goods in Virginia, Alexandria and Fairfax County merchants petitioned the legislature in 1772: "Setting forth the bad Condition of the Roads from the Mountains to the Town of Alexandria, and Praying the House to devise some method for making the roads more useful." One hundred thirty years later we're still trying to make roads more useful.

In 1785, George Washington wrote to Virginia Governor Patrick Henry, "our great roads leading from one public place to another should be shortened, straightened and established by law." Washington claimed road construction was a necessary government expense until "turnpikes may with propriety be established." He also wrote that connecting America through good roads was not an "Utopean [sic] scheme."

With Washington's input, an act was passed in 1785 to construct the road and collect tolls. Eleven years later the Fairfax and Loudoun Turnpike Road Company was formed but quickly failed. This venture's failure led to the formation on January 28, 1802 of the Little River Turnpike Company, with a president, four directors and a charter to sell 200 shares of stock for $100 each.

Turnpikes typically required a fifty to sixty foot wide right of way. The actual road measured eighteen to twenty feet in width. Completed on January 11, 1812, the Little River Turnpike measures thirty-four miles and runs from the intersection of Duke Street and Diagonal Road in Alexandria (near the Masonic Temple) to the point in Aldie, Virginia where it crosses the Little River.

Toll rates varied over time (U.S. soldiers and mail carriers exempted). In the early 1800s it cost six cents to ride a horse on the turnpike. A carriage pulled by one horse (called a gimlet) cost ten cents, pulled by two horses (a podanger) was fifteen cents, and pulled by four horses was twenty-five cents. The price of a three-horse cart (a spike) was not listed on the board but likely cost twenty cents. Forty cattle were twenty-five cents and it cost two cents "for every person on foot." Collection of tolls ceased in 1896.

Altogether, seven tollbooths lined the turnpike and it cost $6,292 per mile to build. As of December 2004, it boasted eighty-seven traffic lights and was home to forty gas stations.

Many people opposed paying tolls and considered turnpike gates as "a check to their ideal liberty." According to one old-timer who served as a judge in Frederick and Winchester Counties in Virginia:

"Adventurous youths would sometimes drive as quietly as possible up to an open gate and then whip up the horse and dash through before the keeper could close the gate, leaving the gatekeeper, who had come out expecting to collect the toll, empty-handed and angry. This was called "running the gate," and was a misdemeanor punishable by fine if caught. Another method of beating the toll keeper was to drive boldly through the gate, calling the name of someone who was known to pay for toll by the year. Since the tollgate keepers were usually aged men or women, and not very active or alert, these escapades and deceptions were usually successful."

Eventually obstacles were set up near the tolls making it difficult to avoid without paying. But despite setting the tolls at strategic locations such as river crossings and entrances to mountain passes, the most persistent turnpike problem were travelers who evaded (or shunned) paying the tolls by temporarily getting off the turnpike and traveling on nearby side paths and trails at the point where the toll booths were set up. Once past the toll booths, these "shunpikers" got back on the turnpike.

The employees were sometimes a problem too. Just like the metro parking attendants caught stealing money a few years ago, three tollbooth operators were caught stealing in the year 1809 alone.

In 1815 there were about fifty-five turnpike companies in Virginia, but most never made a road or a profit. The Little River Turnpike, by far the most successful, did both. In profitable years (record annual receipts were $30,719 in 1818), dividends were paid, with the highest reaching 6.7%. There were eighty-three stockholders in 1850, the vast majority owning one to three shares each.

The men who built the turnpike represented a diverse group. The third and last principal turnpike engineer (from 1822-1843) was Claudius Crozet, a former artillery officer from Napoleon's Army. He had personally learned the importance of good roads the hard way. Bad roads in Belgium caused Captain Crozet an unfortunate and critical delay in getting ammunition to Napoleon at Waterloo. The first two engineers were Laommi Baldwin Jr. (1816-1818) and Thomas Moore (1818-1822).

Slave labor was used to build the road. The news accounts of the day are pretty revealing. One advertisement in the *Alexandria Gazette* offered a reward for returning a slave who ran away from his work on the turnpike road. In another notice an individual reported he had hired out his slave to work on the road for $100.

White males over age sixteen were also conscripted to work on the road, but only on that part of it that came within three miles of their house. These "tithables" could escape duty if they could find and pay someone to take their place.

An instant cachet, addresses along the turnpike were very desirable, much like being near a metro stop today results in higher rents and sales prices. An 1840 advertisement in the *Alexandria Gazette* proudly noted a two story brick house available for rent "on the Little River Road, near Gate No. 1" (about where the George Washington Masonic Temple is currently located.)

More than twenty years after the road had been deeded over to the government an engineer provided this vivid observation:

"...approaching Fairfax, it has degenerated into a road poorly maintained and only for the use of residents along its borders. Through Fairfax it is the main street and passes between the old brick tavern and the courthouse, in which is kept the will of George Washington. Westerly from the courthouse, the Washington trolley cars follow its edge for three quarters of a mile, after which the old turnpike again becomes the neglected country road. At the foot of a hill it splashes in a ford across the brook where ducks swim peacefully within the limits of the road. At different places where the road passes over steep hills, narrow cuts sufficient for only one vehicle have been dug in the side, often fifteen feet deep."

Today, only a seven-mile stretch of the road between Annandale and the City of Fairfax carries the name Little River Turnpike. Other parts of the road are called Duke Street, Main Street, Lee-Jackson Memorial Highway and the John S. Mosby Highway.

Send Books to Soldiers: WWI Posters

"A poster should be to the eye what a shouted demand is to the ear."   Charles Buckles Falls

Advertising wars on colorful posters went over the top and began on a massive scale in World War I, at a time when the cutting edge of technology was a piece of paper. Perhaps Cro-Magnon man etched recruitment slogans on cave walls or ancient Egyptians used hieroglyphics to buy swords to fight Romans. But in America, it started with posters during the Great War. (In the English language, Charles Dickens introduced the word *poster* in 1839 in *The Life and Adventures of Nicholas Nickleby*.)

Poster campaigns bought the weapons, ammunition and supplies needed to quench thirsty war machines. However, these efforts were not without controversy. Some complained posters glamorized war, others thought the images too horrific. Advertising war felt--some even whispered 'propaganda'--unseemly. War, they cried, should not be sold like soap. George Creel, a Denver newspaper editor appointed by President Wilson to head the 'Committee on Public Information,' acknowledged in his memoirs (*How we Advertised America*) that posters were indeed propaganda, but only as it meant a "propagation of faith." Whether called advertising or its evil twin propaganda, these 1,500 or so artworks certainly galvanized support and helped secure victory. Creel's poster-war experience later translated to political campaigning: in 1934, he ran unsuccessfully for the Democratic nomination for governor of California.

I WANT YOU is probably the best known. Sired by James Montgomery Flagg, this granddaddy of American posters (with approximately four million copies distributed in WWI), singlehandedly bolted Uncle Sam from a frail senior citizen to an electrifying leader striking his finger like lightning directly into the faces of millions. A precocious artist, Flagg had his artwork published by the age of fourteen in *Life Magazine.*

In all, he contributed forty-six paintings to the war effort. And like the other artists, Flagg was not paid and did not want to be paid for his efforts. In fact, it was reported that Flagg once "angrily left a meeting after an artist even dared to suggest some form of payment."

Idyllic images ranging from pictures of children and eagles, sunsets and sunrises to historic legends like George Washington and Abraham Lincoln to American icons like Lady Liberty, the Statue of Liberty, and the Liberty Bell reached emotions and got results. The chord of patriotism- *Remember! The Flag of Liberty--Support it!* pushed civilians to dig deep into their wallets. Those playing on patriotism: *Your Country Needs You!* prodded young men to hurry to enlistment boards.

Civilians at home were encouraged to: *Use Less Fuel, Save Coal!* and *Save Scrap Metal, Knit a Bit, Send Smokes to Sammy* and those wanting to supersize their contribution could: *Build a Silo.*

With regard to food alone, posters asked: *Are You a Victory Canner?* Cut down on sweets because: *Sugar Means Ships.* For victory's sake, please: *Plant More Potatoes* because *Food is Ammunition.* If you *Don't Waste While Your Wife Saves,* the United States would surely *Farm to Win 'Over There.'* If people at home would only *Buy Fresh Fish, Eat Victory Bread, Save Seed Corn, Eat Cane Syrup and Molasses,* and *Make Every Egg Count,* then we'd have *War Gardens Victorious!* Efforts to *Collect Bottles! Can Fruit and the Kaiser too, Collect Acorns and Chestnuts! Stop Cantaloupe Losses,* and *Collect Apple and Pear Peelings,* would certainly *Sow the Seeds of Victory.* Remember: *Food Will Win the War* if civilians would *Save a Loaf a Week, Raise More Poultry,* and *Eat More Cottage Cheese.*

But foodstuffs alone did not ensure poster victory. Civilians were advised that *Women of America Work for Victory, Knowledge Wins, Your Work Means Victory* and *Morale Hastens Victory.* If you can't do anything else, then *Sing for Victory.*

Women were urged to save hair clippings (for industrial products like driving belts and insulation pads) and daylight needed saving too (more time to garden). People were persuaded to send goodies to the troops, including tobacco, musical instruments, socks, wine and chocolate. They were also asked to donate books so soldiers could *Read to Win the War.*

The hugely successful WW I poster effort made an encore appearance a little more than two decades later in the Second World War.

Thoughts Inspired by a War-Time Billboard
By: Wallace Irwin

"I stand by a fence on a peaceable street
And gaze on the posters in colors of flame,
Historical documents, sheet upon sheet,
Of our share in the war ere the armistice came.

And I think about Art as a Lady-at-Arms;
She's a studio character most people say,
With a feminine trick of displaying her charms
In a manner to puzzle the ignorant lay.

But now as I study that row upon row
Of wind-blown engravings I feel satisfaction
Deep down in my star-spangled heart, for I know
How Art put on khaki and went into action.

There are posters for drives—now triumphantly o'er—
I look with a smile reminiscently fond

As mobilized Fishers and Christys implore
In a feminine voice, "Win the War—Buy a Bond!"

There's a Jonas Lie shipbuilder, fit for a frame;
Wallie Morg's "Feed the Fighter" lurks deep in his trench;
There's Blashfield's Columbia setting her name
In classical draperies, trimmed by the French.

Charles Livingston Bull in marine composition
Exhorts us to Hooverize (portrait of bass).
Jack Sheridan tells us that Food's Ammunition—
We've all tackled war biscuits under that class.

See the winged Polish warrior that Benda has wrought!
Is he private or captain? I cannot tell which,
For printed below is the patriot thought
Which Poles pronounce "Sladami Ojcow Naszych."

There's the Christy Girl wishing that she was a boy,
There's Leyendecker coaling for Garfield in jeans,
There's the Montie Flagg guy with the air of fierce joy
Inviting the public to Tell the Marines.

And the noble Six Thousand—they count up to that—
Are marshaled before me in a battered review.
They have uttered a thought that is All in One Hat
In infinite shadings of red, white, and blue.

And if brave Uncle Sam—Dana Gibson, please bow—
Has called for our labors as never before,
Let him stand in salute in acknowledgement now
Of the fighters that trooped from the studio door."

Thomas Jefferson said he couldn't live without books and our soldiers shouldn't have to either. Although the Internet, cable news and the fraction 24/7 have driven these ubiquitous artworks into a no-man's land of history, our soldiers are still wonderful and deserving of whatever books or other supplies you can send them. ***Please Do So!***

Dissent in Wartime

There is an adage that a country needs the 'trinity' of its people, army and politicians working together to win at war. In America, this trinity is often MIA, wartime dissent neither new or unusual. Entire volumes have been written about the controversy at home during wartime but here are just a few examples of things said and done to fuel what Abraham Lincoln referred to as "the fire in the rear."

It is widely believed that about a third of Americans were avidly against the American Revolution, another third in favor, and the rest, according to John Adams, "mongrels." Adams remarked that had Virginia and the New England states not pressed the other states, it's likely that New York and Pennsylvania would have joined the British.

A committee of the Continental Congress warned in October 1776 that: "If America falls, it will be owing to [Loyalists] more than the force of our enemies." An unidentified soldier agreed: "The people at home are destroying the army...much faster than [the British] can possibly do." Renowned historian Arthur Schlesinger opined (in 1963) that of all American wars, the Revolution had the "most determined body of opinion arrayed against the government."

Thirty years later, the War of 1812 hit and Federalists, especially in New England vehemently dissented in many colors of hot, but not red, white and blue. Daniel Webster declared: "We in New England are no patriots—we will do what is required—no more." He accused

305

the administration of intentionally withholding information to make war more likely. The *Connecticut Courant* estimated that more than two thirds of Northerners "had loathed [the war] from the beginning and almost all of them at the end." The Federalists in Congress denounced it as a "party not a national war," fomented by a "divided people."

The Massachusetts Senate proclaimed the war was "founded in falsehood" and "declared without necessity." A Massachusetts reverend protested: "It is a war unexampled in the history of the world, wantonly proclaimed on the most frivolous and groundless pretences." New Englanders even threatened to secede from the Union over the war.

Hardened Federalists hurled a tsunami of invectives against two of their most despised opposition—Thomas Jefferson, and the president during the war years, James Madison. A few years earlier, in the build up to war, Federalists in New York had celebrated the 4th of July by burning an effigy of Jefferson. This relentless wave of opposition caused Madison to complain that dissenters were worse than the enemy, even after the British had destroyed much of Washington City: "To see the capital wrecked by the British does not hurt so deeply as to know sedition in New England."

A Baltimore newspaper charged that the war, started "without funds, without an army, navy or adequate fortifications," would lead to "the prostration of civil rights and the establishment of a system of terror." This same editor claimed he welcomed war because the ensuing horrible results would cause the "idiots who bellow in public bodies," to eventually "be sent to Bedlam, and imposters to the stocks."

The Mexican War later struck and the dissenters struck back. The war they cried, was "treason against God" started by Southern politicians. The *Kennebec (Maine) Journal* suggested that no other country "ever resorted to justificatory reasons which were so false and hypocritical as those alleged for our aggressions on Mexico." The *Xenia (Ohio) Torch Light* asserted the Mexicans were in the right and the United States was in the wrong. "They may appeal...to the God of Battles, but if we look for aid...it must be to the infernal machinations of hell." One Boston clergyman proudly announced if he enlisted it would be with the Mexicans.

Three thousand Unitarians submitted a thirty-six yard long anti-war petition to Congress. A group of Quakers obtained 9,000 signatures for their anti-war screed. In Hudson, New York 2,500 "Friends of Peace, Commerce, and the Constitution" gathered to protest the war. The *Washington Union* reported "the war is branded with every abusive epithet, and the president of our country...is denounced as a bloody tyrant and murderer." Four New England states' legislatures characterized the war as "hateful," and the U.S. House of Representatives condemned it as "unnecessarily and unconstitutionally begun by the President of the United States."

"Allow the President to invade a neighboring nation whenever he shall deem it necessary to repel an invasion," a little-known Illinois Congressman warned, "and you allow him to make war at pleasure." For President Polk's handling of the war, Mr. Lincoln berated him as "a bewildered, confounded, and miserably perplexed man," whose "mind, tasked beyond its power, is running hither and thither, like some tortured creature, on a burning surface, finding no position on which it can settle down." Congressman Lincoln called the Mexican War: a war of conquest fought to catch votes.

And then the Civil War came. President Lincoln, having the tables turned on him, was publicly vilified as a: "despot, liar, usurper, thief, monster, perjurer, ignoramus, swindler, tyrant, fiend, butcher and pirate." And that's only a partial list.

Many people, Lincoln included, might have worried more about war critics at home than the enemy on the battlefield, like the Union surgeon who lamented: "It is a common saying here that if we are whipped, it will be by Northern votes, not Southern bullets."

"King Lincoln," according to one congressman, waged the "wicked, cruel and unnecessary" war to "crush out liberty and erect a despotism." Another congressman stated that in watching the "the melancholy spectacle" of war he was seeing "a free government die." Lincoln and the Republicans were accused of "invok[ing] the storm which has since rained blood upon the land. They courted the whirlwind which has prostrated the progress of a century in ruins...

They danced with hellish glee around the babbling cauldron of civil war and welcomed with ferocious joy every hurtful mischief which flickered in its lurid and infernal flames."

The La Crosse (Wisconsin) Democrat, which referred to Lincoln as a "widow-maker" and an "orphan-maker," had this to add as Lincoln sought a second term: "May Almighty God forbid that we are to have two terms of the rottenest, most stinking, ruin-working smallpox ever conceived by fiends and mortals, in the shape of two terms of Abe Lincoln's administration."

The *Bangor (Maine) Democrat* printed this little verse in 1863:

You saw those mighty legions, Abe,
And heard their manly tread;
You counted hosts of living men-
Pray—can you count the dead?
Look o'er the proud Potomac, Abe,
Virginia's hill along;
Their wakeful ghosts are beck'ning you,
Two hundred thousand strong.

Northern newspapers scolded the Lincoln Administration for concealing military losses in "a sickening flow of partisan delusion," and predicted the country was headed for military dictatorship. "Under the pretence of saving the Union, these bloody-minded scoundrels have been doing their utmost to destroy it."

Presidents have long known the power of the press to shape popular opinion. Lincoln, in fact, compared *New York Tribune* editor Horace Greeley's support to having an army of 100,000 men in the field.

The most apt summary remark might be this line uttered by Robert Livingstone in 1787: "Let us watch with vigilant attention over the conduct of those in power; but let us not...restrain their effort to be useful."

One person who truly didn't think war necessary, and who paid very dearly for his dissent was Henry 'Light Horse Harry' Lee. Former congressman, governor of Virginia and loyal friend of George

Washington, he was a hero in the American Revolution. A few years later he helped quell a rebellion in Western Pennsylvania over taxes on whiskey. He was a proud member of the Lees, of whom George Washington proclaimed: "I know of no country which...can produce a family all distinguished...as our Lees." (And this was before Robert E. Lee's debut in the next generation).

Ironically, the War of 1812 was really not necessary. 'Not necessary,' not in the pacifist or dissent sense, but not necessary because a couple days before it started, England had repealed its embargo, the primary cause of the war. Unfortunately, however, in this era of pre 24/7 time, news from England traveled only as fast as the winds and currents would take it across the ocean.

At the twilight of his illustrious life, the fifty-six-year-old war hero who had spent almost a lifetime riding hard saddles should have been feted in comfort with occasional rides down memory lane. The road would pass adoring and appreciative crowds throwing flowers, slowed only by an occasional ceremony to collect well-deserved laurels. That's what should have happened.

But it didn't. Instead, by 1810, he had gambled and lost on just about every sort of project and scheme--coal mines, canals, currency transactions, speculative property, interest-bearing loans, and the eponymously-named Dismal Swamp land deal. Eventually, the only chips the former hero had were a bankrupt reputation, acres of debt, and eleven months in debtor's prison.

Incredibly though, the hard times got even harder. In July 1812, a month after the war started, Lee traveled to Baltimore to lend support to his friend Alexander Hanson, whose political views had put his life and his livelihood in danger. Lee and Hanson were both ardent Federalists and furious war critics. Hanson owned and published his own newspaper to loudly voice his war complaints. He railed in his *Federal Republican* against President Madison, charging, among other things, the war as: "unnecessary, inexpedient, and entered into from...motives...of undisguised foreign influence."

Lee added his own inflammatory comments, claiming war against England would mean "every possibility of the most disastrous defeat and scarcely a possibility of the slightest success."

On July 28, Lee and Hanson were holed up in a house at 45 Charles Street. A rabid mob skulked its way over to make the reviled pariahs pay for their disloyalty. With the prey inside, the 'treasonous' newspaper ink now dry, the 300 to 500 fervently mad Marylanders eager to war against England were ready to unleash unspeakable wrath and fury upon anyone who wasn't.

Under a military force, Lee, Hanson and twenty-one other intrepid Federalist war critics were whisked away to the safety of a nearby Baltimore jail. Safe, that is, only as long as the guards stayed in position. But before long, however, the security forces slipped home or to local taverns, leaving the prison wall, like a poorly-constructed levee, the only thing protecting the inside calm from the wicked storm. It didn't hold long.

A screaming hurricane named Terror broke through. Quickly indentifying Lee: "the damned old Tory general!" the mob madly swung, poked, clubbed, slashed, kicked and stabbed. When they finally fled the bloody fracas, Lee was believed dead. They were not wrong about thinking they had killed James Lingan, another Revolutionary War veteran, ardent Federalist, and former congressman.

The following remarks were included in George Washington Parke Custis's remarks delivered at a memorial service for James Lingan:

> "Why are Federalists a persecuted race? Must they leave their Egypt, and under the conduct of another Moses, seek a new Canaan? Can they boast of no virtues, no services, to entitle them to the joys of liberty's land? Who reared the Temple of National Freedom? Who kindled the sacred flame on its alters? Whose virtues, whose services have contributed to nourish that flame? Go! Untie the scroll of Fame! Peruse the list of American Worthies, and tell me if any *Federalists* are there!
>
> Go to the hard fought field of the Revolution-kneel on their sacred earth, which tells no lies, and ask her, if on the memorable days, when we fought for Liberty, no Federalist blood moistened her bosom? Nay, persecuted as we are, perhaps at this moment some gallant, sailor climbs the shattered mast

to nail the flag of my Country to its stump-My life on it, *that fellow is a Federalist!*

Perhaps some gallant soldier may yet scale the Heights of Abraham, to wreathe Liberty's standard around Montgomery's tomb-I tell you the first foot which presses the classic ground, *will be a Federalist's!*"

After his injuries to what President Madison called "barbarians and hypocrites," Lee moved to the West Indies, where for the remaining six years of his life he didn't know a single healthy day. He died and was buried on Cumberland Island, Georgia in March 1818. It was his first trip back to America.

Oval Office Veterans

We may have a military veteran in the Oval Office when the next president is sworn in. Again. The hazards and hardships of military life may just be the most common life experience among the American presidents. Success at soldiering has paved an open road to the White House for thirty of the forty-two men who have held the highest political office (George W. Bush is sometimes referred to as #43 but he is the 42nd person to be president; Grover Cleveland, who served two non-consecutive terms, gets counted twice).

So frequently has a veteran occupied the White House that there has been only one period in American history when more than two consecutive presidents have not served in the military: in the early part of the Twentieth Century with a string consisting of six presidents from William Taft to Franklin Roosevelt.

President Truman, who credited much of his success in politics to his military service, wrote that maneuvers in battle were like political maneuvers. Another leader made a similar connection noting the only difference between war and politics is that the former came with bloodshed. Three presidents were career soldiers (Zachary Taylor, Ulysses Grant and Dwight Eisenhower). Several saw extensive battle, most notably Taylor, who served in four wars.

Eight presidents served during the Civil War (Millard Fillmore, Andrew Johnson, Grant, Rutherford Hayes, James Garfield, Chester Arthur, Benjamin Harrison and William McKinley). Grover Cleveland, who was drafted but paid a thirty-two-year-old Polish immigrant to take his place, made the following unique remark about America and war: "The United States is not a nation to which peace is a necessity." Benjamin Harrison, who was in Sherman's March to Atlanta, later said of his military aspirations: "I am not Julius Caesar, nor a Napoleon, but a plain Hoosier colonel, with no more relish for a fight than for a good breakfast." Grant also claimed to have had little military aspirations: "The truth is I am more of a farmer than a soldier. I take little or no interest in military affairs, and, although I entered the army thirty-five years ago and have been in two wars...I never went into the army without regret and never retired without pleasure." Fillmore did not see any action in the war but organized a Buffalo, New York home guard unit consisting of men over the age of forty-five. The unit primarily saw volunteers off to war, took part in funeral services and marched in parades. As for McKinley: this commendation from a supervising officer certainly showed presidential aptitude: "Young as he was, we soon found that in the business of a soldier, requiring much executive ability, young McKinley showed unusual and unsurpassed capacity."

Seven presidents served during World War II: Eisenhower, John Kennedy, Lyndon Johnson, Richard Nixon, Gerald Ford, Ronald Reagan and George H. W. Bush. Ford served on a ship which took part in almost all major battles of the South Pacific including the assaults on Wake Island and Okinawa. Bush enlisted on his 18th birthday and went on to fly fifty-eight combat missions in a single engine aircraft. Of his original squadron of fourteen pilots, he was one of only four to survive the war.

Five veterans came from the War of 1812: Andrew Jackson, William Henry Harrison, John Tyler, Taylor and James Buchanan. Jackson's famous victory at the Battle of New Orleans occurred after the war ended, but with the communications of the era, the word had not gotten to America in time.

Zachary Taylor used an old war incident as a political slogan. Refusing to retreat at a difficult point in the war, Taylor bristled, "my wounded are behind me, and I will never pass them alive." Years later, the slogan 'Taylor never gives up' was used in his presidential campaign. Harrison's 1811 victory against Indians at the Tippecanoe

Creek earned him the nickname Old Tippecanoe. That moniker, along with the fact that his running mate's surname started with the letter T played nicely into his campaign slogan: 'Tippecanoe and Tyler Too.'

Four veterans were from the American Revolution: George Washington, James Madison, James Monroe and young Andrew Jackson, who primarily served as a messenger. It was from this war that Jackson holds claim to being the only president to have been a prisoner of war. He was captured by the British and held for about two weeks in Camden, South Carolina. Monroe saw extensive action and was involved in the famous Christmas 1776 crossing of the Delaware.

Washington was the only president to lead, while in military uniform, an armed federal military force. That incident occurred in 1794 when he led the federal army to southwestern Pennsylvania to quell the Whiskey Rebellion.

Three veterans from the Mexican Wars became president (Taylor, Franklin Pierce and Grant) and two from the Black Hawk War: Taylor, and Captain Abe Lincoln, who received $125 for his wartime service of trying to track down Chief Black Hawk in what is now Southern Wisconsin. Lincoln later joked that the only blood he lost in defense of his country was to mosquitoes.

Two World War I vets went onto the White House: Truman and Eisenhower. Truman is believed to have fired one of the last rounds before the armistice. Eisenhower's war-time experience convinced him of the importance of good roads, culminating years later in the Eisenhower Highway System in America.

Both Roosevelts requested active duty service during World War I but were denied: Theodore, because of his advanced age and Franklin because President Wilson wanted him to remain in his position as assistant secretary of the navy.

Five wars were represented by one future president each: Washington in the French and Indian War, Jackson in the First Seminole War of 1817-1819, and Taylor in the Second Seminole War of 1837-1840. Theodore Roosevelt fought in the Spanish-American War where he set "a splendid example to the troops" for his gallant charge on San Juan (or Kettle) Hill. Jimmy Carter, who was in uniform during the Korean War, served on one of the first nuclear submarines. Finally, James K. Polk was in the military during peace time and George W. Bush served in the Texas National Guard.

Prior service in the armed forces seems to result on an inside track to the Oval Office, but is certainly no guarantee. Otherwise we would have former chief executives with names like McClellan, Goldwater and McGovern.

The Retrocession of 1846

Like a runaway kid learning the harsh realities of the world and longing for his own bed again, Alexandria returned home to Virginia in 1846. Prior to that time, the land making up present-day Alexandria and Arlington, having been carved out of Virginia forty-six years earlier, fell within the boundaries of the federal city of Washington.

Had it not been for a 19th Century retrocession, it's very possible that people living in Arlington and Alexandria might still be residents of the District of Columbia. The Constitution referred to a District: "… as may, by Cession of particular States, and the Acceptance of Congress, become the Seat of the Government of the United States." The land donated by Virginia, formerly within Fairfax County, became Alexandria County of Washington, DC. The nascent federal government moved from Philadelphia to Washington in 1800.

Debate to retrocede the land back to Virginia began almost immediately. Alexandria merchants felt they did not get the financial support they deserved and needed from Washington. When they looked at their Georgetown neighbors on the other side of the Potomac River they saw prosperity, growth and favoritism. For them, neglect and stagnation ruled. By the early 1840s, going back home to Virginia, where the economic and political grass was much greener, seemed like a very good idea.

As a result, a plebiscite to retrocede the land back to Virginia was held in the City and County of Alexandria in 1840. It passed 537-155.

The results were presented to Congress in 1846 and the movement got a surprise boost because more critical matters, such as impending war against Mexico, limited Congress's ability to debate, delay and deny.

Many people vehemently opposed the hotly contested retrocession. Some believed it unconstitutional. Others were against it because only the citizens south of the Potomac had been allowed to vote rather than all District residents.

Congress passed the Retrocession 32-14 in the Senate and 96-65 in the House of Representatives (two of Virginia's fifteen congressmen voted against). The only remaining obstacle was a final Alexandria County referendum, held September 1st and 2nd. Supporters shouted their enthusiasm in song:

"Come Retrocessionists, give a loud shout
And show the anti's what we're about,
For freemen's lives we are bound to lead
And to Virginia retrocede;
The ladies all cry out, 'God speed,'
Hurrah! We'll retrocede."

Afterwards, the *Alexandria Gazette* reported the results just as enthusiastically:

"For Retrocession 763 / Against Retro'n 222 / 541 Majority!!!

…The large crowd of citizens immediately formed in procession, and headed by a band of young men singing … The young folks lighted their torches and flambeaux, flags, banners and transparencies were produced, the cannon thundered, firearms of all kinds were discharged, rockets, squibs and crackers were let off, and general joy and enthusiasm prevailed."

Inevitably in all matters concerning Alexandria, George Washington somehow seems to weigh in. In this case a letter in the *National Intelligencer* ascribed how Washington might have reacted:

"George Washington, no doubt, looked upon the District with a military eye, and purposely located it in such a manner as to include all the heights which would command the Capitol, the President's house, and the public offices. If the County of Alexandria should be retroceded, Virginia will have all the commanding heights ... from which to bombard the town, the President's house, the public offices, and even the Capitol itself. In short, she would command the city."

Washington's thoughts against retrocession were imputed, but two other presidents used their own words to remove any doubt: "The relinquishment of that portion [of Washington, DC) which lies within the state of Virginia was unwise and dangerous," wrote President Lincoln in 1862. President Taft was even more blunt in contemptuously calling it an "egregious blunder" and "an injury to Washington."

President James K. Polk issued a Retrocession Proclamation on September 7, 1846, making the move back to Virginia official. With the enormous benefit of immediately gaining full Congressional representation for its citizens, it makes you wonder why some or all of the land originally carved from Maryland to form the District has not been retroceded back to Maryland.

When the federal city was originally laid out, forty boundary marker stones, cut from a quarry in Stafford, Virginia, were set in the ground, ten on each side of the square, a mile apart. The first was set into place at Alexandria's Jones Point on April 15, 1791. The stones are about a foot square and about eighteen inches above ground. On the side of the marker facing the district is carved: Jurisdiction of the United States; the rear gives the state, Virginia or Maryland. Another face of the marker gives the year it was placed, 1791 for the Virginia markers and 1792 for the Maryland markers.

The Lee Highway Blues

Today the Lee Highway is just another strip of monotonous, anonymous, and uninspiring pavement whose best description is congested. But it wasn't always that way.

In the 1920s, it was heralded as the center of the greatest civilization of the world, a contribution to the security, unity, development, welfare, greatness and glory of the Republic. Of exceeding magnitude, complexity and scope, it would lead to the tourist gold that made Switzerland, Colorado, California and Florida. It was to be a perpetual memorial to Confederate General Robert E. Lee, a national highway from Washington to San Diego.

Most of these superlatives were mentioned in a 110-page publicity brochure issued by the Lee Highway Commission, replete with photographs of beautiful scenery through the eleven southern states traversed by America's second transcontinental road. The first transcontinental road, completed in 1913, took a northern route and was designated the Lincoln Highway.

The President of the Lee Highway Association wrote: "There are two great names that epitomize an important era of our natural life, Abraham Lincoln and General Robert E. Lee. The more closely these names are linked together, the better for our reunited land."

Like bookends of history, their paths to greatness ran together through the Civil War. Their fates romanticized in Americans' hearts, profiles chiseled in granite on Stone Mountain and Rushmore. Their names were indelibly inscribed in parallel routes that connected the country and heralded the coming of the future, the automobile age.

The first meeting of what became the Lee Highway Association occurred with no fanfare and only fourteen people in Roanoke, Virginia on George Washington's birthday in 1919. Ten months later the association was formed. Its impetus was a small group who had come to Washington in 1918 to try and get a road constructed from Memphis to the nation's Capitol. Unbeknownst to them, a group led by Professor D.W. Humphries of Washington and Lee University had a very similar goal. Once the groups got together it was only a matter of time.

The association worked feverishly with state legislatures, the U. S. Department of Public Roads, and early lobbyist groups such as the Good Roads Association, the American Automobile Association, the Ship by Truck Bureau, and the Lincoln Highway Association. The U.S. Department of War kicked in surplus materials, including 1,118 Dodge touring cars and light-duty trucks as well as eighteen thousand tons of explosives.

In addition to federal and state funds, private contributors purchased annual memberships ranging from $5 for "Active" to the princely sum of $250 for "Founder." In between, $25 and $125 bought Life and Supporting memberships.

President Warren Harding dedicated the Zero Milestone Monument in a ceremony near the White House on June 4, 1923, with about 8,000 people present and more automobiles than ever before assembled in the city. A band played "Hail, Hail, The Caravan!" As the starting point of the Lee Highway, the monument would be where "all road distances in the United States and throughout the Western Hemisphere shall be reckoned." Milestone markers were also placed in Nashville and San Diego.

Once completed, the road became nationally recognized for unifying the country. Harding proclaimed the monument marked "the approximate meeting place of the Lincoln and the Lee Highway... (where) those sections which once grappled in conflict (are) now happily united for all time in the bonds of national fraternity, of a single patriotism, and of a common destiny."

Woodrow Wilson wrote that it "should lead to the obliteration of the sectional lines carved during the bitter civil strife" of the war which had ended fifty-eight years earlier. Bureau of Education textbooks taught "Main Streets across America," featuring the Lee Highway to elementary school students. Signs commemorating Lee Highway were placed on lamp posts in Washington, DC.

Much more recently, a musician named Michael Cleveland composed a bluegrass song about Lee Highway, the former national majestic road that in the last eighty years has lost its name in every state except parts of Virginia, Alabama and Tennessee. Even here in Northern Virginia, the Lee Highway in Fairfax City was renamed Fairfax Boulevard on July 1, 2005. No wonder the song is called the *Lee Highway Blues.*

War Takes a Holiday: WWI Christmas Truce

Ninety years ago this month soldiers fighting World War I shared a Christmas truce. The combatants faced each other, sometimes over only a matter of yards, for approximately 430 miles along France's northern and western borders. On one side, hundreds of thousands of cold, wet soldiers eked out another wretched hour or perhaps another miserable day in filthy, muddy rat-infested trenches. On the other side, the same.

Their only reprieve from this madness came with the order to go over the top and recklessly charge a well-entrenched enemy expecting the attack, with guns ready and perfectly trained. The ground between the armies, the aptly named No-Man's land, was painted with the victims of war, whose dead and dying bodies were more often than not hanging on barbed wire or buried in ubiquitous mud-filled lakes formed from shell craters. These soldiers truly were, as one historian noted, "the last insurable men on earth." In a 1934 *New York Times* story, World War I veteran Valentine Williams wrote:

"The dead were everywhere; the dead of bygone months, the dead of last week, the dead of last night, poor, scarecrow figures, waxen of face and hands, smeared from top to toe with mud like their living comrades. There were corpses built into the parapets; they emerged from the quaking slime beneath men's feet in the trenches; they strewed No Man's Land."

Somehow amidst this blackened tempest of hell came a glowing ray of humanity to illuminate man's desire for compassion. At many places along the front, motivated only by a peaceful holiday wish, the fighting stopped on Christmas Eve. World War I veteran Robert Graves recalled:

"Christmas was a peculiar sort of day, if I ever spent one. Hobnobbing with the Hun, so to speak; swapping fags and rum and buttons and badges for brandy, cigars and souvenirs. Lieutenant Coburg and several of the Fritzes talked English, but none of our blokes could sling a word of their bat."

The truce was not officially sanctioned, and in fact such fraternizing would have been severely punished. After all, the soldiers were in the business of killing. But they were also human. Being at the front was not much different, better or worse than being dead; the warriors took a well-earned holiday because they had nothing left to lose. The worse that could happen is they'd get sent to the front to die, but they were already there doing that. Valentine Williams also explained:

"The rifles were laid aside, hands were grasped in Christmas friendship, cigars and cigarettes handed about, souvenirs exchanged, the hatred between the peoples, under the influence of the 'happy morn,' evaporating like the clouds of tobacco smoke mounting in the sparkling air. Even the German guns that daybreak, refrained from the customary morning hate." (The bombardment to start each day).

But there's more to this unlikely ceasefire, as if it's not surreal enough for warriors to stop killing each other and become friends for a day before they go back to killing each other. The true test of friendship: a soccer game! Yes, the combatants ran, jumped and kicked like schoolboys without a care in the world and all the muddy craters, barbed wire and the recently dug graves proved a mere nuisance to their enjoyment.

The Christmas truce has been vividly captured in literature and music. "The War Game" is a beautifully pictured children's book by Michael Foreman and "Silent Night" by Stanley Weintraub relates the soldiers' thoughts in such detail you feel you know them.

Folksinger John McCutcheon's "Christmas in the Trenches" narrates a British soldier's reminiscent:

"And one by one I noticed they walked into no-man's land
with neither gun nor bayonet, we met there hand to hand
we shared some secret brandy and wished each other well
and in a flare-lit soccer game we gave them hell
The ones who call the shots won't be among the dead and lain
and on each end of the rifle we're the same."

The soldiers along the Western Front could often be heard humming the tune of Auld Lang Syne, with these sad little lyrics:

We're here because we're here, because we're here, because we're here;
We're here because we're here, because we're here, because we're here."

The Lee-Jackson-King
Holiday in Virginia

On Friday, January 14, 2005, Virginia employees will get the day off for the Lee-Jackson holiday. The following Monday, January 17, they will honor Martin Luther King Jr., with another holiday. For sixteen years, these holidays were combined into one. It would be difficult to concoct a more controversial or diverse holiday than the former ill-fated Lee-Jackson-King Holiday.

Start with the Great State of Virginia, home of the Capitol of the Confederacy during the Civil War (after a brief stint in Montgomery, Alabama), where some of the fiercest fighting of the war occurred in places named the Wilderness, Cold Harbor, and the Crater.

Next throw in a state holiday originating in 1889 to the venerable Confederate General Robert E. Lee, who had declined President Lincoln's offer to command the Union Army. Lee, born on January 19, 1807, would not fight against his home state of Virginia.

If George Washington was first in the hearts of Virginians, Robert E. Lee was a close second. To southerners and especially Virginians, Lee was the ideal paragon of integrity and honor. The recent book *April 1865* by Jay Winik makes a persuasive argument that by surrendering his troops and ending the war, Lee saved the country. Absent a definitive cessation of hostilities, the assertion goes, small groups of roaming Confederates could have made successful and very destructive terrorist-type raids all through the Union for a long time with little chance of being stopped or caught.

Now add Confederate General Thomas Jackson, born in Virginia on January 21, 1824. In 1904, for reasons that have been lost to history, the Lee holiday was expanded to include Jackson, the brilliant strategist and military hero. Perhaps best known for his actions in the first major battle of the war-the Battle of Bull Run (also known as the Battle of First Manassas), Jackson earned the sobriquet "Stonewall" for standing fierce and steady when the fire and lead flew fiercely. Other troops were ordered to "rally behind the Virginians!"

Jackson's legend was forever secured, however, with the Confederate victory against overwhelming Union forces at Chancellorsville (outside Fredericksburg) in May 1863. That day the South won the battle, but many argue, may have lost the war because Jackson was wounded by friendly fire. He died a week later. His amputated arm was buried in a different location than the rest of his body.

In the end, the Confederacy lost the war, but Virginia did not lose any of its love or admiration for Lee and Jackson. Coincidentally, in the same month and year that the holiday became the Lee-Jackson, General James Longstreet died. Longstreet ("the War Horse of the Confederacy"), a superb Confederate General, never garnered nearly the same reverence in the South as Lee or Jackson.

Finally, add the great Martin Luther King, Jr., civil rights leader and orator, born January 15, 1929, and you have the Lee-Jackson-King Holiday. Since 2001, the holidays in Virginia for the three leaders have been segregated.

Today in Virginia, the names "Lee-Jackson" are tied in so many ways, not the least of which is a major highway, that the Old Dominion-neophyte who thinks "Lee Jackson" was one person can be forgiven. The Lee-Jackson Foundation of Charlottesville is a charitable organization founded in 1953, and dedicated to increasing educational opportunities for Virginia's youth, primarily by awarding scholarships for outstanding essays which "demonstrate an appreciation of the exemplary character and soldierly virtues of Generals Lee and Jackson."

100th Anniversary of Appomattox Surrender

The Civil War's bloody winding roads mercifully ended at the cul de sac known as Appomattox Court House, a small town ninety miles southwest of Richmond on April 9, 1865. The house was left standing after 1,457 sunsets and 620,000 lives when Confederate General Robert E. Lee surrendered his Army of Northern Virginia to Union General Ulysses S. Grant.

Picture this: At Appomattox on April 9th, Lee and Grant are seated next to each other. Suddenly and unexpectedly, Lee is tapped on the shoulder by a uniformed officer who hands him a telegram. Lee's mind races as he wonders what emergency is so pressing as to interrupt him now on this solemn day in this town where the war came to die. Lee arrived knowing full well what needed to be done and what he was there to do. The telegram shocks him: "Do not sign anything. Await further instructions. Jefferson Davis."

What? Wait a minute. How, you may wonder, does this bizarre, yet true episode comport with the facts of the surrender?

The telegram incident occurred in 1965 at the 100th Anniversary Commemoration of the surrender at Appomattox Court House. The Robert E. Lee in this story is Robert E. Lee IV, the great grandson of the Confederate General; Ulysses Grant (the III) is the grandson of the Union general. The sender of the telegram? A colleague of Lee's with a good sense of humor playing a clever joke on him.

In an April 10, 1965 newspaper article, the New York Times wrote:

> About 5,000 persons gathered under leaden skies in the square of the restored village of Appomattox Court House. There, four bitter years of fratricidal strife came to an end a century ago… The crowd was in a holiday mood, only slightly dampened by occasional showers, and the atmosphere was more that of a country fair than a solemn historic occasion… There was no reenactment of the surrender. A spokesman for the National Park Service said that after the re-enactment of the Battle of Manassas in 1961 'got out of control,' it was decided not to hold centennial re-enactments on national park grounds.

Robert E. Lee IV lives in the Washington, DC metropolitan area and recounted the above story in a recent conversation. At the time of the commemoration, Lee and his family resided in California, where he was an advertising executive for the *San Francisco Chronicle*. He had made the trip to Appomattox Court House without his wife and children. Since he was not expecting a telegram, his immediate concern upon receiving it was of a possible family emergency.

Lee mentioned that sometimes when he identifies himself to people over the telephone they think he's joking and ask him about his horse "Traveler," or the whereabouts of General Grant. The Robert E. Lee line doesn't end at IV; Lee is the proud father and grandfather of Robert E. Lee V and VI.

April 9th marks the 140th anniversary of the end of the war. It lasted almost exactly four years and coincided very closely with Abraham Lincoln's presidency. It started thirty-nine days after he was inaugurated and ended five days before he was assassinated.

The war was fought in many states, as far north as St. Albans, Vermont, as far south as Florida and Texas. With only about 100 miles between the Capitols of the Union and Confederacy, the fiercest fighting took place in places named Manassas, Cold Harbor and the Wilderness. It has been called many names, then and now, including the War Between the States, the War of 1861, the War to Save the

Union, the Second American Revolution, and the War of Northern Aggression.

Preservation groups are working hard to save remaining undeveloped battlefields from becoming ubiquitous shopping centers or gated-condominiums subtly hinting at their historic past with glossy names like Meadows Brigade or Victory Ridge.

I Pledge Allegiance to the Flag

S tarts the famous recitation echoing from schools across our land, whose famous lines were written by Francis Bellamy of Rome, New York, a socialist who penned, never copyrighted, and anonymously published it for the first time in the September 8, 1892 edition of the children's magazine, *"The Youth's Companion,"* to commemorate the 400th anniversary celebration of Columbus's discovery of America at the Chicago Exposition, at a time when the fabric of our most sacred symbol contained forty-four stars. It "should float over every school-house in the land and the exercise be such as shall impress upon our youth the patriotic duty of citizenship," wrote Bellamy, about the flag

Of the United States of America,

which also happens to be the six words added to the pledge in 1923, almost twenty years before the United States Congress made the pledge official, by formal inclusion in the U. S. Flag Code on June 22, 1942, which was followed by the Supreme Court's 1943 ruling that school children could not be forced to recite the pledge to the flag.

And to the Republic for Which it Stands, One Nation

And its American citizens have made numerous court challenges to the pledge, most recently on June 14, 2004, when the Supreme Court reviewed an earlier ruling by the U.S. Ninth Circuit Court of Appeals, which covers California and eight other states when it ruled that the plaintiff, an atheist who had filed suit on behalf of his kindergarten-age daughter, lacked legal standing to make the challenge because he was not the custodial parent. The Supreme Court ruled "the Pledge of Allegiance evolved as a common sense public acknowledgement of the ideals that our flag symbolizes. Its recitation is a patriotic exercise designed to foster national unity and pride in those principals." The plaintiff originally prevailed in 2002, when the Ninth Circuit ruled that the Pledge of Allegiance was unconstitutional, when it contained the words:

Under God,

words added by President Dwight Eisenhower on June 14, 1954, the last time changes were made to the Pledge, with the explanation that "in this way we are reaffirming the transcendence of religious faith in America's heritage and future; in this way we shall constantly strengthen those spiritual weapons which forever will be our country's most powerful resource in peace and war." Of course wars are fought with military and political weapons too, and it was no different one hundred and forty years ago when the Civil War, fought over four terrifying years, over thousands of blood-soaked acres of sacred soil and at the cost of over 600,000 American lives finally ended after having tested, as President Lincoln eloquently said, whether a nation conceived in liberty could long endure, and fortunately for us and for the future, its conclusion proved that the independent States of America would remain united and

Indivisible,

And regardless of the endless contentious and bitter arguments over political matters among strangers and friends, enemies and families in the courts and in offices and taverns, in health clubs and barbershops and wherever else people gather across our great country, we shall all cherish America and our way of life, and strive to ensure that we continue to live in a society with dignity and respect for the aged and infirm; hope and laughter for the youth, honor and courage for our leaders, and most of all,

With Liberty and Justice for All.

Former Holidays in Colonial Virginia

As we celebrate Independence Day this month, consider these five legal holidays enacted in Virginia prior to 1776, two of which related to Indian massacres, and two to the operations of Virginia under the aegis of the King of England.

Great Massacre Day, March 22: Established in 1623 to "solemnize as a holiday" the day that Indian Chief, King Opechancanough's warriors attacked white settlers on Good Friday, March 22, 1622. On this holy day people gathered in churches and homes to "thank God for their deliverance and to pray for and memorialize the dead." The Indians massacred 347 white men, women and children, a staggering figure given the entire Virginia population was approximately 1,200. Jamestown settlers were able to defend themselves and survive the attack because they had been forewarned by an Indian boy named Chanco, who had been taken under the guidance of a white settler. The Indians were reported to have:

"come unarmed into our houses without bowes or arrows... yea in some places, sat down to breakfast with our people at their tables, whom immediately, with their own tooles and weapons, eyther laid downe, or standing in their houses, they basely and barbarously murthered, not sparing eyther age or sexe, man woman or childe...and not being content with taking away life alone, they fell after againe upon the dead, making as well as they could, a fresh murder, defacing, dragging, and mangling the dead carcasses into many pieces, and carrying some parts away in derision, with base and bruitish triumph."

Opechancanough Day, April 18: King Opechancanough was not killed or captured in the Great Massacre. He lived to attack again. He eventually succeeded Powhatan and on this day in 1644, he directed his Indians to attack with "utmost fury," and that "now is the time or never to rout out all the English." King Opechancanough, who was said to be so old and infirm that he needed assistance opening his own eyelids, was captured and killed and the day was celebrated "by thanksgiving for our deliverance from the hands of the Savages."

New England Puritan leader John Winthrop opined the Virginia settlers' problems with the Indians were due to an insufficient level of religion: "It is very observable that this massacre came upon them soon after they had driven out the Godly ministers we had sent them."

Cavalier Day, May 29: This holiday was established to commemorate the re-establishment of royal government:

"Since God of his mercy hath been pleased to restore our late distracted kingdoms to peace and unity and his late depressed majesty to the throne of his royall ancestors, bee itt enacted that in testimony of our thankfulnesse and joy the 29th of May of his majestic birth and happy restitution be annually celebrated as a holy day."

Many of the cavalier class who had sought refuge in Virginia had full freedom to place their imprint upon its social life and provide its later name: the Cavalier State.

Old Dominion Day, January 30: Associated with the Cavalier Day holiday. On this day in 1649, King Charles I of England was beheaded for treason. Eleven years later the House of Burgesses established this holiday to "solemnize with fasting and prayers that our sorrows may expiate our crimes and expiate our guilt."

Birkenhead Day, September 13: Named for an indentured servant named Birkenhead who reported to the Governor of Virginia a planned overthrow of other indentured servants. It's likely the would-be revolutionaries were angry about the lengthy time periods of their indentures. The planned uprising was prevented and Informant Birkenhead received his freedom, 200 pounds stirling, and a holiday in his name. Established in 1663:

"Whereas it is evident that certain mutinous villaines had entred into such a desperate conspiracy as had brought an enevitable ruyne to the country had not God in his infinite mercy prevented it, this grand assembly to testify their thanks to Almighty God for soe miraculous a preservation have enacted that the day this villainous plot should have been putt into execution, be annually kept holy to keep the same in perpetual commemoration."

It has been reported that when the Revolutionary War started, Virginia had 2,754 indentured servants and 1,399 slaves.

White Indentured Servants

Poor and famished pilgrims endure treacherous hardships to emigrate to the United States to grab a sliver of the American pie and find the riches of gold-paved roads, a bountiful food supply, or anything just a little bit better. It's always been that way. Freedom-starved Cubans drowning in shark-infested waters and dirt-poor Latinos suffocating in abandoned trucks while trying to get to America are ghastly reincarnations of yesterday's indentured servants.

Constituting a valuable workforce in early America, indentured servants often bartered their freedom and future toil to whichever stranger paid their ocean passage. The length of the indentures, usually five to seven years, was negotiated and varied slightly depending on age and skill.

Many children were swept away from their families and homes. They found themselves on ships headed to America where they then began a long indenture, forced to labor for someone else for a pittance. Other than the child, a lot of people made money in this arrangement and it became so pervasive that a word was coined to describe it: kidnapped.

For those not kidnapped, arrangements were occasionally made before the servants left home; however, it was more likely their fate lay aboard ships after arrival in an American port. For days or weeks after surviving a brutal eight to eleven week Atlantic Ocean ordeal, they waited. Suffering from hunger and dehydration and diseases contracted from constant exposure to filthy food, contaminated water and sick passengers, who died miserably, or were a vermin-ridden breadcrumb from becoming a corpse thrown overboard, they waited. The survivors met their new masters and bargained away their liberty from positions as weak as their bodies. One witness stated that: "They [the Irish] sell their [indentured] servants here as they do their horses, and advertise them as they do their oatmeal and beef." Another witness recalled:

"Every day (potential buyers) come ... from a great distance, say 20, 30, 40 hours away and go board the newly arrived ship that has brought and offers for sale passengers from Europe, and select among the healthy persons such as they deem suitable for their business and bargain with them how long they will serve for their passage money...Many parents must sell and trade away their children like so many head of cattle...As the parents often do not know where and to what people their children are going, it often happens that such parents and children, after leaving the ship, do not see each other again for many years, perhaps no more in all their lives."

Concerned that excessive discipline might discourage new immigrants, Virginia passed a law in 1661 to limit punishment against servants: "Whereas the barbarous usage of some servants by cruell masters bring soe much scandall and infamy to the country in generall, that people who would willingly adventure themselves hither, are through feare thereof diverted."

Further legal protections added in 1705 required masters to provide "wholesome and competent diet, clothing and lodging ... neither shall, at any time, whip a Christian white servant naked, without an order from a justice of the peace."

Despite these protections, servants sometimes fled their masters and indentures. Rewards were advertised in newspapers, including the *Alexandria Gazette*: Susan, "a servant woman...(with) a wen on the instep of one of her feet" had a $10 bounty for her capture. Eighteen year old Charles Tennison, wearing a brown cloth coat and grey pants when he left home also fetched $10. One cent was promised for three seventeen year old boys in the cabinet making business, and six cents for Andrew J. Day, a twelve year old in the tailoring business.

The return of James C. Bangs, "a stoutly made, round shouldered boy with a light complexion and hard of hearing," guaranteed one dollar. Readers were forewarned at the peril of the law against "harboring or employing the said boy," who had run away from Levi Hurdle, a chair maker. The ad stated Bangs was bound to Hurdle from "the 5th of August 1839 until the 22nd of January 1845, consequently he had 16 or 17 months to serve yet."

Three generations earlier, George Washington had offered $40 for two runaway servants: one with sandy colored hair and wearing "osnabrug trousers," the other a brickmaker born in Scotland who "talks pretty broad."

One historian tabulated the characteristics of runaway advertisements in great detail and found many ads included a notice of the "peculiar marks" of the runaways. "Eighteen Century America," Jonathan Prude wrote, "produced no other compilation of physiological and psychological distortions comparable to these notices. Here were citations to a woman with remarkable large breasts, to an Irish servant whose head jerked with frequent involuntary motions, and to a slave with six-fingered hands." Although fascinating, the descriptions often weren't descriptive enough to apprehend the runaways. The additional descriptor, included in an astonishing three-quarters of the ads, related to the garments the runaways wore or took with them.

At the completion of their indenture, male servants were given ten bushels of Indian corn, thirty shillings and a musket; female servants got fifteen bushels of corn and forty shillings.

As for the intrepid Mr. Bangs, recapture meant an extended period of indenture, a possible whipping and having his head and eyebrows shaven to make him easily recognizable in case he went looking again for freedom in America.

Early American Terror:
Blackbeard

Long before the word terrorist was coined, a man from Accomack County, Virginia created massive fear and panic by murdering, plundering and thwarting the transportation of critical supplies along the Atlantic coast. Yes, Virginia, there really was a well-known man with a beard. But his beard wasn't white and no one considered him jolly.

It was during his service as a privateer, a nautical license to steal, raiding French ships in Queen Anne's War, that Edward Teach (or Thach, Thatch or Tach) tasted the lucrative rewards of his future career in piracy. The war ended in 1713 and Teach took to tying his beard into little pig tails held fashionably snug with black ribbons. This 18th century gang-wear made him look as vicious as his sobriquet sounded: Blackbeard.

In 1718, a William Howard, "not having the fear of God before his eyes nor regarding the allegiancy due to his majesty," was charged with "pyracy and robbery committed on the high seas." The charges mentioned that he and fellow conspirators "Edward Tach and other wicked and desolute persons… did…commit pyracys and depredations upon the high seas." A specific charge related to the pirates' attack on the sloop *The Betty of Virginia* on or about the 29th of September, 1717.

Robbing and plundering ships along a deadly swath of the Atlantic seaboard, Blackbeard was "diabolically clever as well as fierce" and seemingly unstoppable. Complaints to England had been shelved and ignored. Blackbeard moved to North Carolina from Virginia for the protection of safe-haven status. In the former he was a wealthy businessman wanted for his willingness to pay lucrative kickbacks to the governor; in the latter, he was simply wanted.

Although there had been anti-piracy laws on the books in Virginia since 1699, they were tough to enforce against the exile. "Great mischief and depredations are dayly done upon the high seas by pyrates privateers and sea robbers...(for) resistance or refusall to yield obedience to his majestyes authority it shall be lawfull to kill or destroy such person or persons."

The newly elected governor of Virginia, Alexander Spotswood, dealt severely with the evil-doer and got a proclamation passed offering a one hundred pound reward:

"Whereas by an Act of Assembly...begun at the Capital in Williamsburg, the eleventh day of November, in the fifth year of his Majesty's reign, entitled, an Act to Encourage the Apprehending and Destroying of Pirates...it is enacted, that all and every person or persons, whom...shall take any pirate, or pirates, on the sea or land...within one hundred leagues of the continent of Virginia...that is to say, for Edward Teach, commonly called Captain Teach, or Blackbeard..."

With the reward, the terrorist was now hunted and his days of plunder were numbered. "Ships at a distance have every man's wish on board," written by Zora Neale Hurston, aptly describes Commander Henry Maynard of the *Pearl* upon getting his first glimpse of *Queen Anne's Revenge* off the North Carolina coast on the 17th of November 1718. As Maynard had hoped, on board was none other than the elusive Blackbeard.

"Damnation seize my soul if I give a quarter or take any from you!" Blackbeard shouted, before mentioning that only he and Satan could find the treasure he buried.

As a pirate, here are a few more expressions for that time period that Blackbeard and his compatriots would have used: Escaping from a tight situation was a "soft farewell," any theft from the Spanish was called a "a forced loan," leaving a pirate's corpse out as a warning to others was known as "sun-dried," and poking captives with sharp knives as they ran a gauntlet was called a "sweat." "Belly-timber" meant food, "fudled" was drunk and "Davy Jones" or "Davey Jones's locker" meant the bottom of the sea. And finally, red, not black, was the flag color most feared by those who came across pirates. A red flag meant that no quarter would be given to anyone captured. A red flag meant death, no discussion and no exception. A black flag (even with the skull and crossbones), indicated quarter would be given to those who surrendered.

Back to Blackbeard's impending fight and doom. The defiant thug was closer to hell than tomorrow.

Battle ensued and a few minutes later the head formerly spewing the taunts and threats was now proudly mounted to the *Pearl's* bowsprit and the not-so-good *Queen Anne's Revenge* started collecting barnacles on the ocean floor.

Blackbeard died in the "bloody knot of hand to hand combat" and his booty was quickly disposed of: "The effects of Teach the pirate have been condemned by the Court of Vice-Admiralty and sold at public auction."

Blackbeard's fellow surviving pirates were tried, convicted and hanged in Williamsburg. Virginia State Papers include a claim for twenty pounds in which a Henry Irwin sought reimbursement for the cost of two horses that died while transporting witnesses for the trial of "Blackbeard's crew of pirates."

The battle with Blackbeard in North Carolina waters caused some friction between the two colonies; North Carolina believed Virginia unnecessarily intruded and should mind its own matters and patrol its own waters.

History of the OED

Students of history know well the value of the Oxford English Dictionary. It's back-to-school time, which means tons of school supplies are flying off store shelves and onto students' desks. No desktop would be complete without a dictionary; however, few of our young scholars this fall will be sporting the gold standard of reference books, the Oxford English Dictionary. "Word lovers, the Gods are smiling upon you," may express the joy of the OED to aspiring wordmongers and sesquipedalians, but there are no words in the English language to accurately convey the staggering magnitude of the behemothian OED. Just considering its 22,000 pages and over 500,000 defined words makes the OED a sheer delight for even the most hard-core lexicologist. Throw in its 2.5 million quotations, fifty-nine million words and the 540 megabytes needed to electronically store it, and it's clear the OED is the tyrannosaurus rex of the scholarly world. And at 138 pounds, the OED just might weigh more than your student.

Students and their parents looking for a great book to read in their spare time this fall should pick up Simon Winchester's *The Madman and the Professor*, a fascinating tale of how the OED came about, including how an inmate at a criminal insane asylum became a major contributor of words.

The project to compile the OED began in 1857 and was completed seventy years later. It was originally anticipated to take ten years. Five years after starting the editors had made it alphabetically to the word ant. "Among the wonders of the world of scholarship" and "in all probability, the greatest continuing work of scholarship," the hardback OED set sells on the Oxford University Press website for $1,500. Speaking of "set," the OED contains over 150 definitions for just that word alone.

The word 'history' was first used in 1390, and subsequent usages include: History is a "huge Mississippi of falsehood" (1865) and "history is the science of man in his character as a political being" (1886).

You don't have to be a writer to be fascinated by words and how they came about.

Alexander Graham Bell's name for the phone, Roy Jacuzzi for the hot tub, John Stetson's for a hat, French acrobat Jules Leotard for the tights, and Charles Ponzi for a fraudulent scheme to steal money. Generals Burnside and Hooker are recalled because of their Civil War exploits, but it's widely believed their names became words. Whether Thomas Crapper's name led to a word is debatable.

Some people are remembered forever because of what they said or wrote, like politicians and writers. Others became famous because they did something unusual or unique before there was a word to describe it. So their name became the word to describe the event.

Ranchers brand their cattle. Otherwise disputes over the ownership of these wandering beasts would lead to not-so-neighborly friction between farmers. In the 1890s a rancher named Samuel A. Maverick refused to brand and presto, the word maverick was coined! Whether he refused because he didn't think it was necessary or to lay claim to all unbranded cattle is not recorded.

An English landowner messed with his tenants so much that they got together and stopped renting from him anymore. Mr. Charles Boycott's name became mud with his tenants, but today it's a widely known verb or noun. It's not certain, but many believe Patrick Hooligan was the source of the word to describe dangerously rowdy street thugs. A tavern bouncer with a nasty and well-deserved reputation for being out of control, Hooligan killed a policeman in London. Philadelphia whiskey maker E. G. Booz needs no further explanation. Gerrymandering oddly shaped congressional districts comes to us through a portmanteau of Mr. Elbridge Gerry (a congressman and vice president) and the word salamander.

In 1820, a North Carolina Congressman named Felix Walker defended foolish remarks he made in a speech by saying he spoke for the people of his home county—Buncombe County. So buncombe, and later just 'bunk' became synonymous with nonsense.

In 1907 a writer named Gelette Burgess (1866-1951) tried to sell his book, *"Are You a Bromide?"* with a little summary of the book on the cover along with a drawing of a buxom woman he called Miss Blinda Blurb. Future summaries then had a name to them: blurbs.

That ubiquitous red flower that comes out at the end of the year was introduced in the United States in the 1830s by a man who brought it back from his travels to Mexico. The man happened to be a former congressman from South Carolina and Minister to Mexico. His name was Joel R. Poinsett. Add an 'ia' after his surname and you have the Christmas flower. Don't forget William Forsythe, Alexander Garden and French botanist Pierre Magnol for forsythia, gardenia and the magnolia plants.

William Frisbie owned a pie shop in Bridgeport, Connecticut, home of the tin pans that became the Frisbee. Other food related people include opera singer Nellie Melba, Reverend Sylvester Graham and Lemuel Benedict for toast, crackers and a special egg dish.

A bomb goes off on the battlefield and deadly jagged pieces of metal go flying everywhere. Do you think British soldier Henry Shrapnel would have imagined we'd being talking about him a century and a half after he died? Other inventors included Richard J. Gatling and Samuel Colt (not to mention Mr. Remington, Smith and Wesson too) for their guns and Edwin P. Hubble (World War I) for the telescope; Charles Goodyear for making rubber an everyday product; David Buick, Ransom Olds, Henry Ford, Horace Dodge and Walter Chrysler for their cars as well as Mr. Rudolph Diesel (who built a 25 HP engine in 1897) for the motor to run them. And don't forget a couple Frenchmen named Pasteur and Guillotine--one for saving lives, the other for ending them.

There's the Greek God named Pan who instilled fear in people by the scary noises he made, causing widespread panic. And let's not forget the Scandinavian mythological figure named Berserk. Imagine having crazy, irrational behavior named after you.

George Washington Gale Ferris, a Pittsburgh steel inspector came up with the big slow circular ride you take at amusement parks. Also for science, you have Heinrich Hertz, Alessandro Volta and Ernest Mach to thank for radio frequencies, electric voltage and the speed of sound. If something mesmerizes you, thank Austrian physician Franz Mesmer for lending his name. Italian physiologist Luigi Galvani might be thought of when things are galvanized. Weather reports all mention Doppler, Fahrenheit and Celsius, which brings to mind the Austrian scientist Christian Johann Doppler, Dutch instrument maker Daniel Gabriel Fahrenheit and the Swedish astronomer Anders Celsius. Of course to help the blind read, Louis Braille, take a bow.

The first known written usage of the words 'school' and 'teacher' date back to the 10th century; however, regardless of dates and times, students need to pay close attention in their classrooms (first used in 1656), do their homework (1889) and avoid trips to the principal's (this one goes way back to the year 1297) office if they want to get good grades (1886). Of course, staying out of detention (1882) "to meditate over their evil ways" and acing (1959) a few tests (1602, Shakespeare's Hamlet: "It is no madnesses that I have uttered, bring me to the test") would help too. Speaking of Shakespeare, he is the OED's most quoted author with about 33,300 entries.

Next time you see an arithmetic textbook (students: that's next week!), consider the word arithmetic was first known to have been written over 750 years ago! But this sentence from a word usage in 1750 might be considered inappropriate for student textbooks: "Arithmetic is excellent for the gauging of liquors."

Algebra, "the department of mathematics which investigates the relations and property of numbers by means of general symbols; and, in a more abstract sense, a calculus of symbols," was first used over 450 years ago. In a word usage from 1570: "That more secret and subtill part of arithmetike, commonly called algebra." A word usage in 1860 included the simile: "passionless as algebra." The first use of civics (1886) was in the form of a question: "Shall civics be taught in the public schools?"

You and your student-scholar can visit your local library and consult the OED, which has been artfully described by the writer Annie Proulx as "the greatest treasure of words waiting to be assembled into fiery tracts and rants, literary novels, histories, sagas, comic poems, exposes, polemics, tall tales and learned treatises, kids' books, advert copy, reports on busted dams and declarations, all the expressions of a hundred different cultures."

Good luck and happy philology!

A Duel in Virginia

In a long-forgotten historical epoch forty-five presidential elections ago, when politics could be a life-threatening activity, two of America's greatest statesmen, John Randolph of Virginia and Henry Clay of Kentucky. engaged in the 19th Century equivalent of the nuclear option and faced each other with loaded weapons on a meadow in Northern Virginia. Dueling had been in place for many years as the most drastic step to resolve arguments, or more likely, terminating the opponent causing the argument.

It was, however, very controversial. Patrick Henry called dueling "gothic and absurd." Thomas Jefferson claimed: "It is not an inclination in anyone but a fear of the opinion of the world which leads one to the absurd and immoral decision of differences by duel."

In one of the most controversial Presidential nominations in American history, John Quincy Adams selected Henry Clay as his secretary of state in March 1825. Adams had just been sworn in, putting an end to the rule, as it was called by many New Englanders, the "Virginia junto," the incredible string of three Virginians— Jefferson, Madison and Monroe—controlling the White House for twenty-four consecutive years. Adams had won in an incredibly close and controversial race, and in fact, was literally selected in the end for the White House by none other than Henry Clay.

Adams, Clay (who was the most powerful member of the House of Representatives), Andrew Jackson and William Crawford of Georgia competed for the presidency in 1824. Crawford, the

Secretary of Treasury under Monroe probably won have won (had he stayed healthy) as the candidate most factions could live with. He did not draw the animosity and strong passions-for and against—that the other candidates did. But Crawford suffered a major stroke just before the campaign. By keeping the news from the public, Crawford stayed close throughout the race and was in it until the very end.

The vote was close. With the candidates splitting the votes, no one got the required 131 total electoral votes to win. Adams won the New England States- 84 electoral votes and about 31% of the popular vote. Clay won Ohio, Kentucky and Missouri and their 37 electoral votes. Crawford won Georgia and Virginia and captured 41 electoral votes. Jackson won everything else, with 99 electoral votes and 41% of the popular vote.

As per the Constitution, the names of the top three candidates go to the House of Representatives (where candidate Clay happened to be Speaker) to select the winner. Crawford had narrowly edged out Clay to make the triumvirate with Jackson and Adams.

In the House, each of the twenty-four states had a single vote. Henry Clay despised Andrew Jackson, and the feeling was mutual. Clay was diplomatic when he simply said he could not believe that "killing 2500 Englishmen at New Orleans qualifies [Jackson] for the chief magistracy."

Adams did not get a single vote from Kentucky in the 1824 race and upon the matter of the selection going to the House of Representatives to decide, the Kentucky Legislature sent Clay instructions to vote for Jackson. But Clay would not be swayed away from selecting Adams. Speaker Clay twisted enough arms (particularly Stephen van Rensselaer's of New York) and shook enough hands with his colleagues in the House to get Adams selected. Three states which had each given all or most of its electoral votes to Jackson in the November 1824 election gave its single vote in the February 1825 selection in the House of Representatives to Quincy Adams: Illinois, Maryland and Louisiana.

Even before the decision, many Jackson supporters howled about a suspected Adams-Clay conspiracy that end, when the curtain was finally drawn, with Quincy Adams in the White House and

Henry Clay in the second most desirable chair in Washington—that belonging to the secretary of state. In those days and up to that period, the secretary of state was the immediate launching pad to the White House. It was no secret to anybody that Henry Clay had presidential aspirations.

Many believed the Clay nomination was the back end of the corrupt bargain that had been in the works. Although it's possible, most historians, however, do not think it actually happened like that. Adams is viewed as too honest to have engaged in a nefarious deal of that sort. Perhaps he was honest, a positive trait thrown against his highly abrasive personality. Quincy Adams said about himself: "I am a man of reserved, cold, austere and forbidding manners."

It's probable that Adams first offered the job to DeWitt Clinton of New York. When Clinton declined, Clay's experience made him the likely choice. But whether the bargain was corrupt or not, many believed the bargain stank, and its stench wafted through all those political bodies connected to Adams and Clay.

Especially enraged was John Randolph, the "half-mad Virginian," who never liked Adams to begin with, and deeply distrusted Clay, and anyone else from Kentucky, "a race," he characterized as, "inferior to those of the Old Dominion." Randolph, promptly "turn(ed) upon President Adams and Secretary Clay all the batteries of criticism, sarcasm, excoriation and plain vituperation of which he was master." His voice was a "shrill scream when he was giving vent to his turgid philippics. In the heat of debate…his wit and ridicule was unsurpassed."

Randolph's "interminable speeches…constituted a kind of mental lottery in which at any moment the listener was likely to draw a prize in the nature of a saying which he would treasure in his memory for years. It might be a bit of razor-edged sarcasm, a momentary flash of wit, a happy allusion to the classics…but whatever it might be, it was certain to sparkle…Eventually it came to pass that when anything good was said it was assumed to be a quotation from the master of Roanoke…'All the bastard wit of the country has been fathered on me,' he complained once."

Henry Adams described Randolph's tactics: "To spring suddenly, violently, straight in the face of the opponent...In the white heat of passionate rhetoric he could gouge and kick, bite off an ear or a nose, or hit below the waist." Josiah Quincy, a cousin of John Quincy Adams, remarked of Randolph: "Upon the whole, he is a man who will always have more enemies than friends."

Henry Clay, "the Great Statesman of the West," an exceptionally respected orator and politician, was "tall and dignified in bearing... peculiarly winning in his manner (and) united with this suavity was strength of will, an inbred sense of honor." Clay proudly proclaimed he'd rather be right than be President, and with four unsuccessful attempts at the White House, he must have often been right.

The enmity exploded in 1826 when Randolph lambasted the administration and colorfully called Clay "black-legged" (a swindler).

Clay's subsequent request that Randolph explain his verbal assault was contemptuously dismissed: "Puritanic, diplomatic, black-legged administration," Randolph snarled, didn't need further explanation. In response to this "unprovoked attack upon [his] character," Clay suggested he and Randolph have a meeting, a gentleman's euphemism for a duel.

On Saturday, the 8th of April at half past four o'clock, a meeting took place between Mr. Clay and Mr. Randolph. Although dueling was illegal in Virginia, Randolph rationalized his participation by claiming it was not really a duel, because, after checking "the devil in Clay's eye," he did not plan to return fire.

Randolph's assistant had insisted on setting Randolph's pistol with a "hair trigger." The pistol discharged as it was being handed to Randolph. Clay graciously announced it was accidental, thereby allowing Randolph to retain his honor. Both politicians were given their pistols with the verbal command: "Fire-1-2-3-stop."

They both missed. After all, words were their weapons. Clay, complaining "this is child's play!" demanded a do-over. On the second try, Clay's bullet grazed Randolph's oversized coat. Randolph fired in the air and proclaimed, "I do not fire at you, Mr. Clay!"

The relieved warriors shook hands and a witness to the event wrote: "The joy of all was extreme at this happy termination of a most critical affair, and we immediately left with lighter hearts than we brought."

Randolph's animosity toward Clay, however, never changed. Tradition has it that Randolph wanted to be buried facing west so he could keep an eye on Henry Clay. The sight of the duel, where many duels were fought, is "a stone's throw" from one of the old District of Columbia boundary markers near Walker's Chapel Methodist Church on Glebe Road in Arlington.

The hostility from the 1824 election reared its angry guns in other locations in 1826. In a duel in Franklin, Kentucky on September 22, at only fifteen feet apart, Tennessee Congressman Sam Houston, a loyal and close friend of Andrew Jackson, shot and severely wounded General William A. White, a lawyer and a veteran of the Battle of New Orleans.

NASA and the Moon Landing

World War II settled matters on earth but ignited the Cold War to space. Imagination and patriotism propelled the ship, but it was captained by fear, fear over placing second in a must-win race and eventually having to sleep, as President Lyndon Johnson warned, under the light of a Communist moon. An exuberant spirit of youthful daring-do intoxicated Americans to go beyond, to shatter the parameters of caution. Everywhere all systems were go, everything was A-OK. We were entrenched in scorched planetary warfare over what was widely believed to be not mere victory, or control of the heavens, but our very survival. Armed with the scientific know-how and the audacity to dare, we would somehow, someway, control the spacious skies and plant our flag on the high ground of the moon. No naysayer would impede the effort; no bureaucrat worried about a few billion space dollars was going to thwart the free and the brave from its meeting with destiny on a dusty barren surface of which the likes of Galileo, DeVinci and Columbus dreamed about. For centuries or more man has wondered if he'd ever get there, but for a mere twelve years, an infinitesimal sliver of time, from October 1957 when the 184-pound Donna Summer-disco ball named "fellow traveler," otherwise known as Sputnik, frightfully beeped through orbit at 17,000 mph until July 1969 when an Ohio farm boy took a small step, two horses named America and Russia blazed the quarter million mile cosmic track from earth to the moon to try and win the Lunar Derby.

The whole idea goes way back but 1865 might be the best starting point. That was the year Jules Verne wrote *From the Earth to the Moon,* about a rocket carrying three men, blasting off from Tampa, Florida, going up in space and splashing down in the Pacific Ocean, all remarkably close to the actual events of an Apollo mission a century later. The only real difference was that Verne used a count-up that ignited the rocket at forty rather than a countdown to zero. Half a century later Robert Goddard, the father of American space flight, said it would be possible to land on the moon someday. However, he completely dismissed the idea because it would probably cost a million dollars.

The secretive Russians got off to a propitious start. They basked in their successes and hid their failures so that with Sputnik, followed a month later, just for good measure and to prove it wasn't a fluke, with another satellite, they looked invincible. Two years later, in September 1959, they crash landed a rocket on the moon. Sure, it wasn't a man yet, but getting a lot of space debris there, along with several pictures of Lenin was light years ahead of our program, which was grounded by a nasty turf war between the military services, each pushing its own rocketry as the vehicle to space. The Army had its Redstone rockets, the Navy the Vanguard, and the Air Force had Atlas. But in the end, the Army had the brains on its payroll, in the form of Wernher von Braun, a former German scientist, to eventually lead America to the moon.

Sputnik happened less than a year after Nikita Khrushchev banged his shoe on the table and spewed: "Whether you like it or not, history is on our side. We will bury you!" Americans were scared and demanded action. Congress sprayed money at NASA. NASA buzzed with young brash pilots. Pilots trained with the excitement of kids and kids hid under their school desks.

NACA (the National Advisory Committee for Aeronautics) was founded in 1915 as a rider to a navy appropriations bill. With its first annual allotment of $5,000 it planned "to supervise and direct the scientific study of the problems of flight, with a view of their practical solution." By late 1958 change was in order and NACA's five thousand engineers working at five different centers were absorbed into NASA.

No one knew how things would evolve: would it be a civilian or military project? If it involved pilots, would they be from the Navy or the Air Force? Trying to figure things out led only to more questions. It truly was the epitome of uncharted territory. Many believed we had already lost the race and should concentrate on satellites rather than getting a man on the moon. A member of the early planning committee said during a White House meeting that a manned space launch would "only be the most expensive funeral man has ever had."

After grueling batteries of tests, NASA winnowed an original list of 508 test pilots down to seven, three each from the Navy and the Air Force, and one from the Marines. This "Original Seven," selected in April 1959 to commence the space race went down in history as the Mercury 7. Six of them went up in space and one eventually walked on the moon. In Roman mythology, Mercury was the messenger of the gods. Project Mercury replaced another that was lost to history—an Air Force project known as MISS, which stood for "Men in Space Soonest." This was a cool bunch of pilots. One astronaut (Gordo Cooper) fell asleep while awaiting takeoff; another's heart rate never exceeded 105 during his mission in orbit (Scott Carpenter).

Two of them had to make an effort to keep the pounds off. Every extra pound of body weight required an additional one thousand pounds of fuel to launch. In addition, the less they weighed, the more science stuff could be stuffed into the capsule.

But before any of them ascended into space (which officially is 50 miles up—if you travel 49 miles, you are not considered to have gotten there), NASA wanted to send a chimp on the first test voyage. Twenty veterinarians were hired to train forty chimpanzees to select the best candidate to ride the rocket. The winning chimp was introduced as HAM, an acronym for the Holloman Aerospace Medical Center. He made it back safely, as did a later space traveler, another chimp named Enos (Greek for man).

The name of the first spacecraft was Freedom 7, neither an acronym nor Greek. Each of the seven astronauts got to name his own spacecraft and the first one up, Alan Shepard, named his the Freedom 7. The press spun it so the 7 represented the idea that although they went up individually, they were all on a Team of Seven. In reality, there was a 7 after Shepard's spacecraft because it was the seventh spacecraft manufactured by the McDonnell Douglas assembly team. Thirty eight years later, John Glenn, the politician-astronaut, was still spinning the 7 as for team and leaving out of his autobiography the original reason for the 7.

Apparently there is no i in team but there really is a 7 because all the others followed with a 7 -- the Liberty Bell 7, Friendship 7, Delta 7, Aurora 7, Sigma 7, and Faith 7. The Delta 7 never went up because at the 11th hour NASA decided Deke Slayton's previously diagnosed heart problem might not be conducive to space travel. But Slayton, the only Mercury 7 astronaut who stayed grounded through the Mercury program, eventually ended up making a flight into space in 1975 in a joint USA/Russia endeavor. Six Mercury astronauts flew one flight between May 1961 and May 1963, and then had to wait to see if and when they'd get the chance to fly again.

The following is from *The Elephant's Child* by Rudyard Kipling. Certainly he didn't have these six Mercury astronauts in mind, but it seems to fit perfectly:

I keep six honest serving men
(They taught me all I knew):
Their names are What and Why and When
And How and Where and Who.

I send them over land and sea,
I send them east and west,
But after they have worked for me,
I give them all a rest.

Twenty three days after Russia propelled Yuri Gagarin to the title of first man in space, Alan Shepard grabbed his fifteen minutes of fame, a fifteen minute ride into space that officially put America in the race. It also, according to *the London Times*, "exorcised the demon of inferiority that had possessed Americans." After Shepard's flight, beer and liquor sales skyrocketed; according to the *New York Times,* people "were toasting the success of the astronaut's feat." Not surprisingly, technology stocks like IBM and McDonnell Douglas also soared.

The astronauts had financial interests too, and a tax lawyer and owner of the Washington Redskins, provided free service to assist them. Charles Leo D'Orsey was like a Godfather to the "boys" and their families. "It is impossible to overstate Leo's influence on the seven astronauts those first two or three years," one family member wrote. He even referred to them as his boys several times in a newspaper story. Among other things, he negotiated a lucrative deal with *Life Magazine* to provide financial assistance to the astronauts, who after all, were cosmic superstars scrapping by on mere earthly government salaries. When the third one went up (John Glenn), D'Orsey considered buying a $100,000 insurance policy and Lloyd's of London agreed to write a policy for $16,000. D'Orsey, however, didn't want to bet against Glenn so instead wrote out a $100,000 check payable to Mrs. Glenn in case anything happened to her husband.

Astronauts were the big guns in the space war so NASA feverishly collected them. In September 1962, nine more were brought in (called "the Next Nine") followed by groups of fourteen, five, nineteen and eleven in 1963, 1965, 1966, and 1967 respectively. The 1965 and 1967 groups consisted exclusively of scientists, one of whom later walked on the moon. At its peak in the summer of 1967, fifty-six astronauts rode NASA's payroll.

Project Gemini replaced Mercury. Latin for twins, the Constellation Gemini appears like a set of twins, an apt name given that two astronauts flew together in each Gemini flight. From March 1965 through November 1966, Gemini churned out ten manned flights.

Project Apollo then replaced Gemini. Named for the God who carried the fiery sun across the sky in a chariot, Apollo sent eleven crews of three each into space and one to its early death. Apollo One's Gus Grissom, Ed White and Roger Chaffee were killed by carbon dioxide poisoning when their spacecraft caught fire in January 1967, in the unkindest cut of all. Not in space, not on the moon, but on the launch pad during a practice session. Grissom, the commander, had predicted that if anyone died in Apollo, it would be him. The man who later determined which astronaut went up in each mission, wrote years after the accident that Grissom would have been the first one to walk on the moon had he lived. Grissom believed that President Johnson was pushing things too fast in an attempt to offset criticism for the Vietnam War. Grissom said the Apollo One was the worst spacecraft he'd ever seen, going so far as to stick a lemon on it, and ordering someone to leave the lemon on what he considered a piece of shoddy engineering. You lose if you get all lemons on a slot machine and astronauts lose if their space rocket is decked out with a lemon.

NASA had switched contractors for Apollo, dropping the contractor that had safely navigated Mercury and Gemini through space. Worse, however, than just walking away from experienced and proven spacecraft engineers was the widely-held belief that they switched to the new inexperienced contractor for political cronyism, always a terrible reason, especially so with astronauts' lives at stake.

The astronauts of Apollo 7, the first manned mission after the deaths of Apollo 1, still upset with NASA for the deaths of their fellow astronauts as well as for the belief that they were getting make-work unnecessary tasks, refused while in space, a directive from NASA. None of the three from Apollo 7 ever went up in space afterwards.

Charlie Brown and Snoopy did, however, later go into space. These were the names the astronauts of Apollo 10 gave their command module and lunar modules. The mission got to within 47,000 feet of the moon, setting up the Apollo 11 moon walk. At the very same time that Armstrong and Aldrin of Apollo 11 were walking on the moon, the Russians sent up an unmanned spacecraft (Luna 15) to land on the moon, scoop up rocks and bring them back to earth before Apollo 11 returned. In the books that would have been another Russian space victory, but since it crashed on the moon (about 500 miles away from Apollo 11), it's not much talked about. Armstrong didn't talk much either. He was generally so quiet that his fellow astronauts were surprised he said so much in his single sentence about his first step being a small one for man and a giant one for mankind. Aldrin was known as Dr. Rendezvous because, according to another astronaut, "that's all he could talk about, even over a cup of coffee." Fun fact: Aldrin's mother's maiden name was Moon!

Any talk between Apollo spacecraft and NASA came about via three big antennas evenly spaced over the globe in Spain, Australia and the Mojave Desert. For directional navigation, the spacecraft computer contained the celestial coordinates of thirty-seven selected stars.

Incredibly, NASA's financial coordinates froze as things heated up in the late 1960s. The president slashed NASA's budget to 3.83 billion dollars, about 25% below its peak year of 1965. Congress then cut it to $3.69 billion, forcing NASA to terminate about 5,000 jobs at Cape Kennedy. But even if they had all the money in the world they couldn't buy anything better than late 1960s technology. The Apollo 11 lunar module, known as Eagle had a single 17.5 pound Raytheon computer on board with a memory of 36 K, less than today's cell phones. The command module to return them to earth had two of the same computers. The computers held only 38,000 words.

The last person the astronauts saw as they boarded their craft was Guenter Wendt, often referred to by the astronauts as the "Pad Fuehrer." Wendt had been a pilot in the German Luftwaffe during WW II. After the war, he moved to St. Louis, where in 1955, he became an American citizen and an employee of McDonnell Aircraft, the lead contractor for the Mercury program. As a joke he gave parting gifts to the astronauts before each mission. For the Apollo 11 astronauts, Wendt gave them a four-foot long key to the moon.

When Apollo 11 landed on the moon the spacecraft had only 17 seconds of fuel remaining. Just before landing, an alarm code went off indicating a computer overload. A twenty-six year old NASA whiz kid made a quick decision to ignore the warning and go ahead with the landing. For his efforts, Scott Bales later joined the Apollo 11 astronauts in receiving the Medal of Freedom from President Nixon. But despite all these close calls, they landed in fine fettle with Aldrin's heart rate showing a cool 125 when they touched down on the moon. Coming back they traveled at about 25,000 mph through the brief reentry period. As a measure of comparison, a bullet shot out of a rifle goes about 2,000 mph.

At much slower speeds on the moon, the lunar-mobile traveled several miles, an astronaut clubbed a golf ball into forever, and incredibly, none of the astronauts died. Had something gone wrong, there was no way they would survive, no one would rescue them. Everyone knew that, including President Nixon, who had his farewell Neil and Buzz speech ready to go. We all know Armstrong's first soulful words about mankind. The last of the twelve men on the moon, Eugene Cernan, waxed much less eloquently: simply a comment to "get this mother ought of here."

A mother-to-be named Valentina Tereshkova became the first woman in space with 48 orbits in almost three days in 1963, a year before giving birth to a daughter. Cosmonaut Tereshkova was not a pilot or an engineer. She was a factory worker who had joined a sky-diving club. The Russians appeared early on to be winning the space race, but behind the scenes there was serious trouble. When they learned that we would be sending up two astronauts at a time in Gemini, they wanted to send three to gain a space victory. But, the three and their suits and equipment weighed too much. Answer: send the cosmonauts up without their heavy space suits, which is exactly what happened. Incredibly, they pulled it off and the three cosmonauts wearing coveralls and sneakers made it back safely. Cosmonauts on another mission safely landed back on earth but so far off their target that they didn't get picked up (by ski troops) until the next day. They built a campfire to stay warm and to frighten off nearby wolves.

No one remembers much of 1966, but in that year, both countries safely landed (unmanned) space craft on the moon to take pictures. In fact, before Armstrong walked on the moon, America had safely landed five unmanned space craft on the moon's surface, all which sent pictures back to NASA.

Two astronauts planned to take a mystery picture to mess with the earthlings later. They set up a timer to take a picture of both of them in front of their spacecraft. The timer didn't work and the picture didn't get taken. Imagine how that would have fired up the "we never landed on the moon" crowd! It's not recorded whether NASA management was fired up or laughing when they rejected one astronaut's travel voucher (yes they filed vouchers to space) claiming mileage of seven cents a mile, for *all* his miles into space.

They took all sorts of things up there, for laughs and even for profit. They took a corned beef sandwich (so much for special astronaut food!), a couple rolls of dimes to give out later as souvenirs, postal envelopes which were sold to a collector and even Miss December 1972-a Playboy magazine. Neil Armstrong joked about taking rocks from earth to the moon and bringing them back as "moon rocks" just to mess with NASA scientists.

Shortly before Apollo 17 took off in December 1972, a writer named Tom Wolfe penned this for *Rolling Stone Magazine*: "The main thing to know about an astronaut, if you want to understand his psychology, is not that he's going into space but that he is a flyer and has been in that game for fifteen or twenty years. It's like a huge and complex pyramid, miles high, and the idea is to prove at every foot of the way up that pyramid that you are one of the elected and anointed ones who have *the right stuff* and can move even higher and even—ultimately, God willing, one day—that you might be able to join that very special few at the very top, that elite who truly have the capacity to bring tears to men's eye, the very Brotherhood of The Right Stuff itself."

As for weighty remarks about the importance of the space program and its future, Astronaut Cernan summed it up much more professionally and diplomatically than his comment about getting off the moon's surface: "We will go (into deep space) because it is logical to do so, and our curiosity as a species will not allow us to remain locked to our home planet much longer. Humankind must explore, for we want to learn what lies over the hill or around the corner. Inspiration, sweat, challenges, and dreams got us to the moon and they will get us to Mars and beyond. It is our destiny...Lunar exploration was not the equivalent of an American pyramid, some idle monument to technology, but more of a Rosetta Stone, a key to unlock dreams as yet undreamed. Our legacy is that humans are no longer shackled to Earth. We opened the door to tomorrow, and our trips to another celestial body will rank as the ultimate triumph in the Age of Achievement. And for the price, it was the biggest bargain in history."

Scott Carpenter's book about his life in the NASA program includes this quote showing his poetic side: "Be ready in trouble, endeavor to be a jolly companion, remember and tell good and true stories around lonely campfires."

POWs in America
During World War II

Of the millions of soldiers that America fought against in World War II, precisely 435,788 of them ended up here in the United States as prisoners of war, spread out in more than 600 sites in every state except Vermont and Nevada, as well as in the Territory of Alaska.

The first POW of the war, a Japanese officer, was captured on December 8, 1941 on a mini-submarine at Pearl Harbor. The first German POW was a U-boat captain captured off the North Carolina coast in May 1942.

Housed in old Civilian Conservation Corps (CCC) barracks, national guard camps, air bases and numerous other locations where the government owned land and buildings, the 378,898 Germans, 51,455 Italians and 5,435 Japanese each received at least ten cents per day (officers got more) in canteen credits to buy beer, tobacco, candy and toiletries. Rules concerning prisoner treatment had been dictated by the Geneva Convention, which had been signed by forty-six nations in July 1929 and ratified by the United States in January 1932. If the prisoners got hired out to work in the local community they received eighty cents a day. Whoever hired them out actually paid the prevailing rate to the government (forty-three cents per hour per man) with the excess over eighty cents used to fund the camps. In 1944 alone, the government earned $ 22 million for hiring these

POWs out, all of whom wore blue uniforms with PW stenciled in white on the back. As late as February 1945, Congressional representatives were pressuring the military to bring over to America an additional 100,000 POWs "to relieve the farm labor shortage" due to the war. In finalizing its accounts after WW II, the United States Government paid an additional $200 million to these POWs or their dependents for canteen credits which the POWs never got the chance to use, for one reason or another.

One reason that 2,827 of the POWs may have not been able to use their credits is that they were not in camp, that is, they had escaped, albeit most only for a temporary period. One Japanese prisoner, 604 Italians and 2,222 Germans escaped, many in odd and interesting ways. In New Mexico, German POWs dug a tunnel, 178 feet long, where twenty-five of them made their break the day before Christmas 1944. All were soon recaptured.

Several German POWs were unintentionally freed from camp when their Army driver forgot about them, drove off and left them stranded. One escapee from a New Hampshire POW camp was picked up four months later in Manhattan's Central Park, where he was painting and selling pictures. Another-*on four different occasions*-escaped and was recaptured, and one clever POW was recaptured in 1953 in Chicago where he had reinvented himself as a prosperous, respected book dealer.

One escapee, a poet at heart, left a goodbye note to camp authorities which included his rationale, an apology, and even a short poem:

"According to the great philosopher Spinoza every man has to seek happiness. Having not found it in this camp of war prisoners, I must go somewhere else. As you are not supposed to give us a furlough, though, I am taking it myself...I beg you to excuse and forgive me, after a certain lapse of time, if your authorities don't catch me before, I will return myself.

It matters not how straight the gate,
How charged with punishment the scroll,
I am master of my fate,
I am captain of my soul."

This particular prisoner never got the opportunity to turn himself in as the authorities recaptured him first. Several others did get a chance to turn themselves in, including one German who did so in March 1946, three months after he escaped and well after the war had ended. In fine fashion, he traveled by taxi back to the POW camp to turn himself in. Certainly he wasn't there much longer, because almost all the POWs officially left the United States in July 1946. The exception were the forty three POWs that had escaped and not been recaptured, and the 162 who were awaiting trial, having been charged with serious crimes. Altogether fourteen POWs were convicted of murder while in camps and were executed by hanging. Fourteen years after the war ended, in 1959, another escapee turned himself in. But the record belongs to 1985, the year the last POW turned himself in. And no, the year shown is not a typo.

Another German POW was found dead in the Hudson River, under mysterious circumstances, in October 1944. The autopsy cited the cause of death as "drowning by immersion *in salt water.*" Altogether 735 Germans, 99 Italians and 24 Japanese POWs died in camps, most from disease, a few from gunshot wounds as they tried to escape.

Hans Krug escaped from a POW camp in April 1942 and made his way to a Detroit tavern keeper named Max Stephan. For one day, Stephan fed Krug, bought him new clothes and a suitcase, and gave him $40 before getting him on a bus to Chicago, which was to be his next stop on a trip to Mexico. For this day's work, Stephan was convicted and almost hanged. One historian wrote that this was the first case since the Civil War that an American court had sentenced a man to die for treason. Mere hours before the scheduled execution President Roosevelt commuted the sentence to life imprisonment.

Escaping, however, became much easier for them in February 1944 when the camps instituted a "calculated risk" policy, significantly decreasing security. It was believed POWs did not pose a threat and if they escaped it would be relatively easy to recapture them. The worse crime committed by a POW escapee was car theft. Several reports mentioned that civilians, not POWs were the concern:

"The biggest problem is not to keep prisoners from making

advances to people. The problem is to keep the people from fraternizing with prisoners—feelings of sympathy being manifested by attempts to give gifts…Most trouble…is caused by the civilian element rather than a failure of prisoners to observe rules and regulations."

But the strangest escape of all dealt with a Harvard graduate named Dale Maple. The young (born September 10, 1920) San Diego native and United States Army private had made enough Pro-German, anti-American comments to get himself assigned to the 620th Engineer General Service Company, one of three groups where American soldiers with questionable loyalties were dumped. These three groups, consisting of between 1,200 and 1,500 soldiers, didn't carry weapons. If they were assigned guard duty, they were given flashlights and clubs. Mostly they wove camouflage nets, graded landing areas, pulled weeds, transplanted trees and dug ditches. In army reports and correspondence the group was alternately referred to as a "subversive organization" and a "special organization."

By early 1944, the 620th made its home at Camp Hale, a remote post about 120 miles west of Denver, and incredibly, only three hundred yards from a POW camp consisting of about 200 Germans. Through music and languages, Maple had developed a deep affection for all things German, despite the fact that he had never traveled there and had no known German ancestors. With an IQ of 152 and the ability to speak many languages, Maple was off-the-charts smart. He graduated from high school at age sixteen, first in a class of 585, and from Harvard in 1941, *magna cum laude*.

In later court martial records it was revealed that teachers at Maple's San Diego high school were thrilled when he left because his incredible intelligence was "embarrassing to the faculty." A Harvard professor said, "no one brain could withstand" all the information that "Dale was trying to cram into his." Much discussion and trial testimony dealt with Maple's childhood being the cause of his later problems. Maple was an only child. His parents divorced, with his father staying on the west coast and his mother moving to Newport, Rhode Island. A professor of Child Development and Family Relationships used Maple's home life and subsequent army problems as a classroom case study. There was a report that Maple was hit by a car on Easter Sunday in 1929 and carried into a nearby church where "he flopped about like a dying chicken."

One incident reveals Maple's loyalties. Upon getting a three day pass, Maple did not leave Camp Hale. Instead, he secretly managed to get himself into a POW uniform and spent the time in the POW camp with the Germans. He formed a plan to help two of them escape, which he might have pulled off had it not been for trouble with the ten year old faded cream-colored 1934 Reo sedan, the "Flying Cloud" model automobile he purchased for $250 for the project.

On February 15, 1944, two German POWs, who probably walked off a work crew, security being light, hopped into Maple's Reo for the nearly thousand mile road trip to Mexico, where they stood a decent chance of eventually getting to Germany, or at least getting away from North America. It took thirty hours for their absence to be reported, so anyone stumbling upon and helping three guys in a broken down Reo can be excused, which is exactly what happened. The gods of road trips were not smiling upon Maple and his Teutonic buddies. A tire went flat, they got it fixed and another tire went flat. They drove on with the bare rim of the flat tire until they accidently drove off the road into a ditch. An American Customs official stopped and helped them get back on their trip, which didn't last long because a few miles later they ran out of gas. They were about 17 miles from Mexico so their legs had to carry them home, or at least to Mexico. The hapless trio made it to Mexico but caught the eye of a Mexican Customs official who couldn't help but suspect something was out of the ordinary.

Maple was court martialled and sentenced to death by hanging for aiding the enemy. Although he had counsel and was not a lawyer himself, Maple cross examined many of the witnesses at his trial. A note he tried to secretly get to one of his confederates in the plan was intercepted and mentioned that he was going to try the "abused America angle" defense. His sentence was commuted to life in prison, and later to ten years. The POWs were sent back to POW camps. Three American soldiers who had helped Maple formulate the plan were also convicted. In addition, five WACs (Women's Army Corps) were charged in this affair for exchanging romantic notes with German POWs at Camp Hale. After leaving prison, Maple went back to California. He got involved in a venture building commercial fishing boats, which eventually led him into the marine insurance business.

Generally, the guards got along with the POWs and there few incidents. One guard in a South Carolina POW camped reported that the POWs:

> "...were just young boys. They weren't Nazis. Some were well educated, some were not...We had one sergeant, I'll never forget him...He told me he was captured three times. He was caught in Africa, but he escaped in a boat to Sicily. He was captured by the British, and he escaped again to Italy. The Americans got him there, and shipped him over here. I asked him if he was going to take off again, but he said, "Ach, too far to swim." I used to bring the newspaper in every morning and leave it in the orderly room. It was like a ritual. He'd ask if he could look at the paper. I'd say sure and he's sit down and snap open the paper...before you knew it he'd started to form political opinions. There were these article about Roosevelt running for the third time. He said the mothers of America would never re-elect Roosevelt because he had promised to keep their sons out of war, and he didn't do it."

But there were very few examples on the other extreme. In a Salina, Utah camp in July 1945, an America private named Clarence Bertucci opened fire with a 30-caliber machine gun at sleeping German POWs, killing eight and injuring twenty.

Tragically, a German POW named Werner Drechsler was murdered in a POW camp. Drechsler was the ideal prisoner, exceptionally cooperative. He spoke freely and fully to American interrogators. He was so vocally anti-German that it would have been perilous to his life to place him among other German POWs, as he might have been considered a spy or traitor. Word travels quickly everywhere, including the POW community. His life was at such risk that his file included a warning that he *should never be sent to a prisoner of war camp where other German naval prisoners of war were held."* For reasons that have never been determined—not known whether accidental or intentional--he was sent on March 12, 1944 to Arizona's POW camp at Papago Park, ten miles from Tempe. Within six and a half hours, he was dead, murdered by seven other POWs. Those seven were later convicted, and on August 25, 1945--after the war had ended--they comprised the last mass execution by the United States Government.

In Fairfax County, Virginia a total of 199 German POWs were stationed at a camp on Route 29. At the time Fairfax County was the third largest dairy producing county in the United States. A *New York Times* magazine story from September 1945 reported that the POWs often worked twelve hour days and were picked up from the camp by local farmers at 7 a.m. The first POW arrived June 13, 1945 and the last one left on November 16, 1945. In those five months, they worked a total of 111,000 hours at 196 different farms around the county. Altogether, the State of Virginia held approximately 17,000 POWs in twenty-seven installations.

In the First World War, only 1,346 German POWs—officers and crew members of German ships in America ports when the hostilities broke out--were held in the United States.

As for executions of American soldiers, Private Dale Maple may have dodged the noose, but a few years later another soldier named Private John A. Bennett did not.

Private John A. Bennett holds the infamous distinction of being the last soldier executed while serving in the United States military. Bennett was convicted on February 8, 1955, after a five day trial for the rape and attempted murder of an eleven year old girl in Siezenheim, Austria on December 21, 1954. Bennett signed an admission to the offense, in which he stated that before the incident occurred he had spent the day drinking "about six beers, one liter of cognac and a small bottle of gin" with some unidentified friends at a place called Francis's Gasthouse in Siezenheim. After the incident, he returned to Camp Roeder, where he was first contacted by authorities at about 9:00 p. m. while watching a movie.

Between 9:30 a.m. and 5:00 p.m. on the day of the incident he was seen by several witnesses wandering the streets of Siezenheim.

He walked into five witnesses' homes and asked if they knew where he could find a woman he referred to as "Margaret" or "Marget" or "Margie." None of the witnesses knew of such a person. He left each of the homes without incident.

At approximately 5:00 p.m. on December 21, 1954, an eleven-year old girl named Gertie Aigner was returning home by bus from a shopping trip to Salzburg, Austria to buy a calendar and sewing materials for her mother. Gertie later testified the man raped her and threw her in a puddle of water where she pretended to be dead. He then pulled her out of the water and dragged her to a nearby mill stream where he threw her in. The millstream was described in court records as eleven feet wide and three to four feet deep. She again pretended to be dead and he left.

Bennett had been inducted into the army on August 27, 1953, for two years. He was born April 10, 1935, in Chatham, Pittsylvania County, Virginia. He had two brothers in the army. Although single, Bennett had a child living in Chatham, Virginia. He had been found guilty in April 1953, for breach of marital promise and was sentenced to pay $30 per month for child care until the child reached adulthood. In civilian life, Bennett quit school at age fifteen and worked as a farmer. Bennett was a private first class in the Headquarters Battalion, 11th Anti-aircraft Artillery Battalion.

At the United States Disciplinary Barracks, Fort Leavenworth, Kansas, the execution of Prisoner John A. Bennett 'was completed without incident" at 12:21 a.m. Central Standard Time, 13 April 1961.

Afterword

George Orwell wrote that those who control the present control the past and those who control the past control the future. The control Orwell (real name: Eric Blair) spoke about related to history. Controlling history is about teaching and writing it, and unfortunately those disciplines are done using art far more than science. And consciously or unconsciously it is sometimes built on half-truths and myth. As much as Rembrandt masterfully filled his canvas with real-lifes: the historian chooses which colors and scenes- the events and facts of history- to portray. Historians interested in the continuing glorification of everything-Abraham Lincoln for example, can easily conceal the ugly scenes (like imprisoning newspaper editors and destroying their printing presses) in the blurred background of the painting. Indeed they can leave it out altogether. You very well may end up believing in the end that it was a good thing that Lincoln and the North handled matters the way they did. However, that's not for me or any writer of history to decide for you. If we do our jobs properly, we will not ignore or intentionally minimize significant facts and events.

A recent movie about John Adams glossed over the fact that Adams, while running for reelection for president in a very tight race, benefitted and knew he benefited from the most egregious violation of the 1st Amendment in American history, i.e. the Alien and Sedition Acts of 1798. As president he signed the legislation and had to know it would be used exactly as how it was used: to suppress the political speech -at the risk of criminal prosecution and imprisonment- of the opposing party. In a seven-hour HBO television series the only part of this even mentioned gave a very brief sympathetic view that Adams wrestled with his decision to sign. There was no mention whatsoever that it was used exclusively against members of the opposing political party to suppress their speech. Nor was there even a mention that it was highly unconstitutional.

Historians, like today's journalists, choose what to report, what to ignore and how much emphasis to place on each fact or event. Those who tend to emphasize points that coincide with their theories and beliefs while intentionally ignoring or demonizing other aspects give the field a bad name and are the scoundrels Samuel Butler had in mind when he said: "Although God cannot alter the past, historians can." This point has been elucidated by many. Henry Ford said history was bunk; Ralph Ellison called historians "responsible liars;" Napoleon remarked that history is nothing but agreed upon lies; Ben Franklin opined that "historians relate, not so much what is done, as to what they would have believed;" and Mark Twain noted, "the very ink with which all history is written is merely fluid prejudice."

More recently, George Will wrote that some "turn the teaching of history into political preaching...History in the hands of ethnic partisans is not an exercise of intellectual disinterestedness but an instrument of group cohesion and political agendas." What these historians provide, according to Will, are "absurd and poisonous blends of cultural myths and biological determinism of a sort once favored by white supremacists."

C. Vann Woodward, a former president of the Organization of American Historians (OAH) and well-known scholar, lamented, "more and more often...academic historians...address...narrow subjects deemed fashionable or politically correct. Until they recover from these habits the public will have to rely... on others for works traditionally expected and long supplied by historians." He has urged universities to "restore free speech and revive standards."

Another former OAH president made similar remarks about the state of today's professional historians when he complained his fellow scholars needed to "defeat...cowardly administrators and their complicit faculty." He pointed out that in both academia and publishing "anything that [emphasizes] the poor, the oppressed, and the downtrodden passes muster and may expect to be greeted with hosannas, and never mind how absurd the arguments and how blundering the scholarship."

Arthur Schlesinger Jr. charged a "cult of ethnicity" has taken over college campuses, as an "attack on the common American identity." He urges the "great silent majority of professors" to "cry enough and challenge what they know to be voguish nonsense." (And that was almost twenty years ago!)

One big reason for this problem was expressed cleverly in this summary a few years ago: "In the field of American history...a liberal Ph.D. who subscribe[s] to consensus instead of class conflict, or a white male conservative who admires [James] Madison rather than [Karl] Marx, ha[s] about as much chance of getting hired on some faculty as Woody Allen of starting as a point guard for the Knicks."

Dixon Wecter used a reference to the Muse of History when he stated: "The muse called Clio, can be sold down the river to become the handmaid of propaganda, brazenly perverting the truth." A fellow named Hearnshaw wrote in 1923 that "history has, from early times, been the happy hunting ground of the propagandist...History is the memory of the human race, but it is a memory artificially created and sustained. It is the historian who determines, by his method of selection and rejection, which facts or legends are to be perpetuated and in what light they are to be regarded." I couldn't agree more.

Also in 1923, the *New Republic* reported that historians often wrote "with a political purpose, more of less subtly concealed, and political purposes seldom square with truth...History had become present politics."

Facts- "severe, stubborn, notorious facts" -are the foundation needed for historians to construct and retell accurate stories of bygone days. Some are repeated frequently, too much perhaps, while others not at all. But facts matter, whether they're retold once or a million times. Ignoring them, as Aldous Huxley said, does not make them cease to exist.

"Now what I want is facts," starts Charles Dickens's *Hard Times*.

"Teach these boys and girls nothing but facts. Facts alone are wanted in life. Plant nothing else, and root out everything else. You can only form the minds of reasoning animals upon facts: nothing else will ever be of any service to them. This is the principle on which I bring up these children. Stick to the facts, sir!"

Of course, facts do not, as the adage goes, speak for themselves. Facts alone don't prove everything. They don't provide a complete picture and can intentionally or accidently mislead. That is what William Faulkner had in mind when he said facts and truth rarely had anything to do with each other. They need to be paired with their sophisticated and complex twin: analysis. With both you get perspective and understanding. History is the art of putting these together.

Don't be afraid to read well-documented accounts that question the predominant thinking. Keep traveling the history highway, but understand that truth does not come from repetition and consensus.

Notes

Preface

1. "Fiction is history:" attributed to Andre Gide, The Original Knickerbocker, The Life of Washington Irving, by Andrew Burstein, Introduction.

2. "Great dust-heap called history:" attributed to Augustine Birrell, Oxford Dictionary of Quotations, Second edition, page 72.

3. Quotes by Herodotus and Ibn Khaldun: A Brief History of History: Great Historians and the Epic Quest to Explain the Past, by Colin Wells, pages 1 and 99.

4. "We need to know...can bring to life:" The Life and Letters of John Hay, by William Roscoe Thayer, Volume I, page 136.

5. "Pleasure is a shadow...peace and happiness:" attributed to DeWitt Clinton, in Famous American Statesmen and Orators, edited by Alexander K. McClure, Volume II, pages 192-193.

6. "Past is prologue:" The Tempest, by William Shakespeare.

7. "The past is never dead, it's not even past:" Requiem for a Nun, by William Faulkner, page 80.

8.   "So we beat on...into the past:" The Great Gatsby, by F. Scott Fitzgerald.

9.   "If the mad impossible...on your fiddle:" attributed to Bernard DeVoto, in American Traveler, by James Zug, page 174.

Benjamin Church: Revolutionary War Doctor Spy

10. "Witty, high strung and bombastic:" *Paul Revere & the World he Lived in,* Esther Forbes, page 120.

11. "The noisiest patriot in Boston," Ibid, page 135.

12. "Make use of every precaution:" *The Codebreakers: The Story of Secret Writing,* David Kahn, page 176.

13. "You may as well...chains of decency:" *Paul Revere & the World he Lived in,* Esther Forbes, page 296.

14. "The first American...as well:" *The Codebreakers: The Story of Secret Writing,* David Kahn, page 176.

15. Church's wife received British pension: *Invisible Ink-Spycraft of the American Revolution,* by John A. Nagy, page 50.

16. Information about the history of cryptology: *Invisible Ink-Spycraft of the American Revolution,* by John A. Nagy.

17. "Exceeding dirty and nasty:" *Almost a Miracle—the American Victory in the War of Independence,* by John Ferling, page 77.

18. Articles of War amended to include death penalty: *The Tree of Liberty: A Documentary History of Rebellion and Political Crime in America*, edited by Nicholas N. Kittrie and Eldon D. Wedlock, Jr., page 52.

John Champe's Audacious Adventure

19. "Of all the Americans...the most enterprising and dangerous." *On the Trail of Benedict Arnold,* by W.D.

Wetherell, published in The American Heritage Magazine, April/May 2007.

20. Information about angry mob in Philadelphia: *Treason at West Point: The Arnold-Andre Conspiracy,* by J. E. Morpurgo.

21. "First in peace...his fostering hand:" Henry Lee, *Famous American Statesmen and Orators,* Volume I, edited by Alexander K. McClure, page 368.

22. "The carefully calculated...to strike back:" *Light–Horse Harry Lee and the Legacy of the American Revolution,* by Charles Royster, page 21.

23. Description and information about Champe: *Memoirs of the War in the Southern Department of the United States,* by Henry Lee.

24. Reference to Baldwin: *George Washington, A Life,* by Willard Sterne Randall.

25. "My aim is to make an example of him:" *The Writings of George Washington,* edited John C. Fitzpatrick, Volume 20.

26. British executed 275 prisoners in New York City: *Nathan Hale, The Life and Death of America's First Spy,* by M. William Phelps, page 184.

27. "Ignominy of desertion:" *Memoirs of the War in the Southern Department of the United States,* by Henry Lee.

28. "Reputation would be protected:" Ibid.

29. "Hailed as the avenger:" Ibid.

30. "Excited thirst for fame:" Ibid.

31. Had to zig-zag: Ibid.

32. "His Excellency, Sir Henry Clinton has authorized me... who are disposed to join me:" *Broadsides & Bayonets—the Propaganda War of the American Revolution,* by Carl Berger, pages 33-34.

33. Flotilla of 42 ships and 1600 soldiers: *The Day the Revolution Ended*, by William H. Hallahan.

34. Information about pension: *The Sergeant Major's Strange Mission*, by George F. Scheer, American Heritage, October 1957.

35. Information about codes: *Invisible Ink-Spycraft of the American Revolution,* by John A. Nagy.

36. Poem: *Songs and Ballads of the American Revolution,* edited by Frank Moore.

The Newburgh Conspiracy

37. "The predicament...as critical and delicate as can well be conceived:" *The Writings of George Washington,* Volume 26, John C. Fitzpatrick, editor, page 186.

38. "A gulph of civil horror:" Ibid, page 217.

39. Debt estimated at $25 million: *E Pluribus Unum: The Formation of the American Republic,* by Forrest McDonald, page 51.

40. "The forebodings of evil:" *The Writings of George Washington,* Volume 26, John C. Fitzpatrick, editor, page 186.

41. "The privilege of asking for everything...prerogative of granting nothing:" George Washington and the Newburgh Conspiracy, by Carol Berkin, published in *I Wish I'd Been There,* American Historical Publications, Inc., page 36.

42. "Pay must be found for the army...God knows:" *Benjamin Lincoln and the American Revolution,* by David B. Mattern, page 139.

43. "Be so deeply stung by the injustice and ingratitude of their country as to become...tygers and wolves:" Ibid, page 142.

44. "Tremble[d] for his country:" Ibid, page 134.

45. "Distressing beyond description:" *The Writings of George*

Washington, John C. Fitzpatrick, editor, Volume 26, page 217.

46.   "Starved, ragged...to help themselves:" *Private Yankee Doodle, Being a Narrative of Some of the Adventures, Dangers and Sufferings of a Revolutionary Soldier by Joseph Plumb Martin*, edited by George E. Scheer, page 279.

47.   "The insults and neglects...part with a dollar for their army:" *A Respectable Army: The Military Origins of the Republic 1763-1789*, by James Kirby Martin and Mark Edward Lender, page 149.

48.   "The coldness and severity of government...chair of independence:" *The Inside History of the Newburgh Conspiracy: America and the Coup d'état*, by Richard H. Kohn; The William and Mary Quarterly, 1970, Series 3, Volume 27, page 207.

49.   "Tramples upon your rights, disdains your cries and insults your distresses:" *Presidents Under Fire: Commanders in Chief in Victory and Defeat*, James R. Arnold, page 37.

50.   "I have often thought...but this by the by:" *The Writings of George Washington*, Volume 26, edited by John C. Fitzpatrick, page 185.

51.   "Give one more...patient virtue:" Ibid, page 38.

52.   Information about Washington's speech: *George Washington under Fire-1783*, published in Almost History, by Roger Bruns.

53.   "Who harbour wicked designs...to lessen [Washington's] popularity in the Army:" *Letters of Delegates to Congress*, Volume 19, Paul H. Smith, editor, page 746.

54.   "I have grown grey and now find myself going blind:" *The Inside History of the Newburgh Conspiracy: America and the Coup d'état*, by Richard H. Kohn; The William and Mary Quarterly, 1970, Series 3, Volume 27.

55.   "Disrobed [the Temple] of its mantle of purity:" attributed

to Benson Lossing in *Landmarks of the Revolution*, by Mark M. Boatner III, page 267.

The Plot to Kidnap George Washington

56. Guard's qualifications of "sobriety, honesty and good behavior...from 5' 8" to 5' 10"...handsomely and well made...clean and spruce:" *The Commander-In-Chief's Guard,* by Carlos E. Godfrey, page 20.

57. "A network of corruption and treachery:" *Life of George Washington,* by Washington Irving, page 106.

58. The going offer was 5 guineas and the promise of 200 acres of land for the recruit and 100 acres for his wife: Ibid, page 108.

59. William Collier reported the comments he heard at the *Sergeant Arms Tavern*: *The Commander-In-Chief's Guard,* by Carlos E. Godfrey, page 23.

60. Got bewitched after hard money:" *Summer Soldiers: A Survey & Index of Revolutionary War Courts-Martial,* by James C. Neagles, page 27.

61. Believed to have been printing counterfeit currency on its vessels blockading New York: *George Washington: A Biography,* by Douglas S. Freeman, Volume 4, page 119.

62. Quotes from George Washington and Thomas Paine about British counterfeiting: *Outfoxing the Counterfeiters,* by Stephen Mihm; published in the *Wall Street Journal,* April 24, 2010, page W1.

63. Hanged from a tree near the present day intersection of Christie and Grand Streets: *The Commander-In-Chief's Guard,* by Carlos E. Godfrey, page 32.

64. Fellow convict Isaac Ketchum claimed he was so "deeply imprest with shame and confusion ...entirely on another subgyt:" *Turncoats, Traitors and Heroes,* by John Bakeless, page 101.

65. "Damnably corrupted:" *George Washington: A Biography*, by Douglas S. Freeman, page 119.

66. Committee formed "for the hearing and trying of disaffected persons and those of equivocal characters:" Ibid, page 115.

67. Information about Loyalists trials: *History of the State of New York*, edited by Alexander C. Flick, New York Historical Association, 1933, Volume 3, pages 338-341.

68. "Durst not show their heads:" Ibid, page 259.

69. "Exciting and joining in a mutiny and sedition, and treacherously corresponding with, enlisting among, and receiving pay from the enemies of the United American Colonies:" *The Commander-In-Chief's Guard*, by Carlos E. Godfrey, page 27.

70. "This country was sold...the enemy would soon arrive, and it was best for us old countrymen to make our peace ... or they would kill us all:" Ibid, page 29.

71. Information about Hickey's defense: "get some money from them:" *The Papers of George Washington*, edited by W. W. Abbot, Volume 5, page 113.

72. "Unhappy fate:" Ibid, page 129.

73. "Produce many salutary consequences and deter others from entering into like traitorous practices:" *The Writings of George Washington*, John C. Fitzpatrick, editor, Volume 5, page 193.

74. "Lewd women...first led [Hickey] into practices which ended in an untimely and ignominious death:" *The Papers of George Washington*, edited by W. W. Abbot, Volume 5, page 129.

75. "Officers...will take every precaution...to prevent an inundation of bad women from Philadelphia:" *The Papers of George Washington*, Philander D. Chase, editor, Volume 11, page 55.

76.   Aaron Burr quote about women spies: *Invisible Ink-Spycraft of the American Revolution,* by John A. Nagy, page 182.

77.   "Hellish:" *Letters of Delegates to Congress: 1774-1789,* Paul H. Smith, editor, Volume 4, page 410.

78.   "Vile:" Ibid, page 301.

79.   "Horrid:" Ibid, page 342.

80.   "Most barbarous and infernal:" *The Spirit of 'Seventy-Six,* edited by Henry Steele Commager and Richard B. Morris, page 736.

81.   George Washington was to have been stabbed in the plot: *The Commander-In-Chief's Guard,* by Carlos E. Godfrey, page 33.

82.   "The whole Bay was full of shipping…I thought all London was afloat:" *George Washington: A Biography,* by Douglas S. Freeman, page 127.

83.   Crowd estimated at 20,000: *The Papers of George Washington,* W. W. Abbot, editor, Volume 5, page 130.

84.   Hickey was first soldier executed in Revolution: *The Pictorial Field-Book of the Revolution,* by Benson J. Lossing, Volume II, page 595.

85.   Estimated 100 soldiers executed during the American Revolution: *Almost a Miracle: The American Victory in the War of Independence,* by John Ferling, page 334.

86.   "Are destroying the army…do by their fighting:" *Less than Glory, A Revisionist's View of the American Revolution,* by Norman Gelb, page 142.

87.   "Tories…measured their loyalty…towards the Whigs:" *Ethan Allen and the Green Mountain Heroes of '76,* by Henry W. Depuy, page 227.

88.   "A Loyalist is a thing…neck needs stretching:" *Less than Glory, A Revisionist's View of the American Revolution,* by Norman Gelb, page 160.

89.   "The sun never shined…greater worth:" *Our Nation's*

Archives: The History of the United States in Documents, edited by Erik Bruun and Jay Crosby, page 143.

90. "Let them call me rebel…and this is one:" Ibid, page 155.

91. "In a chariot of light…our Liberty Tree:" *The Patriot's Handbook,* edited by George Grant, page 115.

92. "Fought independence bitterly…some foreign tyrant:" *History of the State of New York,* edited by Alexander C. Flick, New York Historical Association, 1933, Volume 3, pages 332-333.

93. "Ye Tories all rejoice and sing… And curse the haughty Congress:" *The Tree of Liberty: A Documentary History of Rebellion and Political Crime in America,* edited by Nicholas N. Kittrie and Eldon D. Wedlock, Jr., page 55.

An Early American Health Care Crisis

94. "The smallpox! The smallpox! what shall we do with it?" *John Adams,* by David McCullough, page 141.

95. "King of Terror:" Ibid, page 141.

96. Benedict Arnold believed it would cause "the entire ruin" of the army: *Pox Americana: The Great Smallpox Epidemic of 1775-1782,* by Elizabeth A. Fenn, page 67.

97. George Washington: its "calamitous consequences…the sword of the enemy:" Ibid, pages 87 and 92.

98. Two thirds of all American casualties due to smallpox: *His Excellency George Washington,* By Joseph J. Ellis, page 86.

99. "It raged in the streets and cantonments:" *The War of the Revolution, by Christopher Ward,* edited by John Richard Alden, page 114.

100. "The smallpox raged in a violent manner… a little distance from the town:" *The Autobiography of a Yankee Mariner: Christopher Prince and the American Revolution,* edited by Michael J. Crawford, page 91.

101. Information about the Slave Onesimus: *John Adams,* by David McCullough, page 142.

102. "Pus from the ripe postules:" Ibid, page 142.

103. "Venom:" *Paul Revere & the World He Lived In,* by Esther Forbes, page 78.

104. Information about the Committee of Thirty Six and efforts in Boston: *After the Siege: A Social History of Boston, 1775-1800,* by Jacqueline Barbara Carr, pages 136-137.

105. Paul Revere refused to allow his daughter to be sent to the pesthouse: *Paul Revere & the World He Lived In,* by Esther Forbes, page 77.

106. "Inoculation-Mad:" *Pox Americana: The Great Smallpox Epidemic of 1775-1782,* by Elizabeth A. Fenn, page 54.

107. "Such a spirit of inoculation…as they can hold:" *Benjamin Lincoln and the American Revolution,* by David B. Mattern, page 26.

108. "PS I fear the Small Pox…God only knows:" *The Old Revolutionaries: Political Lives in the Age of Samuel Adams,* by Pauline Maier, page 157.

109. "You dog, I'll inoculate you with this, with a pox to you:" *Paul Revere & the World He Lived In,* by Esther Forbes, page 74.

110. Benjamin Franklin quote: "The expense of having the operation…of America:" *Pox Americana: The Great Smallpox Epidemic of 1775-1782,* by Elizabeth A. Fenn, page 41.

111. A third of the army ill with smallpox at one time: *The War of the Revolution, by Christopher Ward,* edited by John Richard Alden, page 320.

112. "As this was against orders…in the same condition:" contained in Josiah Sabin's pension application, *The Revolution Remembered, Eyewitness Accounts of the War for Independence,* edited by John C. Dann, page 19.

113. Private Martin's reminisce: I was soon …joined the

regiment:" *Private Yankee Doodle, Being a Narrative of Some of the Adventures, Dangers and Sufferings of a Revolutionary Soldier by Joseph Plumb Martin*, edited by George E. Scheer, pages 65-67.

114. "You have erased from the calendar...has been extirpated:" *Thomas Jefferson Writings*, edited by Merrill D. Peterson, page 1163.

Christopher Ludwick: the Baker-General

115. "He [King George III] is at this time transporting large armies of foreign Mercenaries to compleat the works of death, desolution and tyranny: *The Declaration of Independence.*

116. "Slavish Hessian guards...cruelty and desolation:" *Ethan Allen and the Green Mountain Heroes of '76*, by Henry W. Depuy, page 253.

117. "I know our situation well...whose father we shall doubt of:" *Our Nation's Archives: The History of the United States in Documents*, edited by Erik Bruun and Jay Crosby, page 155.

118. The first treaty was signed on January 9, 1776 with the Duke of Brunswick: *The German Allied Troops in the North American War of Independence*, by J. G. Rosengarten, page 16.

119. "Such a pittance of troops as Great Britain...insure disappointment:" from a letter written by Johnny Burgoyne, according to news accounts of Sotheby auction: reported in the *New York Times*, March 23, 2010, page C4, and in *Military History Magazine*, July 2010, page 8.

120. England leasing Hessians soldiers was nothing new; by 1776 it had already been done five times in the 18th Century: *The Hessian Mercenary Troops in the American Revolution*, a dissertation by Thomas Ryan Stephens, May 1998, Texas A & M University.

121. "The poor Hessians who end[ed] their lives unhappily...by nothing but dirty selfishness:" *The Hessians and the Other German Auxiliaries of Great Britain in the Revolutionary War,* by Edward J. Lowell.

122. "The Treasury...was filled with blood and tears:" *The German Element in the War of American Independence,* by George Washington Greene, page 200.

123. "Damnable money:" *The Course of Empire,* by Bernard DeVoto, page 225.

124. "Far outweigh the hatefulness of the business...have conquered our worst enemy—our debts:" *The Hessians and the Other German Auxiliaries of Great Britain in the Revolutionary War,* by Edward J. Lowell.

125. "All countries, especially all German countries...in a merciless, carnivorous manner:" *The German Element in the War of American Independence,* by George Washington Greene, page 176.

126. "The skulls and other bones...in a foreign land:" *Private Yankee Doodle, Being a Narrative of Some of the Adventures, Dangers and Sufferings of a Revolutionary War Soldier, by Joseph Plumb Martin,* edited by George E. Scheer, page 134.

127. "The many Hessians...are so well pleased to be in this country... the dreary abodes of bondage from whence they came:" *Christopher Ludwick: Patriotic Gingerbread Baker,* by William Ward Condit, published in the Pennsylvania Magazine of History and Biography, Volume 81, Number 4, October 1957, page 377.

128. "A complete farm...the frau:" *The American Home Front,* by James L. Abrahamson, page 13.

129. "America is a wonderful land... when nothing else is to be done, they hit a ball:" *A Hessian Report as Noted in the Diary of Chaplain Philip Waldeck,* translated by Bruce E. Burgoyne, pages 65-66.

130. "The Americans are bold, unyielding and fearless...

indomitable ideas of liberty:" *Broadsides & Bayonets—the Propaganda War of the American Revolution,* by Carl Berger, page 193.

131. "Encourage Hessians...to quit [their] iniquitous service:" *Christopher Ludwick: Patriotic Gingerbread Baker,* by William Ward Condit, published in the Pennsylvania Magazine of History and Biography, Volume 81, Number 4, October 1957, page 374.

132. "Choose to accept lands, liberty...dangers of a long and bloody war:" *Secret History of the American Revolution,* Carl Van Doren, page 15.

133. Offered 50 acres for any Hessian to desert... 800 acres, four oxen, one bull and two cows: *The Hessians and the Other German Auxiliaries of Great Britain in the Revolutionary War,* by Edward J. Lowell, page 286.

134. "An excellent opportunity for our hired troops...lands and protection:" *Broadsides & Bayonets—the Propaganda War of the American Revolution,* by Carl Berger, page 120.

135. "Christian Gentlemen and Fellow Brethren...sharpest orders not to give a single one of you quarter:" *The Journal of the Johannes Schwalm Historical Association,* Volume 1, Number 4, pages 13-14.

136. "The difference between the privilege and manner...the German counties of Pennsylvania:" *An Account of the Life and Character of Christopher Ludwick,* by Benjamin Rush, M.D., page 13, published in 1831; provided by the Historical Society of Pennsylvania.

137. "So fraught with a love of liberty...between them and the British:" *Maxims of Washington,* edited by John Frederick Schroeder, page 155.

138. Information about bread and flour: *Bread and the Superintendent of Bakers of the Continental Army,* John C. Fitzpatrick, published in the Daughters of the American Revolution Magazine, September 1922, Volume 56.

139. "The [flour] mixed with cold water...and scorched on one

side:" *Private Yankee Doodle, Being a Narrative of Some of the Adventures, Dangers and Sufferings of a Revolutionary War Soldier, by Joseph Plumb Martin,* edited by George E. Scheer, page 77.

140. "Hard enough to break the teeth of a rat:" Ibid, page 24.

141. "Riddled with hunger...cursing the deadly place:" *Western Star,* by Stephen Vincent Benet, page 96.

142. "Glutted gutts...to pasteboard:" *The American Reader: From Columbus to Today,* by Paul M. Angle, page 111.

143. "His deportment...proofs of his integrity and worth:" *The Writings of George Washington,* edited by John C. Fitzpatrick, Volume 29, page 201.

144. Epitaph on Ludwick's tombstone: *Christopher Ludwick, Baker-General in the Army of the United States During the Revolutionary War,* page 347, author unidentified, published in the Pennsylvania Magazine of History and Biography, Volume 16, Number 3, 1892, courtesy of the Historical Society of Pennsylvania.

145. Location of Ludwick's residence: *The Guide Book of Germantown,* published in 1904, page 80.

The English-language Controversy

146. All information and quotes about the German-English language issue: Speaking American, by Friederike Baer, published in the *American History Magazine,* August 2007, pages 60-64.

147. President Teddy Roosevelt quote that all immigrants "should be required to learn English...or leave the country: *The American Treasury: 1455-1955,* edited by Clifton Fadiman, page 26.

148. "Money! Money! Money! I want money so much that I would do almost anything for some:" *Records of the Revolutionary War Containing the Military and Financial Correspondence of Distinguished Officers*, edited by W.T.R Saffell, pages 82 and 84.

149. "May entirely cease:" Ibid, page 76.

150. "If the evil is not immediately remedied… must absolutely break up:" *American Aurora: A Democratic Republican Returns*, edited by Richard N. Rosenfeld, page 261.

151. "I think the game is pretty near up:" Ibid, page 307.

152. "Starve, dissolve or disperse:" Ibid, page 343.

153. "A dissolution of the Army…is unavoidable:" Ibid, page 377.

154. "If our condition should … all the consequences:" Ibid, page 377.

155. "The aggravated calamities …are beyond description:" Ibid, page 399.

156. "A foreign loan …cannot be kept together:" Ibid, page 405.

157. "But why need I run… our deliverance must come:" Ibid, page 405.

158. Thomas Paine didn't believe had enough money to transport provisions: Ibid, page 402.

159. "We could not afford it:" Ibid, page 317.

160. Franklin not joking about bows and arrows: *John Adams and the American Revolution*, by Catherine Drinker Bowen, page 550.

161. "The public treasury empty, public credit exhausted:" *Liberty's Blueprint: How Madison and Hamilton Wrote the Federalist Papers, Defined the Constitution, and Made*

Democracy Safe for the World, by Michael I. Meyerson, page 17.

162. "There was not a single dollar in the treasury:" *The Critical Period of American History,* by John Fiske, page 167.

163. Poem: "He made our wives and daughters fine…flip and toddy:" *The Power of the Purse: A History of American Public Finance, 1776-1790,* by E. James Ferguson, page 25.

164. New Jersey money no good in Pennsylvania, "and so on:" *A Financial History of the United States,* by Margaret G. Myers, page 38.

165. "Ninepences and fourpence… and French sous:" *The Critical Period of American History,* by John Fiske, page 165.

166. War cost $135-$170 million: *The Critical Period of American History,* by John Fiske, page 166—estimated cost at $170 million; *A Financial History of the United States,* by Margaret G. Myers, page 50--estimated cost at $135 million.

167. "The consequence was that no salt was brought to market:" *Tom Paine and Revolutionary America,* by Eric Foner, page 243.

168. "Reprobated by many and obeyed by few:" *The Revolutionary Generation 1763-1790,* by Evarts Boutell Greene, page 263.

169. "As active and wicked as the Devil himself:" Ibid, page 269.

170. "To hang them all on a gallows higher than Haman:" *The Critical Period of American History,* by John Fiske, page 164.

171. "Non-sensical quackery:" *Tom Paine and Revolutionary America,* by Eric Foner, page 152.

172. "Naked as the day they were born:" *Patriot Pirates: The Privateer War for Freedom and Fortune in the American Revolution,* by Robert H. Patton, page 211.

173. "Tasted the cruelties...know not what it is to suffer:" *The American Home Front,* by James L. Abrahamson, page 27.

174. "We vent[ed] our spleen...for an ungrateful people:" *A Respectable Army: The Military Origins of the Republic, 1763-1789,* by James Kirby Martin and Mark Edward Lender, page 149.

175. "One hypothesis has been piled...crumbled away:" *Currency in the Era of the American Revolution,* by Joseph Albert Ernst, dissertation, University of Wisconsin, 1962, page 397.

176. Taxes were the "radical cure...my books, or clothes or oxen, or your cows, to pay it:" *A Financial History of the United States,* by Margaret G. Myers, page 32.

177. Massachusetts debt at 11 million pounds: *John Hancock: Merchant King and American Patriot,* by Harlow Giles Unger, page 292.

178. "There is not a shilling ... nor is it probable there will be..." *Fragments of Revolutionary History*, edited by Gillard Hunt, page 23.

179. Amount of currency printed ($38 million in first 5 years, $188 mil in 1778 and 1779): *The American Home Front,* by James L. Abrahamson.

180. "A waggon load of money could scarcely buy a waggon-load of provisions:" *Liberty's Blueprint: How Madison and Hamilton Wrote the Federalist Papers, Defined the Constitution, and Made Democracy Safe for the World,* by Michael I. Meyerson, page 17.

181. "When a rat...expenses of the army:" *Washington: The Indispensible Man,* by James Thomas Flexner, page 128.

182. By 1779, the Continental dollar had lost 97%: *Patriot Pirates: The Privateer War for Freedom and Fortune in the American Revolution,* by Robert H. Patton, page 60.

183. Corn increased in price by 1255 % in one year: *Tom Paine and Revolutionary America*, by Eric Foner, page 161.

184. $4,000 Continentals were needed to buy one dollar in gold: *Patriot Pirates: The Privateer War for Freedom and Fortune in the American Revolution,* by Robert H. Patton, page 203.

185. $1,200 for a quart of rum: *Private Yankee Doodle: Being a Narrative of Some of the Adventures, Dangers and Sufferings of a Revolutionary Soldier, by Joseph Plumb Martin,* edited by George F. Scheer, page 242.

186. Sam Adams spent $2,000 for $20 worth of clothes: *John Hancock: Merchant King and American Patriot,* by Harlow Giles Unger, page 293.

187. $300 for a pair of socks: *Tom Paine and Revolutionary America,* page 243.

188. $150,000 for a cavalry horse: *The War of the Revolution,* page 866.

189. "Running all over Europe, asking to borrow money:" *A Financial History of the United States,* by Margaret G. Myers, page 35.

190. "A man in the midst of the ocean negotiating for his life among a school of sharks:" Ibid, page 36.

The Revolutionary War Lottery

191. "That none can reap...plough the Lottery main:" *Fortune's Merry Wheel: The Lottery in America,* by John Samuel Ezell, page 101.

192. "The Realme...publique good workes:" *Continental Lottery, 1776,* by Doris M. Reed, published in the Indiana Quarterly, Volume 3, July 1947, page 52.

193. "For the more effectual...of said Plantation:" Ibid.

194. "Reall and substantiall...hath been nourished:" *The Lottery in Colonial America,* by John Ezell, published in The William and Mary Quarterly, Third Series, April 1948, Volume V, page 187.

195. "The Merchants of Virginia...in this Land:" *Fortune's Merry Wheel: The Lottery in America*, by John Samuel Ezell, page 5.

196. "Such... evil sports and games:" *Nation of Gamblers*, by J. M. Fenster, published in the American Heritage Magazine, September 1994.

197. Pennsylvania: "mischievous and unlawful games ...poor families:" *The Lottery in Colonial America*, by John Ezell, published in The William and Mary Quarterly, Third Series, April 1948, Volume V, page 193.

198. Georgia: "idle, loose...dissolute course of life:" Ibid.

199. Massachusetts: "children, servants... foolish expense of money:" Ibid.

200. Wagers Charles Fox...by Christmas Day, 1777:" *The Germanic People in America,* by Victor Wolfgang von Hagen, page 165.

201. "These cursed...lotteries... all to themselves:" *The Lottery in Colonial America*, by John Ezell, published in The William and Mary Quarterly, Third Series, April 1948, Volume V, page 190.

202. Number (157) of pre-war lotteries: *Fortune's Merry Wheel: The Lottery in America*, by John Samuel Ezell, pages 55-59.

203. "The silly man may buy a ticket...but fortune deifies:" Ibid, page 29.

204. "Those who will not...they've neglected to obtain:" Ibid, page 89.

205. Information about soldiers gambling for acorns and the quote: "All officers, non-commissioned officers and soldiers...vice and immorality:" *Gambling—Apple Pie American and Older than the Mayflower*, by Ed Crews, published in the *Colonial Williamsburg Magazine*, Volume XXX, Number 4, Autumn 2008, pages 67-72.

206. "Gaming corrupts our dispositions:" *The Jefferson Cyclopedia*, edited by John P. Foley, page 372.

207. "Useful in certain occasions:" *What Would the Founders do Today?* by Richard Brookhiser, published in the American Heritage Magazine, June/July 2006.

208. "A few Continental lottery tickets to be sold at the Orderly Office:" *The Writings of George Washington*, edited by John C. Fitzpatrick, Volume 11, page 313.

209. "A few tickets …Adventurers are requested to apply:" Ibid, Volume 13, page 274.

210. "For carrying on the present…lives, liberties and property:" *Continental Lottery, 1776*, by Doris M. Reed, published in the Indiana Quarterly, Volume 3, July 1947, page 55.

211. Information on value of high prizes: *The United States Lottery*, by Lucius Wilmerding, Jr., published in the New York Historical Society Quarterly, January 1963, Volume XLVII, page 11.

212. "Thanks to the state… and the Blanks but few:" *Fortune's Merry Wheel: The Lottery in America*, by John Samuel Ezell, page 152.

Revolutionary War Privateers

213. "At Johnny Bull's expense:" *The Maritime History of Massachusetts*, Samuel Eliot Morison, page 29.

214. "Thousands of schemes for privateering … some profitable projects will grow:" *The Revolutionary Generation, 1763-1790*, Evarts Boutell Greene, page 266.

215. "Privateering mad:" Ibid, page 114.

216. "Oh what prizes these cruisers brought in…welcoming tavern doors:" *Stage-Coach & Tavern Days*, Alice Morse Earle, page 189.

217. "Come all you young fellows …will clothe you with gold:"

Patriot Pirates: The Privateer War for Freedom and Fortune in the American Revolution, Robert H. Patton, page 90.

218. "All you that cannot…join our ship's crew:" *The Old Revolutionaries: Political Lives in the Age of Samuel Adams*, by Pauline Maier, page 96.

219. "Brave boys…private ship whatever:" *After the Siege, a Social History of Boston 1775-1800*, by Jacqueline Barbara Carr, page 164.

220. "Lumber, spars, pitch and tar…glassware, linens and dry goods:" *War, Profit, and Privateers along the New Jersey Coast*, Richard J. Koke, published in the New York Historical Quarterly Report, Volume XLI, 1957, page 287.

221. "In a most rapid manner:" *Patriot Pirates: The Privateer War for Freedom and Fortune in the American Revolution*, Robert H. Patton, page 47.

222. "Could not find a rope in the night:" Ibid, page 125.

223. Fourteen-year old who received, from a single voyage, one ton of sugar, 30 to 40 gallons of rum…and about $700: *The Memoirs of Andrew Sherburne: Patriot and Privateer of the American Revolution*, page 22.

224. Residents of Tom's River: dividing their share in prizes: *War, Profit, and Privateers along the New Jersey Coast*, Richard J. Koke, published in the New York Historical Quarterly Report, Volume XLI, 1957, page 287.

225. "There were a great many persons … dejected on the return of peace:" *Patriot Pirates: The Privateer War for Freedom and Fortune in the American Revolution*, Robert H. Patton, page 233.

226. Poem: "Brave Manly he is stout… our bold privateer:" *Fired by Manley Zeal: A Naval Fiasco of the American Revolution*, Philip Chadwick Foster Smith, page 14.

227. "Fisherman, husbandmen…unfortified places:" *Thomas Jefferson Writings*, edited by Merrill D. Peterson, page 56.

228. Double and triple money for sailor(s) who first sighted and

boarded the prize: *John Adams and the American Revolution*, Catherine Drinker Bowen, page 548.

229. Thomas Jefferson: "A British prize would be a more rare phenomenon [in Virginia] than a comet:" *The Case of the 'Three Friends:' an Incident in Maritime Regulation During the Revolutionary War,* Randolph B. Campbell, published in the Virginia Magazine of History and Biography, April 1966, page 194.

230. Information about man going up the masthead to check for other ships in sight: *The Prize Game: Lawful Looting on the High Seas in the Days of Fighting Sail,* by Donald A. Petrie, page 153.

231. Information about the decrease in navy vessels and increase in privateers from 1778-1782: *The Old Revolutionaries: Political Lives in the Age of Samuel Adams,* by Pauline Maier, page 93.

232. "Chimerical and phantastick:" *John Adams and the American Revolution,* by Catherine Drinker Bowen, page 546.

233. "Think," urged one dissenter, "of the effect privateering would have on the morals of American seamen! They would grow mercenary, bloodthirsty altogether:" Ibid, page 547.

234. "Eat[ing] out the vitals of British commerce:" *The Jefferson Cyclopedia,* edited by John P. Foley, page 724.

235. "The dagger which strikes at the heart of their enemy:" Ibid.

236. French-owned and staffed mostly by Irish Smugglers--captured 114 British vessels: *Ben Franklin's Privateers,* William Bell Clark, page 173.

237. A British citizen observed 82 captured English ships in port: *Patriot Pirates: The Privateer War for Freedom and Fortune in the American Revolution,* Robert H. Patton, page 71.

238. The *General Mifflin* captured six prizes in the Irish Sea: Ibid, page 163.

239. The *Pilgrim* took eight prizes in one cruise off the Irish coast: "A short, easy and infallible method:" *The Naval History of the American Revolution,* Gardner W. Allen, Volume II, page 50.

240. "A short easy and infallible method...to a conclusion:" Ibid.

241. In February 1778...the House of Lords in England heard a report that seven hundred and thirty-three ships had been captured or destroyed by American privateers: *A History of American Privateers,* by Edgar Stanton Maclay, page xiii.

242. "Had it not been for our privateers...swept from the seas:" *Patriot Pirates: The Privateer War for Freedom and Fortune in the American Revolution*, Robert H. Patton, page 215.

243. Single most important factor related to ending the war: *A History of American Privateers,* Edgar Stanton Maclay, page xiii.

244. "Piratical sea-dogs:" *Smuggling in the American Colonies at the Outbreak of the Revolution*, William Smith McClellan, page 6.

245. "We expect to make their merchants...and nothing gained:" *The Old Revolutionaries: Political Lives in the Age of Samuel Adams*, by Pauline Maier, page 91.

The Revolutionary War Draft in Virginia

246. "It is an old maxim...for War:" *The Writings of George Washington*, edited by John C. Fitzpatrick, Volume 19, page 410.

247. "When the Capital...in the Enemy's hands:" Ibid, Volume 9, page 385.

248. "Five feet four inches...or subject to fits:" *Laws of Virginia*, edited by William W. Hening, Volume 9, page 81.

249. "By no means punctually filled:" *The Writings of George Washington*, edited by John C. Fitzpatrick, Volume 9, page 385.

250. "In the warmest...the continental army:" *Laws of Virginia*, edited by William W. Hening, Volume 9, page 347.

251. Promised 100 acres: Ibid, Volume 10, page 24.

252. Exemption from taxes "during their service:" Ibid, Volume 9, page 91.

253. Promised 300 acres: Ibid, Volume 10, page 331.

254. Exemption from taxes, "during life:" Ibid, Volume 9, page 456.

255. $12,000 bounty: Ibid, Volume 10, page 331.

256. "Unhappy depreciated...the money:" *The Writings of George Washington*, edited by John C. Fitzpatrick, Volume 13, page 145.

257. "A gill of spirits per day gratis:" *Laws of Virginia*, edited by William W. Hening, Volume 9, page 446.

258. "Experience has shewn...the only effectual one:" *The Writings of George Washington,* edited by John C. Fitzpatrick, Volume 19, page 408.

259. "We have only to decide... by coercive methods:" Ibid, Volume 8, page 77.

260. "The most unpopular...of all oppressions:" *The Writings of Thomas Jefferson*, edited by Andrew Lipscomb, Volume 4, page 286.

261. "May produce convulsions in the people:" *The Writings of George Washington*, edited by John C. Fitzpatrick, Volume 8, page 78.

262. "Many incentives of immediate interest...once for all:" Ibid, Volume 19, page 411.

263. "The hopes of the people...measures of vigor:" Ibid, Volume 18, page 418.

264. "It would not be deemed a hardship:" Ibid, Volume 9, page 387.

265. "The people would not complain:" Ibid, Volume 10, page 319.

266. "Standing on too precarious…a footing:" Ibid, Volume 17, page 127.

267. "It is of the greatest moment…and Yohogania:" *Laws of Virginia*, edited by William W. Hening, Volume 9, page 275.

268. 1777 draft quotas: Ibid, Volume 9, page 339.

269. 1780 draft quotas: Ibid, Volume 10, page 327.

270. Information about drawing out of a hat: Ibid, Volume 9, page 341.

271. Deserting "with public arms:" Ibid, Volume 10, page 418.

272. "One moiety… to the commonwealth:" Ibid, Volume 10, page 336.

273. "Sixty pounds and one dollar per mile:" Ibid, Volume 10, page 263.

274. "Civilly dead:" Ibid, Volume 10, page 414.

The Raid on Monkton and Weybridge, Vermont

275. Raid team consisted of 354 British soldiers and officers and 100 Indians: *Otter Creek: the Indian Road*, James E. Petersen, page 70.

276. Christopher Carlton married to an Indian: Ibid, page 69.

277. "I mean still to prosecute…irreparable this season:" Ibid.

278. "Are in every respect…induce them to relinquish it." Haldimand Papers, The Public Archives of Canada, Ottawa.

279. "This extensive province…are excellent marksmen:" Ibid.

280. "Under the Command of James Bentley…guarding them

to Ticonderoga:" *Vermont, the Green Mountain State,* by Walter Hill Crockett.

281. "Approaching the place in Monkton...and his detachment:" Ibid.

282. "Voluntarily and cheerfully...whatsoever in our power:" Haldimand Papers, The Public Archives of Canada, Ottawa.

283. "A country unpeopled...like a gathering storm on my left:" *The Rangers, or, a Tory's Daughter,* author unidentified, published in 1851, Volume II, page 7.

284. "My principal motive...the Indian interpreter:" *Carlton's Raid,* by Ida H. Washington and Paul A. Washington.

285. "Repelled the Indians...and spared the stacks:" *History of Monkton, Vermont 1734-1961,* the Vermont Historical Society, page 17.

286. "Having in the meantime...no other one attempted it:" *Lake Champlain: Key to Liberty,* by Ralph Nading Hill, page 141.

287. "There remain no more of these traitors...rid ourselves of these neighbors:" Haldimand Papers, The Public Archives of Canada, Ottawa.

288. Hoyt showing up in the 1810 census in Swanton, Vermont: *Carlton's Raid,* by Ida H. Washington and Paul A. Washington, page 74.

289. George Washington letter to Ethan Allen: "Sir, I have been...well grounded:" *Collections of the Vermont Historical Society,* Volume II, page 64.

290. "The Indians have demanded...to take some scalps:" Haldimand Papers, The Public Archives of Canada, Ottawa.

291. "Contain themselves...be suffered to go:" Ibid.

292. General Carlton's journal: *Carlton's Raid,* by Ida H. Washington and Paul A. Washington.

293. Lt. John Enys's journal: *The American Journals of Lt. John Enys*, Elizabeth Cometti, editor.

294. Esther Bishop's statement: The Daughters of the American Revolution library, Washington, DC.

295. Claudius Brittle's plea for release: "We were captured... took the oath of Allegiance:" *Carlton's Raid*, by Ida H. Washington and Paul A. Washington, page 71.

296. Claudius Brittle pension application: The National Archives, Washington DC.

297. Poem-Monkton Cannon: *The Vermont Historical Gazetteer*, edited by Abby Maria Hemenway, Volume I, page 66.

298. No area hit harder than the Otter Creek: *Otter Creek: the Indian Road*, James E. Petersen, page 78.

299. Ethan Allen quote: "Vaunt no more, Old England...the hire of the Hessians:" *Ethan Allen and the Green-Mountain Heroes of '76,* by Henry W. Depuy, page 275.

The Words of Cato in the American Revolution

300. Made its way across the Atlantic by 1736: The Virginia Historical Magazine of History and Biography, Volume 26, page 180 has a reference that the play was advertised (performance at William & Mary University) in the *Virginia Gazette* on September 3 and 10, 1736.

301. Cato's Utica and Caesar's Rome resembled the relationship between America and Europe: *Joseph Addison and Richard Steele: a Reference Guide,* by Charles A. Knight.

302. A Roman soul is bent on higher views...And break our fierce barbarians into men:" *The Radicalism of the American Revolution,* by Gordon S. Wood, page 217.

303. Washington called "the very Bible of Republican idealism," saw it many times and had it performed for his troops at Valley Forge: *Joseph Addison and Richard Steele: a Reference Guide,* by Charles A. Knight, page 231.

304. "Behold these locks that are grown white beneath a helmet in your father's battles:" Cato.

305. "The American founders honored Addison, "for [his] elegance of thought and pertinacious wit; even after the founding era, every young man of substance read [him]:" *The Original Knickerbocker: The life of Washington Irving,* by Andrew Burstein, page 21.

306. John Adams: "We cannot insure success, but we can deserve it:" *John Adams,* by David McCullough, page 91.

307. George Washington letter to Nicholas Cooke dated October 29, 1775: *The Writings of George Washington,* edited by John C. Fitzpatrick, Volume 4, page 53.

308. George Washington letter to Benedict Arnold dated December 5, 1775: Ibid, page 148.

309. "'Tis not in mortals to command success, but we'll do more, Sempronius, we'll deserve it:" *Cato: A Tragedy, and Selected Essays by Joseph Addison,* edited by Christine Dunn Henderson and Mark E. Yellin.

310. "What pity is it that we can die but once to serve our country!" *Cato: A Tragedy, and Selected Essays by Joseph Addison,* edited by Christine Dunn Henderson and Mark E. Yellin.

311. "It is not now a time to talk of aught, but chains or conquest, liberty or death:" *Cato: A Tragedy, and Selected Essays by Joseph Addison,* edited by Christine Dunn Henderson and Mark E. Yellin.

312. Ben Franklin: "Here will I hold… if there is a power above us:" *Benjamin Franklin Writings*, edited by J. A. Leo Lemay, page 1388

313. Thomas Paine quoted from Addison in the *Age of Reason*, (*Thomas Paine, Collected Writings*, edited by Eric Foner, page 688)

314. Thomas Jefferson: "Oh liberty! Thou goddess heav'nly bright…Giv'st beauty to the sun, and pleasure to the day:"

Writings of Thomas Jefferson, edited by Merrill D. Peterson, page 617.

315. Cato "When vice prevails and impious men bear sway, the post of honour is a private station." *The Radicalism of the American Revolution,* by Gordon S. Wood, Page 143. Washington used this line in letters to David Humphreys (June 12, 1796) and Thomas Pickering (July 27, 1795)

316. Washington talked an officer, John Thomas, out of resigning in part with a line from Cato. In their struggle, "surely every post ought to be deemed honorable in which a man can serve his country." *1776,* by David McCullough, page 53.

317. Voltaire proclaimed that Addison was "the first English writer who composed a regular tragedy and infused a spirit of elegance through every part of it." *English Men of Letters,* edited by John Morley, page 121.

318. Poor Richard's Almanac: "The 19th of this month, 1719, died the celebrated Joseph Addison... than those of all other English pen whatever." *Benjamin Franklin Writings,* edited by J. A. Leo Lemay page 1248.

The Presidential Cheese Caper of 1802

319. Most information about the cheese caper, including the poem: *Of Bigotry in Politics and Religion,* by Constance B. Schulz, published in the *Virginia Magazine of History and Biography,* January 1983, Volume 91, Number 1, pages 80-81.

320. Quotes: Two bottles of water...far from being good:" *Ambitious Appetites—Dining, Behavior, and Patterns of Consumption in Federal Washington,* by Barbara G. Carson, page 137.

321. Ford proposal to impeach Judge Douglas: *Impeachment: The Constitutional Problems*, by Raoul Berger, pages 86-94.

322. Fell into disgrace by using privileged information obtained as a member of Congress to attempt to enrich himself in the flour market: *America Afire*, by Bernard A. Weisberger, page 217.

323. "Abrasive, arrogant and overbearing:" *Perilous Times*, by Geoffrey R. Stone, page 58.

324. "Abounds with good humor ...I like him hugely:" *The Trial of Samuel Chase*, Samuel H. Smith and Thomas Lloyd, page 289.

325. "There is nothing...destruction of the government:" *America Afire*, by Bernard A. Weisberger, page 217.

326. "All they contained was misrepresentation ... or mosquitoes:" *Crisis in Freedom*, by John C. Miller, page 79.

327. "I would sooner... dressed by a dog ... than to a Democrat:" Ibid, page 40.

328. Jefferson Inaugural Address: *Inaugural Addresses of the Presidents*, edited by John G. Hunt.

329. "I shall take no other revenge...no resurrection for it:" *American Aurora*, edited by Richard N. Rosenfeld, page 902.

330. "Nothing but their eternal hatred:" *Sister Revolutions*, by Susan Dunn, page 80.

331. "Republican ascendancy:" *Jefferson and Madison: The Great Collaboration*, by Adrienne Koch, page 212.

332. "Keep people...in the right:" Ibid, page 135.

333. "Outrage of decency:" *Quarrels That Have Shaped the Constitution*, edited by John A. Garraty, page 10.

334. "I can say with truth…his own Choice:" *The Jeffersonian Crisis*, by Richard E. Ellis, page 32.

335. "That the leaders of the federal party… through the storm:" *Gentleman Revolutionary: Governour Morris*, by Richard Brookhiser, page 168.

336. "Wise men …at the helm:" James Madison, Federalist Number 10.

337. Sedition Act: *The Tree of Liberty: A Documentary History*, edited by Nicholas N. Kittrie, page 86.

338. Massachusetts Federalists: "More degenerated from… Union:" *Crisis in Freedom*, by John C. Miller, page 122.

339. Only two members from States south of the Potomac River: Ibid, page 70.

340. "The head of a respectable opposition…enlightened people:" Ibid, page 141.

341. "What… are you going to do with Virginia?" *American Aurora*, edited by Richard N. Rosenfeld, page 581.

342. "Would teach the lawyers of Virginia…of the press:" Ibid, page 805.

343. "I wish it were possible … our sedition law:" *The Tree of Liberty: A Documentary History*, edited by Nicholas N. Kittrie, page 87.

344. "Now hark ye, sweet Liberty boys:" *Alexandria Advertiser and Commercial Intelligencer*, February 3, 1801.

345. "When questioned whether… steel will turn:" *Patrick Henry: The Last Years*, by Patrick Daily, page 190.

346. "Men were prosecuted… the behind:" *Responses of the Presidents to Charges of Misconduct*, edited by C. Vann Woodward, page 25.

347. "He is not for us, is against us:" *Perilous Times*, by Geoffrey R. Stone, page 29.

348. "Advertisements contain…in a newspaper:" *The American Treasury*, edited by Clifton Fadiman, page 217.

349. "Our opponents are so disposed...out of your hands:" *Of Bigotry in Politics and Religion,* by Constance B. Schulz, *The Virginia Magazine of History and Biography,* January 1983, Volume 91, Number 1, page 86.

350. "When President Adams sat to have his likeness taken...his becoming unpopular:" *The William and Mary Quarterly: A Magazine of Early American History and Culture,* October 1988, Third Series, Volume XLV, Number 4, page 772.

351. "A little patience...reign of witches...true principles:" *American Aurora,* edited by Richard N. Rosenfeld, page 136.

352. "Restore our judiciary...was its object:" *The Jeffersonian Crisis,* by Richard E. Ellis, page 52.

353. "The Constitution was no more," and that Jefferson was, "determined at all events to destroy the Independence of the Judiciary & bring all the powers of Government in to the House of Representatives:" Ibid, page 57.

354. Its short tenure resulted...brought to trial were convicted: *Perilous Times,* by Geoffrey R. Stone, page 63.

355. "Travesties of justice dominated... of Republican sentiments:" *Sister Revolutions,* by Susan Dunn, page 79.

356. "The Federalists have retired ... and erased:" *Grand Inquests,* by William H. Rehnquist, page 49.

357. "The judges were antidemocratic...to the attack:" *The Democratic Republic: 1801-1815,* by Marshall Smelser.

358. "Chase's bloody circuit:" *Perilous Times,* by Geoffrey R. Stone, page 69.

359. Not one Republican judge in the entire federal judiciary: *The Trial of Samuel Chase,* Samuel H. Smith and Thomas Lloyd, page 303.

360. "The most formidable...land in his courtroom:" *American Sphinx,* by Joseph J. Ellis, page 268.

361. "Oppressive and disgusting:" *The Democratic Republic: 1801-1815,* by Marshall Smelser, page 69.

362. Judges were "objects of national fear:" *Perilous Times*, by Geoffrey R. Stone, page 52.

363. "History shows... passion than of justice:" *Impeachment: The Constitutional Problems*, by Raoul Berger, page 79.

364. Information about impeachment of Judge Pickering: *The Jeffersonian Crisis*, by Richard E. Ellis, page 75.

365. "As a trial judge on circuit, Chase... had no peer:" *The Trial of Samuel Chase*, Samuel H. Smith and Thomas Lloyd, page 289.

366. In 1803, Chase delivered ...threatening the courts' independence: *Aaron Burr--Conspiracy to Treason*, by Buckner F. Melton, Jr. page 63.

367. Campaigned openly for Adams in the election of 1800: *The Trial of Samuel Chase*, Samuel H. Smith and Thomas Lloyd, page 284.

368. Notice of the pending impeachment: *National Intelligencer & Washington Advertiser* Newspaper Abstracts 1800-1805, edited by Joan M. Dixon.

369. "Wickedest tongue...and courage and wit to use it:" *Randolph of Roanoke: A Political Fantastic,* by Gerald W. Johnson, page 15.

370. Information on Randolph/Clay duel: *Dueling in the District of Columbia*, by Myra L. Spaulding, Records of the Columbian Historical Society, Volumes 29-30.

371. "Like a mackerel...shines and stinks:" *Randolph of Roanoke: A Political Fantastic,* by Gerald W. Johnson, page 16.

372. Randolph description: "A shrill scream...meteor of Congress:" *Dueling in the District of Columbia*, by Myra L. Spaulding, Records of the Columbian Historical Society, Volumes 29-30, page 159.

373. Lyon background: *Perilous Times*, by Geoffrey R. Stone, page 19.

374. "Unbounded thirst...and selfish avarice:" *American Aurora*, edited by Richard N. Rosenfeld, page 527.

375. Prison cell description: "the common receptacle for horse-thieves:" *Perilous Times*, by Geoffrey R. Stone, page 51.

376. Vote tally in the House: *The Trial of Samuel Chase*, Samuel H. Smith and Thomas Lloyd.

377. The charges against Chase: *Committee on the Judiciary, House of Representatives, Ninety-Third Congress, consideration of impeachment charges against President Nixon.*

378. Oath of Supreme Court Justice Chase: *The Trial of Samuel Chase*, Samuel H. Smith and Thomas Lloyd, page 402.

379. Tax of July 4, 1798: Ibid.

380. Fries was convicted of treason and sentenced to hang: *Grand Inquests*, by William H. Rehnquist, page 49.

381. Chase lecture to Fries that: "...It cannot escape observation: *The Tree of Liberty: A Documentary History*, edited by Nicholas N. Kittrie, page 94.

382. "The most villainous compound of... matter conceivable:" Ibid, page 95.

383. "Painful is the idea of taking the life of a man:" *John Adams*, by David McCullough, page 540.

384. "...This particular situation of Pennsylvania... of human affairs:" *The Tree of Liberty: A Documentary History*, edited by Nicholas N. Kittrie, page 97.

385. Hamilton information against Adams-20,000 word pamphlet and quote: *America Afire*, by Bernard A. Weisberger, pages 243 and 249.

386. "Callendar was a Scot...Madison and Thomas Jefferson:" Ibid, page 207.

387. Callendar: "the happy privilege of an American, that he may prattle and print, in what he pleases, and without any one to make him afraid:" *Crisis in Freedom*, by John C. Miller, page 83.

388. Callendar: "A little reptile...a dirty, little toper with shaved head and greasy jacket...the scum of party filth"

who "deserved... the gallows:" *Perilous Times*, by Geoffrey R. Stone, page 61.

389. Callendar: "had once been physically removed from the halls of Congress because he was covered with lice and filth:" *Crisis in Freedom*, by John C. Miller, page 215.

390. "Professed aristocrat... British interest:" *The Trial of Samuel Chase*, Samuel H. Smith and Thomas Lloyd, page 57.

391. "Has never opened his lips, ... who differs from his opinions:" *Perilous Times*, by Geoffrey R. Stone, page 62.

392. "A French war ...and consequences of debt and despotism:" Ibid.

393. "A repulsive pedant...nor the courage of a man?" *John Adams*, by David McCullough, page 537.

394. Description of Chase's conduct in Callendar trial: *Impeachment: The Constitutional Problems*, by Raoul Berger, page 246.

395. "Sowing discord among... an attack the people themselves:" *Perilous Times*, by Geoffrey R. Stone, page 62.

396. Callendar fell off a ferry in a drunken seizure and drowned: *Crisis in Freedom*, by John C. Miller.

397. "Twistifications:" *American Sphinx*, by Joseph J. Ellis, page 208.

398. "When conversing with Marshall...I can't tell:" *Aaron Burr--Conspiracy to Treason*, by Buckner F. Melton, Jr., page 63.

399. Chase comments on article: "I have just received the articles of impeachment:" *The Papers of John Marshall*, edited by Charles F. Hobson.

400. "It is, emphatically, the province and duty of the judicial department, to say what the law is." (The Supreme Court Historical Society)

401. "It was the practice in Courts of Justice to arraign the murderer before the Judge, but now we behold the Judge

before the murderer!" *Aaron Burr--Conspiracy to Treason*, by Buckner F. Melton, Jr., page 65.

402. Articles of Impeachment: *The Trial of Samuel Chase*, Samuel H. Smith and Thomas Lloyd.

403. Nicholson quote on "Good Behavior:" Ibid, page 342.

404. Cesar Rodney quote on "Good Behavior:" Ibid, page 388.

405. Randolph quote: Ibid, page 481.

406. "He began a speech…lost his notes:" *The Jeffersonian Crisis*, by Richard E. Ellis, page 101.

407. House Manager Campbell quote: *The Trial of Samuel Chase*, Samuel H. Smith and Thomas Lloyd, page 387.

408. Burr: "conducted himself and the trial "with the dignity and impartiality of an angel, but with the rigor of a devil:" *Grand Inquests*, by William H. Rehnquist page 19.

409. Senate vote tally: *The Trial of Samuel Chase*, Samuel H. Smith and Thomas Lloyd.

410. "There is not a Constitutional majority… on any one article:" Ibid.

411. "Cursed of thy father / Scum of all that's base / Thy sight is odious / and thy name is ---." *Aaron Burr--Conspiracy to Treason*, by Buckner F. Melton, Jr., page 65.

412. "No party that ever… destroyed them:" *American Aurora*, edited by Richard N. Rosenfeld, page 901.

413. "Although the Sedition Act…of this Court:" Ibid, page 907.

414. "I like the dreams…history of the past:" *American Sphinx*, by Joseph J. Ellis, page 273.

Virginia (Finally) Joins the Confederacy

415. Congressman Lincoln quote: "Any people anywhere, being inclined and having the power…a most sacred right:" *The*

Collected Works of Abraham Lincoln, edited by Roy P. Basler, Volume I, page 438.

416. "American history has known few events more momentous than the secession of Virginia:" *The Coming Fury,* by Bruce Catton, page 330.

417. "The course taken in Virginia was the most important." Remarks to Congress July 4, 1861, published in the *Congressional Globe for the 37th Congress.*

418. Virginia was the most influential of the Border States: *Reveille in Washington,* by Margaret Leech, page 29.

419. "Without Virginia, the Southern Confederacy could not have hoped to win ...hopes were not half bad:" By Bruce Catton, page 330.

420. Henry Adams quote: "The great and decisive struggle rested always in Virginia...settle the fact of disunion: *Henry Adams: the Great Secession Winter of 1860-1861 and Other Essays,* edited by George E. Hochfield, pages 24-25.

421. "The little impudent vixen [South Carolina] has gone beyond all patience....so they would only do it by sea, and not pester us:" Attributed to Robert L. Dabney in *the Secession Movement in Virginia, 1847-1861,* by Henry T. Shanks, page 135.

422. Charleston, South Carolina newspaper, "Virginia will never secede now:" *The Impending Crisis, 1848-1861,* by David M. Potter, page 508.

423. A delegate from the western portion of Virginia wrote to Secretary of State Seward: "We have scarcely left a vestige of secession in Western Virginia...she will never join them:" *The Secession Movement in Virginia, 1847-1861,* by Henry T. Shanks, page 153.

424. Diplomat William Thayer reported that Seward, "is jubilant over the elections in Virginia and Tennessee...will save the Border States:" *Politicians in Crisis: The Washington Letters of William S. Thayer, December 1860-March 1861,* edited

by Martin Crawford, published in *Civil War History*, Volume 27, Number 3, page 240.

425. A *New York Tribune* reporter: "As to Virginia seceding, that need not be thought of in any event...who prefer the Southern Confederacy:" *The Secession Movement in Virginia, 1847-1861,* by Henry T. Shanks, page 256, footnote number 19.

426. "President Lincoln indulged the hope...a great majority of the people [of Virginia] were opposed...positive, active and violent:" *Gideon Welles Diary*, Volume 1, page 39.

427. President Lincoln: "It may well be questioned whether there is to-day a majority ... of the so-called seceded states:" Remarks to Congress July 4, 1861, published in the *Congressional Globe for the 37th Congress.*

428. Poem: Virginia to the North—"Thus speaks the sovereign Old Dominion....when I have a mind to:" *The Rebellion Record: a Diary of American Events*, edited by Frank Moore, page 4.

429. Roger Pryor of Virginia: "I will tell you, gentlemen, what will put Virginia in the Southern Confederacy in less than an hour by Shrewsbury clock—strike a blow:" *History of the Civil War, 1861-1865*, by James Ford Rhodes, page 24.

430. Virginia was to provide three regiments made up of 2,340 men: *War of the Rebellion: Official Records of the Union and Confederate Armies,* hereafter referred to as "OR", Series III, Volume I, page 69.

431. The proclamation "knocked Virginia straight out of the Union:" *The Coming Fury,* by Bruce Catton, page 330.

432. "A blaze of excited indignation:" OR, Series I, Volume 51, Part II, page 11.

433. William N. H. Smith, a Whig member of Congress: "The Union feeling was strong up to the recent proclamation. This War manifest extinguishes it, and resistance is now on every man's lips...Union men are now such no longer:"

Dissent in the Confederacy: the North Carolina Experience, by Marc W. Kruman, published in *Civil War History,* Volume 27, Number 4, page 296.

434. Another Whig politician "up to the time of Lincoln's proclamation...I then saw that the South had either to submit to abject vassalage or assert her rights at the point of the sword:" Ibid.

435. Virginia Governor John Letcher: "...the militia of Virginia will not be furnished... as determined as the Administration has exhibited toward the South:" OR, Series III, Volume I, page 76.

436. Tennessee Governor Isham Harris: "Tennessee will not furnish a single man ...and those of our Southern brethren:" OR, Series III, Volume I, page 81.

437. Kentucky Governor Boriah Magoffin: "I say emphatically Kentucky will furnish no troops for the wicked purpose of subduing her sister Southern States:" OR, Series III, Volume I, page 70.

438. North Carolina Governor John Ellis: "I regard the levy of troops made by the Administration for the purpose of subjugating the States of the South ...You can get no troops from North Carolina:" OR, Series III, Volume I, page 72.

439. Missouri Governor Jackson: "Your requisition...is illegal, unconstitutional and revolutionary... to carry on any such unholy crusade:" OR, Series III, Volume I, page 82.

440. Arkansas Governor Rector: "In answer to your requisition for troops from Arkansas to subjugate the Southern States... against Northern mendacity and usurpation:" OR, Series III, Volume I, page 99.

441. "Lincoln had said that to trade a fort for a state, Sumter for Virginia...Virginia's departure was almost automatic:" *The Coming Fury,* by Bruce Catton, page 330.

442. Information about Lincoln's statements to Rives and Summers, as well as Hay's journal entry: *The War for the*

Union: the Improvised War, 1861-1862, by Allan Nevins, page 47.

443. "Men seldom, or rather never for any length of time and deliberately, rebel against anything that does not deserve rebelling against:" attributed to Thomas Carlyle in *Unleashed at Long Last,* by W. H. T Squires, page 154.

444. "Vote against secession in Virginia of 89-45 on April 4, 1861: *The Borderland in the Civil War,* by Edward Conrad Smith, page 162.

445. Ten members absent: *The War for the Union: the Improvised War, 1861-1862,* by Allan Nevins, page 93.

446. Fairfax vote on secession: *Conditional Unionism and Slavery in Virginia 1860-1861: the Case of Dr. Richard Epps,* by Shearer Davis Bowman, published in *the Virginia Magazine of History and Biography,* Volume 96, Number 1, January 1988, page 49.

447. Information about Henry Brookes abruptly stopping his writing: *Annandale, Virginia, a Brief History,* by Robert Morgan-Moxham and Estella K. Bryans-Munson, editor, page 58.

448. "The command marched in column...silently advanced across the bridge:" attributed to the *Biographical Memorial of General Daniel Butterfield* (page 24) by Charles O. Paullin, in his Oration of April 15, 1924 before the Columbia Historical Society, page 113.

449. "Most conspicuous of all...and many never came back:" *The Life and Letters of John Hay,* by William Roscoe Thayer, Volume I, page 116.

450. "Emancipation without deportation...this Southern Confederation:" *A Virginia Village Goes to War: Falls Church During the Civil War,* by Bradley E. Gernand, page 214.

451. "Nearly every prominent hill...to many residents:" *Alexandria County in 1861,* by Charles O. Paullin, Oration

of April 15, 1924 before the Columbia Historical Society, page 125.

452. "Southerner could lick five Northern mudsills...blocks of five:" Charles E. Davis, *Three Years in the Army*, cited in *The Civil War Archive: the History of the Civil War in Documents*, edited by Henry Steele Commager, page 219.

453. "It was not so very...blocks of five:" Ibid.

454. Information about pre-war Northerners moving to Fairfax and driving up real estate prices: *A Virginia Village Goes to War: Falls Church During the Civil War*, by Bradley E. Gernand, pages 116-117.

455. Information about shell hitting the home of Mr. Pullman: *Alexandria Gazette*, August 6, 1864.

456. "The moral condition...would hardly know the place:" *Alexandria Gazette*, August 25, 1862 and August 25, 1864.

457. "The convalescent camp...confusion and dissatisfaction:" *Alexandria Gazette*, October 3, 1862.

458. William J. Crossley quote: " July 17th, we arrived at Fairfax where some of the smart ones...without cause or provocation;" *Personal Narratives of Events in the War of the Rebellion, Being Papers Read Before the Rhode Island Soldiers and Sailors Historical Society*, Sixth Series, Number 4; on file at the Virginia Historical Society, E 464.R47.

459. Anthony Trollope quote about Alexandria—"we saw as melancholy...man can conceive:" *Alexandria During the Civil War*, by William B. Hurd, page 101, published in *Alexandria: A Composite History*, published by the Alexandria Bicentennial Commission.

460. "A reign of terror...mercy of the maddening throng:" Ibid.

461. "Destruction here stares...return to them:" *Courage and Betrayal: The Union Loyalist in Lewinsville*, by Kenneth A. Link, pages 7-8, published in the *Northern Virginia*

Heritage, A Journal of Local History, February 1986, Volume VIII.

462. "The streets are so shockingly filthy...wrong to tell:" The Civil War Diary of Anne Frobel, edited by Peter R. Henriques, published in the *Northern Virginia Heritage, A Journal of Local History,* February 1987, Volume IX.

463. "Even in her present aspect of decay...memory of some exile:" *A Virginia Village Goes to War: Falls Church During the Civil War,* by Bradley E. Gernand, page 142.

464. "The government bakery is here...the government stores:" Letter from Private Alfred Bliss dated February 29, 1864, as published in the Alexandria Historical Society Newsletter, October 1989.

Devilry on Duke Street: The Alexandria Slave Pen

465. Information about ownership and uses of the building: *Prison Life in Civil War Alexandria,* by T. Michael Miller, published in the Northern Virginia Heritage, October 1987, Volume IX, pages 9-13.

466. Information about Armfield and Franklin: *The Local Career of an Alexandria Slave Trader,* by Henry A. Wise, Jr.

467. "There were none so despised...of negro-trader:" attributed by Henry A. Wise Jr., in an unpublished paper called *The Local Career of an Alexandria Slave Trader,* in *Slavery: A Problem in American Institutional and Intellectual Life,* by Stanley Elkins.

468. "Exceedingly strange looking...piratical and repulsive:" attributed by Henry A. Wise Jr., in an unpublished paper called *The Local Career of an Alexandria Slave Trader,* page 12, to *Isaac Franklin, Slave Trader and Planter of the Old South,* by Wendell Stephenson.

469. I found it...he finally died: *Forgotten Valor, the Memoirs, Journals & Civil War Letters of Orlando B. Wilcox,* edited by Robert Garth Scott.

470. "The building was used...dunking them:" *Legends and Folk Tales of Old Alexandria, Virginia,* by Ruth Lincoln Kaye.

471. "Jeered at the Union troops...once too often:" Ibid.

472. "Its outside presented only the appearance...shadow of the Capitol! *Twelve Years a Slave, by Solomon Northup,* edited by Sue Eakin and Joseph Logsdon, page 23.

473. "When a new hand...to his respective chores:" *Twelve Years a Slave, by Solomon Northup,* edited by Sue Eakin and Joseph Logsdon, pages 124-127.

474. "The Slave Pen is now used...service than whites:" Letter from Private Alfred Bliss dated February 29, 1864, as published in the Alexandria Historical Society Newsletter, October 1989.

475. "Cotton was well adapted...the death of an Irishman was a small matter:" *The Growth of Southern Civilization--1790-1860,* by Clement Eaton, pages 27-28, 64.

476. Lincoln quote: "He watches your necessities...death for the slave trader:" *The Collected Works of Abraham Lincoln,* edited by Roy P. Basler, Volume II, pages 264-265.

The Attempted Slave Insurrection in Fairfax

477. DeTocqueville quote: *The Liberator,* by Ira Berlin, published in *Days of Destiny,* edited by James McPherson, page 122.

478. Advertisement for Vincent: *Alexandria Gazette,* September 3rd and 9th, 1833.

479. Advertisement for Simon: *Alexandria Gazette,* September 3rd, 7th and 9th, 1833.

480. Advertisement for 40 or 50 slaves: *Alexandria Gazette,* September 7th and 9th, 1833.

481. Slave population in Fairfax: Northern Virginia Slavery: *A Statistical and Demographic Investigation,* by Donald

M. Sweig, 1982, submitted as dissertation to College of William & Mary.

482. Slave Riot in New York: *The Great Riots of New York*, edited by Joel Tyler Headley, 1970.

483. William Lloyd Garrison started his newspaper, The Liberator: *1831, Year of Eclipse,* by Louis P. Masur.

484. Nat Turner's slave insurrection in Southampton County: Ibid.

485. Weather in Fairfax on September 5, 1833: Meteorological Observations, by T. Mountford, published in *Alexandria Gazette*, October 4, 1833.

486. Windover's encounter with slaves: Letter to the Governor published in *Virginia Calendar of State Papers*.

487. Windover's arrest: *Alexandria Gazette*, September 20, 1833.

488. Windover charged for his attempt to burn the jail and escape: Virginia Court Records.

489. Windover's escape from jail: *Alexandria Gazette*, May 9, 1834.

490. Information about George Boxley: *"Poor Deluded Wretches—the Slave Insurrection of 1816,"* by William H. B. Thomas, published in the *Louisa County Historical Magazine,* Winter 1974-1975, Volume 6, Number 2.

491. Report of Mr. Dodson's activities: *Richmond Dispatch Newspaper*, as provided the University of Richmond.

492. Report of Mr. Vaughn's activities: Ibid.

Frank Padget: Virginia's Honored Slave

493. "Many persons...more such scenes:" *Shipwreck in the Mountains: The Loss of the Canal Boat Clinton and the Heroism of Boatman Frank Padget,* by Alexander Crosby Brown, *The American Neptune*, Volume 16, January 1956.

494. "The river life...from Virginia:" The Amherst County

Story, by Alfred Percy, The Amherst County (Virginia) Chamber of Commerce, 1961

495. Other information obtained regarding Frank Padget from the following sources:

496. *In Memory of Frank Padget*, by Robert L. Scribner, *The Virginia Cavalcade*, Volume 3, Winter 1953.

497. *A History of Rockbridge County Virginia*, by Oren F. Morton, Regional Publishing Company, 1980.

498. *Rockbridge County, Virginia Heritage Book, 1778-1997*, The Rockbridge Area Genealogical Society, 1997.

499. *Journey on the James: Three Weeks Through the Heart of Virginia*, by Earl Swift, The University Press of Virginia, 2001.

500. *A Hard Life on the Water*, by Gary Robertson, The Richmond Times-Dispatch, September 26, 1999.

501. *Glasgow, Virginia: One Hundred Years of Dreams,* by Lynda Mundy-Norris Miller, Rockbridge Publishing Company.

502. Information about Alex Kean Monument: *Monument Erected to a Faithful Slave,* by Doniphan Purcell Howland, published in the *Louisa County (Virginia) Historical Magazine,* Spring 2004, Volume 35, page 56.

Peyton Anderson: First Confederate Wounded

503. Instruction to fire two warning shots: Peyton Anderson Biography, *The Rappahannock News,* May 25, 1961.

504. Anderson later joined Mosby's Rangers: 6th Virginia Cavalry, by Michael P. Musick, *The Virginia Regimental Histories Series*, page 93.

505. Information about the monument: *The Confederate Veteran Magazine,* 1927, page 273.

506. James Robey summary of the incident: Letter to the United Daughters of the Confederacy, retained in Virginia Research Room, Fairfax County Public Library.

507. Anderson born on the 4th of July: *6th Virginia Cavalry*, by Michael P. Musick, The Virginia Regimental Histories Series, page 93.

508. Information on the deaths of Peyton and Louemma Anderson: Peyton Anderson biography, *The Rappahannock News*, May 25, 1961.

The Battle Hymn of the Republic

509. "An enormous hamper of fried chicken...a very special picnic." *Willard's of Washington*, by Garnett Laidlaw Eskew, page 91.

510. Information about Frederick Brown: *Memories of Many Men and Some Women: Being Personal Recollections*, by Maunsell B. Field, published in 1874, pages 291-292.

511. "The first thing in the morning is drill...and have a roll-call." *The Civil War: A Book of Quotations*, edited by Bob Blaisdell, page 27.

512. "At evening parade all Washington appears...but as men of the world." Theodore Winthrop, *Life in the Open Air, and Other Papers*, cited in *The Civil War Archive: the History of the Civil War in Documents*, edited by Henry Steele Commager, page 217.

513. "On Tuesday we marched...gulf of despair:" Charles O. Paullin, in his Oration of April 15, 1924; *Columbia Historical Society*, page 126.

514. Information about William Irwin court-martialed: *Tarnished Eagles, The Courts-Martial of Fifty Union Colonels and Lieutenant Colonels*, by Thomas P. Lowery, MD.

515. "We were no exception to the generality of mankind... the largest return for our admiration." Charles E. Davis, *Three Years in the Army*, cited in *The Civil War Archive: the History of the Civil War in Documents*, edited by Henry Steele Commager, page 221.

516. Each shareholder took turns carrying it... in the barrel of

428

the musket. *Detailed Minutiae of Soldier Life in the Army of Northern Virginia*, cited in *The Civil War Archive: The History of the Civil War in Documents*, edited by Henry Steele Commager, page 226.

517. "Snow-ball battles were sometimes fought...that might be contained in them." *Where Men Only Dare to Go or the Story of a Boy Company, C.S.A.*, by Royall W. Figg, pages 100-101.

518. Willard's was the first American hotel to provide writing facilities for its guests in every room: *Willard's of Washington*, by Garnett Laidlaw Eskew, page 93.

519. "Gave original draft... with notation, Willard's Hotel." *The Story of the Battle Hymn of the Republic*, by Florence Howe Hall, Books for Libraries Press, 1916.

520. "As I lay waiting for the dawn." *The Song that Wrote Itself,* by Louise Hall Tharp, American Heritage Illustrated, The Magazine of History, Volume 8, December 1956.

521. "The instrument for the righting of the wrong." *The Story of the Battle Hymn of the Republic,* by Florence Howe Hall, Books for Libraries Press, 1916.

522. "In the midst of the blare and glitter." Ibid.

523. "As if a heavenly ally were descending with a song of succor." Ibid.

524. "In the words of the Battle Hymn, we hear...our great Republic:" Ibid.

525. Information about James E. Kerrigan court-martial: *Tarnished Eagles, The Courts-Martial of Fifty Union Colonels and Lieutenant Colonels,* by Thomas P. Lowery, MD.

526. 'Despite warnings...treat their superiors with disdain:" *Five Points: the 19th Century New York City Neighborhood that Invented Tap Dance, Stole Elections, and Became the World's Most Notorious Slum*, by Tyler Anbinder, pages 297-301.

527. Information about Kerrigan's length of service in the military and Congress: *Biographical Directory of the*

American Congress 1774-1971, compiled by Lawrence F. Kennedy, page 1229.

Professor Lowe's Flying Machine

528. Information on newspaper reporter saying 200 feet: *Reveille in Washington,* by Margaret Leech, page 84.

529. "Expressed their dislike...throwing bombs at it:" *The Confederate Blockade of Washington, D.C., 1861-1862,* by Mary Alice Wills, page 132.

530. Information about silk dress balloon: *A Civil War Treasury of Tales, Legends and Folklore,* edited by B. A. Botkin, page 127.

531. Information about using a white flag: *A Virginia Village Goes to War: Falls Church During the Civil War,* by Bradley E. Gernand, page 93.

532. "The signals from the balloon ... will revolutionize the art of gunnery." Arlington and Fairfax Counties: Land of Many Reconnaissance Firsts, by Dino A. Brugioni, published in the *Northern Virginia Heritage, a Journal of Local History,* February 1985, Volume VII.

533. Information about William Paulin, William Small and Dan Sickles: *The Confederate Blockade of Washington, D.C., 1861-1862,* by Mary Alice Wills, pages 127-132.

534. Information about Zeppelin: *The Germanic People in America,* by Victor Wolfgang von Hagen, pages 342-346.

535. "It was a weird spectacle...the imperturbable mariner continued to spy out the land." Townsend, *Campaigns of a Non-Combatant,* cited in *The Civil War Archive: the History of the Civil War in Documents,* edited by Henry Steele Commager, page 243.

536. Lowe was indeed the first American "spy in the sky." Arlington and Fairfax Counties: Land of Many Reconnaissance Firsts, by Dino A. Brugioni, published in

the *Northern Virginia Heritage, a Journal of Local History,*
February 1985, Volume VII.

537. "Every day the Yankees sent up a balloon…was burned by
the Yankees:" *Mrs. Tinsley's War Recollections, 1862-1865,*
by Mrs. Fannie Gaines Tinsley, published in the *Virginia
Magazine of History and Biography,* Volume 35, page 396.

538. Lowe leaving in May 1863 and being named a colonel
by Lincoln: *The Unknown Civil War: Odd, Peculiar, and
Unusual Stories of the War Between the States,* by Webb
Garrison, page 150.

539. Information about French balloon flights: *Footnotes to
World History, a Bibliographic Source Book,* by Harold S.
Sharp, pages 296-297.

Northern Slave Traders

540. Information about Captain Gordon: *Hanging Captain
Gordon: The Life and Trial of an American Slave Trader,* by
Ron Soodalter; *The Suppression of the African Slave-Trade
to the United States of America 1638-1870,* by W. E. B.
Dubois; and *Complicity—How the North Promoted,
Prolonged, and Profited from Slavery,* by Anne Farrow, Joel
Lang, and Jenifer Frank.

541. Lincoln quote: "When southern people tell us…I
acknowledge the fact:" *The Collected Works of Abraham
Lincoln,* edited by Roy P. Basler, Volume II, page 255.

542. Cotton was king, but "he was a puppet monarch:" *King
Cotton and His Retainers—Financing & Marketing
the Cotton Crop of the South, 1800-1925,* by Harold D.
Woodman, page 359.

543. "The physical existence [of New York City] depend[ed]
upon… the continuance of slave labor and the prosperity of
the slave master:" *The Epic of New York City—A Narrative
History,* by Edward Robb Ellis, page 285.

544. "The nest of slave pirates:" attributed to Horace Greely-*Ibid*, page 286.

545. The 34th Congress of the United States: "Almost all the slave expeditions... chiefly at New York." *The Suppression of the African Slave-Trade to the United States of America 1638-1870*, by W. E. B. Dubois, page 180.

546. The United States attorney: "New York [is at] the head and front of the slave trade." *Hanging Captain Gordon—the Life and Trial of an American Slave Trader*, by Ron Soodalter, page 75.

547. Marshal for New York: "the principal depot for vessels in this traffic:" *Hanging Captain Gordon—the Life and Trial of an American Slave Trader*, by Ron Soodalter, page 241.

548. Most of money invested in the slave trade by New Yorkers: *American Slavers and the Federal Law, 1837-1862*, by Warren S. Howard, page 154.

549. New York Times: "their sense of the wickedness...blood-stained gains:" *Hanging Captain Gordon—the Life and Trial of an American Slave Trader*, by Ron Soodalter, page 227.

550. Christian Intelligencer: "New York has long enough borne the disgrace...negro stealing business:" *Hanging Captain Gordon—the Life and Trial of an American Slave Trader*, by Ron Soodalter, page 225.

551. "The City of New York had been until of late...only second to her in that distinction:" *The Suppression of the African Slave-Trade to the United States of America 1638-1870*, by W. E. B. Dubois-page 179.

552. "The money manipulators of New York dominated every phase of [slavery], from plantation to market:" *The Epic of New York City—A Narrative History*, by Edward Robb Ellis, page 287.

553. "The number of person engaged...is notorious:" *The Slave-Trade in New York*, published in *The Continental Monthly*, January 1862, pages 86-90.

554. "For the hideous truth is that...mart in the world: *The New York Tribune,* September 29, 1860, according to *John C. Calhoun: American Portrait,* by Margaret L. Coit, page 333.

555. "Not so much from the slave state...commercial interests of New York:" Ibid, page 333.

556. Northern businesses set the price...left narrow margins of profit for the planter." *Black Reconstruction in America 1860-1880,* W. E. B. DuBois, page 37.

557. Frederick Douglas: "The South was fighting to take slavery out of the Union, and the North fighting to keep it in the Union:" *Ibid,* page 61.

558. Charles Sumner, "the lords of the lash and the lords of the loom...traffickers of New England:" *Complicity—How the North Promoted, Prolonged, and Profited from Slavery,* by Anne Farrow, Joel Lang, and Jenifer Frank, page 37.

559. Ralph Waldo Emerson: "The cotton thread is the Union:" *Ibid,* page 37.

560. By 1860, New England was home to 472 cotton mills: *Ibid,* page 6.

561. In 1860, nearly 50% of all the textiles produced in the United States came from mills located in Massachusetts and Rhode Island: *Ibid,* page 26.

562. New York newspaper: "That plucky little state [Rhode Island] will at once abandon...set down at $50,000,000 annually:" Published in the *New York Tribune* on April 1, 1861, according to *Prologue to Sumter: the Beginnings of the Civil War from the John Brown Raid to the Surrender of Fort Sumter,* by Philip Van Doren Stern, page 219.

563. In 1858 those three products accounted for 66% of all exports. The following year the figure was a whopping 71%: *King Cotton Diplomacy,* by Frank Lawrence Owsley, pages 13-14.

564. Information about revenue from Southern and Northern

Customs Houses in the period June 1858-June 1859: *Lifeline of the Confederacy: Blockade Running During the Civil War,* by Stephen R. Wise, page 228.

565. Information about the 79% of all imports to Great Britain being from Southern States: *King Cotton Diplomacy,* by Frank Lawrence Owsley, page 3.

566. New York was the center of the international slavery trade according to W. E. B. DuBois: *The Suppression of the African Slave-Trade to the United States of America 1638-1870,* by W. E. B. Dubois, page 178.

567. W. E. B. Dubois reported that New York harbors fitted out 85 slaving vessels, transporting 30,000-60,000 slaves annually. *Ibid,* pages 179 and 185.

568. Information about Northern slavers in the 1850s: *The Suppression of the African Slave-Trade to the United States of America 1638-1870,* by W. E. B. Dubois-Appendix C; and *Complicity—How the North Promoted, Prolonged, and Profited from Slavery,* by Anne Farrow, Joel Lang, and Jenifer Frank.

569. Information about Northern slavers in the 1850s and 1860s: *The Suppression of the African Slave-Trade to the United States of America 1638-1870,* by W. E. B. Dubois-Appendix C; and *Complicity—How the North Promoted, Prolonged, and Profited from Slavery,* by Anne Farrow, Joel Lang, and Jenifer Frank.

570. Information about the slaving vessels: Julia Moulton, Orion, Splendide, Bonito, Merchant, Falmouth, Oregon, William Lewis, Jasper: *American Slavers and the Federal Law, 1837-1862,* by Warren S. Howard.

571. Information about the *J. Harris* and *Wildfire* slaving vessels: *Revelations of a Slave Smuggler: Being the Autobiography of Captain Richard Drake, an African Trader for Fifty Years,* by Richard Drake, page 100.

572. Information about Farnum: *The Wanderer—the Last*

American Slave Ship and the Conspiracy that set its Sails, by Erik Calonius, page 242.

573. New Orleans Picayune: "It is believed that the slaver... in Cuba before she was burned:" *Revelations of a Slave Smuggler: Being the Autobiography of Captain Richard Drake, an African Trader for Fifty Years,* by Richard Drake, page vi.

574. "Who conducts our commerce...first to Boston or New York!" *The Wanderer—the Last American Slave Ship and the Conspiracy that set its Sails,* by Erik Calonius, page 33.

575. Lincoln lost NYC by greater than 2:1 margin in 1864: *Remember Your Country and Keep up its Credit: Irish Volunteers and the Union Army, 1861-1865,* by Susannah Ural Bruce, published in the *Journal of Military History,* April 2005, page 358.

576. In 1864, the *Huntress* from the North delivered slaves to Cuba: *The Suppression of the African Slave-Trade to the United States of America 1638-1870,* by W. E. B. Dubois- Appendix C.

577. Poem—The Guinea Captain-- "Lives there a savage ruder... hurries back for more!: *Revelations of a Slave Smuggler: Being the Autobiography of Captain Richard Drake, an African Trader for Fifty Years,* by Richard Drake, page v.

Blenker's Germans

578. Information about Nast and Teddy Roosevelt: *The Germanic People in America,* by Victor Wolfgang von Hagen, page 340.

579. At least 20,000 Germans in the November 1861 Falls Church Grand Review. *My Diary North and South,* by William Howard Russell, page 328.

580. "We Germans...are prepared to defend our American home as the blessed place of freedom." *The Blessed Place*

of Freedom: Europeans in Civil War America, by Dean B. Mahin.

581. "From the same motives which brought Von Kalb and Steuben…as the right cause." Ibid.

582. "Take the Dutch out of the Union army and we could have whipped the Yankees easily:" Ibid.

583. Germans represented "the most reliable and consistent supporters of the Union cause:" Ibid.

584. Information about Lincoln secretly purchasing a German-America newspaper: *The Fourth Horseman: One Man's Mission to Wage the Great War in America*, by Robert Koenig, page 13.

585. Information about newspaper story claiming the sixteen Finch brothers joined the same Ohio regiment: *The Rebellion Record: a Diary of America Events, Volume 1,* edited by Frank Moore, page 95.

586. "All known and unknown lands… army of the grand Duchess of Gerolstein." *Annandale, Virginia, a Brief History,* by Robert Morgan Moxham and edited by Estella K. Bryans-Munson, page 46.

587. "Circus or opera…as varied and brilliant as the colors of the rainbow." Ibid.

588. "In reply to their challenge…or Esquimaux or Chinese:" Ibid.

589. Blenker subsequently transferred to Fremont's Mountain Department where his military resume consists of falling off his horse and being involved in the Union defeat at the Battle of Cross Keys. *Reveille in Washington*, by Margaret Leech, page 432.

590. Information about Colonel Emil von Schoenig court martial: *Tarnished Eagles, The Courts-Martial of Fifty Union Colonels and Lieutenant Colonels,* by Thomas P. Lowery, MD.

591. Eighty-two German-American Civil War soldiers received

the Medal of Honor: *The Fourth Horseman: One Man's Mission to Wage the Great War in America,* by Robert Koenig, page 12.

592. General McClellan said "few were of the slightest use to us...so often men without character." *McClellan's Own Story,* cited in *The Civil War Archive: the History of the Civil War in Documents,* edited by Henry Steele Commager, pages 245-246.

Vice Crackdown

593. I would rather be farther off from town...an increase of sickness in camp," *The Story the Soldiers Wouldn't Tell: Sex in the Civil War,* by Thomas P. Lowery, MD, page 32.

594. "But now the evils of this place... I have not been able to reach [General] Grant to protest these matters. *The Civil War Archive: the History of the Civil War in Documents,* edited by Henry Steele Commager, page 373.

595. "Picket pockets flourished...the bullies and the roistering soldiers, the drabs bedizened the police courts." *Reveille in Washington,* by Margaret Leech, pages 260-266.

596. Information about Miss Maude Roberts and H. C. Burtenett: Ibid, pages 267-270.

Some Californians--aka: the Second Massachusetts Cavalry, fight in Fairfax

597. *The War in the Far West 1861-1865: an Informal History of the Part Played by the Western States in the Civil War,* by Oscar Lewis.

598. Information about the Pony Express: *Orphans Preferred: The Twisted Truth and Lasting Legend of the Pony Express,* by Christopher Corbett.

599. Approximately 101 ships sank off the California coast: *Encyclopedia of Civil War Shipwrecks,* by W. Craig Gaines, pages 24-31.

600. Information about Wakefield Chapel and Elhanan Winchester Wakefield: *Wakefield Chapel*, by D. Anne A. Evans.

601. *The Great Diamond Hoax and other Stirring Incidents in the Life of Asbury Harpending*, by Asbury Harpending.

602. "The sun is gold...with Mosby's stamp:" Herman Melville, *The Scout Toward Aldie*.

603. "I have the honor to report all quiet...and shot at 12 this noon." *Mosby's Rangers: A Record of the Operations of the Forty-Third Battalion Virginia Cavalry*, by James J. Williamson, page 426.

604. Most information about Ormsby and the Second Massachusetts: The Sojourn of the Second Massachusetts Cavalry in Vienna, by Noel Harrison, published in the *Northern Virginia Heritage: a Journal of Local History*, June 1985, Volume VII, pages 11-12.

605. Other information from *The Nature of Sacrifice: A Biography of Charles Russell Lowell, Jr., 1835-64*, by Carol Bundy.

606. "I do not respect the service in which Mosby was engaged... are secondary consideration." *Anguish of a Virginia Unionist: The Civil War Diary of Edward Carter Turner*, edited by Peter R. Henriques, published in the *Northern Virginia Heritage, A Journal of Local History*, June 1979, Volume I.

607. "Led blindly into a war from...and accomplished thy ruin:" *Ibid.*

Colonel John S. Mosby

608. 'Mosby has annoyed me considerably.' *A Virginia Village Goes to War: Falls Church During the Civil War*, by Bradley E. Gernand, page 200.

609. "As a Command we had no knowledge ...to obey orders and to fight." *Reminiscences of a Mosby Guerilla*, cited in *The Civil War Archive: the History of the Civil War in*

Documents, edited by Henry Steele Commager, pages 251-252.

610. So I have had the distinction of having had negro babies and dogs named after me." *Mosby's Memoirs,* by Colonel John S. Mosby, page 167.

611. "...Your treatment and (that of) your men to us...a bad disturber." *Ibid,* page 189.

612. "When I can shoot my rifle clear...When his buttermilk is gone:"*A Civil War Treasury of Tales, Legends and Folklore,* edited by B. A. Botkin, page 396.

613. "Deception is the ethics of war:" *Mosby's Memoirs,* by Colonel John S. Mosby, page 203.

614. "The very name was enough... Mosby was everywhere." *Fairfax County, A History,* Fairfax County Board of Supervisors, 250th Anniversary Commemorative Edition, page 353.

615. "His sleepless vigilance and unceasing activity...*petite guerre* in any age." *Mosby's Memoirs,* by Colonel John S. Mosby, pages 269-270.

616. Information about Mosby using the turnpike and the last casualty on the turnpike: *History of the Little River Turnpike,* Part II, 1861-1979, by D'Anne Evans, published in the Globe, July 19, 1979.

617. Information about skirmishes in Annandale involving Mosby: *The Cyclopedia of Battles,* page 32.

618. "Mosby had had a skirmish near Gooding's Tavern... slaughter houses in Alexandria:" *Echoes of History: Pioneers of America Society,* September 1972, interview of Fairfax resident Alexander L. Haight by H. H. Douglas, page 35.

619. Poem: How We Rode from Annandale: *Southern Bivouac Magazine,* September 1886.

Edwin Stoughton: The Luckless Sleeper in Fairfax

620. Stoughton stationed at Gunnell House: *Mosby's Fighting Parson: The Life and Times of Sam Chapman*, by Peter A. Brown, page 96.

621. Snow was falling: *The Affair at Fairfax Court-House*, by Thomas J. Evans, published in the April-May 1984 issue of the Kepi, page 13.

622. "Luckless sleeper at Fairfax:" *Gray Ghost: The Life of John Singleton Mosby*, by James A. Ramage, page 71.

623. "The Affair at Fairfax Courthouse:" *The Affair at Fairfax Court-House*, by Thomas J. Evans, published in the April-May 1984 issue of the Kepi, page 11.

624. "Do their deviltry:" *Ranger Mosby*, by Virgil Carrington Jones, page 91.

625. "I had no reputation to lose...Adventures to the adventurous:" *The Memoirs of Colonel John S. Mosby*, page 172.

626. "All the horses had...riders had a saber and two pistols:" *Mosby's Capture of Stoughton*, by Virgil Carrington (Pat) Jones, page 65, published in "Fairfax County and the War Between the States", reprinted 1987.

627. Details of Mosby waking up Stoughton: *The Guerrilla War 1861-1865*, by Albert Castel, published in the October 1974 issue of Civil War Times Illustrated, page 17.

628. "When a light was struck...he has caught you" *Mosby's Rangers: A Record of the Operations of the Forty-Third Battalion Virginia Cavalry*, by James J. Williamson, pages 39-40.

629. Mosby writing his name on the wall: *Gray Ghost: The Life of John Singleton Mosby*, by James A. Ramage, page 69.

630. Mosby captured 32 men and 58 horses: *Fairfax, Virginia: A City Traveling Through Time*, by Nan Netherton et al,

History of the City of Fairfax Round Table, 1997, page 30.

631. "The night was dark and rainy...in a reckless manner:" *Alexandria Gazette* Newspaper, March 10, 1863.

632. "Take the place of the Gen. Caught at Fairfax last night:" *The Collected Works of Abraham Lincoln*, Volume VI, page 129.

633. "I can make a much better brigadier in five minutes...$125 a piece:" Ibid.

634. "I fear more the raids of Stevens on the treasury than those of Mosby on our lines:" *John Sherman's Recollections of Forty Years in the House, Senate and Cabinet, an Autobiography*, by John Sherman, published in 1895, Volume I, page 359.

635. "There is a woman...full of bad whiskey:" *Mosby's Capture of Stoughton*, by Virgil Carrington (Pat) Jones, published in "Fairfax County and the War Between the States," reprinted 1987, page 67.

636. In response to these attacks up on Stoughton... offered $250 to the *New York Times* to release the author's identity: The Antonia Ford Mystery, by Linda J. Simmons, published in the *Northern Virginia Heritage: a Journal of Local History*, October 1985, Volume VII, pages 3-6.

637. "I knew I could not revenge...so I took the Major: *All the Daring of the Soldier: Women of the Civil War Armies*, by Elizabeth D. Leonard, page 50.

638. Stoughton soon after left Army and died: *Gray Ghost: The Life of John Singleton Mosby*, by James A. Ramage, page 71.

639. "Inasmuch as I have never...instrumental in getting me captured? Copy of letter in files at the Virginia Room of the Fairfax County Public Library.

640. Antonia Ford "innocent as Abraham Lincoln:" *Gray Ghost: The Life of John Singleton Mosby*, by James A. Ramage, page 74.

641. "To whom it may concern...all lovers of a noble nature:" *Willard's of Washington,* by Garnett Laidlaw Eskew, page 73.

642. Quote from church rector*: An Account of Mosby's Raid, By One of Stoughton's Men: As Told to Herbert A. Donovan,* Historical Society of Fairfax County, Virginia, Inc., Yearbook, Volume 4 (1955), page 72.

643. Information and quotes from two 1928 letters to Mrs. Willard: In files at the Virginia Room of the Fairfax County Public Library.

644. "For years and years...that's what they used to do:" *Echoes of History: Pioneers of America Society,* September 1972, interview of Fairfax resident Alexander L. Haight by H. H. Douglas, page 30.

Catastrophe on the Potomac

645. "Perfectly clear summer evening:" *Loss of the West Point, in the History of the 6ᵗʰ New Hampshire Regiment in the War for the Union,* by Captain Lyman Jackman, 1891.

646. Information re: value and lease contracts of the West Point and the George Peabody: National Archives, Washington, DC.

647. "Very old and hardly sea-worthy:" description of the West Point: *Washington Evening Star,* August 15, 1862.

648. "The first thing...for two days:" *A Memoir of the Embarkation of the Sick and Wounded from the Peninsula of Virginia in the Summer of 1862.*

649. "Dreadful Disaster on the Potomac:" Information about collision from the New York Herald (August 15 and 16, 1862); *New York Times* (August 15, 1862); and *Washington Evening Star* (August 15 and 18, 1862).

650. "At first it was supposed...joyous exclamations:" *New York Herald,* August 16, 1862.

651. "The water was full of struggling humanity…never hear again:" Lyman Jackman.

652. "The air was rent…at last engulfed:" *New York Herald*, August 16, 1862.

653. "The scene which followed…kept his promise:" Lyman Jackman.

654. "Near death's door:" Reunion of the 100th Pennsylvania Regiment.

655. "The scene of this terrible…for all coming time:" *Washington Evening Star*, August 18, 1862.

656. "Mismanagement and corruption… inspection and safeguards:" *History of the Great American Fortunes*, by Gustavus Myers, 1907, page 290.

657. "Amaze and sicken…injustice and extortion:" Ibid.

658. "Dead-horse claims:" Ibid, page 552.

659. "Unconscionable…and extortion:" Ibid.

660. Information about the Steamship *Illinois:* Ibid, page 543.

661. "Shockingly bad condition…to hold a nail:" Ibid, page 295.

662. Q and A re: Marshall Roberts: Ibid, page 401.

663. No foreign capitalists were interested: Ibid, page 290.

664. "Due more to luck than anything else." Ibid, page 290.

Shipwrecks and the Blockade

665. Unless otherwise noted, all information is from *Encyclopedia of Civil War Shipwrecks*, by W. Craig Gaines.

666. The Confederate government sent a buyer to Britain which resulted in the acquisition of eighteen cruisers: *The Civil War Archives: The History of the Civil War in Documents,* edited by Henry Steele Commager.

667. The federal government built their navy by purchase or

construction: *The Blockade and the Cruisers*, by J. Russell Soley, pages 17-19.

668. Information and quotes of Gideon Welles: *The Diary of Gideon Welles*, Volume I, 1861-March 30, 1864.

669. Information about number of miles and harbors covered by the blockade: *A Short History of the United States Navy*, by Carroll S. Alden.

670. Chances of getting caught by blockade runners: *The Civil War Archives: The History of the Civil War in Documents*, edited by Henry Steele Commager.

671. Information about the *Ruth*: *The Loss of Government Greenbacks on the Steamer Ruth*, by Ronald Horstman, published in *the Missouri Historical Review*, Volume 70, October 1975, page 87.

672. Information about Rose O'Neal Greenhow: *Reveille in Washington*, by Margaret Leech, page 441.

673. "The weather is warm and the scene delightful... army looking for an enemy." *All for the Union: The Civil War Diary and Letters of Elisha Hunt Rhodes*, page 53.

674. "The battle of Memphis was, in many respects...never before witnessed." *The Civil War Archives: The History of the Civil War in Documents*, edited by Henry Steele Commager.

675. In 1865 President Lincoln remarked that after the Civil War ended, "we could call [on Britain] to account for the embarrassments she had inflicted on us." *One War at a Time: the International Dimensions of the American Civil War*, by Dean B. Mahin.

676. Information about sinking of CSS Alabama and Cherbourg, France: *Civil Service*, by Dan Carlinsky, published in the *Smithsonian Magazine*, February 2005, pages 27-30.

677. Information about USA/British claims: *Ibid.*

678. Excerpt of January 15, 1866 letter: "The Virginians, I take it...are glad that slavery is dead." *A British Report on Postwar*

Virginia, edited by Wilbur Devereux Jones, Published by the Virginia Historical Society, in the July 1961 *Magazine of History and Biography*, pages 346-352.

Corruption in the Civil War

679. "There is no kind of dishonesty... defrauding the government:" Benjamin Franklin, *The 2,548 Best Things Anybody Ever Said*, edited by Robert Byrne.

680. "Shamelessly hurried to the assault on the Treasury, like a cloud of locusts:" *Four Years with the Army of the Potomac*, by Regis de Trobriand, as quoted in 'The Blue and The Gray, edited by Henry Steele Commager.

681. "Men there were by the hundred thousand...and they made use of it:" Henry S. Olcott, *The War's Carnival of Fraud*, included in *Annals of the War*, edited by Alexander K. McClure.

682. Pactolus River in Turkey: "once famous for...Midas having bathed there:" *Brewer's Dictionary of Phrase & Fable*, by Ivor H. Evans, 14th Edition, page 813.

683. Types of frauds based on geographic regions: Ibid.

684. "Paying ruinous prices:" Ibid.

685. Information on volume of goods purchased, i.e. 325,000 mess pans, etc: *Recollections of the Civil War*, Charles A. Dana, page 162.

686. Number of arms contracted from August 1861-January 1862: *Responses of the Presidents to Charges of Misconduct*, edited by C. Vann Woodward, page 114.

687. "The problem of the war was not men, but money:" *Recollections of Forty Years in the House, Senate and Cabinet, an Autobiography*, John Sherman, 1895, page 268.

688. "National bankruptcy is not an agreeable prospect... effecting its own ruin:" Ibid, page 281.

689. "At one of the gloomiest periods...the Union Now!"

Personal Recollections: *Memories of Many Men and of Some Women*, Maunsell B. Field, 1873, pages 312-313.

690. Information of multiple bounties jumpers: LaFayette Baker, *The Secret Service in the Late War*, published in *The Blue and The Gray*, edited by Henry Steele Commager.

691. "Shadows sliding without a light...Fashionplates, quinine and history:" *John Brown's Body*, Stephen Vincent Benet, Rinehart & Co., Inc., page 150.

692. "A compound...aroma of coffee:" *History of the Great American Fortunes*, by Gustavus Myers, 1937, page 403.

693. "In every regiment...in the sutler's tent:" Charles B. Johnson, *Muskets and Medicine*, as quoted in *The Blue and The Gray*, edited by Henry Steele Commager.

694. Information about withholding portion of requisitioned goods: Ibid.

695. "No back rations...commissary's response:" Ibid.

696. "Fraudulent inferiority:" Ibid.

697. "Could better keep dry...than under:" History of the Great American Fortunes, by Gustavus Myers, 1937, page 403

698. "A fraud upon...they were shoddy:" Ibid.

699. "The world has seen its iron age...this is the age of shoddy:" *Capital City: New York City and the Men Behind America's Rise to Economic Dominance, 1860-1900*, page 39.

700. "For nursing and subsisting...David's Island:" Henry S. Olcott, as quoted in "The War's Carnival of Fraud," included in *Annals of the War*, edited by Alexander K. McClure.

701. "Shoes which were...upon the Government:" *Ibid*, page 548.

702. "Dishonest mixture of oats and Indian corn:" *Recollections of the Civil War*, Charles A. Dana, page 162.

703. "Frauds were...it is well known...for a few hours": *History*

of the Great American Fortunes, by Gustavus Myers, 1937, page 297.

704. "More danger…than to the enemy:" Ibid, page 543.

705. Information about selling and repurchasing carbines: *Responses of the Presidents to Charges of Misconduct,* edited by C. Vann Woodward, page 113.

706. "Dishonest parasite:" Henry S. Olcott, as quoted in "The War's Carnival of Fraud," included in *Annals of the War,* edited by Alexander K. McClure.

707. "Without having bought a gallon…the year's transactions!" Ibid.

708. Information and quote from Whitelaw Reid, ""Put it up in the counting room…necessary to get clothes here:" *A Radical View: The "Agate" Dispatches of Whitelaw Reid, 1861-1865,* edited by James G. Smart, Volume I, pages 14-15.

709. Poem: "The world is flush…can't be mended:" *The Rebellion Record: A Diary of American Events,* edited by Frank Moore, 1862, Volume I, page 115.

710. "General Dix is pressing schemes…position as honesty:" Gideon Welles, *Diary of Gideon Welles, Volume I, Secretary of the Navy under Lincoln and Johnson, 1861-March 30, 1864,* page 177.

711. "A charge of bribery against a Senator…shall again commit the offense:" Ibid, pages 489, 522.

712. Information about women lobbyists: *Reminiscences of Sixty Years in the National Metropolis,* Ben Perley Poore, 1886, Volume II, pages 48-49.

713. "Presents of horses…politer name than bribery:" Henry S. Olcott, as quoted in "The War's Carnival of Fraud," included in *Annals of the War,* edited by Alexander K. McClure.

714. "A little money…went a long way:" Ibid.

715. Information about Henry Clay Dean: *Henry Clay Dean,*

"The Orator of Rebel Cove," by Edgar White, published in the *Missouri Historical Review,* Volume 22, October 1927, page 450.

716. "The quartermaster cheated the government...every imaginable species of fraud:" *Crimes of the Civil War and Curse of the Funding System,* by Henry Clay Dean, pages 94-95.

717. "It is impossible...take proper measures:" *Inside Lincoln's Cabinet, The Civil War Diaries of Salmon P. Chase,* edited by David Donald, page 32.

718. "Colossal graft...individual aggrandizement:" *Responses of the Presidents to Charges of Misconduct,* edited by C. Vann Woodward, page 114.

719. "The starving, penniless man...fruits of their crime": *History of the Great American Fortunes,* by Gustavus Myers, 1937, page 292.

720. "It is as important to the government as the winning of a battle:" Ascribed to Edwin Stanton, Henry S. Olcott, "The War's Carnival of Fraud," included in *Annals of the War,* edited by Alexander K. McClure.

721. "In the early history of the war...with the Government:" *History of the Great American Fortunes,* by Gustavus Myers, 1937, page 402.

722. Information about the False Claims Act in March 1863: *Recollections of Forty Years in the House, Senate and Cabinet, an Autobiography,* John Sherman, 1895, Volume I.

723. Definition and background on Qui Tams: *The Oxford English Dictionary.*

724. "The leniency ...history never explain:" *History of the Great American Fortunes,* by Gustavus Myers, 1937, page 552.

725. "Twenty to twenty-five percent...tainted with fraud:" Henry S. Olcott, "The War's Carnival of Fraud," included in *Annals of the War,* edited by Alexander K. McClure.

726. "Carnival of Fraud:" Ibid.

727. "Boundless resources…recuperative methods:" Ibid.

728. "Every dollar…sapping of ancient virtues:" Ibid.

729. "And should war and hell…both are as full of profiteers:" *John Brown's Body*, Stephen Vincent Benet, Rinehart & Co., Inc., page 151.

Civil War Pensions

730. In 1592, England provided pensions "for reliefe of Soldiours…Virginia in 1624 and the Plymouth Colony in 1636: *Federal Military Pensions in the United States*, by William H. Glasson.

731. 143,644 total pensions before the Civil War: Ibid.

732. Mexican War pensions were not approved until 1887: Ibid.

733. Union Enlistments totaled 2,898,304: *Numbers and Losses in the Civil War in America, 1861-1865,* by Thomas L. Livermore, page 1.

734. "These soldiers are not paupers…they must apply for aid:" Congressional Record, 48th Congress, 1st session, April 11, 1884, as quoted in *Beyond Sorrowful Pride: Civil War Pensions and War Widowhood 1862-1900*, dissertation (Ohio University, 1997) by Changsin Lee.

735. Established rating system for various disabilities: *Federal Military Pensions in the United States*, by William H. Glasson.

736. An 1888 list of disabilities by occurrence: Ibid.

737. Making these medical determinations were 1237 examining boards: *An Inside View of the Pension Bureau*, by A.B. Casselman, published in the Century Magazine, 1893, Volume 46.

738. In 1895 alone, the pension bill was $140 million: *Federal Military Pensions in the United States*, by William H. Glasson.

739. Act of July 1862 ...brothers and fathers in 1866: *Civil War Pensions and the Reconstruction of Union Families*, by Megan J. McClintock, published in the Journal of American History, September 1996, Volume 83.

740. A law in March 1873 allowed pensions to the parent if the son had indicated "a willingness or desire" to provide support: *Ibid.*

741. The law was expanded in 1890 to allow pensions to any parent who needed the money, Ibid.

742. Index cards caused the floor of Ford's Theatre to collapse in 1893, killing twenty-two government workers: *Numbers on top of Numbers—Counting the Civil War Dead*, by Drew Gilpin Faust, published in the Journal of Military History, Volume 70, October 2006.

743. In 1881 the Grand Army of the Republic (GAR) officially started a lobbying Congress: *Federal Military Pensions in the United States*, by William H. Glasson.

744. In 1890: 7,178 GAR posts with 427,981 members: *Civil War Military Pensions-1885-1897,* by Donald L. McMurry, unpublished thesis, 1921, University of Wisconsin, page 46.

745. General B. F. Butler told GAR members in 1890 that acting together, they could make "politicians dance like peas on a hot shovel." Ibid, page 47.

746. Every claimant would get "a favorable recommendation": *An Inside View of the Pension Bureau*, by A.B. Casselman, published in the Century Magazine, 1893, Volume 46.

747. A pension employee reviewed 250 consecutive claims in the 1890s: Ibid.

748. Almost a million pensioners on the rolls: *Federal Military Pensions in the United States*, by William H. Glasson.

749. By 1893, about 40% of the federal budget: *Civil War Pensions and the Reconstruction of Union Families*, by Megan

J. McClintock, published in the Journal of American History, September 1996, Volume 83.

750. For the thirty years from the end of the war until 1895, the pension tally exceeded $1.6 billion: *Federal Military Pensions in the United States*, by William H. Glasson.

751. Information about the last Union and Confederate veterans: *Our Last Civil War Veterans*, by Jay S. Hoar, published in the Blue and Gray Magazine, May 1985, Volume II, Issue 5.

752. A pension office employee estimated 30% of all pension resulted from fraud: *An Inside View of the Pension Bureau*, by A.B. Casselman, published in the Century Magazine, 1893, Volume 46.

753. "An open door to the treasury for the perpetration of fraud": *Federal Military Pensions in the United States*, by William H. Glasson.

754. An "avowedly political machine:" Ibid.

755. "A hideous wrong...prostituted and degraded...a crime against all honest soldiers:" *Civil War Pensions*, by Paul W. Davis, 1932 thesis, Oklahoma Agricultural and Mechanical College.

756. "The chimera of madmen...legislative insanity:" *Federal Military Pensions in the United States*, by William H. Glasson.

757. "Conceived in sin and brought forth in iniquity... and cowardice of the American Congress:" *Ibid.*

758. Investigated 1263 claims...5,131 claims were investigated, of which 28% were determined to be fraudulent: *Civil War Pensions*, by Paul W. Davis, 1932 thesis, Oklahoma Agricultural and Mechanical College.

759. Vampires who suck the very life-blood ...who ever lived:" *History of the Civil War Military Pensions, 1861-1865*, by John William Oliver, doctoral thesis published in the Bulletin of the University of Wisconsin, 1917, page 33.

760. "The friends of the soldiers...and feed upon them:" *Civil War Military Pensions-1885-1897,* by Donald L. McMurry, unpublished thesis, 1921, University of Wisconsin, page 142.

761. Information about George E. Lemon: *History of the Civil War Military Pensions, 1861-1865,* by John William Oliver, doctoral thesis published in the Bulletin of the University of Wisconsin, 1917, page 99.

762. In November 1868, the pension commissioner requested discretionary power to respond to flagrant violations of morality: "others live openly in prostitution for the same object:" Ibid, page 33.

763. Congress denied the request advising it was not responsibility of the federal government to "take care of the morality of its citizens:" *Civil War Pensions and the Reconstruction of Union Families,* by Megan J. McClintock, published in the Journal of American History, September 1996, Volume 83.

764. In 1877 a Philadelphia widow was investigated for collecting a pension even after she had remarried (this was not allowed: *Ibid.*

765. By 1882, Congress enacted measure terminating pensions of CW widows who cohabitated: Ibid.

766. The federal government did not pay any Confederate pensions ... The eleven states of the Confederacy paid state pensions to Confederate soldiers, with Georgia paying the most per year, followed by Alabama. *Encyclopedia of the American Civil War: a Political, Social and Military History,* edited by David S. Heidler and Jeanne T. Heidler.

The Bogus Proclamation of 1864

767. Only known instance of Lincoln ordering arrest and imprisonment of press editors: *Lincoln and the Press,* by Robert S. Harper, page 289.

768. Lincoln's order: "You are to arrest and imprison...any further publication therefrom:" *The Collected Works of Abraham Lincoln*, edited by Roy P. Basler, Volume VII, page 348.

769. "Admirably calculated to deceive:" *Lincoln in the Telegraph Office*, by David Homer Bates, page 232.

770. "The work of a skilled hand:" A Reminiscence of the Arrest and Incarceration of Five New York Telegraphers, Charged with Conspiracy Against the Government in 1864, published in *The Telegraph Age*, February 1, 1905, page 56.

771. May 19th as steamer day and no transatlantic cables until 1866: Ibid, page 231.

772. Information about war news being timed to match schedule of steamers to Europe: *Public Sentiment is Everything: The Union's Public Communications Strategy and the Bogus Proclamation of 1864*, by Menahem Blondheim, published in the Journal of American History, December 2002, Volume 89, Number 3, page 800.

773. Information about Lincoln's real proclamation placed in desk drawer: *The Collected Works of Abraham Lincoln*, edited by Roy P. Basler, Volume VII, page 344.

774. Information about Joseph Howard reporting "scotch plaid cap...military cloak:" *Lincoln and the Press*, by Robert S. Harper, page 295.

775. Information about Howard's pranks: *Encyclopedia of the American Civil War: A Political, Social and Military History*, edited by David S. Heidler and Jeanne T. Heidler, page 1007.

776. "Unnecessary and mischievous:" *Lincoln and the Press*, by Robert S. Harper, page 289.

777. "The most malignant...of all the assailants of the president:" Ibid, page 290.

778. "Thrown into violent fever:" *Abraham Lincoln: A History*, by John G. Nicolay and John Hay, Volume 9, page 48.

779. Howard asked gold merchants about the effect on gold prices of such a proclamation: *Why did President Lincoln Suppress the Journal of Commerce?* by Alice Scoville Barry, page 23.

780. Other papers running correction which quieted the mob: *The Gangs of New York: an Informal History of the Underworld*, by Herbert Asbury, page 156.

781. Information that Samuel Cunard delayed departure of the Scotia: *Public Sentiment is Everything: The Union's Public Communications Strategy and the Bogus Proclamation of 1864*, by Menahem Blondheim, published in the Journal of American History, December 2002, Volume 89, Number 3, page 885.

782. Story picked up in the New Orleans Picayune: Ibid, page 294.

783. "Soothe the righteous anger:" *The Nation's Newsbrokers*; Richard A. Schwarzlose, page 98.

784. Gideon Welles quote: "hasty, rash, inconsiderate and wrong:" *The Fate of Liberty: Abraham Lincoln and Civil Liberties*, by Mark E. Neely, Jr., page 104.

785. Information about Letter to Lincoln: "You know you would not...different law for your opponents and for your supporters?" *Lincoln and the Press*, by Robert S. Harper, page 300

786. "Shock to the public mind:" *Joseph Howard: The Bogus Proclamation*, by Anthony J. Cali, page 17, unpublished thesis.

787. "Hanging a man in advance of the trial:" *Joseph Howard: The Bogus Proclamation*, by Anthony J. Cali, page 19, unpublished thesis.

788. Resolution for censure: "In violation...civil liberty:" *Why*

did President Lincoln Suppress the Journal of Commerce? by Alice Scoville Barry, page 37.

789. One of first columnists to be syndicated: *Encyclopedia of the American Civil War: A Political, Social and Military History,* edited by David S. Heidler and Jeanne T. Heidler, page 1008.

790. "Golden bitters—are the best tonic in town!" Ibid, page 298.

791. *News over the Wires: The Telegraph and the Flow of Public Information in America, 1844-1897,* by Menahem Blondheim, pages 118-140.

792. *Memoirs of John Adams Dix,* Volume II, pages 96-97.

793. *Blue & Gray in Black & White: Newspapers in the Civil War,* by Brayton Harris, page 105.

794. *Constitutional Problems under Lincoln,* by J. G. Randall, pages 497-499.

795. *American Journalism: A History of Newspapers in the United States Through 250 years, 1690 to 1940,* by Frank Luther Mott, pages 350-352.

796. *History of Journalism in the United States,* by George Henry Payne, page 322.

797. The draft of July 18, 1864 resulted in 385,163 new enlistments: *Numbers and Losses in the Civil War in America, 1861-1865,* by Thomas L. Livermore, page 50.

798. Union General Irwin McDowell suggested war correspondents should wear white uniforms: *The First Casualty: From the Crimea to Vietnam: the War Correspondent as Hero, Propagandist, and Myth Maker,* by Phillip Knightley.

799. Henry Adams: "People have become so accustomed...all confidence in us is destroyed:" *Ibid,* page 22.

800. There were seventeen daily papers in New York City alone when the war started: *American Journalism: A History of*

Newspapers in the United States through 250 Years, 1690 to 1940, by Frank Luther Mott, page 339.

801. One reporter shamelessly noted in a letter home that he had received $50 from a Northern artillery officer. *The First Casualty: From the Crimea to Vietnam: the War Correspondent as Hero, Propagandist, and Myth Maker*, by Phillip Knightley.

802. A Congressional committee learned the Lincoln Administration used the wire service to disseminate false information: *News over the Wires*, Menahem Blonheim, page 135.

803. Telegraph man and former congressman from Maine: "The press had more power to make and unmake presidents than either party:" *Public Sentiment is Everything*, Menahem Blondheim, page 878.

804. President Lincoln: "Public sentiment is everything. With it, nothing can fail; against it, nothing can succeed. Whoever moulds public sentiment, goes deeper than he who enacts statutes, or pronounces judicial decisions:" *The Collected Works of Abraham Lincoln,* Roy P. Basler, editor, Volume II, page 553.

805. Reporters conspiring to not mention General Meade's name: *The First Casualty: From the Crimea to Vietnam: the War Correspondent as Hero, Propagandist, and Myth Maker*, by Phillip Knightley, pages 27-28.

Shocking Advertisement Leads to Arrest

806. Testimony of Cantlin and Graves: *The Assassination of President Lincoln and the Trial of the Conspirators*, compiled and arranged by Benn Pittman, page 51.

807. *As Luck Would Have it: Chance and Coincidence in the Civil War*, by Otto Eisenschiml and E. B. Long.

808. *Cahaba: A Story of Captive Boys in Blue*, by Jesse Hawes.

809. Information about number of witnesses and dates of Lincoln

conspirators' trial: *Blood on the Moon: the Assassination of Abraham Lincoln,* by Edward Steers, Jr.

810. *Life in Dallas County During the War,* by Anna G. Fry, published in the Confederate Veteran Magazine, May 1916, Volume XXIV.

811. *History of Alabama and Dictionary of Alabama Biography,* by Thomas McAdory Owen, page 646.

812. Information about Gayle as U. S. attorney: *Bicentennial Celebration of the United States Attorneys.*

813. "To pander to fanatical malignity:" *Reminiscences of Public Men in Alabama: for Thirty Years,* by William Garrett, published in 1872.

814. Poem: Memoirs of Old Cahaba: *Memories of Old Cahaba,* by Anna M. Gayle Fry.

815. "But those beautiful scenes are no more…in its soft, mellow light:" Ibid, pages 69-70.

Civil War Graffiti

816. "I have just been to a village…Mine is there." A Virginia Village Goes to War: Falls Church During the Civil War, by Bradley E. Gernand, page 183.

817. Fairfax City Blenheim House: (703) 591-0560.

818. Brandy Station Graffiti House: (540) 727-7718. www.brandystationfoundation.com

819. Massaponax Baptist Church: (540) 898-0021.

820. Winchester Old Court House Museum: (540) 542-1145 www.civilwarmuseum.org.

821. Information about J. Egbert Farnum and the *Wanderer: The Wanderer: the Last American Slave Ship and the Conspiracy that set its sails,* by Erik Calonius.

822. Information about J. Egbert Farnum and the *Wanderer: The Slave Ship Wanderer,* by Tom Henderson Wells, pages 63-71.

823. "How dearly I loved the Soldiers Home"...Lincoln's Sanctuary, Abraham Lincoln and the Soldiers' Home, by Matthew Pinsker.

824. Size of home as 10,000 square feet—author's interview with Angela Brown, Education Coordinator of President Lincoln and Soldiers' Home National Monument, March 1, 2005.

825. Dates when Lincoln first and last visited the Soldiers Home—Pinsker, page 13.

826. "Where Kings might dwell:" Washington Sunday Chronicle, attributed by Ibid, page 171.

827. Number of months Lincoln spent at the Soldiers Home: Ibid, page 5.

828. Origins of the Home: *The United States Soldiers Home, A History of its First Hundred Years,* by Colonel Paul R. Goode, 1957.

829. Walt Whitman's description of Lincoln's travel; Pinsker, Introduction.

830. Travel going past tavern, brothels and contraband camp: Ibid, page 68.

831. Toll booth operator letter to Lincoln regarding no charge: *Dear Mr. Lincoln-Letters to the President,* edited by Harold Holzer.

832. Lincoln's poems from 1846; Lincoln's Speeches and Writings, 1832-1858, American Poetry-The Nineteenth Century, Volume I-Freeman to Whitman --from poem entitled "My Childhood –Home I See Again."

833. "The saddest face I ever painted" F. B. Carpenter, *The Inner Life of Abraham Lincoln,* 1880.

834. "The tycoon... him where he is." Pinsker, page 110.

835. "We could ill afford to spare just now"—*Lincoln Observed-*

Civil War Dispatches of Noah Brooks, edited by Michael Burlingame, page 126.

836. "The worst rebel you ever saw:" Pinsker, page 144.

837. "Assassination is not an American practice:" attributed to Edwin Stanton, in Ibid, page 50.

838. Number of veterans at the Soldiers Home -author's interview with Angela Brown, March 1, 2005.

839. Financed through military and not tax dollars—Ibid.

Abraham Lincoln's Personal Finances

840. "Now vere ...married folks:" *The Collected Works of Abraham Lincoln,* edited by Roy P. Basler, Volume VII, page 106.

841. Never had enough money to fret about: *The Inner Life of Abraham Lincoln,* F. B. Carpenter, 1880, page 252.

842. Didn't bring anything with him and not taking anything out: Roland T. Carr & Hugh Morrow, We Found Lincoln's Lost Bank Account, *The Saturday Evening Post,* February 14, 1953.

843. First earnings as an 18-year old: Carpenter, page 97.

844. Deposit $310 on March 1, 1853: *The Personal Finances of Abraham Lincoln,* by Harry E. Pratt, 1943, page 122.

845. Seventeen loans for $12,000: Pratt, page 82.

846. Riggs was Treasurer of 1860 Democratic National Committee: Carr & Morrow.

847. Early history of Riggs Bank: Charles O. Gridley & Hugh Morrow, "Big Shots Have Money Troubles Too," *The Saturday Evening Post,* September 18, 1918.

848. Disposition of forty-nine paychecks: Pratt, page 124.

849. Total of 234 checks for $40,000: Carr & Morrow.

850. "Colored man with one leg" -check and description: PNC Archives.

851. Description of check to "Tad, when he is well enough": Carr & Morrow.

852. Tad "get well check" sold at auction in NYC for $5,500: *32 President's Square—Part I of a Two-Part Narrative of the Riggs Bank and its Founders,* by Roland T. Carr, page 233.

853. Description of uncashed check to Isaac Heilprin: Ibid.

854. Account balance of $78.85 when wrote the Heilprin check: *32 President's Square—Part I of a Two-Part Narrative of the Riggs Bank and its Founders,* by Roland T. Carr, page 245.

855. Information about being overdrawn until July 9: Ibid.

856. Description of $50 check sent to wife in New York: Collected Works, Volume VII, page 320.

857. "Tell Tad the goats are well," Ibid.

858. Information about John Summerfield Staples: *Who Was Who in the Civil War,* by Stewart Sifakis, page 617; and *Abraham Lincoln's Substitute in the Civil War,* by Rev. E.S. Walker, published in the April 1912 edition of the Journal of the Illinois Historical Society, Volume 5.

859. Payee on Gideon Welles check: Gridley & Morrow.

860. Description of Lincoln bringing in money to Chase's office: Maunsell B. Field, *Memories of Many Men and of Some Women,* 1874, page 283.

861. On April 13, 1865, Lincoln wrote and cashed $800 check to himself as well as $500 check from lawyer named Eli K. Price: *32 President's Square—Part I of a Two-Part Narrative of the Riggs Bank and its Founders,* by Roland T. Carr, page 253.

862. Description of rates of investments on government securities: Pratt, page 125.

863. Info about tax revenues, whiskey tax and national debt in October 1865: *John Sherman's Recollections of Forty Years in the House, Senate and Cabinet, an Autobiography,* by John Sherman, published in 1895, Volume I, pages 304-305, 377.

864. "To-day begins a new day" analysis: *New York Herald*, September 1, 1862.

865. Lincoln's heirs receiving refund of income taxes: Pratt, pages 126-127.

866. Received $200 for Cooper Union speech: Ibid, pages 109, 163.

867. Amounts in estates and final dispositions: Ibid, pages 141, 184-185.

Abraham Lincoln's Favorite Poem

868. Information about Lincoln and the poem: *Lincoln's Melancholy*, by Joshua Wolf Shenk, pages 120-123.

869. Poem: "Oh, Why Should the Spirit of Mortal Be Proud?" published in book form, by William Knox, Lee and Shepard Publishers, 1883.

870. Information about Francis Carpenter: *The Inner Life of Abraham Lincoln, Six Months at the White House*, by F. E. Carpenter, pages 58-61.

The Saga of Wilmer and Virginia McLean

871. The author appreciates the fine work done by Frank P. Cuble, in his "Biography of Wilmer McLean," H. E. Howard Inc., 1987. With few exceptions, the information in this story was obtained from Mr. Cuble's book.

872. April 22, 1950 edition of the *Saturday Evening Post.*

873. Discussion with neighbors: Author's personal contact.

874. Virginia Hooe McLean's pre-nuptial agreement: Prince William Courthouse records, Manassas, Virginia.

875. Virginia Hooe McLean obituary: *Alexandria Gazette*, August 30, 1893.

876. *The Real Estate of Wilmer McLean*, by Dorothy Ulrich

Troubetzkoy, published in the *Virginia Record,* April 1965.

877. Information about whereabouts of the surrender chairs and tables: *Lucy's Bones, Sacred Stones, & Einstein's Brain—The Remarkable Stories Behind the Great Objects and Artifacts of History, from Antiquity to the Modern Era,* by Harvey Rachlin, pages 241-242.

878. "When I first joined the Army...on the other side:" *A Civil War Treasury of Tales, Legends and Folklore,* edited by B. A. Botkin, page 491.

879. *Wilmer McLean: the Centreville Years,* by Carol Drake Friedman, published in the *Historical Society of Fairfax County Yearbook,* Volume 23.

880. *Prince William: The Story of Its People and Its Places,* compiled by the Writers Program of the Work Projects Administration.

The 27th Michigan Regiment's Fighting Indian

881. *The Cherokee Nation in the Civil War,* by Clarissa W. Confer.

882. Born "ready-made:" *Lincoln's Ready-Made Soldiers: Saugatuck Area Men in the Civil War,* by Kit Lane, page 8.

883. "Nearly all tall and good looking fellows...sharpshooters can be easily made:" *These Men Have Seen Hard Service: The First Michigan Sharpshooters in the Civil War,* Raymond J. Herek, page 36.

884. Twenty-five Saint Regis Indians enlisted in the 98th New York Infantry: *Warrior in Two Camps—Ely S. Parker, Union General and Seneca Chief,* by William H. Armstrong.

885. George Copway offered to raise from the Great Lakes area a regiment of "young men, inured to hardship... runners for the army:" Ibid, page 24.

886. "Some of the deadliest rifles:" Ibid, page 118.

887. "All the go:" Ibid, page 67.

888. "Best squirmishers in the division:" Ibid, page 118.

889. "A typical English dude…We captured not one of them:" Ibid, page 36.

890. "When driven into the open…not one of them:" Ibid, page 121.

891. "A long way from the cool air and giant whispering pines of Michigan's North Country:" Ibid, page 226.

892. "After meeting the soldier…remarried since his death:" *Beyond Sorrowful Pride: Civil War Pensions and War Widowhood 1862-1900*, dissertation (Ohio University, 1997) by Changsin Lee.

893. All military information about Michael White: Pension and enlistment papers, National Archives.

The 27th Michigan Regiment Quells a Race Riot

894. Information about Detroit race riot: *Detroit Free Press*, August 9, 1908, courtesy of Detroit Public Library.

895. *New York Tribune*, March 9, 1863: story entitled: "The Great Riot in Detroit."

First Woman on American Currency

896. Edward Elmore information, including his duel with a Richmond newspaper editor: Confederate Currency and Stamps—Official Acts of Congress Authorizing Their Issue, edited by Claud D. Fuller, page 50.

897. Information about William Crittenden of Kentucky and his death in Cuba in August 1851: *Queen of the Confederacy: the Innocent Deceits of Lucy Holcombe Pickens*, by Elizabeth Wittenmyer Lewis, page 43.

898. Information about the *Free Flag of Cuba*, penned under the psydonum H. M. Hardimann: *Ibid*, page 47.

899. Mary Boykin Chestnut wrote that Lucy "is very clever but affects silly, fine lady airs, for reasons of her own--& it seems to pay:" *The Private Mary Chestnut—the Unpublished Civil War Diaries,* edited by C. Vann Woodward and Elisabeth Muhlenfeld, page 54.

900. Mary Chestnut's diary about Lucy bad-mouthing officers born in New York: *A Diary from Dixie, by Mary Boykin Chestnut,* edited by Ben Ames Williams, page 206.

901. Her marriage at the age of 25: *Confederate Currency and Stamps—Official Acts of Congress Authorizing Their Issue,* edited by Claud D. Fuller, page 48.

902. In the 1860 census, Pickens reported $300,000 worth of assets, not including plantations in Mississippi and Alabama and 300 slaves: *Lucy Holcombe Pickens, Southern Writer,* by Georganne B. Burton and Orville Vernon Burton, published in the *South Carolina Historical Magazine,* October 2002, Volume 103, Number 4, page 305.

903. Lucy remarked in a letter to her mother that she was marrying Pickens to pay off her father's debts: *Ibid,* page 304.

904. Holcombe Legion: *Queen of the Confederacy: the Innocent Deceits of Lucy Holcombe Pickens,* by Elizabeth Wittenmyer Lewis, page 143.

905. Information about Major Jones and the poem called Lines on the Back of a Confederate Note: "Representing nothing on God's earth now...hope of success-it passed:" *Tyler's Quarterly Magazine,* Volume 19, July 1937, page 62.

906. Lucy founded the Maxcy Gregg Chapter of the United Daughters of the Confederacy: *Lucy Holcombe Pickens, Southern Writer,* by Georganne B. Burton and Orville Vernon Burton, published in the *South Carolina Historical Magazine,* October 2002, Volume 103, Number 4, page 306.

907. The Washington DC Chapter of the DAR called themselves the Lucy Holcombe Chapter: *Ibid,* page 306.

908. "Texas fever! Mexico fever! Brazilian fever!" *The Confederate Carpetbaggers*, by Daniel E. Sutherland, page 10.

909. Charles Dickens' quote: "Standing among the crowded ghosts of many miserable years:" *Unleashed at Long Last*, by W. H. T. Squires, page 114.

910. Mary Boykin Chestnut wrote about Confederates moving to Mexico and Brazil: *The Private Mary Chestnut—the Unpublished Civil War Diaries,* edited by C. Vann Woodward and Elisabeth Muhlenfeld, page 244; *The Lost Cause—The Confederate Exodus to Mexico*, by Andrew F. Rolle, page 9.

911. Scarlett O'Hara twice considered the idea of fleeing to Latin America in the epic novel *Gone with the Wind: The Lost Colony of the Confederacy*, by Eugene C. Harter, page 77.

912. Southern girl's diary: "The men are all talking about going to Mexico and Brazil:" *The Confederate Carpetbaggers*, by Daniel E. Sutherland, page 11.

913. Another Southern girl's diary: "There is complete revulsion in public feeling. No more talk about help from France or England...We are irretrievably ruined:" *The Elusive Eden-Frank McMullan's Confederate Colony in Brazil*, by William Clark Griggs, page 13.

914. Quote: "You folks made our lives so impossible in the United States that we had to leave:" *The Lost Colony of the Confederacy*, by Eugene C. Harter, page 9.

915. Felt like an exile and stranger in his own home: *The Confederate Carpetbaggers*, by Daniel E. Sutherland, page 15.

916. An estimated three million of them left their homes in the former Confederate states: *The Lost Colony of the Confederacy*, by Eugene C. Harter, page 11.

917. Mathew Fontaine Maury quote: "The Amazon reminds us

of the Mississippi...an everlasting summer and its harvest perennial:" Ibid, page 27.

918. Popular ditty "Oh, give me a ship with a sail and with wheel...And receive in return, "Welcome, Old Hoss!" *The Lost Colony of the Confederacy*, by Eugene C. Harter, page 39; *The Elusive Eden-Frank McMullan's Confederate Colony in Brazil*, by William Clark Griggs, page 55.

919. Brazilian Emperor Dom Pedro II had agents meet with prospective colonizers at offices in New York and Washington. He subsidized passage...and accelerated and simplified the naturalization process: *The Confederados— Old South Immigrants in Brazil*, by Cyrus B. Dawsey and James M. Dawsey, page 16; *The Lost Colony of the Confederacy*, by Eugene C. Harter, pages 16 and 37; *Os Confederados*, by Robert L. Hoover and David N. Hoover, published in the *Civil War Times Illustrated*, January/ February 1993, page 26.

920. In 1866 a group of Brazilians established the International Society of Immigration to encourage legislation for new and beneficial immigration programs: *The Elusive Eden-Frank McMullan's Confederate Colony in Brazil*, by William Clark Griggs, page 15.

921. "Emigration to Brazil! Notice to members of the Pioneer Colony...and all should provide themselves with provisions for about six months:" *The Lost Colony of the Confederacy*, by Eugene C. Harter, pages 26-27.

922. A former Alabama cotton grower quote: "Move here and buy land, which you can do on four year's credit...and before you can join us, shall have a steamer on the river:" Ibid, pages 14-15.

923. Nearly all Southern newspapers were against the emigration: *The Confederate Carpetbaggers*, by Daniel E. Sutherland, page 22.

924. General Robert E. Lee and former President of the Confederacy Jefferson Davis vociferously urged against it:

The Lost Colony of the Confederacy, by Eugene C. Harter, pages 19-21; The *Confederate Carpetbaggers*, by Daniel E. Sutherland, page 23; *The Confederados—Old South Immigrants in Brazil*, by Cyrus B. Dawsey and James M. Dawsey, page 160.

925. A Brazilian newspaper reported in 1867 that Confederados were living on every block of Rio de Janeiro: *The Lost Colony of the Confederacy*, by Eugene C. Harter, page 23.

926. Emigrant's letter: "Neither too hot nor cold, and where frost is never known...everything grows, and grows well:" *The Elusive Eden-Frank McMullan's Confederate Colony in Brazil*, by William Clark Griggs, page 26.

927. Another wrote: "The war worn soldier, the bereaved parent...of harrowing scenes of sorrow and death:" *The Lost Colony of the Confederacy*, by Eugene C. Harter, page 14.

928. Quote: "A happy band of emigrants:" Ibid, page 37.

929. Many Brazilians still carry names like Lee, Jefferson and Washington: Ibid, page 105.

930. The most popular Brazilian singer in 1984 was named Rita Lee: Ibid, page 74.

931. Georgia Governor Jimmy Carter visited in 1972; both he and his press secretary remarked how the Confederados sounded and seemed just like Southerners: Ibid, pages xii-xiii; *The Confederados—Old South Immigrants in Brazil*, by Cyrus B. Dawsey and James M. Dawsey, page 210.

932. Poem: "With what joy our hearts were burning...May God ever bless Brazil! *The Elusive Eden-Frank McMullan's Confederate Colony in Brazil*, by William Clark Griggs, page 147.

Book Review: DeLorezno

933. Quotes attributed to James Webb: *Born Fighting: How The Scots-Irish Shaped America,* by James Webb, pages 211 and 223.

934. Quote on tariff question: attributed to The Northern British Review, Edinburgh, in *Those Dirty Rotten Taxes,* by Charles Adams, page 79.

935. "The varnishers and veneerers... human weaknesses out of him:" *The Vintage Mencken*, edited by Alistair Cooke, page 78.

936. H. L. Mencken quote: "Lincoln has become...no longer possible:" attributed to Mencken in *Those Dirty Rotten Taxes,* by Charles Adams, page 95.

Anti-Immigrant Fury in World War One

937. Billy Sunday: "If Hell could be turned upside down:" *Over There-The United States in the Great War, 1917-1918*, by Byron Farwell, page 51.

938. "Everything that is pro-German must go:" *Dry Manhattan—Prohibition in New York City,* by Michael A. Lerner, page 32.

939. Teddy Roosevelt: "hyphenated Americans:" *The Last Days of Innocence—America at War, 1917-1918,* by Meirion & Susie Harries, page 39.

940. Woodrow Wilson: "poured the disloyalty into the very arteries...must be crushed out:" *Ibid.*

941. U.S. War Department banned 75 books it called German propaganda: *Over There-The United States in the Great War, 1917-1918*, by Byron Farwell, page 126.

942. *NY Times:* "Any book whatever that comes to us from a German printing press...between its covers:" *The Last Days of Innocence—America at War, 1917-1918,* by Meirion & Susie Harries, page 295.

943. Peace conference: "Behind the chair ... the shadow of the spiked helmet." *Ibid, page 295.*

944. German composers such as Bach, Beethoven and Wagner was prohibited. *Over There-The United States in the Great War, 1917-1918*, by Byron Farwell, page 125.

945. German actors and opera singers found it almost impossible to get work: *Ibid, page 125.*

946. The Metropolitan Opera refused to perform German operas: *Dry Manhattan—Prohibition in New York City*, by Michael A. Lerner, page 32.

947. German churches began conducting services in English: *Ibid, page 32.*

948. Approximately 1,200 German-Americans were placed in internment camps, including Carl Muck: *Over There-The United States in the Great War, 1917-1918*, by Byron Farwell, page 125.

949. Dachshunds became liberty dogs and in many places in the United States, stones were thrown at them: *The Last Days of Innocence—America at War, 1917-1918*, by Meirion & Susie Harries, page 295.

950. Berlin, Maryland to Brunswick, and Berlin, Michigan to Marne: *Over There-The United States in the Great War, 1917-1918*, by Byron Farwell, page 124; *Names on the Land*, by George R. Stewart, page 373.

951. Examples of renamed cities, streets: *Names on the Land*, by George R. Stewart, *page 373.*

952. NYC's German Hospital and Dispensary changed name to Lenox Hill Hospital and Germania Life Insurance Company became the Guardian Life Insurance Company: *Dry Manhattan—Prohibition in New York City*, by Michael A. Lerner, page 32.

953. Hamburger was renamed salisbury steak. Sauerkraut and frankfurters became liberty cabbage and liberty sausage. German measles were called liberty measles, hasenpfeffer

and wiener schnitzel were banned from restaurants and beer halls no longer offered pretzels: *Over There-The United States in the Great War, 1917-1918*, by Byron Farwell, page 125; also *The Last Days of Innocence—America at War, 1917-1918*, by Meirion & Susie Harries, page 295.

954. Information about mob lynching Robert Prager: *The Last Days of Innocence—America at War, 1917-1918*, by Meirion & Susie Harries, page 296; *Perilous Times: Free Speech in Wartime*, by Geoffrey R. Stone, page 188; *Latah (Idaho) County Historical Society*.

955. The mob's ringleaders wore red, white and blue ribbons in their buttonholes and were all acquitted: *The Last Days of Innocence—America at War, 1917-1918*, by Meirion & Susie Harries, page 296.

956. NH Senator Jacob Gallinger remark that the solution was to reduce the availability of grain in the manufacture of beer: *Perilous Times: Free Speech in Wartime*, by Geoffrey R. Stone, page 188.

957. DOJ prosecuted more than 2,000 dissenters during the war: *Ibid, page 170.*

958. Thirty German Americans in SD convicted for sending a petition to the governor asking for reforms in the selective service procedure: *Ibid, page 172.*

959. A man in Iowa was sentenced to a year in jail for attending a meeting, applauding, and contributing twenty-five cents: *Ibid, page 173.*

960. A resident of Latah County, Idaho recalled draft deferments were tarred and feathered. This witness also recalled that a prominent and wealthy shop owner "gathered up everything [from his store] ... all over the county:" *Latah (Idaho)* County Historical Society.

961. In Willard, Ohio, a Mr. and Mrs. Zuelch compelled to salute and kiss an American flag: *The Last Days of Innocence—America at War, 1917-1918*, by Meirion & Susie Harries, page 296.

962. Information about John Deml: Latah (Idaho) County Historical Society.

963. In Oklahoma, a former minister who opposed the sale of war bonds was tarred and feathered: *Perilous Times: Free Speech in Wartime,* by Geoffrey R. Stone, page 156.

964. A brewery-worker in California who made pro-German remarks was tarred and feathered: *Ibid, page 156.*

965. In Texas, six farmers were horsewhipped because they declined to donate to the Red Cross: *Ibid, page 156.*

966. People were warned to keep an eye out for "gloaters:" *Over There-The United States in the Great War, 1917-1918*, by Byron Farwell, page 125.

967. Widow and son of Geronimo purchased many of these bonds: *Ibid, page 128.*

968. Germans were said to be putting ground glass into food, and poison on Red Cross bandages. The flashes of light refracted from a New York apartment along the Hudson River were believed to be signals to German submarines skulking in water below." *The Last Days of Innocence— America at War, 1917-1918,* by Meirion & Susie Harries, page 295.

969. German brewers in this country…have rendered thousands of men inefficient and are thus crippling the Republic:" *Dry Manhattan—Prohibition in New York City,* by Michael A. Lerner, page 31.

970. "How can any loyal citizen…vote for a trade that is aiding a pro-German alliance?" *Ibid, page 31.*

971. "We have German enemies in this country …Pabst, Schlitz, Blatz and Miller:" *Ibid, page 31.*

972. "Liquor is the Kaiser's mightiest ally!" *Over There-The United States in the Great War, 1917-1918,* by Byron Farwell, page 290.

973. President of Brown University neatly summed up the sentiment: "Prohibition spells Patriotism!" *Ibid, page 290.*

Ulysses, the Poem

974. *The Top 500 Poems*, edited by William Harmon, pages 645-646.

The Little River Turnpike

975. "When the Indian trail...a vent for industry:" attributed to Ralph Waldo Emerson, *Historic Turnpike Roads and Toll-Gates*, by Major Fred J. Wood, published in the *Daughters of the American Revolution Magazine*, January 1919, Volume LIII, page 1.

976. Information about turnpikes in England in 1235 and 1346: *The Turnpikes of New England and Evolution of the same through England, Virginia and Maryland*, by Frederic J. Wood, page 4.

977. "Setting forth the bad conditions..."- *Beginning of the Turnpike Movement in Northern Virginia*, by Philip Terrie.

978. "Our great roads...be established"- *The Papers of George Washington*, edited by W.W. Abbot, Volume 3.

979. "Utopean scheme:" *The Writings of Washington*, Volume 27, page 489.

980. Little River Turnpike stock certificates are retained in Box 240 at the Alexandria Public Library, Queen Street, Alexandria, Virginia.

981. Turnpike completed on 1/11/1812-*Calendar of State Papers and Other Manuscripts: January 1, 1808-December 31, 1835; The Origins of the West End*, Timothy Hills.

982. Mail and troops exempt-*A History of Roads in Fairfax County, Virginia*, Heather Crowl.

983. Rates for usage: An Act to Incorporate-Alexandria Advertiser and Commercial Intelligencer July 23, 1802; *The Turnpike Movement in Virginia: 1816-1860*, Robert F. Hunter 1957.

984. Seven toll booths-*A History of Roads in Fairfax County, Virginia*, Heather Crowl.

985. Cost of $6,292 per mile-*The Turnpike Movement in Virginia: 1816-1860*, Robert F. Hunter, 1957.

986. Number of traffic lights and gas stations today- author counted on December 5, 2004.

987. "Check to their ideal liberty:" *The Turnpike Movement in Virginia*, Robert F. Hunter; *A History of Roads in Fairfax County, Virginia*, Heather Crowl.

988. "Adventurous youths...usually successful," *Candid Reminiscences of a Comfortable Life*, by Philip Williams, published in the Winchester-Frederick County Historical Society Journal, Volume VI, 1991-1992, page 77.

989. Strategic locations-*A History of Roads in Fairfax County, Virginia*, Heather Crowl.

990. Evasion the biggest problem for the tollbooth operators-*The Turnpike Movement in Virginia*, Robert F. Hunter.

991. Shunpikes-*The Turnpike Movement in Virginia*, Robert F. Hunter-*A History of Roads in Fairfax County, Virginia*, Heather Crowl; Turnpike Tourism in Western Virginia: 1830-1860, Virginia Cavalcade.

992. Three turnpike tollbooth collectors charged-*A History of Roads in Fairfax County, Virginia*, Heather Crowl; *The Origins of the West End*, Timothy Hills.

993. Fifty-five turnpike companies-*A History of Roads in Fairfax County, Virginia*, Heather Crowl; *The Turnpike Movement in Virginia*, Robert F. Hunter.

994. Highest receipts in 1818-*The Turnpike Movement in Virginia*, Robert F. Hunter.

995. Highest Dividend of 6.7%-Ibid.

996. Eighty-three stockholders-D. Anne Evans, *The Globe*, July 12, 1979.

997. Crozet-A story of Roads in Virginia: Virginia Department

of Highways and Transportation, edited by Albert W. Coates, Jr.; *The Virginia Cavalcade, Spring 1963, Volume 4, "Colonel Claudius Crozet"* by Ullrich Troubetzkoy.

998. Information about turnpike engineers: *A Story of Roads in Virginia,* published in the Virginia Department of Highway and Transportation Magazine, edited by Albert W. Coates, Jr.

999. Indication of slave labor-*The Origins of the West End,* Timothy Hills.

1000. Tithable labor-Ibid.

1001. Advertisement for house to rent along the Turnpike: *Alexandria Gazette,* October 12, 1840.

1002. "Approaching Fairfax, it has degenerated...fifteen feet deep:" *The Turnpikes of New England and Evolution of the same through England, Virginia and Maryland,* by Frederic J. Wood, page 8.

Dissent in Wartime

1003. "The fire in the rear:" *Copperheads: The Rise and Fall of Lincoln's Opponents in the North,* by Jennifer L. Weber, page 12.

1004. "Treason against God:" Schlesinger, page 178.

1005. "Ever resorted ...aggressions on Mexico:" Ibid.

1006. "They may appeal... the infernal machinations of hell:" Ibid.

1007. "The war is branded... tyrant and murderer:" Ibid, page 179.

1008. Four New England states..."hateful:" Ibid.

1009. "Unnecessarily and unconstitutionally...the United States:" Ibid.

1010. "Allow the President to ... war at pleasure:" *The House: The History of the House of Representatives,* by Robert V. Remini, page 135.

1011. "A bewildered…perplexed man:" *The Collected Works of Abraham Lincoln*, Roy P. Basler, editor, Volume I, pages 441-442.

1012. Lincoln: A war of conquest fought to catch votes: *The Collected Works of Abraham Lincoln*, Roy P. Basler, editor, Volume I, pages 476.

1013. "Despot, liar, usurper, thief, monster…butcher and pirate:" *Perilous Times: Free Speech in Wartime*, page 129.

1014. "It is a common saying…not Southern bullets:" *Copperheads: The Rise and Fall of Lincoln's Opponents in the North*, by Jennifer L. Weber, page 68.

1015. "King Lincoln…Wicked, cruel and unnecessary:" *Perilous Times: Free Speech in Wartime*, by Geoffrey R. Stone, page 101.

1016. "Crush out liberty and erect a despotism:" Schlesinger, page 181.

1017. "The melancholy spectacle…free government die:" *Copperheads*, page 129.

1018. "Invoked the storm…which flickered in its lurid and infernal flames:" *Ibid*, page 129.

1019. "Widow maker…orphan-maker…May Almighty God forbid … of Abe Lincoln's administration:" *Ibid*, pages 159 and 142.

1020. "A sickening flow of partisan delusion:" *Ibid*, page 140.

1021. Poem: "You saw those mighty legions…two hundred thousand strong": *Perilous Times: Free Speech in Wartime*, by Geoffrey R. Stone, page 131.

1022. "Under the pretence of saving … their utmost to destroy it:" *Ibid*, page 141.

1023. Statement about having Greeley's support like having 100,000 more soldiers: *Orphans Preferred: The Twisted Truth and Lasting Legends of the Pony Express*, by Christopher Corbett, page 14.

1024. "Let us watch…to be useful:" Robert Livingstone, quoted in *Famous American Statesmen & Orators*, edited by Alexander K. McClure, Volume I, page 281.

1025. "I know of no country…as our Lees:" *R. E. Lee: A Biography*, by Douglas Southall Freeman, Volume I, page 164.

1026. "Barbarians and hypocrites:" *Light Horse Harry Lee: A Biography of Washington's Great Cavalryman*, by Noel B. Gerson, page 237.

Oval Office Veterans

1027. The Complete Book of U.S. Presidents, by William A. Degregorio.

1028. *To the Best of My Ability: The American Presidents,* by James M. McPherson.

The Retrocession of 1846

1029. John Hammond Moore, The Retrocession Act of 1846, Alexandria and Arlington Return to the Fold, published in the *Virginia Cavalcade,* Winter 1976, Volume 25.

1030. Mark David Richards, The Debates over the Retrocession of the District of Columbia, 1801-2004, unpublished doctoral dissertation, *Hope and Delusion: Struggle for Democracy in the District of Columbia.*

1031. Debate to retrocede started almost immediately: Richards.

1032. Plebiscite results: Moore, Richards.

1033. Vote in Congress: Moore, Richards.

1034. Retrocessionists' fight song: Richards.

1035. Alexandria Gazette report on results of vote and quote "The large crowd … enthusiasm prevailed" Richards.

1036. National Intelligencer: "George Washington...command the city." Moore, Richards.

1037. President Lincoln quote: "The relinquishment...and dangerous." Moore, Richards.

1038. President Taft quote: "Egregious blunder .. injury to Washington" Richards.

1039. President Polk issuing Proclamation on September 7, 1846: Moore, Richards.

1040. Information about boundary markers: *Revisiting Washington's Forty Boundary Stones, 1972*, by Edwin Darby Nye, published in the *Records of the Columbia Historical Society of Washington, DC,* 1971-1972.

The Lee Highway Blues

1041. "Center of the greatest civilization...of the world"-- *Views along the Lee Highway, A Main Street of the Nation,* Lee Highway Commission (Virginia Historical Society- HE 356.v8. L33), page 47.

1042. "Contribution to the security...glory of the Republic"— *Report of the Initial Activities for Lee Highway Association, April 20-June 19, 1920* (Virginia Historical Society- HE 356 v8. L3).

1043. "Of exceeding magnitude...and Florida"— Ibid.

1044. "A perpetual memorial to Robert E. Lee"— Weingroff, Richard: Department of Transportation, Zero Milestone Washington, DC. (www.fhwa.dot.gov)

1045. "There are two great Americans...our reunited land"— Eleanor Lee Templeman: *Lee Highway: King of the Road,* Washington Post, January 16, 1969.

1046. Information contained in paragraph starting: the association worked feverishly-- *Views along the Lee Highway, A Main Street of the Nation,* Lee Highway Commission (Virginia Historical Society- HE 356.v8. L33), pages 38-43.

1047. Information on surplus war contributions-- *Ibid*, page 48.

1048. Information about memberships-- *Ibid*, page 44.

1049. Information about President Harding dedicating the Zero Milestone-- *Ibid*, page 43.

1050. "The approximate meeting place...common destiny"— Weingroff, Richard: Department of Transportation, Zero Milestone Washington, DC." (www.fhwa.dot.gov).

1051. Wilson "Should lead to the obliteration...bitter civil strife"— *Views along the Lee Highway, A Main Street of the Nation*, Lee Highway Commission (Virginia Historical Society- HE 356.v8. L33), letter from Wilson dated January 5, 1921.

1052. Information about textbook and lamp posts with Lee Highway—*Ibid*, pages 43 and 47.

1053. Musician named Michael Cleveland- compact disc containing the song "Lee Highway Blues."

War Takes A Holiday: WWI Christmas Truce

1054. "The last insurable men on earth": *In Flanders Fields—the 1917 Campaign,* by Leon Wolff, page 301.

1055. "The dead were everywhere..." Valentine Williams- *The Greatest of all Christmas Tributes,* New York Times, December 23, 1934.

1056. "Christmas was a peculiar sort of day..." Robert Graves-Short story entitled *Christmas Truce.*

1057. "The rifles were laid aside..." Williams.

1058. "And one by one..."-John McCutcheon-Christmas in the Trenches.

1059. "The soldiers along the Western Front...because we're here:" *In Flanders Fields—the 1917 Campaign,* by Leon Wolff, page 5.

Former Holidays in Colonial Virginia

1060. "Solemnize as a holiday...pray for and memorialize..." Charles E. Gilliam, *Legal Holidays Peculiar to Colonial Virginia*, published in the William and Mary Historical Magazine, October 1943.

1061. "Come unarmed...brutish triumph:" Richard L. Morton, *Colonial Virginia, Volume I: The Tidewater Period, 1607-1710*, Virginia Historical Society, page 75.

1062. "Utmost fury...Now is the time...rout all the English:" Ibid, page 153.

1063. Chief so infirm he needed assistance to open his eyes: Morton, page 154.

1064. "By Thanksgiving...the savages:" Charles E. Gilliam, *Legal Holidays Peculiar to Colonial Virginia*, published in the William and Mary Historical Magazine, October 1943.

1065. "It is very observable...we had sent them:" Morton, page 152.

1066. "Since God...holy day:" *Legal Holidays Peculiar to Colonial Virginia*, by Charles E. Gilliam, published in the William and Mary Historical Magazine, October 1943.

1067. "Solemnize with fasting...our guilt:" Ibid.

1068. "Whereas it is evident...commemoration:" Ibid.

1069. Figures of 2,754 indentured servants and 1,399 slaves: Thomas M. Preisser, *White Servant Labor in Colonial Alexandria, 1749-1776*, Northern Virginia Heritage, June 1982.

White Indentured Servants

1070. Died miserably." Gottlieb Mittelberger: *On the Misfortune of Indentured Servants, in Readings in American History, America Firsthand*, Volume I, edited by Robert D. Marcus and David Burner.

1071. "They [the Irish] sell their servants here... oatmeal and beef:" *Birthright-The True Story That Inspired Kidnapped,* by A. Roger Ekirch, page 62.

1072. "Every day... no more in all their lives:" Ibid.

1073. 1661 law: *Laws of Virginia,* edited by William Waller Hening.

1074. 1705 law: Ibid.

1075. Advertisement for Susan: *National Intelligencer,* November 20, 1839.

1076. Advertisement for Charles Tennison: *Alexandria Gazette,* November 16, 1840.

1077. Advertisement for three seventeen year old boys: *Alexandria Gazette,* March 9, 1841.

1078. Advertisement for Andrew J. Day: *Alexandria Gazette,* November 27, 1839.

1079. Advertisement for James C. Bangs: *Alexandria Gazette,* September 4, 1843.

1080. George Washington's ad: *The Papers of George Washington,* edited by W. W. Abbot, Volume 10, from the Virginia Gazette, May 5, 1775.

1081. Information about peculiar marks and garments: *To Look upon the Lower Sort; Runaway Ads and Appearance of Unfree Laborers in America, 1750-1800,* by Jonathan Prude, published in the Journal of American History, June 1991.

1082. Information that servants were given corn and shillings: *Laws of Virginia,* edited by W. W. Hening.

1083. Information that indenture had his head and eyebrows shaven after attempting to escape. By: John A. Cantwell, Northern Virginia Indentured Servants: A Sampling, in *Northern Virginia Heritage Magazine,* October 1987.

Early American Terror: Blackbeard

1084. "Not having ...the High Seas:" *Calendar of Virginia State Papers*, Volume I, 1652-1781, edited by William Palmer, page 196; also Tyler's Quarterly Magazine, Volume I, page 36.

1085. "Diabolically clever as well as fierce," John C. Vitale, Virginia vs. Blackbeard, in the *Iron Worker Magazine*, Winter 1964.

1086. "Great mischief ...person or persons:" *Laws of Virginia*, Edited by William W. Hening.

1087. "Whereas by an Act of Assembly...or Blackbeard:" John C. Vitale, Virginia vs. Blackbeard, in the *Iron Worker Magazine*, Winter 1964.

1088. "Ships... on board:" Zora Neale Hurston, *Their Eyes Were Watching God: Novel Openers*, edited by Bruce L. Weaver.

1089. "Damnation seize my soul...from you!" John C. Vitale, Virginia vs. Blackbeard, in the *Iron Worker Magazine*, Winter 1964.

1090. Only Blackbeard and Satan knew where treasure buried: *The People's Chronology*, edited by James Trager, page 282.

1091. Information about pirate's jargon and flag colors: *Empire of Blue Water: Captain Morgan's Great Pirate Army, the Epic Battle for the Americas, and the Catastrophe that Ended the Outlaws' Bloody Reign*, by Stephan Talty, pages 107 and 113.

1092. "Bloody knot of hand to hand combat:" John C. Vitale, Virginia vs. Blackbeard, in the *Iron Worker Magazine*, Winter 1964.

1093. "The effects of Teach... sold at public auction:" Ibid.

Information about claim for two horses: *Calendar of Virginia State Papers*, Volume I, page 200.

History of the OED

1094. The Oxford English Dictionary, Oxford University Press.

1095. A Guide to the OED, by Donna Lee Berg.

1096. *The Madman and the Professor,* by Simon Winchester.

1097. Origin of words from Graham, Walker, Melba, Hooligan, Forsyth, Garden. Booz, Benedict, Diesel, Blurb and Volta are from *Anonyponymous, the Forgotten People Behind Everyday Words,* by John B. Marciano.

A Duel in Virginia

1098. "Killing 2500 Englishmen at New Orleans qualifies [Jackson] for the chief magistracy:" *The American Talleyrand-the Career and Contemporaries of Martin Van Buren, Eighth President,* by Holmes Alexander, page 214.

1099. Kentucky Legislature sent Clay instructions to vote for Jackson: Ibid, page 218.

1100. John Quincy Adams: "I am a man of reserved, cold, austere and forbidding manners:" Ibid, page 222.

1101. Secretary of State nomination originally offered to DeWitt Clinton: Ibid, page 234.

1102. "Gothic and Absurd:" *The Code Duello in America,* by Jeannette Hussey.

1103. "It is not an inclination...differences by duel:" *The Code Duello: With Special Reference to the State of Virginia,* by A. W. Patterson.

1104. "Corrupt Bargain:" *The Encyclopedia of American History,* edited by John M. Faragher, page 462.

1105. "Half-mad-Virginian:" *Gentlemen's Blood,* by Barbara Holland, page 121.

1106. A race inferior to those of the Old Dominion:" *Dueling in the District of Columbia,* by Myra L. Spaulding, included in the Records of the Columbia Historical Society, Volume 29, page 159.

1107. "Turn(ed) upon President ... he was master:" *Randolph of Roanoke: A Political Fantastic,* by Gerald W. Johnson, page 231.

1108. "Shrill scream...his wit and ridicule was unsurpassed:" *Dueling in the District of Columbia,* by Myra L. Spaulding, included in the Records of the Columbia Historical Society, Volume 29, page 159.

1109. "Interminable speeches...Senate fathered on me:" *Randolph of Roanoke: A Political Fantastic,* by Gerald W. Johnson, pages 233-236.

1110. "To spring suddenly...an opponent:" attributed to Henry Adams, in *America's Jubilee,* by Andrew Burstein, page 173.

1111. "Upon the whole...than friends:" Ibid, page 176.

1112. "The Great Statesman of the West ...an inbred sense of honor:" *Dueling in the District of Columbia,* by Myra L. Spaulding, included in the Records of the Columbia Historical Society, Volume 29, page Spaulding, page 158.

1113. Randolph called Mr. Clay "black-legged:" Ibid, page 164.

1114. Definition of black-legged: *Oxford English Dictionary.*

1115. "Puritanic, diplomatic...administration:" *Dueling in the District of Columbia,* by Myra L. Spaulding, included in the Records of the Columbia Historical Society, Volume 29, page 165.

1116. "Unprovoked attack upon his character:" Ibid, page 161.

1117. "On Saturday, the 8th of April...Mr. Randolph:" *Alexandria Gazette,* April 11, 1826.

1118. "The devil in Clay's eyes:" *Dueling in the District of Columbia,* by Myra L. Spaulding, included in the Records of the Columbia Historical Society, Volume 29, page 168.

1119. Verbal command: "Fire-1-2-3-stop:" Ibid, page 173.

1120. "This is child's play!" Ibid, page 175.

1121. "I do not fire at you, Mr. Clay!" *Alexandria Gazette*, April 11, 1826.

1122. "The joy of all…than we brought:" *Gentlemen's Blood*, by Barbara Holland, page 126.

1123. "Randolph wanted to buried facing West:"—*Henry Clay, The Man Who Wouldn't Give Up*, by Katherine E. Wilkie, page 166.

1124. Sight of the duel and proximity to boundary marker: *A History of Arlington County, Virginia,"* by Dorothy Ellis Lee, page 146.

1125. Information about duel involving Sam Houston and William White: *The Raven-a Biography of Sam Houston*, by Marquis James, page 66.

NASA and the Moon Landing

1126. "Under the light of a Communist moon:" The Right Stuff, by Tom Wolfe, page 400.

1127. "Fellow traveler," otherwise known as Sputnik: *Live From Cape Canaveral: Covering the Space Race, from Sputnik to Today*, by Jay Barbree, page 4.

1128. *From the Earth to the Moon and Round the Moon*, by: Jules Verne.

1129. Robert Goddard said it would be possible to land on the moon someday but dismissed the idea because it would probably cost a million dollars: *Carrying the Fire, an Astronaut's Journeys*, by Michael Collins.

1130. The Army had its Redstone rockets, the Navy the Vanguard, and the Air Force had Atlas: *Light This Candle, the Life and Times of Alan Shepard*, by Neal Thompson, page 182.

1131. Khrushchev threat… "History is on our side. We will bury you!" *The Dictionary of War Quotations*, edited by Justin Wintle, page 356.

1132. NACA was founded in 1915 as a rider on a navy appropriations bill. With its first annual allotment of $5,000 it planned "to supervise and direct the scientific study of the problems of flight, with a view of their practical solution:" *North Star Over my Shoulder, A Flying Life*, by Bob Buck, page 372.

1133. NACA's 5,000 engineers at five locations absorbed into NASA: *Deke!* by Donald K. Slayton, page 68.

1134. A NASA member said during a White House meeting that a manned space launch would "only be the most expensive funeral man has ever had:" *For Spacious Skies: The Uncommon Journey of a Mercury Astronaut*, by Scott Carpenter and Kris Stoever, page 214.

1135. NASA winnowed an original list of 508 test pilots down to seven: Deke! page 69.

1136. Air Force project known as MISS, which stood for "Men in Space Soonest:" Wolfe, page 74.

1137. Gordo Cooper fell asleep while awaiting takeoff: *Schirra's Space*, by Wally Schirra, page 84.

1138. Scott Carpenter heart rate never exceeded 105 during his mission in orbit: Wolfe, page 376.

1139. Two of them had to make an effort to keep the pounds off. Every extra pound of body weight required an additional one thousand pounds of fuel to launch. In addition, the less they weighed, the more science stuff could be stuffed into the capsule: Carpenter, page 239.

1140. Space is officially is 50 miles up—if you travel 49 miles, you are not considered to have gotten there: Wolfe, page 414; *Riding Rockets: the Outrageous Tales of a Space Shuttle Astronaut*, by Mike Mullane, page 276.

1141. Twenty veterinarians were hired to train forty chimpanzees to select the best candidate to ride the rocket: Wolfe, page 194.

1142. In reality, there was a 7 after the name because it was the seventh spacecraft manufactured by the McDonnell Douglas assembly team: Thompson, page 245; Deke! page 97.

1143. Thirty eight years later, John Glenn, the politician astronaut, was still spinning the 7 as for team and leaving out of his autobiography the original reason for the 7: *John Glenn, a Memoir,* by John Glenn and Nick Taylor, by John Glenn, page 238.

1144. "I keep six honest serving men...I give them all a rest:" *The Elephant's Child* by Rudyard Kipling.

1145. *The London Times* reported, "exorcised the demon of inferiority that had possessed Americans:" Thompson, page 266.

1146. After Shepard's flight, beer and liquor sales skyrocketed; according to the *New York Times,* people "were toasting the success of the astronaut's feat." Not surprisingly, technology stocks like IBM and McDonnell Douglas also soared: Thompson, page 262.

1147. Information about Charles Leo D'Orsey: Carpenter, page 202: Glenn, page 254: Wolfe, page 139.

1148. "It is impossible to overstate Leo's influence on the seven astronauts those first two or three years," one family member wrote years later: Carpenter, page 203.

1149. He even referred to them as his boys several times in a newspaper story: *The St. Petersburg Times*: June 2, 1963.

1150. At its peak in the summer of 1967, fifty-six astronauts rode NASA's payroll: Collins, page 181.

1151. Grissom, the commander, had predicted that if anyone died in Apollo, it would be him: Deke! pg 193.

1152. The man who later determined which astronaut went up in each mission, wrote years after the accident that Grissom would have been the first one to walk on the moon had he lived: Ibid; page 191.

1153. Grissom believed that President Johnson was pushing

things too fast in an attempt to offset all the criticism directed at him for the Vietnam War: Thompson, page 315.

1154. Grissom said the Apollo One was the worst spacecraft he'd ever seen: Ibid.

1155. Shortly before the fire, Grissom had complained about the quality of the craft, going so far as to stick a lemon on it, and ordering someone to leave the lemon on what he considered a piece of shoddy engineering: Barbree, pages 121-123; Carpenter, pages 325-327; Cernan, pages 5-8, 161.

1156. NASA had switched contractors for Apollo, the widely-held belief that the reason for the switch to a new inexperienced contractor was for political cronyism: Barbree, page 135; Schirra, page 178.

1157. The astronauts of Apollo 7, refused while in space, a directive from NASA: Barbree, page 134; *The Book of the Moon*, by Rick Stroud, page 218; Schirra, pages 207-208.

1158. Aldrin was known as Dr. Rendezvous because, "that's all he could talk about, even over a cup of coffee:" *The Last Man on the Moon*, by Eugene Cernan and Don Davis, page 78.

1159. Talk between Apollo spacecraft and NASA came about via three big antennas evenly spaced over the globe in Madrid, Spain, Eastern Australia and the Mojave Desert: Collins, page 403.

1160. For directional navigation, the spacecraft computer contained the celestial coordinates of thirty-seven selected stars: Ibid, page 286.

1161. NASA's financial coordinates froze as things heated up in the late 1960s. The president slashed NASA's budget to 3.83 billion dollars, about 25% below its peak year of 1965. Congress then cut it to $3.69 billion, forcing NASA to terminate about 5,000 jobs at Cape Kennedy: Cernan, page 236.

1162. The Apollo 11 lunar module, known as Eagle had a single 17.5 pound Raytheon computer on board with a memory of 36 K, less than today's cell phones. The command module had two of the same computers on board: *Rocket Men: The Epic Story of the First Men on the Moon*, by Craig Nelson, page 221.

1163. The computers held only 38,000 words: Collins, page 431.

1164. Information about Guenter Wendt: Wendt obituary in *The Wall Street Journal*, May 5, 2010, page A9.

1165. Their fuel tank held, when they landed on the moon, only 17 seconds more of fuel: Nelson, page 258.

1166. A twenty-six year old NASA whiz kid made a quick decision to ignore the warning and go ahead with the landing. For his efforts, Scott Bales later joined the Apollo 11 astronauts in receiving the Medal of Freedom from President Nixon: Thompson, page 335.

1167. Coming back they traveled at about 25,000 mph through the brief reentry period. As a measure of comparison, a bullet shot out of a rifle goes about 2,000 mph: Nelson, page 300.

1168. Eugene Cernan said, "get this mother ought of here:" Cernan, page 338.

1169. Valentina Tereshkova became the first woman in space with 48 orbits in almost three days in 1963: Ibid, page 64.

1170. Tereshkova was not a pilot or engineer, but a factory worker who had joined a sky-diving club: *Men From Earth,* by Buzz Aldrin, page 109.

1171. Three cosmonauts in space in coveralls and sneakers: Ibid, page 110.

1172. Cosmonauts waited a day to be picked up by ski troops: Ibid, page 123.

1173. Two astronauts planned to take a mystery picture of both of them in front of their spacecraft. The timer didn't work and the picture didn't get taken: Stroud, page 233.

1174. One astronaut's travel voucher claimed seven cents a mile, for *all* his miles into space: Collins, page 253.

1175. They took a corned beef sandwich: Nelson, page 298.

1176. Took a couple rolls of dimes: Wolfe, page 284.

1177. Took postal envelopes which were later sold to a collector: Cernan, page 271.

1178. Took Miss December 1972-a Playboy magazine: Ibid, page 309.

1179. Neil Armstrong joked about taking rocks from the earth to the moon and bringing them back as "moon rocks" just to mess with NASA scientists: Nelson, page 76.

1180. Tom Wolfe penned this for *Rolling Stone Magazine*: "The main thing to know about an astronaut...the very Brotherhood of The Right Stuff itself:" Cernan, page 302.

1181. Astronaut Cernan: "We will go (into deep space) because it is logical to do so...And for the price, it was the biggest bargain in history:" Ibid, pages 343-344.

1182. Be ready in trouble, endeavor to be a jolly companion, remember and tell good and true stories around lonely campfires: Carpenter, page 332.

POWs in America During World War II

1183. Number of POWs in America: Hitler's Soldiers in the Sunshine State, by Robert D. Billinger, Jr., page 8.

1184. In more than 600 sites, in every state except Vermont and Nevada, as well as in the Territory of Alaska: *Hitler's Soldiers in the Sunshine State*, by Robert D. Billinger, Jr., notes of the preface section.

1185. First POW (Japanese) captured December 8, 1941 and first German POW in May 1942: *The German POWs in South Carolina*, by Deann Bice Segal page 25.

1186. Housed in old CCC barracks, national guard camps, air bases and numerous other locations where the government owned land and buildings: *The Faustball Tunnel—German POWs in America and Their Great Escape,* by John Hammond Moore, page 57.

1187. Received at least ten cents per day (officers got more) in canteen credits to buy beer, tobacco, candy and toiletries: Ibid, page 57.

1188. Information about dates and ratification of Geneva Convention: *The German POWs in South Carolina,* by Deann Bice Segal page 23.

1189. Information about treatment of prisoners under the Geneva Convention: *Axis Prisoners of War in the Free State, 1943-1946,* by Richard E. Holl, published in the *Maryland Historical Society Magazine,* Volume 83, Summer 1988, page 145.

1190. The excess over eighty cents used to fund the camps: *The Barbed-Wire College: Reeducating German POWs in the United States During World War II,* by Ron Robin, page 6.

1191. Prevailing rate at 43 cents per hour per man: *Hitler's Wehrmacht in Virginia, 1943-1946,* by John Hammond Moore, published in *The Virginia Magazine of History and Biography,* page 267.

1192. In 1944 alone, the government earned $ 22 million for hiring these POWs out: *Bronzed Bodies behind Barbed Wire: Masculinity and the Treatment of German Prisoners of War in the United States During World War II,* by Matthias Reiss, published in *The Journal of Military History,* April 2005, page 6.

1193. As late as February 1945, Congressional representatives were pressuring the military to bring over to America an additional 100,000 POWs "to relieve the farm labor shortage:" *The Barbed-Wire College: Reeducating German*

POWs in the United States During World War II, by Ron Robin, page 6.

1194. The U. S. Government paid an additional $200 million to these POWs or their dependents, for unused canteen credits: *The Faustball Tunnel—German POWs in America and Their Great Escape,* by John Hammond Moore, page 241.

1195. 2,827 POWs escaped, 1 Japanese prisoner, 604 Italians and 2,222 Germans: *Bronzed Bodies behind Barbed Wire: Masculinity and the Treatment of German Prisoners of War in the United States During World War II,* by Matthias Reiss, published in *The Journal of Military History,* April 2005, page 7.

1196. In New Mexico, German POWs dug a tunnel, 178 feet long, where twenty-five of them made their break two days before Christmas 1944: *The Faustball Tunnel— German POWs in America and Their Great Escape,* by John Hammond Moore.

1197. Several German POWs were unintentionally freed from camp when their Army driver forgot about them: Ibid, page 71.

1198. One escapee from a New Hampshire POW camp was picked up in Manhattan's Central Park, where he was painting and selling pictures: Ibid.

1199. Another-*on four different occasions*-escaped and was recaptured: *Nazi POWs in the Tar Heel State,* by Robert D. Billinger, Jr., page 136.

1200. One POW was recaptured in 1953 in Chicago: *The Faustball Tunnel—German POWs in America and Their Great Escape,* by John Hammond Moore, page 242.

1201. *"According to the great philosopher Spinoza every man has to seek happiness...I will return myself...It matters not how straight the gate...I am captain of my soul:"* Nazi POWs in the Tar Heel State, by Robert D. Billinger, Jr., page 126.

1202. One German turned himself in by taxi in March 1946, three months after he escaped: Ibid, page 139.

1203. The last of the POWs officially left the United States in July 1946: *Bronzed Bodies behind Barbed Wire: Masculinity and the Treatment of German Prisoners of War in the United States During World War II*, by Matthias Reiss, published in *The Journal of Military History*, April 2005, page 493.

1204. Forty three POWs successfully escaped and 162 awaiting trial: *Hitler's Wehrmacht in Virginia, 1943-1946*, by John Hammond Moore, published in *The Virginia Magazine of History and Biography*, page 271.

1205. Fourteen POWs executed for murder: *Stalag: USA—The Remarkable Story of German POWs in America*, by Judith M. Gansberg, page 52.

1206. In 1959, a POW escapee turned himself in: *Nazi POWs in the Tar Heel State*, by Robert D. Billinger, Jr., page xiv.

1207. In 1985, last POW escapee turned himself in: *Hitler's Soldiers in the Sunshine State*, by Robert D. Billinger, Jr., notes of the preface section.

1208. German POW was found dead in the Hudson River, by "drowning by immersion *in salt water*." *Nazi POWs in the Tar Heel State*, by Robert D. Billinger, Jr., page 132.

1209. Altogether 735 Germans, 99 Italians and 24 Japanese POWs died in camps, most from disease, a few from gunshot wounds as they tried to escape: *The Faustball Tunnel—German POWs in America and Their Great Escape*, by John Hammond Moore, page 71.

1210. Information about Max Stephan and Hans Krug: *Treason-The Story of Disloyalty and Betrayal in American History*, by Nathaniel Weyl, page 342.

1211. In February 1944 when the camps instituted a "calculated risk" policy, significantly decreasing security: "*Bronzed Bodies behind Barbed Wire: Masculinity and the Treatment of German Prisoners of War in the United States During*

World War II, by Matthias Reiss, published in *The Journal of Military History*, April 2005, page 493.

1212. Worse crime committed by POW escapee was car theft: *Stalag: USA—The Remarkable Story of German POWs in America*, by Judith M. Gansberg, page 44.

1213. The biggest problem is not to keep prisoners from making advances to people. ... to observe rules and regulations:" *Bronzed Bodies behind Barbed Wire: Masculinity and the Treatment of German Prisoners of War in the United States During World War II*, by Matthias Reiss, published in *The Journal of Military History*, April 2005, page 493.

1214. The 620th Engineer General Service Company, one of the three groups where American soldiers with questionable loyalties were dumped: E. J. Kahn Jr., *The New Yorker*, March-April 1950.

1215. Information about Maple and the road trip to Mexico: Ibid.

1216. Maple cross examined many of the witnesses at his trial. A note he tried to secretly get to one of his confederates in the plan was intercepted and mentioned that he was going to try the "abused America angle" defense.

1217. Five WACs charged: newspaper articles posted on the Metropolitan State College of Denver's website: www.mscd.edu/~history/camphale.

1218. Information about Maple after release from prison, as marine insurance agent: *Suspects in Sturgis—a plot to free German prisoners of war was hatched at Fort Meade*, by Paul Higbee, published in the November/December 2000 edition of the *South Dakota Magazine*, pages 47-50.

1219. Information about Maple's court martial-including high school teachers happy he graduated; Harvard professor saying no brain could withstand what Maple was trying to cram into his; 620th called "subversive" and "special" organizations; Carried into church "flopped about like a dying chicken"; and professor of Child Development using

Maple as case study: Army court martial records, U. S. Army.

1220. "Were just young boys...keep their sons out of war, and he didn't do it:" *The German POWs in South Carolina*, by Deann Bice Segal, page 32.

1221. Information about Clarence Bertucci killing eight German POWs and wounding twenty: *Martial Justice—The Last Mass Execution in the United States*, by Richard Whittingham, page 259.

1222. Information about Werner Drechsler and the execution of seven German POWs: *Martial Justice—the Last Mass Execution in the United States*, by Richard Whittingham.

1223. Information about Fairfax POW camp: *The Fairfax Camp: German Prisoners of War in Fairfax County During World War II*, by Adam D. Herman and Christopher F. Jones, published in Yearbook, Number 23, 1991-1992, the Historical Society of Fairfax County, Virginia.

1224. Information about 12 hour days and *New York Times* story: *Hitler's Wehrmacht in Virginia, 1943-1946*, by John Hammond Moore, published in *The Virginia Magazine of History and Biography*, page 267.

1225. Virginia held 17,000 POWs in 27 installations: *Axis Prisoners of War in the Free State, 1943-1946*, by Richard E. Holl, published in the *Maryland Historical Society Magazine*, Volume 83, Summer 1988, page 145.

1226. Only 1,346 German POWs in USA during the First World War: *The German POWs in South Carolina*, by Deann Bice Segal page 11.

1227. Information about Private John A. Bennett: Freedom of Information Act records obtained by the author from the U. S. Army.

Afterword

1228. "God cannot alter the past:" *The Life and Letters of John Hay,* by William Roscoe Thayer, Volume I, page 111.

1229. "History is bunk:" by Henry Ford, *The Oxford Dictionary of Quotations,* Oxford University Press, Second edition, page 209.

1230. Napoleon quote about history being agreed upon lies: *Words of Wisdom,* edited by Mick Farren, page 95.

1231. "Historians relate...would have believed:" *Less than Glory,* by Norman Gelb, introduction.

1232. "The very ink...fluid prejudice:" attributed to Mark Twain by Dixon Wecter, in *How to Write History,* published in *"Sense of History: The Best Writing from the pages of American Heritage,* page 39.

1233. George Will quote: *The Leveling Wind: Politics, the Culture and Other News,* by George F. Will, pages 173-174.

1234. "More and more often...restore free speech and revive standards:" *Clio, Canons, and Culture,* by Lawrence W. Levine, published in the *Journal of American History,* December 1993, page 851.

1235. "Defeat...cowardly administrators...blundering the scholarship:" Ibid.

1236. "Cult of ethnicity...voguish nonsense:" Ibid, page 852.

1237. In the field of American history...point guard for the Knicks:" Ibid.

1238. "The muse called Clio:" Dixon Wecter, in *How to Write History,* published in *A Sense of History: The Best Writing from the pages of American Heritage,* page 39.

1239. "History has from early times...they are to be regarded:" attributed to F.J.C. Hearnshaw, in *Hoaxes,* by Curtis D. MacDougall page 160.

1240. "With a political purpose...history had become present politics:" Ibid, page 161.

1241. "Severe, stubborn, notorious facts:" *Jefferson and Hamilton, A Classic Study of America's Greatest Antagonists*, by Claude G. Bowers, page 174.

1242. Aldous Huxley: "Facts ...cease to exist:" *Treasury of Wit & Wisdom*, compiled by Jeff Bredenberg, page 171.

1243. "Now what I want is facts...facts, sir!" *Hard Times*, by Charles Dickens, page 11.

Index

CPSIA information can be obtained at www.ICGtesting.com

261153BV00003B/11/P